Cooking For Blokes
Flash Cooking For Blokes

Also by Duncan Anderson and Marian Walls

FOREIGN COOKING FOR BLOKES

COOKING FOR BLOKES OMNIBUS

Cooking For Blokes
Flash Cooking For Blokes

DUNCAN ANDERSON &
MARIAN WALLS

SPHERE

This omnibus edition first published in Great Britain by
Time Warner Paperbacks in 2002
Reprinted 2005
Reprinted by Time Warner Books in 2005
Reprinted 2006
Reprinted by Sphere in 2007, 2008

Cooking For Blokes Omnibus Copyright © Duncan Anderson &
Marian Walls 2002

Previously published separately:
Cooking For Blokes first published in Great Britain in 1996 by Warner Books
Reprinted 1996 (four times), 1997 (twice), 1998 (three times),
1999 (twice), 2000 (twice), 2001, 2002
Copyright © Duncan Anderson & Marian Walls 1996

Flash Cooking For Blokes first published in Great Britain in 1999 by Warner Books
Reprinted 2000
Copyright © Duncan Anderson & Marian Walls 1999

The moral right of the authors has been asserted.

A CIP catalogue record for this book is available from the British Library.

ISBN 978-0-7515-3275-3

Printed and bound in Great Britain by Clays Ltd, St Ives plc

Papers used by Sphere are natural, renewable and recyclable
products made from wood grown in sustainable forests and certified
in accordance with the rules of the Forest Stewardship Council.

Mixed Sources
Product group from well-managed
forests and other controlled sources
www.fsc.org Cert no. SGS-COC-004081
© 1996 Forest Stewardship Council

FSC

Sphere
An imprint of
Little, Brown Book Group
100 Victoria Embankment
London EC4Y 0DY

An Hachette Livre UK Company
www.hachettelivre.co.uk

www.littlebrown.co.uk

Cooking For Blokes

CONTENTS

INTRODUCTION

The First Rule of this book is don't panic.

We hope all the instructions are clear and simple and the recipes are easy to follow. You don't need to know anything about cooking to use this book and it is good to remember that there is nothing mysterious about cooking. It is not some religious discipline requiring years of study, a funny haircut, a massive kitchen, thousands of spoons, a working knowledge of French, or an account at your local speciality food emporium. Millions of people have been doing it for years and most have survived.

If someone has bought you this book then you are probably going to have to make one of our recipes. We have included recipes which don't need any cooking at all, so if you are at all nervous about cooking, this may be a good place to start. Each chapter is graded with the easier recipes at the front and the more difficult ones last. None is really difficult, and all of them will taste good and look good.

All of the recipes are flexible and forgiving. You do not need to be obsessional about getting the exact amount of an ingredient to the nearest gram. Lots of the ingredients come in packs, tins or tubs in standard sizes. Recipes take advantage of this. Some use half a standard pack, for instance for dried pasta. With meat and fish just ask for the amount you want at the shop, or look for a pack of about the same size. We have tried to suggest quantities that won't cause a lot of waste, but sometimes it has been impossible to use a whole can or jar or packet in a recipe. You may have left-overs of cooked foods too. We have tried to use some of these in other recipes.

Cooking for yourself means you can take control of what you eat, and it won't be money that makes you decide between Mexican and Indian or a pizza, it'll be your taste buds. Think about it. You can eat what you like. I like Mexican food. I can go to a restaurant and get some over-priced beer and tortillas which may be either too hot or not hot enough, or I can have a go at it myself. OK, the first time I try it may be too hot or not hot enough, but the next time it will be better.

It's a lot cheaper to cook for yourself than live on take-aways, oven-ready meals or eating out in restaurants. I had a friend who over the years gradually made more money, but was always broke. Whenever he needed to eat, it was corn flakes, muesli or toast, or something bought. A bought sandwich, a take-away. He had a series of girlfriends that he was trying to impress and they couldn't cook either. Restaurants every night can lead to financial ruin, and he couldn't drink because he had to drive, so he spent his life deciding which take-away to go to.

Is cooking easy? Yes.
Does it save you money? Yes.
Does it give you control over what you eat? Yes.
Is it an impressive thing to be able to do? We think so.
Is it enjoyable? 95% of the time.

We have tried to think of everything you would need to know to start cooking easy and exciting recipes.

Just like any other activity you need a few tools to get started. There is a section on tools you will need, and some you don't need but might like because they make some things that much easier. You may need an electric drill to put up shelves but you only need a knife and a couple of pans and a set of measuring spoons to get started cooking.

You don't need a set of scales; instead, wherever possible, we use spoons and cups for measuring. There are standard measuring spoons and cups that come in sets in plastic or metal. Those you eat and drink from may not be standard.

In case you decide to brave it without even the measuring cups or spoons, a measuring cup is about the same size as a half-pint (250 ml) mug. There are a bunch of recipes where you won't even need the spoons or cups.

There is a 'How to ...' section which deals with general things like cooking vegetables, rice and pasta. Defrosting has a small space to itself because you will probably find frozen food reasonably priced and convenient if you shop for more than a day at a time.

There's a list of basic cheap food items you could think of keeping for stand-by.

Recipes are grouped together. We have started with starters and snacks, and then some grouped by food type: eggs, chicken, fish, meat, vegetarian and desserts. The second part takes food from the take-away and restaurant. Chinese stir-fry and satay, Italian pasta and pizza, Tex-Mex ribs, tacos, sauces and beans, Indian curries and sauces, parties and drinks.

Give it a go.

HOW HOT IS YOUR OVEN?

Ovens and temperatures

Every recipe that needs an oven has got the correct cooking time and oven temperature in the recipe. We have gathered all the temperatures from various cookers here. Approximate equivalent temperatures are shown below for different ovens.

140°C, 275°F, Gas mark 1
150°C, 300°F, Gas mark 2
170°C, 325°F, Gas mark 3
180°C, 350°F, Gas mark 4
190°C, 375°F, Gas mark 5
200°C, 400°F, Gas mark 6
220°C, 425°F, Gas mark 7
230°C, 450°F, Gas mark 8
240°C, 475°F, Gas mark 9

Gas ovens and fan-assisted ovens get hotter quicker than standard electric ones.

In most ovens the top is hotter than the bottom. Most things are best cooked in the middle. Roast potatoes and vegetables are best cooked at the top if you like them crispy.

Fan-assisted ovens have less of a difference between top and bottom and need different cooking times. Please refer to your instruction book.

Microwave cooker

There are no recipes for microwave cookers in this book. Please write to the publisher and demand the commissioning of a slim companion volume, 'Cooking for Blokes (the Microwave Years)'.

TOOLS

THE BASICS

In this book all the tools you need for a particular recipe are listed after the ingredients. The information in this chapter should help you decide which are the most suitable for you.

Sharp knives

Knives are the most important tools. They must be sharp. They do not need sharpening every day or even every week, but they will eventually get blunt. Just like some tools are better than others, and generally more expensive, so it is with knives. Within reason, more expensive knives last longer and keep an edge longer.

If you only buy one knife choose a 'kitchen knife'. The blade should be about 16 to 20 cm (6½ to 8 inches) long with a comfortable handle. It should have a gently curved edge. It should have a smooth chopping blade rather than be serrated. This size and kind of knife can be used for chopping vegetables and meat as well as carving.

The next most important kind is a small knife for cutting up smaller things. This can double as a vegetable peeler. The blade should be about 10 cm (4 inches) long.

6

Knife sharpeners

Buy a cheap one and follow the instructions.

One kind looks like crossed fingers. You pull the knife through a few times and it puts an edge on both sides of the knife at the same time.

'Butcher's steels' (the long pointed sharpeners with a handle) need a lot of practice to use properly and can lead to injury in the overconfident starter.

Electric sharpeners, like a lot of time-saving ideas, are an expensive waste of space.

Chopping boards

These should be made of plastic.

A plain round wooden board is all right for cutting bread on, but unhygienic for meat, fish or vegetables.

Basic hygiene and the state of some food (remember salmonella in eggs and chickens) gives two rules for using chopping boards. First, keep them clean. Wash them every time you use them. Second, chop the vegetables, salad or cheese before chopping any meat or fish. This is because the salad may get infected with bugs from the meat. The bugs are killed by cooking.

Measuring spoons & cups

Recipes in this book use spoonfuls or cupfuls rather than weights for most things. If you look in any kitchen you will see that teaspoons and cups come in several sizes. This means the amounts and so the taste may be very different if you just use any cup or spoon. To get round this problem, buy a set of spoons and cups in standard sizes. Look in the cooking section of your local supermarket. They come in plastic or stainless steel.

One teaspoonful is 5 ml.
One tablespoonful is 15 ml.

The cup set looks like a very large spoon set, and has four sizes:

1 cup	250 ml	approx. 9 fluid ounces
Half a cup	125 ml	4 fl oz
Third of a cup	80 ml	3 fl oz
Quarter cup	60 ml	2 fl oz

This makes from some easy conversions. A pint is 20 fl oz, and is approximately two and a quarter cups.

Some cups are based on 240 ml to the cup. Either sort will do. The difference between them is only about five per cent and well within the tolerance of the recipes.

Wooden spoons, spatulas and other spoons

Minimum requirements are a wooden spoon and a spatula (it gets into the corners better).

Next most important is a cooking spoon for getting stuff out of pans and on to plates.

Next is a fish slice and a spoon with holes in it for draining.

If you buy a set, make sure it is not going to melt if it gets warm or scratch your nice aluminium non-stick pans.

Bowls

You need bowls to mix things in. If the bowl looks OK you can use it to serve food in as well. Choose a plastic or glass one and make sure it is big enough.

Vegetable peelers

A small sharp knife will do, but there are some specially made vegetable peelers which are slightly safer and easier to use.

One is a bit like a knife and sometimes has an apple corer at the end furthest from the handle.

Another looks a bit like a letter D with the straight edge of the D being a slotted blade.

Pans – overall advice

Buy a cheap set and then go looking in street markets or car boot sales for second-hand cast-iron pans with enamelled insides. This is where being a bloke will be an advantage. People buy these and then decide they don't like using them because they are too heavy. You, on the other hand, will have no trouble with them.

The cheapest sets are aluminium non-stick.

Saucepans

Buy pans with lids.

How many?
At least one and preferably two.

What size?

22 cm (8½ inches) across. 2 litres (3½ pints). This is big enough to cook pasta or rice or stew.

16 cm (6½ inches) across. 1 litre (1¾ pints). This is big enough for tomato sauce for pasta, custard or frozen peas.

Stick or non-stick?

Go for non-stick. Most aluminium pans have a non-stick coating. But remember, this is easy to remove with forks, metal implements and scouring pads. It can also make an interesting chemical burning smell if you heat it up too much with nothing in the pan, which may put you off eating for some time.

What metal?

Aluminium: The cheap ones will wear out in a couple of years. By this time you will have decided if you want to continue to cook and whether to keep buying cheap ones or go for something better.

Stainless steel: Very shiny. Quite expensive. Longer lasting. Thicker bases distribute the heat more evenly. This means that if you forget to stir, the food sticks evenly to the bottom of the pan rather than in the shape of the heating element. Thinner bases mean more stirring. Stainless steel saucepans can be soaked in hot soapy water and burnt-on food will come away fairly easily.

Cast iron with enamel interior (eg Le Creuset): These are expensive, very durable and heavy. They cook very evenly. The enamel lining makes them practically non-stick. They do not like being heated up with nothing in them and the enamel may crack if you move them too quickly from heat to cold water. They can be soaked in water but the wooden handles don't like it. The handles can char if you cook on too high gas. Handles and casserole lids can be bought separately and replaced.

Frying-pans

General advice as to sort of metal is as above.

Size should be about 25 to 28 cm (10 to 11 inches across).

If you want to cook a lot of omelettes buy a smaller one as well, say 20 cm (8 inches).

Casserole with lid

There are three sorts: pottery, ovenproof glass or cast iron. These are used for cooking in the oven. Cooking this way is an easy option because you can just put the food in the oven and leave it to cook while you do something else.

If you go and look in a shop you will see some ovenproof glass (Pyrex type) casseroles. These and the pottery ones are both OK. Don't get them really hot and then put them in cold water or they may crack.

There are a bewildering number of sizes, but get one that holds at least 2 litres or 4 pints.

Our personal recommendation must be for a cast-iron casserole. The ideal size is a 25 cm oval casserole with straight sides. It holds 4 litres (7 pints) and can take a chicken, a small leg of lamb or most beef roasts, as well as being OK for all the casserole dishes in the book. It is fairly foolproof. It also means there is lots of juice for making gravy.

Large ovenproof dish

These come in all sizes. They can be made from pottery, ovenproof glass or metal. If you get a big enough one it can be used as a roasting dish as well.

The most useful one we use is 30 cm by 18 cm (11$\frac{1}{2}$ by 7$\frac{1}{2}$

inches) and 6 cm (2 inches) deep and made of ovenproof glass. It is big enough to roast a chicken in, or make Lasagne or Shepherd's Pie.

Round ovenproof glass dish 25 cm (10 inches) diameter

This is used for cooking tarts and quiches, and doubles as something you can roast chicken pieces on.

Metal baking sheet about 25 cm (10 inches) across

This can be used for quickly warming things in the oven or cooking things that don't create a lot of liquid. It will also do as a tin to cook or heat pizzas and pizza bases.

Colander or sieve

This is useful for draining vegetables after they have been washed, and again after they have been cooked or for draining cooked pasta.

Colanders come in metal and plastic, with and without bases. The ones with bases will stand up on their own so you can put them in the sink and keep your hands away from the boiling substances you pour in. Plastic ones are cheaper.

Sieves can do most of what a colander does. They don't come with stands, but do have long handles. You can drain rice in them. You can also use a sieve as a fine strainer, to get the lumps out of gravy or sauce.

Grater

These are made from metal or plastic and have a range of cutting surfaces for getting different sizes of gratings. Use these for grating cheese, carrot or whatever.

Pie dish (if you want pies)

A metal dish, coated with non-stick material. It should be about 22 cm (8½ inches) across, with sloping sides at least 3 cm (1 inch) deep. Some have lots of holes in the bottom which help make the pastry base crisp. Other dishes are pottery. This dish is for making pies, which have a pastry lid as opposed to tarts which don't.

BITS THAT MAKE LIFE EASIER

Lemon zester

This is for getting the rind off lemons and oranges. It has four or five holes in a little scraper. There is no other tool which does it as quickly, or that makes such long strips of rind. If you use a knife and then slice it, the shreds come out a bit big. You can try using a grater, but it's not as easy.

Apple corer

A sharp-ended tube on a handle. You push the corer through the apple from the top of the apple where the stalk would be. When you pull it out it takes the core and seeds out.

Garlic crusher

There's not a lot to say about these. You put the peeled garlic in
and squeeze the handles together. The garlic gets pulped up. You
poke the residue out and throw it away.

Garlic is available ready pulped in tubes or jars.

Wok

A wok is like a combination of a frying-pan and saucepan. There
are a number of Wok kits which include the Wok itself (a sort of
metal bowl with a handle), lid, chopsticks, spoon and whatever else
is thought to be useful. They are the best thing to cook Chinese
stir-fry in.

Authentic woks do not have a non-stick coating, but others do.
Get one with a non-stick coating, but remember not to use metal
tools on it. Also, buy one with a flat bottom (round ones can be
unstable).

Larger woks are particularly useful. You can use them to cook
larger quantities of food like chilli con carne or curries.

GET A CUPBOARD

It is worth having some ingredients that you keep in store. There is no need to go and get them all at once but if you buy a few at a time you will have enough stuff to cook at least a meal. The idea is that you can cope with emergencies, like forgetting you have someone coming round, or coming in late, starving hungry.

There are some things which you don't use up every time you cook a recipe which includes it.

Cans and things

Salt and pepper, preferably a pepper grinder
400 g tin of plum tomatoes
500 g pack of pasta
Sunflower oil
Olive oil
Tikka powder
Packet of mixed Mediterranean herbs
Pack of Mexican chilli seasoning
400 g tin of red kidney beans
Tin of baked beans
200 g tin of tuna
Carton of custard

Fridge

Tube of garlic paste
Mayonnaise
Small bottle of lemon juice
Butter or low fat spread
Eggs
Tomato purée

Frozen food

1 pack of chicken pieces (thighs, breasts or quarters)
1 pack of white fish (Cod, Hake or Hoki)

Vegetables

Onions
Potatoes
Red pepper

There are the basics for pasta and tomato sauce, Mediterranean Fish or Italian Roast Chicken.

When you have used up any of the ingredients, replace it.

HOW TO COOK VEGETABLES

Frozen

For frozen peas, sweet corn and other vegetables, follow the instructions on the bag. In general these will include adding the vegetables to boiling water with half a teaspoon of salt, and cooking for a few minutes. Cooking times are approximately 3 minutes for sweet corn (off the cob) and 5 minutes for peas.

Fresh

Fresh vegetables take a bit more preparation than frozen and sometimes take longer than frozen vegetables to cook. There are times in the year when fresh vegetables will be much cheaper than frozen, and other times when they will be more expensive or simply unavailable.

Wash all fresh vegetables thoroughly. Throw away any leaves which are slimy and cut out any bits that look bad.

Potatoes

Potatoes are probably the most widely used and versatile vegetable. They can be boiled, baked, roasted, mashed, deep fried as chips or pan fried in butter.

New potatoes have thin flaky skins which almost come off when the potatoes are scrubbed. They are smaller, often called 'Jersey Royals' or 'Cyprus'. They are good for boiling or salads.

Old potatoes are larger, go under such names as Whites, King Edwards, Désirée Reds or Romanos. Good for mashing, roasting or baking.

Boiled potatoes

Potatoes can be cooked with their skins on or off. They are better for you with the skins on. If you are leaving their skins on be sure to give them a thorough wash or scrub and dig out any eyes or unpleasant looking bits.

Cook small to medium potatoes whole. Large ones should be cut in half or quarters, so that all the pieces of potatoes in the saucepan are about the same size. Generally speaking the smaller the potato piece the quicker it will cook. Put the potatoes in a saucepan of water with 1 teaspoon of salt, bring to the boil, turn the heat down and simmer for 20–25 minutes. Test them with a fork to see if they are done. When they are done the fork will easily pierce the potato. If they start to fall apart they are overdone. When they are done drain off the water and serve.

Mashed potatoes

Peel and cook as for boiled potatoes (above), and then drain off the water. Put them in a bowl or return them to the saucepan, then mash the potatoes up with a fork or a potato masher. Add small blobs of butter or margarine and fresh ground pepper to taste. If you like them creamier add a little milk (1 tablespoon) and mix well into the mashed potatoes.

Baked potatoes

Pick large old potatoes for this. Get about three potatoes to the kilogram. Do not peel, but give them a good scrub. Stick a metal skewer through each potato, it helps them to cook in the middle. If you like the skin very crispy then prick the skin with a fork and place on the top shelf of the oven on 230°C, 450°F, Gas mark 8 for about an hour.

To check if they are done, cover your hand, preferably with an oven glove, to protect it from the heat and squeeze the sides gently. If it gives easily, it is done. If you like it less crispy, cover in tin foil and remove ten minutes before taking from the oven. If not crispy at all, leave the tin foil on.

Roast potatoes

Peel the potatoes, cutting away any nasty bits, and cutting out any eyes. Chop the potatoes in half if medium sized or into quarters if large. Put the potatoes in an ovenproof dish with some sunflower oil. Turn over the potatoes to coat them in oil. Cook in the top of a preheated oven at 180°C, 350°F, Gas mark 4 for 60 minutes or so if you like them really well done. Turn over half-way through cooking.

You can heat the oil first by putting the dish with the oil in the oven for about 10 minutes before adding the vegetables. It helps to reduce sticking.

Pan fried potato in butter

This is a good way of using up cooked, left-over potato. Just put a couple of spoons of butter in a frying-pan. Slice the potato and fry for about 10 minutes.

Chips

We are not going to cover chips in this book; there are so many kinds of oven chips and frozen chips available and so many chip shops that it is not worth the hassle and risk of cooking them. Chip pans are the most common cause of household fire in the country.

Carrots

This is a vegetable that is good eaten raw. Add grated carrot to salad, or cut them into large match-stick shapes to dip into things like guacamole.

They are good roasted, and can be peeled and cooked together in the same dish as a joint of meat.

To cook separately, just peel and chop into quarters lengthways and put in an ovenproof dish with half a cup of water, a tablespoon of butter and a teaspoon of sugar. Cover with foil and cook in a preheated oven at 180°C, 350°F, Gas mark 4 for 30 minutes.

Small, young carrots can be boiled whole for 10 minutes or steamed whole for 20 minutes.

Cauliflower or broccoli

Break into 'florets' then cook in 5 cm (2 inches) of water with a teaspoon of salt for about 10 minutes. Test the florets with a fork to check if they are ready. Cauliflower and broccoli can be eaten raw, and the longer you cook them, the softer they get.

Cabbage

This comes in several colours: red, white and green. Treat them all the same. Throw away any nasty looking outer leaves. Cut out the central hard core and discard. Chop the cabbage roughly and cook in 2 cm (1 inch) of water with a teaspoon of salt for about 10–20 minutes.

Red and white cabbage are good shredded raw in salads particularly in the winter when lettuces are very expensive or hard to find.

Spinach

This is good raw as a salad leaf or lightly cooked. It shrinks when cooked so you will need at least 500g (1 lb) of spinach for two people.

First wash the spinach, shake out the excess water. Put the spinach into a saucepan with salt to taste and a blob (the size of a small walnut) of butter. There is no need to add any more water. Cook the spinach in a medium-sized saucepan over a medium heat. As soon as the water on the leaves starts to hiss and bubble, and the butter to melt, stir the spinach gently. When it is floppy and transparent, two to three minutes later, it is cooked. Strain off the liquid and serve.

Broad beans, runner beans, fine beans, sugar snaps and mange tout

All these small beans and peas are eaten in the pod. Cut off both ends, and pull any stringy bits from down the side. Cut them into pieces, except the sugar snaps and mange tout which should be cooked whole. Just cover with water, add salt to taste and boil rapidly for five to ten minutes until tender, testing them with a fork. Sugar snaps and mange tout only take three minutes.

Corn on the cob

This is a cheap vegetable in the summer and almost a meal in itself. There are several ways to cook corn: it can be boiled, baked or barbecued.

If boiling, pull all the leaves off and boil in salted water for 20–30 minutes. Check with a fork to see if the corn is soft enough to eat. The fork should pierce the corn easily. Serve with a blob of butter and freshly ground black pepper.

If barbecuing, keep the leaves on, and barbecue for 10–20 minutes turning a couple of times. If the leaves have been removed by the shop, don't worry, just turn the corn more often.

If baking the corn, pull the leaves off as for boiling, place on a baking tray, put a little oil or butter on the corn, sprinkle with salt and pepper and bake for about 45 minutes.

Courgettes

Courgettes are quick and easy to cook. Wash them and slice either across or lengthways. Put them in a pan with some oil or butter and some seasoning. Cook on a medium heat for about five minutes and serve.

HOW TO COOK RICE

The most important thing to know about cooking rice is that you should use twice as much water as you do rice. Below is a recipe for plain boiled rice for two people.

Serves 2   ℗ *Preparation 1 min, Cooking time depends on sort of rice – Easy*

INGREDIENTS
1 cup rice
2 cups water
1 teaspoon salt

EQUIPMENT
Saucepan with lid
Measuring cups and spoons

METHOD
Read the packet to get the correct cooking time. Put the rice, water and salt in the pan. Bring the water and rice to the boil, stirring once to stop the rice sticking to the bottom of the pan. Turn down the heat to low. Put the lid on the pan. Cook for the correct time until the fluid is absorbed (see below for different timings). Do not stir!

After the cooking time, take it off the heat and let it stand for a couple of minutes. Fluff it up with a fork to separate the grains and serve.

TIPS
The cup referred to is a standard measuring cup of 250 ml. It is approximately the same as a mug. For larger quantities just use 1 cup of water and half a cup of rice per person.

Basmati is more fragrant than long grain, and also more forgiving, because it holds together during cooking.

Approximate cooking times (read the packet for more accurate timings):

Basmati	10 minutes
American long grain	15 minutes
Organic long grain brown rice	30–35 minutes
Brown quick cook	20–25 minutes

HOW TO COOK NOODLES

Serves 2   ① *Preparation 1 min, Cooking 4 min – Easy*

INGREDIENTS
2 sheets dried noodles
1 tablespoon sesame oil

EQUIPMENT
Saucepan
Sieve or colander to drain the noodles

METHOD
Check the cooking time on the packet. Boil at least a pint of water in a saucepan. Put the noodles in the water. Boil for about 4 minutes. Drain the noodles. Return to the pan. Add a tablespoon of sesame oil and stir round. Serve.

TIPS
You get three sheets of noodles in a 250 g pack of Sharwoods medium noodles.

HOW TO COOK PASTA

Serves 2   ⏱ *Preparation 1 min, Cooking 2–10 min – Easy*

INGREDIENTS

250 g dried pasta (generally half a pack or two and a half cups)
1 teaspoon salt

EQUIPMENT

Saucepan
Wooden spoon
Sieve or colander

METHOD

Read the packet for the correct cooking time. Put at least a pint of water into the saucepan and bring to the boil. Put the pasta in the water. Stir the pasta once to stop it sticking to the bottom of the pan. Bring back to the boil and simmer for as long as the packet says. Add the salt.

The best way to judge if the pasta is cooked is to bite it. This is tricky, because if you fish out a bit and stick it in your mouth you may burn your mouth with the boiling water. Wait a bit and blow on it, then bite it.

You can trust the cooking time if you want to or put a bit on a plate and cut it with the edge of a fork. If it is hard it needs longer. If it is like mush it is overcooked.

HOW TO ROLL PASTRY

INGREDIENTS
Half a 500 g pack of pastry, chilled or frozen
2 tablespoons flour

EQUIPMENT
Rolling pin

METHOD
Make sure the pastry is well thawed, four hours in the fridge being typical. Keep the pastry in the fridge before rolling. Make sure that the surface that you are going to roll on is clean, dry and flat. Pastry can stick to the surface or rolling pin unless it is kept dry, so sprinkle the surface and the pastry with flour.

Roll and then turn the pastry through a quarter of a circle. Roll and turn, scattering more flour if needed.

It is remarkably easy.

HOW TO BAKE A PASTRY CASE

METHOD
A few recipes need a pre-cooked pastry case to work. If you put the filling in the raw pastry case it will not cook properly. If you just cook the case in the oven it will distort and shrink. So part cook it without the proper filling but lined with greaseproof paper and with some dried beans to keep the pastry in place.

Roll out the pastry, as shown above. Line the dish. Pastry is fairly flexible so you can push it into place. If it tears patch it with a spare bit, moistening with a bit of water to make sure it sticks. Pastry shrinks when it cooks so if you trim it to the top of the rim it will shrink below that level. So cut it high.

Prick the bottom of the pastry with a fork at least five times to let steam out. Cut a piece of greaseproof paper and press gently on to the pastry. Fill the bottom with a layer of cheap dried beans, for instance butter beans. Cook the pastry case at 200°C, 400°F, Gas mark 6 for 15 minutes until the top edges go golden.

Take the pastry case out of the oven.

HOW TO MAKE DRIED BEANS TURN OUT SOFT AND NOT LIKE BULLETS

① Preparation 5 min, Cooking time depends – Easy

INGREDIENTS

1½ cups of dried beans or chick peas – equivalent to 2 (440 g) tins

EQUIPMENT

Saucepan with lid
Bowl

METHOD

Check over the dried beans. Throw away any stones or odd looking ones. Put the beans in a plastic bowl or one made from heatproof glass. Pour boiling water on top of them, and cover to a depth of about 5 cm (2 inches). (Don't add any salt until the beans are cooked.) This takes about a litre or two pints. Leave the beans for 1 to 2 hours to swell up, preferably in a fridge. Drain and rinse the beans.

Put them in a saucepan with at least a pint of fresh water. Bring to the boil and boil vigorously for 10 minutes. Turn down the heat until the water is just simmering gently. Cook the beans till they are soft. This may take anything between 30 minutes and two and a half hours depending on the variety. Add more water if it gets low.

When the beans are done, take off the heat. Drain the beans and leave to cool down.

ADDITIONS & ALTERNATIVES

Approximate cooking times (read the packet for more accurate timings):

Red kidney beans	60–90 minutes
Chick peas	150 minutes
Rose coco (Borlotti) beans	150 minutes
Red split lentils	30 minutes
Green lentils with skin on	90 minutes

TIPS

Parsley is reputed to reduce the wind generating capacity of beans.

HOW TO DEFROST THINGS

Chicken pieces

Overnight in the fridge or six hours at room temperature.

Chicken livers (200 g or 8 oz tub)

Four hours at room temperature or overnight in the fridge.

Lamb chops

Defrost in a single layer for four hours at room temperature or overnight in the fridge.

Half leg of lamb

Overnight in the fridge or four hours at room temperature.

Whole chicken (1.5 kg or 3 lb)

24 hours in fridge, 12 hours in a cool room.

Packet of extra large prawns

Three hours at room temperature.

Plaice, cod and haddock

Cook from frozen.

CHILLI

FRESH CHILLI – A WARNING! When you chop up the chillies be careful to avoid getting juice on your hands. It will sting. If you touch your eyes, mouth or other sensitive areas even an hour after chopping them they will smart and burn. So wash your hands or wear rubber gloves.

STARTERS

TUNA MAYONNAISE

Makes a small bowl   ① *Preparation 5 min – Easy*

INGREDIENTS
200 g tin of tuna
2 or 3 spring onions
2 tablespoons mayonnaise
Salt and pepper to taste

EQUIPMENT
Tin opener
Small bowl
Sharp knife
Chopping board
Fork
Set of measuring spoons

METHOD
Open the tin of tuna. Drain the liquid from the tin. Put the tuna in the bowl and mash it up with the fork.

Get the spring onions and take off the outer leaves. Cut off the root end and trim off the green leaves and any other unsavoury bits. Wash the spring onions and dry. Chop the onions into thin rings with the knife.

Mix the onions and the mayonnaise in with the tuna. Add salt and pepper, if you wish.

ADDITIONS & ALTERNATIVES

This can be used as a pasta sauce. Mix the tuna mayonnaise in with freshly cooked and drained pasta shapes or spaghetti. Sprinkle with grated Parmesan cheese and fresh ground pepper, and serve with fresh warm bread and salad.

Use it as a filling for baked potato.

Use in an avocado pear as below.

AVOCADO VINAIGRETTE, PRAWN OR TUNA

2 servings   ① *Preparation 10 min – Easy*

INGREDIENTS

1 ripe avocado
3 tablespoons olive oil
1 tablespoon lemon juice or wine vinegar
Salt and pepper

EQUIPMENT

Sharp knife
Chopping board
Set of measuring spoons
Small jam jar with lid

METHOD

Cut the avocado in half. Discard the stone.

Put the oil, lemon juice, salt and pepper in a jam jar and shake vigorously. It will go thick and creamy. Pour into the hole left by the avocado stone.

31

ADDITIONS & ALTERNATIVES

Serve with brown bread and butter.

You can buy many different ready-made vinaigrette sauces.

Try making different flavour vinaigrettes using walnut or sunflower oil instead of olive oil, or orange juice instead of the lemon, or adding a crushed clove of garlic, half a teaspoon of French mustard or herbs.

Use Tuna mayonnaise instead of the vinaigrette.

Put a few thawed prawns in the hole and serve with vinaigrette. You can use prawns and prawn cocktail sauce, which fortunately is the next recipe.

TIPS

Ripe avocados are still green and are not hard, but should 'give' a bit when gently pressed.

Make this just before you want to eat. If you cut the avocado too soon it will discolour.

PRAWN COCKTAIL

2 big or 4 small servings   ① *Preparation 10 min – Easy*

INGREDIENTS

Iceberg lettuce
250 g pack of frozen or fresh cooked prawns
2 tablespoons mayonnaise
2 tablespoons low fat yoghurt (or 2 more tablespoons
    of mayonnaise)
1 or 2 teaspoons tomato ketchup
1 or 2 teaspoons lemon juice
$\frac{1}{2}$ teaspoon paprika
1 lemon, sliced

EQUIPMENT
Small mixing bowl
Set of measuring spoons
Sharp knife
Chopping board
2 small cereal or soup bowls or 4 wineglasses

METHOD
Wash and dry a few leaves of iceberg lettuce. Put the lettuce in the bottom of a wineglass or small bowl. Divide up the prawns and put them on the lettuce, keeping a few aside to dangle over the side of the bowl.

Mix the mayonnaise, yoghurt, ketchup, lemon juice and paprika in the bowl. Pour some on each portion. Finish off with a couple of good-looking prawns and a slice of lemon.

ADDITIONS & ALTERNATIVES
Serve with toast or brown bread.

Use white crab meat or lobster bits chopped up instead of prawns.

If you like a more spicy sauce add two drops of Tabasco sauce or a pinch of cayenne pepper to it.

This is a very flexible sauce and can be used with avocado and prawn. It also makes a good dip for Kettle chips.

Add a small pot of cottage cheese and some prawns, and eat it with salads. This is also good with crisps or tortilla chips.

MELON & PARMA HAM

Serves 4   ① *Preparation 5 min – Easy*

INGREDIENTS
1 ripe Galia or Honeydew melon
8 thin slices Parma or Serano ham

EQUIPMENT
Sharp knife
Chopping board

METHOD
Cut the melon into quarters. Scrape away the seeds with a spoon and discard. Cut the melon away from the skin and chop into neat large cubes.

Arrange the melon and the ham on four plates.

ADDITIONS & ALTERNATIVES
Parma and Serano ham should be cut very thin so they are translucent. They are available in packets or from the delicatessen counter or specialist shops. Serano is slightly moister and pinker. It should not be hard.

If the counter does not sell much it can be like an old boot. Don't let them give you the dried out top slices.

Try other melons.

TIPS
Ripe melons smell sweet and are slightly softer, particularly at the end where the stalk comes out.

You can get a small scoop which makes melon balls.

SMOKED MACKEREL PATÉ

Serves 2 or 4   ① *Preparation 10 min – Easy*

INGREDIENTS
2 smoked mackerel fillets with peppercorns
2 to 3 tablespoons butter or soft margarine
1 teaspoon lemon juice
Toast or crusty bread

EQUIPMENT
Fork
Bowl
Set of measuring spoons

METHOD
Pull the skin off the mackerel fillets. Break the fish into lumps, put in bowl and mash up with the butter and lemon juice until smooth enough to spread.

If not spreadable, mash more or add a bit more butter.

Serve with toast or fresh crusty bread.

SMOKED SALMON SALAD

Serves 2   ① *Preparation 15 min, Cooking 12 min – Easy*

INGREDIENTS
1 egg
4 lettuce leaves
100 g packet smoked salmon
100 g pot lumpfish roe, red or black
1 lemon
Bread and butter or toast
Freshly ground pepper to taste

EQUIPMENT
Saucepan
Sharp knife
Chopping board

METHOD
To hard boil the egg, put it in a small saucepan nearly full of water. Bring to the boil, and boil for ten minutes. Cool the egg by putting it in cold water.

When the egg is cold, take off the shell. Chop the egg up. It is easier to chop the white separately then lightly mash the yolk.

Wash the lettuce leaves. Shake dry. Arrange the clean lettuce leaves on two plates. Arrange the salmon artistically in a manner befitting the plate and the occasion. Put half the egg on each plate and a teaspoon of lumpfish roe on top. Cut the lemon in quarters and put one or two on each plate.

Serve with bread and butter or toast and freshly ground pepper.

ADDITIONS & ALTERNATIVES
Assemble the ingredients into a sandwich.

Use smoked salmon trout. It tastes just as good and is cheaper.

TIPS
The egg may be prepared earlier. Leave it in its shell till ready to make the rest of the salad.

STUFFED TOMATOES WITH PESTO

Serves 4   ① *Preparation 3 min – Easy*

INGREDIENTS
4 large tomatoes
190 g jar basil pesto
Salt and freshly ground pepper to taste
2 tablespoons olive oil
Bread and butter
Green salad

EQUIPMENT
Sharp knife
Chopping board
Set of measuring spoons

METHOD
Cut the tomatoes in half. Scoop out the seeds. Put a teaspoon of pesto in each half. Season with salt and pepper. Dribble a little olive oil on each one.

Serve with bread and a little green salad.

STUFFED TOMATOES WITH SPICED FILLING

Serves 4   ① *Preparation 5 min, Cooking 10 min – Easy*

INGREDIENTS

1 egg
1 tablespoon hot mango chutney
2 tablespoons mayonnaise
Salt and freshly ground pepper to taste
4 medium to large tomatoes
Bread and butter
Green salad

EQUIPMENT

Saucepan
Bowl
Sharp knife
Fork
Chopping board
Set of measuring spoons

METHOD

To hard boil the egg, boil it in the saucepan for ten minutes, then cool it down by running cold water over it for five minutes.

Put the hot mango chutney in the bowl. Chop up any lumps.

Peel the egg and mash up with the chutney. Add the mayonnaise. Mix together and season.

Cut the tomatoes in half. Scoop out the seeds. Put a teaspoon of the filling in each half.

Serve with bread and a little green salad.

GRILLED GRAPEFRUIT

Serves 2   ① *Preparation 2 min, Cooking 5 to 10 min – Easy*

INGREDIENTS
1 grapefruit
1 tablespoon port or brandy (optional)
2 tablespoons brown sugar

EQUIPMENT
Sharp knife
Chopping board
Grill
Set of measuring spoons

METHOD
Cut the grapefruit in half. Dig out any visible pips. Loosen the
segments by cutting between them. Put half the port or brandy on
each half. Sprinkle the sugar over the top. Cook under a moderate
grill for five to ten minutes.

ROCKET & GOAT'S CHEESE SALAD

Serves 4 as a starter   ① *Preparation 10 min – Easy*

Good as a starter for four or as a summer meal with other salad.

INGREDIENTS
1 packet of Rocket about 100g
175 g (6 oz) of mild goat's cheese
1 clove of garlic
3 tablespoons olive oil
1 tablespoon lemon juice

39

Salt and pepper
1 teaspoon of ground almonds (optional)

EQUIPMENT
Sharp knife
Chopping board
Garlic crusher
Jam jar with lid
Set of measuring spoons

METHOD
Look at the leaves and throw away any slimy ones. Wash the rest in water and then drain and pat dry between kitchen towel. Lay them out on a plate. Cut the goat's cheese into chunks. Distribute them on the Rocket leaves.

Peel and crush the garlic into the jam jar. Put all of the other dressing ingredients in the jam jar and shake for 30 seconds. Pour over the salad.

ADDITIONS & ALTERNATIVES
Use Camembert or Brie instead of the goat's cheese.
Use salad and basil leaves or watercress instead of the Rocket.
Add two shredded sun-dried tomatoes to the dressing.
There's a cooked version where the cheese is left to stand for half an hour in the dressing then dipped in breadcrumbs and put in the oven at 180°C, 350°F, Gas mark 4 for three minutes.

TIPS
Prepared garlic is sold in tubes and jars. Just read the tube or jar for the suggested equivalent amount. It keeps for six weeks in the fridge.

Rocket is a spicy, peppery green herb. It tastes similar to watercress. Larger supermarkets have it for sale already prepared.

SMOKED SALMON ROLL

Serves 4   ① *Preparation 10 min, Cooking 5 min – Moderate*

INGREDIENTS

2 eggs
1 tablespoon milk
Salt and freshly ground pepper to taste
1 tablespoon butter for frying
100 g (4 oz) packet of smoked salmon or smoked salmon trout
Green salad leaves (lettuce)

EQUIPMENT

Bowl
Set of measuring spoons
Fork
20 cm (8 inch) frying-pan
Egg/fish slice (to turn the omelette over)
Chopping board
Sharp knife

METHOD

First make an omelette. Break eggs into bowl and add milk. Add
a pinch of salt and pinch of pepper. Beat with a fork until mixed.

Melt the butter in the frying-pan over a medium heat. Add the
egg mixture. After 30 seconds it will be solid underneath and can
be turned over for another minute or so. Put the omelette on the
chopping board. Let it cool down a bit.

Put the salmon slices on the omelette. Roll up the omelette so
you have a kind of Swiss roll effect. Cut the roll into slices and
arrange on plates with the salad leaves.

ADDITIONS & ALTERNATIVES

Put a tinned anchovy on each roll.

GARLIC MUSHROOMS

Serves 4   ① Preparation 3 min plus an hour in the fridge,
Cooking 5 min – Easy

INGREDIENTS

2 tablespoons chopped parsley
350 g (13 oz) mushrooms
3 cloves garlic
2 tablespoons wine vinegar
2 tablespoons olive oil
Salt and pepper
2 tablespoons tomato purée

EQUIPMENT

Sharp knife
Chopping board
Saucepan
Set of measuring spoons
Bowl

METHOD

Wash, drain, dry and finely chop the parsley. Wipe the mushrooms clean. Discard any nasty ones. Chop the end off the stalks.

Peel and chop the garlic. Put the garlic, vinegar, oil, salt and pepper in the pan together with about half a cup of water. Boil the mixture. Add the mushrooms and the tomato purée. Boil for five minutes, stirring.

Take the pan off the heat. Allow to cool and put in a bowl with the parsley in the fridge. Leave to get really cold.

ADDITIONS & ALTERNATIVES

Try lemon juice instead of vinegar.

Add 1 teaspoon of Mediterranean mixed herbs.

TIPS

Prepared garlic is sold in tubes and jars. Just read the tube or jar for the suggested equivalent amount. It keeps for six weeks in the fridge.

Tomato purée comes in tubes. It keeps for four weeks in the fridge.

CHICKEN LIVER PATÉ

Serves 2 to 4   ① *Preparation 5 min, Cooking 12 min – Easy*

INGREDIENTS

225 g (9 oz) tub frozen chicken livers
2 small to medium onions
2 cloves of garlic
1 tablespoon butter for cooking
$\frac{1}{2}$ teaspoon mixed herbs
Salt and freshly ground pepper to taste
Toast

EQUIPMENT

Sharp knife
Chopping board
Frying-pan
Wooden spoon
Set of measuring spoons
Bowl

METHOD

Defrost chicken livers. This takes four hours at room temperature or overnight in the fridge.

Chop the onions and garlic. Melt the butter in the frying-pan on a low flame. Add the onions and garlic and gently cook till they are soft. Add the chicken livers and herbs. Cook together gently for ten minutes, mashing it a bit with the spoon to check it is cooked through. If you cook too high it will turn out like rubber.

Put it all in the bowl and mash it together until it is spreadable and to your taste. Some like it chunkier than others. Season to taste.

Serve cold with toast.

ADDITIONS & ALTERNATIVES

Add 1 tablespoon of sherry to the frying-pan when it is nearly cooked through.

TIPS

This will keep in the fridge for a day.

Prepared garlic is sold in tubes and jars. Just read the tube or jar for the suggested equivalent amount. It keeps for six weeks in the fridge.

FRIED CAMEMBERT & CRANBERRY SAUCE

Serves 2–4   ⏲ *Preparation 5 min, Cooking 3 min – Moderate*

INGREDIENTS

A small Camembert cheese (not ripe and runny, and keep it in the
    fridge before use)
1 tablespoon flour
1 beaten egg
2 tablespoons breadcrumbs
Oil
Green salad
300 g (11 oz) jar of cranberry sauce

EQUIPMENT
Knife
Set of measuring spoons
3 small bowls
Frying-pan

METHOD
Cut the cheese into eight segments. Roll the cheese in the flour, dip into the beaten egg and then coat in breadcrumbs.

Heat the oil in the frying-pan. Fry the cheese for about three minutes till golden brown.

Serve immediately with a green salad and cranberry sauce.

ADDITIONS & ALTERNATIVES
You can grate or food-process your own breadcrumbs.

Use Brie instead of Camembert

Use gooseberry preserve instead of cranberry sauce.

HOT WHISKY SMOKED FISH

Serves 4 or eat two yourself for a main course

⏲ *Preparation 15 min,*
Cooking 40 min – Moderately fiddly and messy but worth it

INGREDIENTS
500 g (1 lb) smoked haddock
1 cup milk for cooking the haddock in
1 medium carton (284 ml or 10 fl oz) of single cream
2 tablespoons whisky
400 g tin plum tomatoes
4 tablespoons grated Parmesan cheese
Salt and freshly ground pepper to taste

EQUIPMENT
Sharp knife
Chopping board
Saucepan
Small bowl
Fork
4 ovenproof ramekins or an ovenproof dish
Set of measuring spoons
Tin opener

METHOD
Peel the skin off the haddock. Put the milk and the haddock in the saucepan and bring to the boil. The fish will go firm within a couple of minutes. Take the fish off the heat. Drain off the milk and put the fish into the bowl. Let it cool down. Flake it apart and divide it into the four ramekins

Put the single cream and the whisky in the bowl and mix together.

Open the tin of tomatoes and drain off the juice. Lift out the tomatoes. Cut each one in half and discard the seeds. Put a piece of tomato on top of each portion of fish. Pour the cream and whisky into the ramekins. Put about one tablespoon of Parmesan cheese on top of each ramekin and season. Cook in a preheated oven at 200°C, 400°F, Gas mark 6.

ADDITIONS & ALTERNATIVES
Use grated Pecorino cheese. Both it and Parmesan can be bought in packets.

TIPS
Prepare this a while before you want to eat it. Letting the fish stand in the whisky makes the flavour even better.

A ramekin is a small circular pot roughly 5 cm (2 inches) tall, and 8 cm (3 inches) across. They are also good for making individual desserts in like chocolate mousse or cream caramel.

SNACKS

PRAWN DIP

*Enough for large pack of crisps
or tortilla chips*   ① *Preparation 2 min – Easy*

INGREDIENTS
Half a 250 g pack of frozen prawns
1 medium carton (about 227 g or 8 oz) cottage cheese
1 tablespoon tomato ketchup
1 teaspoon paprika
1 tablespoon lemon juice

EQUIPMENT
Bowl
Set of measuring spoons

METHOD
Thaw the prawns for at least two hours, or according to the pack.
If you are in a hurry, put them in a sieve and run them under
COLD water, then squeeze dry. Mix in the rest of the ingredients.

ADDITIONS & ALTERNATIVES
Serve with crisps, Kettle chips, tortilla chips, or chopped vegetables.

Can be a meal with salad.

TAHINI CREAM DIP

Makes a small bowl   ⏱ *Preparation 2 min – Easy*

INGREDIENTS
1 small carton (142 ml or 5 fl oz) of unsweetened
    Greek yoghurt
1 tablespoon Tahini

EQUIPMENT
Bowl
Fork
Set of measuring spoons

METHOD
Mix the Tahini and the yoghurt together. It will make the yoghurt thicker.

ADDITIONS & ALTERNATIVES
Tahini Cream is a sauce for falafel (spicy fried chick pea balls). Serve with salad and hot pitta bread.

It also makes a good salad dressing.

Adjust the ratio of Tahini to yoghurt.

Try adding lemon juice and sesame oil to thin it a bit.

Add fresh chopped herbs, particularly coriander, parsley, mint or chives.

TIPS
Tahini is a paste made up of crushed sesame seeds. It is available from health food shops and larger supermarkets.

HUMMUS & PITTA BREAD

Serves 4   ① *Preparation 5 min – Easy*

INGREDIENTS
250 g pot hummus
1 tablespoon Tahini
1 tablespoon olive oil
Pitta bread

EQUIPMENT
Plate
Set of measuring spoons
Spoon
Grill
Sharp knife
Chopping board

METHOD
Spoon the hummus on to a plate. Use the back of a spoon to level the hummus. Make a slight depression in the middle of the plate and fill it with the Tahini. Make another slight indentation round the plate near the edge. Fill this with the olive oil.

Grill the pitta bread and cut into slices.

Serve.

ADDITIONS & ALTERNATIVES
Put a couple of olives and a teaspoon of chopped parsley on top.

Eat with tortilla chips.

BASIC CHEESE ON TOAST

Serves 1   ① *Preparation 2 min, Cooking 3 min – Easy*

INGREDIENTS
1 slice toast
Cheddar cheese (about 50 g or 2 oz)
Enough butter for a slice of toast

EQUIPMENT
Sharp knife
Chopping board
Grill

METHOD
Butter the toast. Slice the cheese and put it on the toast. Grill the cheese until it is runny and brown.

SMART CHEESE ON TOAST

Serves 1   ① *Preparation 3 min, Cooking 3 min – Easy*

INGREDIENTS
1 slice toast
Enough butter for a slice of toast
Cheddar cheese (about 50 g or 2 oz or a cup of grated cheese)
1 tablespoon milk
1 teaspoon paprika

EQUIPMENT
Sharp knife
Cheese grater
Bowl

Set of measuring spoons
Grill pan

METHOD

Butter the toast. Grate the cheese. Mix it with the milk and paprika in the bowl. Spread the mixture on the toast. Grill the cheese until it is runny and brown.

ADDITIONS & ALTERNATIVES

Use ready grated cheese.

LATE CHEESE ON TOAST

Serves 1   ① *Preparation 3 min, Cooking 3 min – Easy*

INGREDIENTS

1 slice bread
Enough butter for the bread
1 small to medium onion
Cheddar cheese (about 50–75 g or 2–3 oz)
1 tablespoon HP Sauce

EQUIPMENT

Sharp knife
Chopping board
Set of measuring spoons
Grill

METHOD

Toast one side of the bread. Take it from under the grill. Butter the untoasted side.

Peel and chop the onion finely and sprinkle on the bread. Grill for a minute or so. Slice the cheese and put it on the toast. Grill the cheese until it is runny and brown. Pour HP sauce on the top.

ADDITIONS & ALTERNATIVES
Use ready grated cheese.
  Use cheese spread.

LATE TOASTED CHEESE SANDWICH

Serves 1   ⏲ *Preparation 3 min, Cooking 3 min – Easy*

INGREDIENTS
2 slices bread
2 tablespoons butter
HP Sauce
$\frac{1}{4}$ to $\frac{1}{2}$ onion
Cheddar cheese (about 50–75 g or 2–3 oz)
2 slices tomato

EQUIPMENT
Sharp knife
Chopping board
Grill
Set of measuring spoons

METHOD
Toast one slice of bread. Butter it. Toast one side of the other slice of bread. Take it from under the grill. Butter the untoasted side.
  Spread with HP Sauce.
  Peel and chop the onion finely and sprinkle on the bread. Grill for a minute or so. Slice the cheese and put it on the toast. Grill the cheese until it is runny and brown. Put the tomato and second slice of toast on top.

ADDITIONS & ALTERNATIVES
Use ready grated cheese.
  Add chopped ham.

FRIED CHEESE & ONION SANDWICH

Serves 1   ① *Preparation 2 min, Cooking 5 min – Easy*

INGREDIENTS
2 slices bread
Enough butter for the bread
Sliced cheese (about 50 g or 2 oz)
2 slices of onion
1 tablespoon oil

EQUIPMENT
Sharp knife
Chopping board
Frying-pan
Set of measuring spoons

METHOD
Butter the bread. Make a cheese and onion sandwich.

Put the oil in the frying-pan. Heat. Fry the sandwich, turning once, till the cheese starts to melt.

Serve hot with a green salad, or on its own.

BACON & AVOCADO TOASTED SANDWICH

Serves 2   ① *Preparation 5 min, Cooking 10 min – Easy*

INGREDIENTS
1 ripe avocado (ripe ones are not hard, but give a little at the end
    when gently pressed)
8 rashers bacon

53

4 slices bread
Freshly ground pepper
1 tablespoon mayonnaise

EQUIPMENT

Sharp knife
Chopping board
Grill
Set of measuring spoons

METHOD

Cut the avocado in half. Take out the stone.

Peel the avocado. Cut the avocado into slices. If it is really hard or horribly brown, throw it away and eat something else, like bacon and lettuce and tomato sandwich.

Cut nicks in the bacon rind every couple of centimetres (inch). This stops the bacon curling up. Grill for about five minutes a side, till cooked. Meanwhile, grill the bread. Put the bacon on two slices of toast. Put the avocado slices on the bacon. Grind some pepper on top. Spread a little mayonnaise on the other two slices of toast. Put these on top. Eat.

ADDITIONS & ALTERNATIVES

Bacon bought by the slice from the butcher is generally tastier than pre-packed bacon. There is quite a lot of extra water in pre-packed bacon, which gets added to make it sizzle, and a lot of salts.

You can fry bacon, but it does come out more oily.

If you like bacon less salty, cook it for two minutes, then run it under water. Return and continue cooking.

CLUB SANDWICH

Serves 2   ⏱ *Preparation 5 min, Cooking 10 min – Easy*

INGREDIENTS
A few lettuce leaves
1 ripe tomato
1 cup cooked chicken
4 to 6 rashers bacon
6 slices bread
2 tablespoons mayonnaise
2 tablespoons cranberry sauce
Pepper
A pack of Kettle chips

EQUIPMENT
Sharp knife
Chopping board
Grill
Set of measuring spoons
Set of measuring cups

METHOD
Wash and drain the lettuce. Wash and slice the tomato. Break up the chicken. Cut nicks in the bacon rind every couple of centimetres (inch). This stops the bacon curling up. If you prefer, just cut the rind off. Grill for about five minutes a side, till cooked.

Meanwhile, toast the bread. Spread a little mayonnaise on a slice of toast. Put on half the chicken and lettuce.

Spread some cranberry sauce on another bit of toast. Put this, cranberry side down, on the chicken. Put half the bacon on the top and then some sliced tomato. Grind some pepper on top. Spread a third bit of toast with some mayonnaise and place on top.

Repeat the assembly process for the second sandwich.

Serve with Kettle chips.

ADDITIONS & ALTERNATIVES

You can use turkey instead of chicken.

Bacon with rind is better than without. Bacon bought by the slice from the butcher is generally tastier than pre-packed bacon. There is quite a lot of extra water in pre-packed bacon, which gets added to make it sizzle, and a lot of salts. You can fry bacon, but it does come out more oily. If you like bacon less salty, cook it for 2 minutes, then run it under water. Return and continue cooking.

CHEAT'S CHOCOLATE CROISSANTS

Serves 2   ① *Preparation 5 min, Cooking 20 min – Easy*

INGREDIENTS

375 g pack of ready rolled puff pastry
1 tablespoon butter
2 large chocolate flakes
1 teaspoon milk

EQUIPMENT

Sharp knife
Chopping board
Set of measuring spoons
Baking sheet

METHOD

Thaw the pastry according to the instructions on the packet. Four hours in the fridge seems typical. Unfold and cut into four pieces. Spread the pieces with a thin layer of butter.

Cut the flakes in half. Put one piece of flake on one piece of pastry. Roll it up. Seal the edge with a little milk. Do the other three. Put on a baking sheet and cook in a preheated oven at

200°C, 400°F, Gas mark 6 for about 15 to 20 minutes, until puffed up and golden brown.

ADDITIONS & ALTERNATIVES
Use chocolate bars or chocolate nut spread instead of flakes.

MINI GOURMET PIZZA

*Serves 4 as starter or summer
lunch with salad*

① *Preparation 5 min,
Cooking 10 min – Easy*

INGREDIENTS
1 ciabatta loaf
1 jar or tube sun-dried tomato paste
56 g (2 oz) tube of anchovy paste
Small (100 g) Mozzarella cheese
2 tablespoons olive oil
Salt and freshly ground pepper to taste
Salad of exotic leaves

EQUIPMENT
Sharp knife
Chopping board
Set of measuring spoons
Baking tray

METHOD
Cut 8 slices of ciabatta bread. Spread about a teaspoon of the sun-dried tomato sauce on each one. Spread an inch squirt of anchovy paste on each slice. Top off with a slice of Mozzarella cheese. Season with salt and pepper.

Wipe the baking tray with a little oil. Put the slices on the baking tray. Cook in a preheated oven at 200°C, 400°F, Gas mark

6 until the cheese is melted and slightly brown, about ten minutes.
Serve with a salad of some exotic leaves.

MINI PIZZA

Makes 6   ① *Preparation 5 min, Cooking 10 min – Easy*

INGREDIENTS
1 French loaf
200 g tube tomato purée
1 teaspoon oregano or mixed Mediterranean herbs
100 g Mozzarella cheese
50 g tin anchovies
1–2 tablespoons olive oil

EQUIPMENT
Sharp knife
Chopping board
Set of measuring spoons
Baking tray

METHOD
Cut the French loaf in half lengthways. Cut each slice into three.
Spread each piece with tomato purée. Sprinkle the herbs on the
tomato purée.

Cut the Mozzarella cheese into twelve slices. Arrange the
Mozzarella two slices to each 'pizza'. Put the anchovies on the top.
Brush the top with the oil. Cook in a preheated oven at 200°C,
400°F, Gas mark 6 until the Mozzarella is melted and slightly
brown, about 10 minutes.

ADDITIONS & ALTERNATIVES
Grill it.

Olives, sweet pepper rings or onion slices, all make good
toppings.

AUBERGINE WITH CHEESE

Makes a plateful ℗ *Preparation 20 min, Cooking 15 min – Easy*

INGREDIENTS
2 medium aubergines
Olive oil
Cheese: Parmesan, Gouda, Monterey Jack or Cheddar

EQUIPMENT
Sharp knife
Chopping board
Frying-pan
Slotted spoon
Kitchen roll
Grill

METHOD
Slice the aubergines. Soak in water for 20 minutes, then drain and dry with kitchen paper.

Heat the oil in the frying-pan. Put some aubergine slices, so they do not overlap, in the hot oil. Cook and turn till they are golden on both sides, about three to five minutes. Lift out the aubergine slices and drain on a plate covered in kitchen roll. Cook the rest of the slices the same way.

Slice the cheese thinly and put one slice on each piece of aubergine. Put these on a grill pan and grill till the cheese is melting and brown.

These can be eaten hot, or cold as a summer meal with other Tapas and salad.

ADDITIONS & ALTERNATIVES
Dutch aubergines do not need soaking.

GRILLED SARDINES

Serves 4   ⏱ *Preparation 3 min, Cooking 20 min – Easy*

INGREDIENTS
10 fresh large sardines
1 tablespoon oil
1 lemon
Salt and pepper

EQUIPMENT
Knife
Grill
Set of measuring spoons

METHOD
Buy fresh sardines. Wash the fish under flowing water. Allow to dry. Put the sardines on a grill pan. Brush the sardines with a little oil. Cook for about ten minutes each side. Serve with lemon quarters, salt and pepper.

ADDITIONS & ALTERNATIVES
It goes well with salad.

TIPS
If you don't like fish heads, cut them off before cooking or buy them headless.

SALADS & DRESSINGS

Salads are quick and easy, and are some of the simplest things to experiment with. Salads may be just a few lettuce leaves but can be more complicated classic salads like Salad Niçoise, Waldorf Salad or Caesar Salad. This chapter has recipes for salad dressings and some brilliant salads.

Here is a bit of information on some salad ingredients, followed by some more unusual things you can use in salad. After that there are recipes for some classic and not so classic combinations.

Lettuces

The simplest salad is lettuce. There are a lot of different lettuces. Each has its own characteristics but they all make a good base for a green salad. Green salads are a lot less hassle than vegetables.

Go to your local street market or supermarket. Look at different lettuces, smell them and try them.

Iceberg lettuce is crisp and has a neutral taste. It can be sliced or cut into chunks. It keeps well in the fridge.

Webb's wonder is a crispish round lettuce.

Cos lettuce has long, crisp leaves good for dipping in things.

Round lettuce has more floppy leaves.

Oak leaf has crisp bitterish, brown and green leaves.

Radicchio is small and slightly bitterish, the colour of red cabbage with white veins.

Frisee and lollo rosso have wobbly edges to the leaves. The lollo rosso has purple or red edges to the leaves. Both are very decorative 'designer' lettuce.

Mixing together lettuces of different colour and textures works well.

If lettuce is not available, try shredding white or red cabbage.

Herbs

Fresh herbs can be used in salads, either as decoration or to give a more interesting flavour.

Basil is an aromatic herb, often used in Italian food.

Rocket has small leaves with a distinct taste like watercress.

Other herbs like parsley and coriander work well in salads.

Tomatoes

Ordinary tomatoes can be a bit tasteless but are available all year.

Cherry tomatoes are small, sweet and expensive.

Beef tomatoes are large and good with steak.

Italian plum tomatoes are good for pasta sauces. They are the ones usually sold in tins but now often available fresh in supermarkets.

Other ingredients

You can combine almost anything to make a salad. Other standard salad ingredients include: cucumber, green, red or yellow peppers, spring onions, olives, and shredded carrot.

If you want a substantial salad try adding hard-boiled eggs, fish like tuna, cheese or ham.

Fruit such as chopped apples, pears, oranges or bananas.

Walnuts, peanuts or even a few pecan nuts, cashew nuts or almonds.

Dried fruit like a couple of tablespoons of sultanas, raisins, apricot & dates.

Cooked vegetables like potato, green beans or French beans.

VINAIGRETTE

① Preparation 1 min – Easy

INGREDIENTS
3–5 tablespoons olive oil
1 tablespoon white wine vinegar
Salt and pepper
1 teaspoon mustard (optional)
1 garlic clove (optional)

EQUIPMENT
1 screw-top jar
Garlic crusher
Set of measuring spoons

METHOD
Peel and crush the garlic into the jar. Put all the other ingredients in the screw-top jar and shake vigorously. The vinaigrette will go opaque and thick. It will keep in the fridge for three weeks.

ADDITIONS & ALTERNATIVES

Try mixing half and half ordinary and extra virgin olive oil.

Substitute sunflower oil or walnut oil for the olive oil.

Substitute lemon juice, orange juice or herb vinegar for the wine vinegar.

Try combinations of the ingredients with different salads. All combinations taste good.

TIPS

Prepared garlic is sold in tubes and jars. Just read the tube or jar for the suggested equivalent amount. It keeps for six weeks in the fridge.

Olive oils vary in taste. Extra virgin is more fruity, and interesting than ordinary olive oil but also more expensive. Different brands of extra virgin even taste different, just like different wines.

By the way, extra virgin is too good to fry in, the extra flavour just evaporates.

Good vinegars to use are white or red wine, cider or even ones that have had herbs added. Don't use malt vinegar, it is cheap but only good for chip shops, or making pickles.

BLUE CHEESE DRESSING

Enough for a big bowl of salad   ⓘ *Preparation 5 min – Easy*

INGREDIENTS

Vinaigrette
2 tablespoons of crumbly blue cheese like Roquefort or Stilton

EQUIPMENT

Bowl
Set of measuring spoons

METHOD

Break up the cheese and stir thoroughly into the vinaigrette if you like it lumpy or beat it if you like it smooth.

TIPS

This will keep for a couple of days in a tightly sealed jar in the fridge.

AMERICAN THOUSAND ISLAND DRESSING

Enough for a big bowl of salad   ⏱ *Preparation 10 min – Easy*

INGREDIENTS

1 tablespoon chives
1 tablespoon parsley
2 tablespoons olives, stoned or stuffed
1 tablespoon green pepper
1 cup mayonnaise
3 tablespoons tomato ketchup

EQUIPMENT

Sharp knife
Chopping board
Bowl
Set of measuring spoons
Set of measuring cups

METHOD

Wash and dry the chives and parsley. Chop the olives, green pepper, chives and parsley. Mix the mayonnaise and the ketchup. Put all the ingredients in the bowl and mix together.

Use as a dressing on sliced iceberg lettuce or eggs.

APPLE, ORANGE & CHEESE SALAD

Serves 2 to 4 ⓘ *Preparation 7 min – Easy*

INGREDIENTS
2 oranges
2 crisp eating apples
200 g (8 oz) Edam or Gouda cheese in a piece
1 tablespoon lemon juice or juice of half a lemon

EQUIPMENT
Sharp knife
Chopping board
Serving bowl
Vegetable peeler (optional)
Set of measuring spoons

METHOD
Peel the oranges with the knife. Dig out the pips. Cut the orange into 1 cm (half-inch) cubes. Put into the bowl.

Peel the apples. Cut in half and take out the core. Cut into cubes. Put in the bowl with the orange and the lemon juice and mix together, otherwise the apple will go brown.

Peel the skin off the cheese and cut into cubes. Just before you want to serve the salad put it into the bowl with the apple and orange and mix together.

ADDITIONS & ALTERNATIVES
This is a great salad with kebabs, or grilled meat like steak or chops.

BEAN SPROUT SALAD WITH YOGHURT DRESSING

Serves 4   ① *Preparation 5 min – Easy*

INGREDIENTS
200 g pack alfalfa or other sprouted seeds
2 spring onions
1 tablespoon parsley
Small carton (142 ml or 5 fl oz) yoghurt
Salt and freshly ground pepper to taste
Bread
Green salad

EQUIPMENT
Sharp knife
Chopping board
Wooden spoon
Bowl
Set of measuring spoons

METHOD
Wash and drain the sprouts.

Clean and prepare the spring onions. Cut the root end off, trim the leaves. Peel off and discard any dried up or slimy leaves. Chop into thin slices.

Wash, drain and chop the parsley. Put the spring onions and parsley into the bowl with the yoghurt. Mix together. Season with salt and pepper. Add the sprouts. Stir the sprouts in the yoghurt mixture until they are coated.

Serve with bread and green salad.

CHEDDAR CHEESE, WALNUT, CELERY & RAISIN SALAD

Serves 4   ① *Preparation 10 min – Easy*

INGREDIENTS
200 g (8 oz) Cheddar cheese
2 sticks celery
1 or 2 eating apples
Few mint leaves
4 tablespoons Greek yoghurt
3 tablespoons raisins
About 10 shelled walnuts, chopped

EQUIPMENT
Sharp knife
Chopping board
Small bowl
Set of measuring spoons

METHOD
Cut the cheese into cubes. Wash and clean the celery. Cut off the ends and leaves. Cut into slices. Peel and cube the apples, discarding the core and seeds. Cut the mint into tiny bits and mix in the bowl together with the yoghurt. Put the cheese, celery, apples, raisins and walnuts into the bowl. Stir it round so the ingredients are covered in the yoghurt. If it looks too dry put in more yoghurt.

ADDITIONS & ALTERNATIVES
Try using vinaigrette instead of the yoghurt and mint. There's a recipe for vinaigrette on page 63.

WATERMELON & FETA CHEESE SALAD

Serves 4 to 6   ① *Preparation 5 min – Easy*

INGREDIENTS

1 small to medium watermelon (about 2 kg or 4 lbs)
200 g (8 oz) pack Feta cheese

EQUIPMENT

Sharp knife
Chopping board
Bowl

METHOD

Cut the watermelon into large slices. Peel off the green skin and the pale inner layer. Cut the flesh into large chunks. Put in a bowl.

Chop the Feta cheese into small chunks. Put on top of the watermelon and serve.

ADDITIONS & ALTERNATIVES

Try drained cottage cheese instead of Feta.

TIPS

Ripe watermelon should be red with black seeds (unless they are seedless).

CHICK PEA SALAD

Serves 2 to 4 but good for parties   *① Preparation 15 min – Easy*

INGREDIENTS
2 × 400 g tins or jars of chick peas
Small bunch coriander or parsley
2 tablespoons olive oil
1 tablespoon lemon juice
Pitta bread

EQUIPMENT
Tin opener
Bowl
Sharp knife
Chopping board
Set of measuring spoons
Wooden spoon

METHOD
Open the tins or jars of chick peas. Drain. Put in the bowl. Wash and chop the coriander or parsley. Put the coriander, oil and lemon juice in with the chick peas. Mix together.

Serve with other salads and pitta bread.

ADDITIONS & ALTERNATIVES
Add sweet corn, chopped up sweet red peppers, onions or olives.

If you are going to make a lot of this for a party it is easy to cook the chick peas. There are full instructions in the 'How to' chapter.

GARLIC SAUSAGE & AVOCADO SALAD

*Serves 1 or 2 depending on
what you eat it with* ⏱ *Preparation 5 min – Easy*

INGREDIENTS
1 ripe avocado
200 g (8 oz) garlic sausage in a lump, not sliced up
1 small carton (142 ml or 5 fl oz) of natural unsweetened
  Greek yoghurt
Bread or toast
Green salad

EQUIPMENT
Sharp knife
Chopping board
Spoon
Small bowl

METHOD
Cut the avocado in half and take out the stone. Peel it and cut into
1 cm (half-inch) cubes. If it is really hard or horribly brown, throw
it away and eat something else, like garlic sausage sandwich.

Peel and cut the garlic sausage into 1 cm (half-inch) cubes. Put
the yoghurt in the bowl. Add the garlic sausage and the avocado.

Serve with toast, bread, lettuce or green salad.

ADDITIONS & ALTERNATIVES
Add chopped parsley or chopped mint for a different flavour.

Use tinned frankfurters chopped up instead of garlic sausage.

TIPS
Ripe avocados are green but not hard; they give a little at the end
when gently pressed.

71

GREEK SALAD

Serves 2   ① *Preparation 5 min – Easy*

INGREDIENTS

100 g (4 oz) pack of Feta cheese
1 large ripe tomato
½ cucumber
100 g (4 oz) black olives
1 tablespoon lemon juice
2 tablespoons olive oil

EQUIPMENT

Sharp knife
Chopping board
Serving dish
Set of measuring spoons

METHOD

Cut the Feta cheese into chunks. Cut the tomato into chunks. Cut
the cucumber into chunks. Put the cheese, tomato, cucumber and
olives in a dish. Pour the oil and lemon juice over the top. Stir and
serve.

BREAD & TOMATO SALAD

Serves 6   ① *Preparation 5 min – Easy*

INGREDIENTS
2 tablespoons parsley
2 cloves garlic
6 large ripe tomatoes
1 small cucumber
3 tablespoons extra virgin olive oil
1 tablespoon lemon juice
1 loaf of ciabatta Italian bread or a French stick

EQUIPMENT
Set of measuring spoons
Sharp knife
Chopping board
Wooden spoon
Bowl

METHOD
Wash, drain and chop the parsley. Peel and chop the garlic. Wash and coarsely chop the tomatoes. Wash, peel and dice the cucumber. Put the cucumber, tomato, parsley, garlic, olive oil and lemon juice into the bowl. Mix round. Break the bread into bite-sized chunks. Add to the bowl. Stir.

ADDITIONS & ALTERNATIVES
Try fresh coriander leaves instead of the parsley.
    Add chopped anchovies.
    Add a drained tin of tuna.
    Add olives.

MOZZARELLA SALAD

Serves 2   ① *Preparation 5 min – Easy*

INGREDIENTS
100g packet of Mozzarella cheese
1 or 2 (very large) beef tomatoes
1 Spanish onion
Freshly ground pepper to taste
2 tablespoons extra virgin olive oil
Fresh basil leaves (optional)
French bread

EQUIPMENT
Sharp knife
Chopping board
Set of measuring spoons

METHOD
Mozzarella cheese is sold in lumps in plastic bags. It is the mild stringy cheese used on top of pizza. Open the pack and drain off the fluid. Slice the cheese.

Wash and slice the tomatoes. Cut the top and bottom off the onion, peel, and slice into rings. Arrange the ingredients on a plate, overlapping the slices. Grind black pepper over the salad, and dribble the olive oil over the salad.

Eat with fresh crusty French bread.

ADDITIONS & ALTERNATIVES
Add fresh basil leaves.
Add some stoned olives.

SALAD NIÇOISE

Serves 4 as an accompaniment   ⏱ *Preparation 5 min,*
Cooking 5–7 min – Easy

INGREDIENTS
250 g (9 oz) French beans
1 crisp lettuce (Iceberg or Webb's Wonderful)
Vinaigrette (see recipe on page 63)

some or all of the following:
2 tomatoes
2 hard-boiled eggs
4 anchovies
1 cup olives (green or black, plain or stuffed)
Onion rings

EQUIPMENT
Sharp knife
Chopping board
Bowl
Set of measuring cups

METHOD
Wash the beans and chop into inch lengths. Boil for 5–7 minutes, drain and throw into cold water, and leave to cool.

Wash, dry and chop the lettuce. Toss the beans in vinaigrette. Put in the bottom of a bowl. Put the lettuce on top. Arrange on top quartered tomatoes, quartered hard-boiled eggs, anchovies and olives and onion rings.

Just before serving pour some more vinaigrette on top.

WALDORF SALAD

Serves 2   ① *Preparation 5 min – Easy*

INGREDIENTS
2 sticks of celery
2 eating apples
Small bunch of seedless grapes (about 200 g or 8 oz)
100 g packet of chopped walnuts or pecan nuts
1 cup of mayonnaise

EQUIPMENT
Sharp knife
Chopping board
Bowl
Spoon
Set of measuring cups

METHOD
Clean and chop the celery. Wash and cut the apples into small dice. Discard the pips and apple core. Mix all the ingredients in the bowl.

COLESLAW

Makes a lot   ① *Preparation 7 min – Easy*

INGREDIENTS
Half a white cabbage
3 carrots
3 or more tablespoons mayonnaise
Salt and freshly ground pepper to taste

EQUIPMENT
Sharp knife
Chopping board
Vegetable peeler
Grater
Bowl
Set of measuring spoons

METHOD
Cut the cabbage into really, really thin slices. Then cut it across, otherwise the bits tend to be a bit long. Alternatively, use a grater and shred the cabbage.

Cut the top, leaves and pointed end off the carrots and discard. Peel them. Grate them up. Mix with the cabbage in the bowl. Add 3 tablespoons of mayonnaise. Mix it thoroughly. If it is not enough to coat the cabbage and carrot add some more. Season to taste.

ADDITIONS & ALTERNATIVES
Use red cabbage instead of white.

Clean and chop 2 sticks of celery and add them.

Add half a cup of raisins

Add a handful of peanuts or other nuts. Use unsalted ones and chop roughly.

Use yoghurt instead of some or all the mayonnaise.

SPINACH, MUSHROOM & BACON SALAD

Serves 4 as an accompaniment   ① *Preparation 5 min,*
Cooking 6 min – Easy

INGREDIENTS

500 g (1 lb) of fresh spinach (small leaves are best)
100–200 g (4 to 8 oz) of mushrooms, about 20 in number
6 rashers of streaky bacon
Vinaigrette (see page 63)

EQUIPMENT

Sharp knife
Chopping board
Frying-pan
Kitchen paper

METHOD

Cut the bacon into small pieces. Fry in the pan until crispy. Take the bacon out of the pan and leave to stand on kitchen paper.

Wipe the mushrooms with a piece of paper. Don't wash them because they will go slimy. Cut the bottom of the stalks off. Slice the mushrooms.

Get the spinach and pull the stalks off. It will pull the main vein from the middle of the leaf. Wash the spinach. Dry it and then shred. Put the spinach in a bowl, then the mushrooms then the bacon.

Just before you serve it top off with vinaigrette.

ADDITIONS & ALTERNATIVES

Substitute croutons for bacon. Croutons are crisp fried cubes of bread. Cut some small 1 cm cubes of bread. Put some oil in a frying-pan with a crushed clove of garlic (optional). Heat the oil. Drop in the bread and stir. It should be cooked in two minutes.

PASTA SALAD

Serves 2 or more   *① Preparation 10 min, Cooking 15 min*
– Moderate

INGREDIENTS

Half a 250 g pack of small to medium-sized dried pasta shapes
    Swirls, shells, coloured or plain are suitable (About 2–3 cups)
2 tablespoons olive oil
1 green or red sweet pepper

EQUIPMENT

Saucepan
Set of measuring cups
Sieve or colander to drain the pasta
Bowl
Set of measuring spoons
Sharp knife
Chopping board

METHOD

Cook the pasta. If you have a problem with this there are full instructions in the 'How to' chapter. Read the packet for the cooking time and instructions for the pasta. Cook in at least a pint of boiling water. Drain the pasta.

Throw the pasta into the bowl with the oil and mix it up while it is still hot. This stops the pasta sticking together in a cold congealed mass. It also stops all the water from evaporating and stops it from drying up.

Meanwhile wash and dry the green or red pepper. Cut it open and throw away the seeds, stalk and top. Cut into small pieces. Put in with the pasta.

ADDITIONS & ALTERNATIVES

Add a small can of drained sweet corn, half an onion chopped small, or about 20 small mushrooms, wiped and sliced.

PASTA SALAD WITH AVOCADO

Serves 2 or more
⏲ *Preparation 10 min, Cooking 15 min – Moderate*

INGREDIENTS

Half a 250 g pack of small to medium-sized dried pasta shapes
   Swirls, shells, coloured or plain are suitable (About 2–3 cups)
1 tablespoon olive oil
250 g (9 oz) pack of bacon
1 eating apple
1 ripe avocado
2 teaspoon lemon juice
Lettuce

EQUIPMENT

Saucepan
Set of measuring cups
Sieve or colander
Bowl
Set of measuring spoons
Grill
Sharp knife
Chopping board

METHOD

Read the pasta packet for the cooking time. For most sorts it is about 10 to 15 minutes. Cook the pasta. If you have a problem with this there are full instructions in the 'How to' chapter. Drain the pasta.

Throw the pasta into the bowl with the oil and mix it up while it is still hot. This stops the pasta sticking together into a cold congealed mass. It also stops all the water from evaporating and stops the pasta from drying up.

Meanwhile grill the bacon. When it is cooked and crispy, chop it up. Wash the apple. Cut the core and pips out and discard. Cut into small pieces. Cut the avocado in half and remove the stone. Peel the skin off the avocado. Cut the avocado into bits. Put the bacon, apple and avocado in with the pasta. Add the lemon juice. Stir everything round.

Serve with lettuce.

ADDITIONS & ALTERNATIVES

Add any of the following:

1 small can of drained sweet corn
½ onion chopped small
100 g (4 oz) of mushrooms, wiped and sliced
150 g olives
2 chopped frankfurters

POTATO SALAD

Serves 2   ① *Preparation 5 min, Cooking 20 min – Easy*

INGREDIENTS

500 g (1 lb) new potatoes
4 spring onions
3 or 4 tablespoons mayonnaise

EQUIPMENT

Sharp knife
Chopping board
Saucepan
Wooden spoon
Set of measuring spoons

METHOD

Clean the potatoes. Scrape off any eyes or shoots. Don't peel them unless you really think they need it. Put them in the pan with water to cover them. Boil for about 15 to 20 minutes. How to tell if potatoes are done: get a fork and stick it into a potato. If it goes in easily they are just right. If they completely fall apart they are overcooked. If they are still hard, give them a couple of minutes more then test again.

Meanwhile cut the top and bottom off the spring onions. Take off the outer leaf and discard any slimy bits. Give the spring onions a wash and cut them into fine rings. Cut up the potatoes. Mix the potatoes, spring onions and mayonnaise.

ADDITIONS & ALTERNATIVES

New potatoes are small, hard and solid.

Try designer potatoes like Pink Fir Apple or Charlotte's.

Add a tablespoon of chopped parsley.

The salad can be pepped up with either a chopped hard-boiled egg, 3 chopped gherkins, or 2 tablespoons of capers.

TABBOULEH

Serves 4 ⏱ *Preparation 5 min plus an hour for the bulgar to soak – Easy*

INGREDIENTS

250 g bulgar wheat (about 2 cups)
1 bunch of parsley
3 medium tomatoes, red and ripe
2 tablespoons of olive oil
1 tablespoon of lemon juice
Pitta bread

EQUIPMENT

Set of measuring cups
Sharp knife
Chopping board
Sieve
Bowl
Set of measuring spoons

METHOD

Wash the bulgar and soak for one hour in cold water. The bulgar will get soft and expand.

Meanwhile wash, dry and chop the parsley. Wash the tomatoes. Chop the tomatoes in half and use your finger to get the seeds out. Then chop them into very small cubes.

Drain the bulgar in a sieve. It should be squeezed to remove the excess water. This can be done by putting kitchen paper on top of the bulgar and pressing with the heel of the hand. Put the bulgar, the chopped tomatoes and parsley into a bowl. Mix them up with the lemon juice and olive oil.

Serve with pitta bread.

83

ADDITIONS & ALTERNATIVES

Substitute coriander for the parsley.

Try this with hummus, taramasalata or lamb kebabs.

THREE BEAN SALAD

Serves 4 to 6 ℗ *Preparation 5 min – Easy*

INGREDIENTS

400 g tin red kidney beans
400 g tin chick peas
400 g tin baked beans
Few sprigs of parsley
2 tablespoons of oil
1 tablespoon of lemon juice, or juice of half a lemon

EQUIPMENT

Tin opener
Bowl
Sharp knife
Chopping board
Set of measuring spoons
Wooden spoon

METHOD

Open the tin of baked beans. Pour them into the bowl. Open the chick peas and the red kidney beans. Drain off the fluid. Put the beans and chick peas into the bowl.

Chop up the parsley. Put into the bowl together with the oil and lemon juice. Mix it all together. Keep in the fridge until ready to eat.

ADDITIONS & ALTERNATIVES

Use a tin of butter beans instead of the kidney beans or flageolet beans instead of the chick peas.

ROSE COCO BEAN SALAD

Serves 4   ① *Preparation 10 min and 2 hours waiting for the beans to swell up, Cooking 150 min – Moderate*

INGREDIENTS

250 g dried rose coco (Borlotti) beans (about 1⅓ cups)
2 carrots
3 tablespoons sultanas
at least 2 tablespoons vinaigrette (see recipe on page 63)
1 small onion (optional)

EQUIPMENT

Set of measuring cups
Bowl
Saucepan
Vegetable peeler
Sharp knife
Chopping board
Grater
Set of measuring spoons
Wooden spoon

METHOD

Wash the beans. Put the beans in the bowl. Pour boiling water on top of them, and cover with about 5 cm (2 inches) of water. Leave them for 1–2 hours to swell up. Then wash the rose coco beans and put in the saucepan with at least a pint of fresh water. Bring to the boil and boil vigorously for 10 minutes. Turn down the heat and simmer till they are soft. This should take about two and a half hours. Add more water if it runs low. Let the beans cool down.

Wash and peel the carrots. Cut off the top and bottom ends. Grate the carrots. Put the rose coco beans, grated carrot, sultana and vinaigrette in the bowl and mix together.

ADDITIONS & ALTERNATIVES

Try the orange vinaigrette made with orange juice instead of vinegar.

This is good with pitta bread and hummus.

TIPS

You can make this some time before you want to eat it. The knack is to boil the beans, then keep them going gently, adding more water when it gets a bit low. The only real difficulty is that you may get distracted, they boil dry, and the pan gets ruined.

EGGS

BOILED EGG

Serves 1 or 2   ⏱ *Preparation 2 min, Cooking 3 min – Easy*

INGREDIENTS
2 eggs
1 teaspoon vinegar

EQUIPMENT
Saucepan

METHOD
This recipe gives you boiled eggs which have a cooked white and a runny hot yolk. Put the eggs in the pan and cover with water. Add a teaspoon of vinegar. Use a stopwatch if you have one.

Bring the water to the boil. Start timing from when the water reaches boiling point. Wait three minutes. Take the eggs out of the water. Eat immediately.

Serve with salt and pepper and toast.

ADDITIONS & ALTERNATIVES
If you like your egg yolks more solid, cook for an extra minute.

Hard-boiled eggs should be cooked for about ten minutes and then cooled off in water before trying to handle them.

TIPS
Use eggs at room temperature. Do not keep eggs in the fridge.

EGG MAYONNAISE

Serves 2   ① *Preparation 3 min, Cooking 10 min – Easy*

INGREDIENTS

3 eggs
1 teaspoon vinegar
2 tablespoons mayonnaise
Salt and freshly ground pepper to taste

EQUIPMENT

Saucepan
Set of measuring spoons
Sharp knife
Chopping board
Bowl
Fork

METHOD

Put the eggs in the pan and cover with water. Add a teaspoon of vinegar. Bring the water to the boil. Cook for about ten minutes and then cool off in water before trying to handle them.

Peel the shell off the eggs and cut in half. Separate the yolks from the whites. Mash the yolk in the bowl. Chop the whites and add to the yolks. Mix the eggs with the mayonnaise.

Add salt and pepper to taste.

ADDITIONS & ALTERNATIVES

Add 2 chopped spring onions.

Add 1 chopped small gherkin.

TIPS

Use eggs at room temperature. There is no need to keep eggs in the fridge.

SCRAMBLED EGG

Serves 1   ⏱ *Preparation 1 min, Cooking 2 min – Easy*

INGREDIENTS
2 eggs
1 tablespoon butter
1 piece buttered toast
Salt and pepper

EQUIPMENT
Set of measuring spoons
Saucepan
Wooden spoon

METHOD
Put a piece of buttered toast on a plate. Put the lump of butter in a small pan and let the butter melt over a medium heat. Break the eggs into the pan. Add some salt and pepper. Stir the eggs to stop it sticking to the bottom of the pan and to scramble. The egg will cook within a couple of minutes. When the eggs are still moist turn them out on to the toast. Eat while hot.

Do not overcook the eggs as they end up like rubber.

ADDITIONS & ALTERNATIVES
Add bacon.

A stunning breakfast for two involves a small packet of smoked salmon trout. Cut it into pieces. Make two bits of buttered toast. Make a double quantity of scrambled eggs. Distribute on the toast. Scatter the smoked salmon trout bits on the top. Serve with coffee, fresh orange juice, champagne, or Bloody Marys.

FRIED EGG

Serves 2   ① *Preparation 1 min, Cooking 2 min – Easy*

INGREDIENTS
2 eggs
Oil

EQUIPMENT
2 cups
Frying-pan
Slotted egg slice

METHOD
Break an egg into each cup. Fish out any bits of shell which have got mixed up with it.

How do you like your eggs? Sunny side up or over easy?

Over easy: heat the oil in the frying-pan. Pour the eggs into the pan. When the white has gone solid, use the spatula to free up the eggs gently from the base of the pan. Flip the eggs over and cook for another thirty seconds.

Sunny side up: this is like over easy, except that when the white starts to cook, flick the hot oil over the yolk. The top will turn white. Free up from the bottom of the pan and serve.

ADDITIONS & ALTERNATIVES
Serve with grilled bacon or sausages, or bread and butter.

When you get better at this you can break the egg directly into the pan. It is, however, somewhat more dangerous to try and fish out bits of shell from hot oil.

The traditional way to cook eggs is to use the fat from the sausages and bacon you have already cooked.

The ultimate cholesterol-high breakfast would include fried bread and fried tomatoes.

OMELETTE

Serves 1   ① *Preparation 3 min, Cooking 1 min – Easy*

INGREDIENTS
2 fresh eggs at room temperature
1 tablespoon butter
Pepper

EQUIPMENT
Bowl
Fork
Frying-pan
Wooden spoon

METHOD
Break the eggs into a bowl and pick out any bits of shell. Add the pepper and mix the eggs up with a fork. (Don't add salt to the uncooked eggs because it makes the omelette tough.)

Heat some butter to grease the bottom of a thick frying-pan. Don't let it get too hot and burn the butter. Pour in the eggs and let them spread. Shake the pan gently and gently stir the eggs with a wooden spoon. In a minute or so the omelette is cooked and can be slid on to a plate.

ADDITIONS & ALTERNATIVES
Add 1 tablespoon of cream, milk or cheese to the mixture.

Add mixed herbs or paprika pepper.

You can fill the omelette with warmed bits of chopped ham, chicken, or cooked mushrooms.

Serve with salad.

TIPS
Let the eggs warm up to room temperature before putting them in the pan. Have the pan hot enough to cook the eggs.

ITALIAN MEATY OMELETTE

Serves 4   ⏱ *Preparation 5 min, Cooking 15 min – Easy*

INGREDIENTS

2 tablespoons freshly chopped parsley
10 mushrooms (about 100 g (4 oz))
Small to medium onion
100 g (4 oz) spicy sausage (salami, chorizo or pepperoni)
2 tablespoons olive oil
6 eggs
50 g (2 oz) grated Parmesan cheese (about 3 tablespoons)
Salad

EQUIPMENT

Sharp knife
Chopping board
Frying-pan
Wooden spoon
Set of measuring spoons
Bowl
Grill

METHOD

Wash, drain and chop the parsley. Wipe and chop the mushrooms in half. Peel and chop the onion. Slice the sausage. Put the oil in the frying-pan. Cook the spicy sausage, onion and mushrooms together for a couple of minutes, giving them the odd stir.

Meanwhile, break the eggs into a bowl and pick out any bits of shell. Add the Parmesan and parsley and mix the eggs up with a fork. Add the egg mixture to the frying-pan, and cook on moderate heat for about five minutes.

Put it under a grill for about three minutes to finish it off. It should go golden on top. Cut into triangular segments.

Serve with salad.

ADDITIONS & ALTERNATIVES

Substitute half a bunch of spring onions for the onion.

Try other cheeses: 50g (2 oz or 1 cup) of grated Cheddar or similar would do.

Try adding vegetables like courgettes or onions. Just wash or peel, chop and fry in a tablespoon of butter for three minutes.

Use chopped smoked sausage or hot dogs instead of spicy sausage.

SPANISH OMELETTE

Serves 4   ① *Preparation 5 min, Cooking 20 min – Easy*

INGREDIENTS

2 large potatoes
1 onion
4 eggs
Freshly ground pepper to taste
2 tablespoons olive oil

EQUIPMENT

Vegetable peeler
Sharp knife
Chopping board
Saucepan
Colander or sieve
Bowl
Fork
Frying-pan
Set of measuring spoons
Wooden spoon
Grill

METHOD

Peel the potatoes. Chop into 1 cm (half-inch) cubes. Boil for about 5 minutes, checking that they do not fall apart. Drain the potato. Peel and chop the onion.

Meanwhile, break the eggs into a bowl and pick out any bits of shell. Add the pepper and mix the eggs up with a fork. Heat the oil in the frying-pan. Fry the onion and the potato. Stir from time to time. When they are golden add the eggs and turn the heat down really low. The omelette should be about 2–3 cm (1 inch) thick. Put a lid on the pan and leave it for at least ten minutes.

To brown the top put it under a grill for a couple of minutes to finish it off. When it is cooked the eggs will not be runny. Cut it into triangular pieces.

ADDITIONS & ALTERNATIVES

Try other fillings of meat and vegetables, cooking them first. Broccoli, peas, mushrooms, garlic sausage and cooked ham work well. Or add chopped cooked streaky bacon to the recipe.

POACHED EGGS ON TOAST

Serves 1 ① *Preparation 1 min, Cooking 2 to 3 min*
– Potentially a fiddle but the best version of solo eggs

INGREDIENTS

2 eggs, as fresh as possible
1 teaspoon of vinegar
1 slice of buttered toast

EQUIPMENT
2 cups
Saucepan
Spoon with holes in it to drain the eggs
Fork to let the water out

METHOD
Put the buttered toast on a plate. Use eggs that have not been kept in the fridge. Break one egg into each cup. Fish out any bits of shell which have got mixed up with it. Put at least a pint of water and the teaspoon of vinegar in the pan and bring to the boil. Stir the boiling water. Turn down the water so it is simmering (not boiling violently). Slide the eggs out of the cup into the water. They will hold together, though there may be some white froth which needs to be scooped off the surface. If the eggs appear to stick to the pan, wait till they are fairly well cooked before trying to dislodge them.

The eggs will be cooked when the white is solid and the yolk runny. This takes about two or three minutes. Fish the eggs out with the spoon. Let out any water which has become trapped in pockets of white with the fork. If the white is still runny put it back in the boiling water and cook for a little longer. Put the cooked eggs on the toast.

ADDITIONS & ALTERNATIVES
Serve with baked beans on toast.

There is a special pan which can poach four eggs at a time. Put the water in the bottom, grease the cups with butter, put the eggs in the indentations, and cook for about three minutes.

WALNUT & LEEK QUICHE

Serves 6   ① *Preparation 15 min, Cooking 45 min*
                – Cooking the pastry in two stages is a bit of a fiddle,
                                    but otherwise no problem

INGREDIENTS

450 g pack pre-rolled frozen shortcrust pastry
100 g (4 oz) grated Cheddar cheese, about 2 cups
3 eggs
2 tablespoons milk
Salt and pepper
4 to 6 slender to medium leeks (about 500g or 1 lb)
1 tablespoon butter
100 g (4 oz) walnut halves (about 20)

EQUIPMENT

Round ovenproof dish about 24 cm (9.5 inches) across
Greaseproof paper
1 pack dried beans to hold the pastry down
Grater
Set of measuring cups
Bowl
Set of measuring spoons
Sharp knife
Chopping board
Wooden spoon

METHOD

Make sure the pastry is thawed. Check the packet for times, but generally about four hours in the fridge.

Lightly grease the dish. Unroll the pastry and place in the dish. Pastry is fairly flexible so you can push it into place. If it tears, patch it with a spare bit, moistening with water to make sure it sticks. Prick the bottom of the pastry with a fork at least five times to let steam out. Cut a piece of greaseproof paper to fit and press gently on to the pastry. Fill the bottom with a layer of cheap dried beans, for instance butter beans. Cook the pastry case at 200°C, 400°F, Gas mark 6 for 10 to 15 minutes until the top edges go golden.

Take the pastry case out of the oven. Wait for it to cool then take out the beans and greaseproof paper.

Meanwhile grate the cheese. Break the eggs into a bowl and pick out any bits of shell. Add the milk, salt and pepper. Mix with a fork.

Clean the leeks. First take off the outer leaves, cut the roots off and trim the top. Split the leeks in half lengthways. Hold the leeks under running water and wash any grit out. Shake them dry. Cut into 1 cm (half-inch) slices.

Put the butter in the pan and melt over a medium heat. Put the leeks in and cook for about three minutes to soften them. Take off the heat.

Put some walnuts on the pastry case. Use the broken ones. Spread the leeks over the walnuts. Scatter the cheese on top. Place the best walnut halves on the cheese. Pour the egg mixture on top.

Cook in a preheated oven at 170°C, 325°F, Gas mark 3 for about 20 to 30 minutes till set and golden brown.

Eat hot or cold.

ADDITIONS & ALTERNATIVES

On leeks: don't use really thick ones as they are tougher.

Try other sorts of cheese like Gouda or even crumbled blue cheese half and half with cheddar.

Various combinations of ingredients work; try chopped up cooked ham and mushroom. Chop the mushrooms in half and fry for one minute in a tablespoon of butter, then put in the pastry case.

BACON & TOMATO QUICHE

Serves 6   ① *Preparation 15 min, Cooking 45 min*
Cooking the pastry in two stages is a bit of a fiddle,
but otherwise no problem

INGREDIENTS

Use the previous recipe but substitute the leek and walnuts with:
8 rashers bacon cooked and chopped
2 medium tomatoes

METHOD

Make the pastry case as in the previous recipe.

Chop up the bacon into 2.5 cm (1 inch) lengths. Fry gently for a couple of minutes to get some of the fat off. Put the bacon in the bottom of the pastry case.

Wash and slice the tomatoes. Keep a couple of slices for decoration and put the rest in with the bacon. Add the cheese followed by the reserved tomato slices. Top with the egg mixture. Cook in a preheated oven at 170°C, 325°F, Gas mark 3 for about 20 to 30 minutes till set and golden brown.

ADDITIONS & ALTERNATIVES

You can substitute a small carton (142 ml or 5 fl oz) of single cream for one of the eggs and the milk.

BIG BREAKFAST PIE

Serves 4–6   ① *Preparation 15 min, Cooking 45 min – Easy*

INGREDIENTS

450 g pack of pre-rolled frozen shortcrust pastry
100 g (4 oz) grated Cheddar cheese, about 2 cups
3 eggs
2 tablespoons milk

Salt and pepper
4 frankfurters (about 100–150 g)
2 large onions
1 tablespoon butter

EQUIPMENT
Round ovenproof dish about 24 cm (9.5 inches) across
1 pack dried beans to hold the pastry down
Greaseproof paper
Grater
Set of measuring cups
Bowl
Set of measuring spoons
Sharp knife
Chopping board
Frying-pan
Wooden spoon

METHOD
Thaw the pastry according to the instructions on the packet. Four hours in the fridge seems typical. Make the pastry case according to the previous Quiche recipe.

Meanwhile grate the cheese. Break the eggs into a bowl and pick out any bits of shell. Add the milk, salt and pepper. Mix round with a fork.

Open the packet of frankfurters. Chop into 2.5 cm (1 inch) lengths. Peel and chop the onions. Put the butter in the frying-pan and heat over a moderate heat. Fry the onion for about three minutes till it is golden, stirring to stop it sticking. Spread the frankfurters and onions over the bottom of the pastry case. Scatter the cheese on top. Pour the egg mixture on top. Cook in a preheated oven at 170°C, 325°F, Gas mark 3 for about 20 to 30 minutes till set and golden brown.

This can be eaten hot or cold.

CHICKEN

CAJUN CHICKEN

Serves 2   ⏱ *Preparation 3 min, Cooking 20 min – Easy*

INGREDIENTS
2 chicken breasts
2 tablespoons Cajun Seasoning
1 or 2 tablespoons butter
Salad or rice to serve

EQUIPMENT
Set of measuring spoons
Frying-pan
Wooden spoon

DEFROSTING
Make sure frozen chicken is completely thawed before use. This means leaving it in the fridge overnight, or out of the fridge, covered, for six hours.

METHOD
Rub the chicken breasts with the Cajun seasoning. Melt the butter in the frying-pan. Gently fry the chicken, turning from time to time. Cook for about 15 to 20 minutes. It is normal for the breast to end up quite dark.

Serve with salad or rice.

CHICKEN BOURSIN & BACON

Serves 1   ① *Preparation 3 min, Cooking 25 to 30 min – Easy*

INGREDIENTS
1 chicken breast
16 g individual portion boursin cheese
1 rasher bacon

EQUIPMENT
Ovenproof dish
Aluminium foil

DEFROSTING
Make sure frozen chicken is completely thawed before use. This means leaving it in the fridge overnight, or out of the fridge, covered, for six hours.

METHOD
Get the chicken breast. If it has skin on, loosen it and spread the cheese between the skin and the meat. Otherwise just spread it on the breast. Put the chicken breast in the ovenproof dish. Put a rasher of bacon on the chicken breast. Cover the dish with foil.

Put into a preheated oven at 180°C, 350°F, Gas mark 4 for 20 minutes. Carefully take the foil off and cook for a further 5 to 10 minutes till browned.

ADDITIONS & ALTERNATIVES
Omit the bacon.
Serve with green salad.

CASSEROLE OF CHICKEN WITH BACON & MUSHROOM

Serves 4   ① *Preparation 7 min, Cooking 65 min – Easy*

INGREDIENTS

200 g (8 oz) button mushrooms (approximately 20)
1 onion
2 tablespoons butter
4 rashers bacon
Salt and pepper to taste
4 chicken quarters or other equivalent chicken pieces
1 stock cube

EQUIPMENT

Sharp knife
Chopping board
Frying-pan
Set of measuring spoons
Wooden spoon
Casserole with lid
Set of measuring cups

DEFROSTING

Make sure frozen chicken is completely thawed before use. This means leaving it in the fridge overnight, or out of the fridge, covered, for six hours.

METHOD

Wipe and slice the mushrooms. Peel and chop the onion. Put 1 tablespoon of butter in the frying-pan and heat over a moderate heat. Fry the onion and mushrooms for about three minutes, stirring to stop them sticking. Remove from heat. Chop the bacon into 2.5 cm (1 inch) pieces. Stir in the bacon, salt and pepper.

Put the chicken quarters in the casserole. Pour the mixture on top. Add the other tablespoon of butter. Add a stock cube and a cup of water. Put lid on the casserole. Cook in a preheated oven for one hour at 180°C, 350°F, Gas mark 4.

ADDITIONS & ALTERNATIVES
Serve with rice or vegetables.

CHICKEN BREASTS WITH LEMON

Serves 2   ① *Preparation 3 min, Cooking 25 to 30 min – Easy*

INGREDIENTS
1 lemon
2 chicken breasts
1 tablespoon oil or butter
Pepper

EQUIPMENT
Sharp knife
Chopping board
Ovenproof dish
Aluminium foil
Set of measuring spoons

DEFROSTING
Make sure frozen chicken is completely thawed before use. This means leaving it in the fridge overnight, or out of the fridge, covered, for six hours.

METHOD
Wash and slice the lemon. Put the chicken breast in the ovenproof dish. Put the oil or butter on the chicken breast. Put the lemon slices on top and season with pepper. Cover the dish with foil.

Put into a preheated oven at 180°C, 350°F, Gas mark 4 for 20 minutes. Carefully take the foil off and cook for a further 5 to 10 minutes.

ADDITIONS & ALTERNATIVES
Serve with green salad.
Use chicken quarters.
Add half a glass of white wine.

CIDER CHICKEN

Serves 4   ① *Preparation 10 min, Cooking 60 min – Easy*

INGREDIENTS
2 large apples
2 large leeks
4 chicken quarters
1 small bottle cider (250 ml or ½ pint)
Salt and pepper
Rice or potatoes

EQUIPMENT
Sharp knife
Chopping board
Casserole dish

DEFROSTING
Make sure frozen chicken is completely thawed before use. This means leaving it in the fridge overnight, or out of the fridge, covered, for six hours.

METHOD
Peel the apples. Remove the core and seeds and chop.

Clean the leeks. First take off the outer leaves, cut the roots off and trim the top. Split the leeks in half lengthways. Hold the leeks under running water and wash any grit out. Shake them dry. Cut into 1 cm (half-inch) slices.

Put the chicken pieces in the casserole. Add the leeks and the apples. Pour the cider on top and season with salt and pepper. Put the lid on the casserole. Cook in a preheated oven at 180°C, 350°F, Gas mark 4 for an hour.

Serve with rice or potatoes.

CHICKEN POT STEW

Serves 4 ① *Preparation 5 min, Cooking 3 hours – Easy*

INGREDIENTS
2 rashers bacon
4 medium potatoes
1 medium onion
4 chicken quarters
500g (1 lb) sausages
250g dried split green peas (half a packet or about 1¼ cups)
1 litre water (about 2 pints or 4 cups)
Salt and pepper

EQUIPMENT
Sharp knife
Chopping board
Casserole with lid
Set of measuring cups

DEFROSTING
Make sure frozen chicken is completely thawed before use. This means leaving it in the fridge overnight, or out of the fridge, covered, for six hours.

METHOD
Cut the bacon slices in half. Peel the potatoes and chop into quarters. Peel and slice the onion. Put all the ingredients in the casserole. Put the lid on. Cook in an oven for three hours at 140°C, 275°F, Gas mark 1.

CHICKEN VEGETABLE CASSEROLE

Serves 4   ① *Preparation 15 min, Cooking 90 min – Easy*

INGREDIENTS

3 large potatoes
3 or 4 carrots
1 large onion
10 mushrooms (about 100 g or 4 oz) (optional)
8 to 12 chicken pieces (thigh, drumstick or small breasts)
1 tablespoon mixed herbs
1 chicken stock cube
Salt and pepper
1 glass wine (optional)

EQUIPMENT

Sharp knife
Chopping board
Casserole dish
Set of measuring spoons

DEFROSTING

Make sure frozen chicken is completely thawed before use. This means leaving it in the fridge overnight, or out of the fridge, covered, for six hours.

METHOD

Peel the potatoes, cutting away any nasty bits, and cutting out any eyes. Chop the potatoes into quarters.

Peel and chop the carrots, cutting off both ends. Peel and slice the onions. Wipe the mushrooms, and chop the end off the stalks.

Put the chicken pieces in the casserole. Add all the vegetables, herbs and stock cube. Just cover the chicken with fluid, either water or water and white wine. Season with salt and pepper. Put the lid on the casserole. Cook in a preheated oven at 170°C, 325°F, Gas mark 3 for about an hour and a half.

ADDITIONS & ALTERNATIVES

Try using small chops instead of the chicken.

Other vegetables can be used with or instead of the carrots and potatoes, like parsnip, peas and beans.

Make the sauce thicker by adding 2 tablespoons of pearl barley or soup mix.

Serve with a green vegetable or salad.

ROAST CHICKEN

Serves 4   ⏱ *Preparation 5 min, Cooking 2 hours – Easy*

INGREDIENTS
1.5 kg (3 lb) chicken
Salt and pepper
3 rashers bacon (see method)
1 tablespoon oil

EQUIPMENT
Cast-iron casserole
or Roasting tin/Ovenproof dish
or Chicken brick
Set of measuring spoons
Set of measuring cups

DEFROSTING
If frozen, make sure the chicken is thawed and that there are no plastic bags of giblets left inside or bits of cardboard underneath. A 1.5 kg (3 lb) chicken takes 24 hours to defrost in the fridge or 12 hours out of it.

METHOD
Season the chicken with freshly ground pepper and salt. If you have a cast-iron casserole (le Creuset or similar) put the chicken in with 1 tablespoon of oil and half a cup of water and roast with the lid on.

If you have a pottery chicken brick, just put the chicken in and roast.

If you are using a roasting dish or ovenproof dish, just put the chicken in with 1 tablespoon of oil and half a cup of water. Cover the breast with 3 rashers of bacon. Cover the top with foil. Cook for 2 hours in a preheated oven at 170°C, 325°F, Gas mark 3.

When the chicken is cooked, take it out of the oven and put it on a plate. Leave it for 5 minutes before carving.

ADDITIONS & ALTERNATIVES

Serve with roast potatoes and vegetables or salad. Put the prepared vegetables in an ovenproof dish with half a cup of oil or so. Cook at the top of the oven for at least an hour. Full instructions are in the vegetarian section.

Cranberry sauce goes well with chicken.

Put an orange cut in half in the body cavity, and sprinkle the chicken with a teaspoon of mixed Mediterranean herbs.

Add a quartered lemon and a tablespoon of fresh tarragon.

Add three small onions and a tablespoon of rosemary.

Add 10 button mushrooms, a drained 250 g (9 oz) tin of sweet chestnuts and a tablespoon of tarragon.

Try Italian roast chicken. It is very quick and easy (see p. 243).

TIPS

Stuffing can be cooked in the oven. If the packet suggests a higher temperature than you are using for the chicken then just cook it for longer.

A recipe for gravy follows, if you need it.

Our personal recommendation must be for the cast-iron casserole method. It is fairly foolproof. It also means there is lots of juice for making gravy. The casserole is very useful for other oven dishes. The ideal size is a 25 cm (10 inch) oval casserole with straight sides. It holds 4 litres (7 pints) and can take a chicken, a small leg of lamb or most beef roasts, as well as being OK for all the casserole dishes.

Club Sandwich, Chicken Curry, Coronation Chicken and Chicken Creole all use left-over cooked chicken.

GRAVY

Serves 4–6   ① *Preparation 2 min, Cooking 10 min – Easy*

INGREDIENTS
2 teaspoons cornflour
2 teaspoons of gravy browning powder (e.g. Bisto)
500 ml (1 pt) water, 2 cups
1 stock cube

EQUIPMENT
Set of measuring spoons
Cup
Wooden spoon
Saucepan

METHOD
Put the cornflour and gravy browning in the cup. Add about 2 tablespoons of water a few drops at a time and stir until you get a smooth paste. If you add the water all at once it will go lumpy.

Put 500 ml (1 pt) water and the stock cube in the saucepan. Put on a medium heat and stir to dissolve. When the water is hot, but before it is boiling, continue to stir with one hand and add the cornflour mixture. Keep stirring to stop it sticking and going lumpy. As the mixture comes to the boil it will thicken. Cook for a minute or so and take off the heat.

This can be reheated when everything else is ready.

ADDITIONS & ALTERNATIVES
Add 1 tablespoon of brandy.
Add 1 glass of wine.
Add the juices from the roast with most of the fat skimmed off.

CHICKEN CREOLE

Serves 2   ⓘ *Preparation 10 min – Easy*

INGREDIENTS
200 g (8 oz) cooked potatoes
200 g (8 oz) cooked chicken or 2 chicken quarters, about 2 cups
    when chopped
1 tablespoon mayonnaise
1 tablespoon Cajun seasoning
150 g can pitted black olives

EQUIPMENT
Ovenproof dish
Sharp knife
Chopping board
Saucepan
Tin opener
Set of measuring spoons
Set of measuring cups

DEFROSTING & COOKING
If you need to cook the chicken, make sure frozen chicken is
completely thawed before use. This means leaving the quarters in
the fridge overnight, or out of the fridge, covered, for six hours.
Then just brush with oil and cook in an ovenproof dish in the oven
for 30 minutes at 200°C, 400°F, Gas mark 6.

METHOD
Cook the potatoes if not already cooked. Clean and peel if needed.
Boil in water for about 20 minutes. Cool and cut into 1 cm (half-
inch) cubes.

Flake or break up the chicken. Mix all the ingredients together.

ADDITIONS & ALTERNATIVES
Serve with salad.
   Use a tin of potatoes instead of the cooked ones.

CHICKEN RICE BAKE

Serves 4   ① *Preparation 10 min, Cooking 90 min – Easy*

INGREDIENTS
4 chicken quarters
2 medium onions
3 medium carrots
$1\frac{1}{2}$ cups of long grain or risotto rice
1 chicken stock cube
3 cups water or white wine and water

EQUIPMENT
Sharp knife
Chopping board
Casserole with lid
Set of measuring cups

METHOD
Make sure frozen chicken is completely thawed before use. This means leaving it in the fridge overnight, or out of the fridge, covered, for six hours.
   Peel and chop the onions. Peel and chop the carrots. Put the chicken, onion and carrot in the casserole. Add the rice. Dissolve the stock cube in the water. Add the stock to the rice. Put the lid on the casserole. Cook in a preheated oven at 150°C, 300°F, Gas mark 2 for 90 minutes.

ADDITIONS & ALTERNATIVES
Serve with a green vegetable.

MOROCCAN CHICKEN

Serves 4   ⏱ *Preparation 10 min, Cooking 50 min – Easy*

INGREDIENTS
8 chicken thighs or drumsticks
2 medium onions
2 tablespoons oil for frying
2 cloves garlic
1 teaspoon turmeric
$\frac{1}{2}$ teaspoon chilli powder
400 g tin tomatoes
2 × 400 g tins chick peas
1 lemon
1 tablespoon parsley or coriander

EQUIPMENT
Sharp knife
Chopping board
Garlic crusher
Big pan or a wok
Wooden spoon
Set of measuring spoons
Tin opener
Cup

DEFROSTING
Make sure frozen chicken is completely thawed before use. This means leaving it in the fridge overnight, or out of the fridge, covered, for six hours.

METHOD

Peel and chop the onions. Put the oil in the pan and put on a medium heat. Peel and crush the garlic into the pan. Add the onion and cook on a medium heat for 5 minutes. Stir from time to time. Add the turmeric and chilli powder. Cook for another three minutes.

Add the chicken pieces and stir round until they start to cook, are covered in the mixture and are golden, about ten minutes. Add the tin of tomatoes, mashing up if required. Open the tins of chick peas. Pour the liquid off into a cup, you may need it later. Add the chick peas to the mixture. Stir it all together and cook on a medium heat (don't burn it) for about 35 minutes. If it starts to get too dry looking, add the chick pea liquid. If this runs out use water.

Just before serving, put in the lemon juice and parsley and/or coriander.

ADDITIONS & ALTERNATIVES

Serve with warm pitta bread (sprinkle them with water and grill for a minute, till they puff up).

Try eating this with tabbouleh (page 83), an appropriate salad.

TIPS

Prepared garlic is sold in tubes and jars. Just read the tube or jar for the suggested equivalent amount. It keeps for six weeks in the fridge.

CORONATION CHICKEN

Serves 2 to 4   ① *Preparation 10 min – Moderate*

INGREDIENTS

Pre-cooked chicken. Can be left over from a roast. 1 breast or 3
    thighs. Can be more or less.
3 tablespoons mango chutney
$\frac{1}{2}$ cucumber
Few coriander leaves (optional)
100 g pack flaked almonds
3 tablespoons mayonnaise

EQUIPMENT

Sharp knife
Chopping board
Bowl
Set of measuring spoons

DEFROSTING & COOKING

If you need to cook the chicken, make sure frozen chicken pieces
are completely thawed before use. This means leaving them in the
fridge overnight, or out of the fridge, for six hours. Then just brush
the portions with oil and cook in an ovenproof dish in the oven for
30 minutes at 200°C, 400°F, Gas mark 6.

METHOD

Get the cooked chicken and cut it up into small pieces. This is
easier if you take it off the bone first. The bits should be about 1 cm
(half-inch) thick. This is not crucial. Size is not, in this instance,
important.

If the chutney has big lumps of mango in it take them out and
chop them up. Wash the cucumber and peel it if you like. Chop
it into little cubes. Wash and cut up the coriander leaves.

CHICKEN

Put the chicken, almonds, coriander leaves and chutney into a bowl with the mayonnaise and mix them all together.

ADDITIONS & ALTERNATIVES

Serve with pitta bread and salad.

Use mixed fruit chutney, lime pickle or peach chutney instead of the mango chutney.

FISH

DEFROSTING

In general white fish do not need to be defrosted before cooking.
Cooked prawns and salmon do. Check the details on the packet.

KIPPERS

Serves 1   ① *Preparation 2 min, Cooking 10 min – Easy*

INGREDIENTS
Pair of kippers
1 tablespoon butter

EQUIPMENT
Grill
Set of measuring spoons

METHOD
Put the kipper skin side down on the grill pan and put a couple of
blobs of butter on the top. Grill for about 5 to 10 minutes
depending on how thick they are.

TIPS
If you find the kippers too salty or smoky, try this trick. Before
cooking, soak the kipper in hot water for a couple of minutes.
Drain the kipper.

CAJUN SALMON

Serves 2   ① *Preparation 3 min, Cooking 10 min – Easy*

INGREDIENTS
2 salmon steaks about 500 g or 1 lb
2 tablespoons Cajun seasoning
1–2 tablespoons butter
Salad or rice to serve

EQUIPMENT
Frying-pan
Wooden spoon
Set of measuring spoons

DEFROSTING
Make sure frozen salmon is completely thawed before use. This means leaving it in the fridge overnight, or out of the fridge, covered, for six hours.

METHOD
Wash and drain the salmon. Rub the salmon steaks with the Cajun seasoning.

Melt the butter in the frying-pan. Fry the salmon, turning from time to time. Cook for about 10 minutes. It is normal for the fish to end up quite dark.

Serve with salad or rice.

SAVOURY SALMON CRÊPES

Serves 2 to 4   ① *Preparation 7 min – Easy*

INGREDIENTS
1 packet crêpes (ready made)
200 g (8 oz) pack smoked salmon or smoked salmon trout
250 g pot Greek yoghurt
100 g jar red lumpfish roe (optional added luxury)
1 lemon
Salad

EQUIPMENT
Sharp knife
Chopping board
Set of measuring spoons

METHOD
Separate the crêpes. Put one on a plate. Put a slice of smoked salmon on the crêpe. Roll up the crêpe. Put half a tablespoon of yoghurt on the crêpe. Put a teaspoon of lumpfish roe on the yoghurt.

Make two for each person. Serve with a slice of lemon and salad.

ADDITIONS & ALTERNATIVES
Substitute cold cooked flaked salmon for the smoked salmon,

Use Parma ham instead of the salmon. Omit the lumpfish roe, and use a chopped-up gherkin or a teaspoon of capers mixed in with the yoghurt.

SALMON BOURSIN

Serves 1   ⏱ *Preparation 3 min, Cooking 20 to 25 min – Easy*

INGREDIENTS
1 salmon steak or cutlet
$\frac{1}{2}$ small boursin cheese or an individual (16g) portion
1 tablespoon oil

EQUIPMENT
Baking dish
Set of measuring spoons
Aluminium foil

METHOD
Put the salmon steak in the baking dish. Spread the cheese on the salmon. Pour the oil on the top. Cover the dish with foil. Put into a preheated oven at 180°C, 350°F, Gas mark 4 for 20 minutes.

ADDITIONS & ALTERNATIVES
Serve with salad or new potatoes.
    Use salmon fillet.

PLAICE WITH WINE

Serves 4 ① *Preparation 1 min, Cooking 15 min – Easy*

INGREDIENTS
600 g pack frozen small plaice (about 5 fillets)
1 tablespoon fresh parsley
Salt and freshly ground pepper to taste
1 tablespoon butter
1 glass white wine

EQUIPMENT
Sharp knife
Chopping board
Ovenproof dish
Set of measuring spoons
Aluminium kitchen foil

METHOD
Wash the fish and drain. Wash, drain and chop the parsley. Put the fish in the ovenproof dish. Season with salt and pepper. Put the butter on the fish in little blobs. Pour the wine into the dish. Cover the dish with aluminium foil. Cook in a preheated oven at 170°C, 325°F, Gas mark 3 for 20 minutes.

When ready to serve spoon the juice over the fish and garnish with the chopped parsley.

ADDITIONS & ALTERNATIVES
Serve with new potatoes, green vegetable or salad.

Add two tablespoons of Greek yoghurt to the juice, and stir and warm through.

FISH IN THE PAN

Serves 2   ⏱ *Preparation 1 min, Cooking 5 min – Easy*

INGREDIENTS
2 fillets of cod, hake or haddock about 500g (1 lb)
2 tablespoons olive oil
Salt and freshly ground pepper to taste

EQUIPMENT
Frying-pan
Fish slice
Set of measuring spoons

METHOD
If cooking the fish from frozen, cook more slowly to begin with. Check it is cooked through to the middle.

Put the oil in the pan and heat up. Place the fish in the pan. Fry for a couple of minutes each side. The fish is cooked when the flesh has changed colour. Season to taste.

ADDITIONS & ALTERNATIVES
Serve with salad.

Add a crushed clove of garlic to the oil.

Use butter, ground black pepper and 1 teaspoon of capers instead of the oil.

TROUT & ALMONDS

Serves 2   ⏱ *Preparation 2 min, Cooking 10 min – Easy*

INGREDIENTS
2 rainbow trout
Salt and freshly ground pepper to taste
1 tablespoon butter
100 g pack flaked almonds
1 lemon

EQUIPMENT
Grill
Aluminium kitchen foil
Set of measuring spoons

METHOD
You can get fish with the head off. Brush butter on the outside of the fish. Cover the grill pan with tin foil. Put the fish on the grill pan. Grill for about 5 minutes.

Turn the fish over. Put more butter on. Sprinkle the flaked almonds on the fish and season with salt and pepper. Grill for about five minutes. It's OK for the skin to get quite dark.

Serve with a segment of lemon.

ADDITIONS & ALTERNATIVES
Serve with salad or new potatoes.

Put some dill inside the fish before cooking.

TIPS
Throw away the tin foil and the grill pan will still be clean.

HOT GARLIC PRAWNS

Serves 3 as a starter ℗ *Preparation 3 min, Cooking 10 min – Easy*

INGREDIENTS
200 g pack frozen extra large prawns
1 lemon
6 cloves garlic
2 tablespoons oil
Bread
Salad

EQUIPMENT
Sharp knife
Chopping board
Frying-pan
Set of measuring spoons

METHOD
Thaw the prawns. If you are in a hurry run cold water over them. Shake them dry.

Cut the lemon into quarters. Peel and slice the garlic.

Put the oil in the frying-pan and cook the garlic for 2 minutes. Add the prawns. Stir and cook for a couple of minutes.

Serve with bread and salad.

TIPS
Prepared garlic is sold in tubes and jars. Just read the tube or jar for the suggested equivalent amount. It keeps for six weeks in the fridge.

POACHED SALMON

Serves 1   ⏱ *Preparation 3 min, Cooking 20 min – Easy*

INGREDIENTS
1 salmon steak or cutlet, about 200 g or 8 oz
1 tablespoon oil
$\frac{1}{2}$ glass of any dry wine
Few sprigs of dill

EQUIPMENT
Baking dish
Set of measuring spoons
Aluminium foil

METHOD
Put the salmon steak in the baking dish. Pour the oil on the top. Add the wine (or a couple of tablespoons of water). Put the dill on top. Cover the dish with foil. Put into a preheated oven at 180°C, 350°F, Gas mark 4 for 20 minutes.

ADDITIONS & ALTERNATIVES
Serve with salad or new potatoes.

   You can cook this in a saucepan over a low heat. Just add a bit more liquid and make sure the saucepan lid fits. Simmer very gently and don't let it boil dry.

BAKED TROUT

Serves 1 ⏱ *Preparation 5 min, Cooking 20 min – Easy*

INGREDIENTS
1 medium trout, gutted and descaled
1 lemon
1 pack fresh dill, or 1 teaspoon dried dill
Salt and freshly ground pepper to taste
1 tablespoon butter

EQUIPMENT
Sharp knife
Chopping board
Set of measuring spoons
Ovenproof dish
Aluminium foil

METHOD
Wash the trout thoroughly. Cut the lemon into slices. Wash and drain two sprigs of dill. Open up the fish and put all the dill and half the lemon slices and butter inside. Add some salt and pepper.

Put the remaining slices of lemon and the butter on the outside of the fish. Wrap in aluminium foil. Put in an ovenproof dish. Cook in the oven at 180°C, 350°F, Gas mark 4 for 20 minutes.

ADDITIONS & ALTERNATIVES
Serve with boiled new potatoes and vegetables or green salad or potato salad.

Substitute orange, grapefruit or lime slices for the lemon.

SALMON IN PASTRY

Serves 2–4   ⏱ *Preparation 5 min, Cooking 20 min – Easy*

INGREDIENTS

375 g pack pre-rolled puff pastry
2 cups pre-cooked salmon or salmon trout or 500g (1 lb) salmon
2 tablespoons freshly chopped parsley
100 g (4 oz) button mushrooms (about 10)
1 tablespoon oil
2 tablespoons milk

EQUIPMENT

Set of measuring cups
Bowl
Sharp knife
Chopping board
Set of measuring spoons
Saucepan
Wooden spoon
Baking tray

METHOD

Thaw the pastry according to the instructions on the packet. Four hours in the fridge seems typical.

Flake the salmon. Discard the skin and bones. Wash and chop the parsley. Wipe the mushrooms clean. Discard any nasty ones. Chop the end off the stalks. Chop coarsely.

Heat the oil in the pan and add the mushrooms and the parsley. Cook for about three minutes, stirring. Add the flaked salmon. Stir and heat for a couple of minutes more. Take the pan off the heat.

Unroll the pastry, and cut in half to make two squares. Take one piece of pastry and lay flat. Put the salmon mixture in a line up the middle. Leave enough pastry at the edge to fold over the top and overlap. Use a finger to moisten the edge of the pastry with milk. Fold the pastry over the top of the salmon and pinch the edges together. You should end up with a small log shape.

Rub some butter or oil on the baking tray. Carefully put the roll on the tray with the join underneath. Brush some milk on the top. Make some small cuts in the top of the pastry.

Cook according to the instructions on the packet of pastry, about 20 to 30 minutes in a preheated oven at 200°C, 400°F, Gas mark 6.

ADDITIONS & ALTERNATIVES

If you need to cook the salmon use the Poached Salmon recipe on page 126.

Substitute a tin of salmon. Break it up and get rid of the bones and skin.

Use puff pastry and roll it yourself. There are full instructions on rolling pastry in the 'How to' chapter.

Use the rest of the pastry for Cheat's Chocolate Croissants (page 56).

SEA PIE

Serves 4 to 6   ⏲ *Preparation 10 min, Cooking 65 min – Easy*

INGREDIENTS

500 g (1 lb) old potatoes (about 6 medium)
Freshly ground pepper
1 tablespoon butter
About 6 tablespoons of milk ($\frac{1}{3}$ cup)
1 medium onion
1 cup milk for cooking the fish
500 g (1 lb) cod, haddock or hake fillet
1 tablespoon freshly chopped parsley

EQUIPMENT

Vegetable peeler
Sharp knife
Chopping board
2 saucepans
Set of measuring spoons
Potato masher
Set of measuring cups
Ovenproof dish
Fork

METHOD

Peel the potatoes, cutting away any nasty bits, and cutting out any eyes. Chop the potatoes into quarters. Boil for 25 minutes until soft. Drain. Add freshly ground pepper and 1 tablespoon butter and 2 tablespoons of milk. Mash thoroughly, making sure with the fork that there are no lumps.

Peel and chop the onion. Put the milk, fish and onion in a saucepan and heat over a moderate heat. Simmer for about 10 minutes. Take the pan off the heat.

Drain the fish and onions. Break the fish into lumps, throwing away any bones or skin, and put it in the bottom of the ovenproof dish with the onion and the parsley. Season with pepper. Spread the potato on top. Use a fork to make swirls and ridges. This increases the surface area and makes the top crisper.

Cook in a preheated oven at 200°C, 400°F, Gas mark 6 for about 30 minutes until crisp and brown.

ADDITIONS & ALTERNATIVES

Add 100 g of thawed pre-cooked pink prawns to the fish, about a cup full.

Add 2 oz grated cheese to the mashed potato.

Add a chopped hard-boiled egg to the fish.

Add 6 chopped button mushrooms to the fish.

Neil's anarchist fish pie: make the pie as above, but before putting in the oven use a teaspoon to make a circle with an 'A' in it. Fill this with tomato ketchup then cook in the oven.

TIPS

Use King Edward's or Désirée Reds potatoes and not new potatoes.

TUNA IN SAUCE

Serves 2   ① *Preparation 5 min, Cooking 25 min – Easy*

INGREDIENTS

1 sweet red pepper
3 tablespoons olive oil
3 cloves garlic
2 medium onions
1 tablespoon chilli sauce
227g small tin tomatoes
1 glass wine (optional)
2 fresh tuna steaks (not tinned)

EQUIPMENT

Sharp knife
Chopping board
Set of measuring spoons
Saucepan
Garlic crusher
Wooden spoon
Tin opener

METHOD

Wash the sweet red pepper. Chop the top off, and remove the seeds. Chop the pepper into very small cubes.

Put a tablespoon of oil in the saucepan. Peel and crush the garlic into the pan. Peel and chop the onion. Fry the onion for about three minutes till it is golden, stirring to stop it sticking. Add the sweet pepper and the chilli sauce and fry for another couple of minutes.

Open the tin of tomatoes. Pour the juice into the saucepan. Use the wooden spoon to mash the tomatoes while they are still in the can. Pour the mashed tomatoes into the pan. Continue to cook, stirring as the mixture boils. If you have wine, add a glass. Turn down the heat till the mixture is simmering. Add the tuna steaks. Cook for another 5 to 10 minutes.

ADDITIONS & ALTERNATIVES

Serve with rice or oven chips and salad, or boiled new potatoes.

Instead of the chilli sauce and the sweet pepper use red Spanish mojo, if you can find it.

Substitute half a teaspoon of chilli powder for the chilli sauce.

TIPS

Prepared garlic is sold in tubes and jars. Just read the tube or jar for the suggested equivalent amount. It keeps for six weeks in the fridge.

TUNA RICE

Serves 2   ① *Preparation 5 min, Cooking 25 min – Easy*

INGREDIENTS

1½ cups rice
Salt
400 g tin chick peas
200 g medium tin tuna
1 small onion
1 clove garlic
2 cm (1 inch) fresh ginger
½ teaspoon turmeric
Soy sauce
Freshly ground black pepper

EQUIPMENT

Sharp knife
Chopping board

Frying-pan
Saucepan
Wooden spoon
Tin opener
Set of measuring spoons
Set of measuring cups

METHOD

Read the instructions on the rice packet for the cooking time (about 20 mins). Cook the rice in 3 cups of water with 1 teaspoon of salt. Bring to the boil. Give it a stir, turn the heat down and put a lid on the pan and simmer. When the rice is cooked and all the water has been absorbed, take the pan off the heat. There are full instructions on cooking rice in the 'How to' chapter.

Open and drain the tins of chick peas and tuna. Peel and chop the onion and garlic. Peel the ginger. Chop into tiny bits.

Fry the onion for a minute, stirring. Add the garlic, ginger and turmeric and cook for another couple of minutes. Take off the heat.

When the rice is cooked add it to the frying-pan with the chick peas and tuna. Stir it round. Warm through.

Serve with soy sauce and black pepper.

STUFFED PLAICE

Serves 4   ① *Preparation 10 min, Cooking 20 min – Easy*

INGREDIENTS

600 g pack frozen small plaice fillets (about 5 fillets)
2 tablespoons fresh parsley
100 g (4 oz) mushrooms (about 10)
Salt and freshly ground pepper to taste
1 tablespoon butter
1 glass white wine

EQUIPMENT

Sharp knife
Chopping board
Set of measuring spoons
Ovenproof dish
Aluminium kitchen foil
Small jug

METHOD

Thaw the fish enough to be able to roll it. Wash the fish and drain. Wash, drain and chop the parsley. Wipe the mushrooms clean. Discard any nasty ones. Cut the end off the stalks. Chop the mushrooms into small bits.

Mix the mushrooms and one tablespoon of parsley together. Get a fish and put a tablespoon of mushroom and parsley in the middle. Roll up the fish, so it is like a sausage. Put the fish in the ovenproof dish. Season with salt and pepper. Put the butter on the fish in little blobs. Pour the wine into the dish. Cover the dish with aluminium foil. Cook in a preheated oven at 170°C, 325°F, Gas mark 3 for 20 minutes. Pour the juice from the ovenproof dish into a small jug and stir in the other tablespoon of parsley.

ADDITIONS & ALTERNATIVES

Serve with new potatoes, green vegetables or salad.

Add a small carton (142 ml or 5 fl oz) of single cream to the wine.

SQUID RINGS IN BATTER

Serves 2 to 4   ① *Preparation 5 min, Cooking about 10 min – Easy*

INGREDIENTS

500 g (1 lb) prepared cleaned medium to large squid tubes
1 pack batter mix
Oil for frying
1 lemon

EQUIPMENT

Sharp knife
Chopping board
Bowl
Frying-pan
Kitchen paper
Slotted spoon or fish slice

METHOD

Cut the squid into rings. Make up the batter mix in the bowl according to the instructions on the packet. Put the squid rings in the batter.

Pour oil in the frying-pan to about 1 cm (half an inch) deep and put on the heat. After a couple of minutes, drip a bit of batter into the oil. If it sizzles and puffs up the oil is hot enough. If not wait.

When the oil is hot enough, put some of the rings in the oil, one at a time. Don't put too many in at a time or they will stick together. After a minute or so, depending on how hot the oil is, turn them over. They are ready when they are golden brown on both sides and the batter looks crisp. Fish the rings out and put on a plate covered in kitchen paper. It helps absorb the oil. If you have an oven you can put them in to keep warm at 140°C, 275°F, Gas mark 1. Serve with lemon.

ADDITIONS & ALTERNATIVES

Great starter for a Greek meal, or main dish with salad.

Use 1 pack of ready-battered squid rings. Read the instructions on the packet. They will probably need to be cooked for about 10 to 15 minutes in a hot oven. Put the squid rings on the baking tray. Spread them out so they don't overlap too much or the ones underneath will still be solid when those on top are crispy. Can be cooked straight from frozen.

TIPS

Cleaned and prepared squid tubes should have no skin and also had the 'quill' (a kind of clear plastic backbone) removed. Check they have before cutting into rings.

FISH STEW WITH CHICK PEAS

Serves 4   ⏱ *Preparation 5 min, Cooking 15 min – Easy*

INGREDIENTS

3 cloves garlic
1 large onion
400 g tin chopped tomatoes
400 g tin chick peas
2 tablespoons chopped parsley
750 g (1½ lb) white fish, cod or hake
1 tablespoon oil
½ teaspoon hot chilli powder

EQUIPMENT

Sharp knife
Chopping board
Tin opener
Set of measuring spoons
Saucepan
Wooden spoon

METHOD

Peel and chop the garlic and onion. Open the tin of tomatoes. Open the tin of chick peas and drain the liquid off. Wash, drain and chop the fresh parsley. Chop the fish into 2.5 cm (1 inch) chunks.

Put the oil in a large pan. Add the onions, garlic and chilli. Fry for a couple of minutes, stirring to stop it sticking. Add the fish and fry for another couple of minutes. Add the tomatoes and cook on a low heat till the fish is almost done, about 5 to 10 minutes. Add the chick peas and cook for another five minutes. Add the parsley and serve.

TIPS

Serve with crusty bread and salad.

Prepared garlic is sold in tubes and jars. Just read the tube or jar for the suggested equivalent amount. It keeps for six weeks in the fridge.

MEDITERRANEAN FISH

Serves 4–6   ① *Preparation 20 min, Cooking 25 min – Moderate*

INGREDIENTS

750 g (1½ lbs) potatoes (about 8 medium)
3 tablespoons oil
500 g (1 lb) white fish (hake, cod or haddock)
2 tablespoons flour
Salt and freshly ground pepper to taste
340 g tin black pitted olives
1 cup frozen peas
500 g bottle of Passata
50 g tin anchovies

EQUIPMENT

Vegetable peeler
Sharp knife
Chopping board
Saucepan
Set of measuring spoons
Large ovenproof dish (30 by 18 cm)
Plastic bag
Frying-pan
Wooden spoon
Kitchen paper roll

Tin opener
Set of measuring cups

METHOD

Peel and chop the potatoes into quarters. Boil them in the saucepan until nearly cooked (about 20 minutes), then drain.

Put a tablespoon of oil in the bottom of the ovenproof dish. Chop the potatoes into 1 cm (half-inch) thick slices. Spread them over the bottom of the dish.

Cut the fish into big bite-sized pieces. Put the flour in the plastic bag with a little salt and pepper. Put a few lumps of fish in the bag and, holding the top tightly closed, shake them up. They will get coated in flour. Pick them out. Repeat till all the fish is coated.

Heat 2 tablespoons of the oil in the frying-pan. Add some of the fish and fry for a couple of minutes on both sides. Don't put too many bits of fish in at a time or they stick together in an unappealing mass. When the fish is golden haul it out and drain on some kitchen towel.

Put the fish on top of the potatoes. Put the olives and peas on the potatoes. Pour passata over the peas and olives. Open the tin of anchovies and drain. Chop them and scatter them on top of the passata. Cook for 20 minutes in a preheated oven at 180°C, 350°F, Gas mark 4.

ADDITIONS & ALTERNATIVES

Try chopped or mashed tinned tomatoes instead of the passata.

MEAT

GAMMON & PINEAPPLE

Serves 1–4   ⏱ *Preparation 2 min, Cooking 15 min – Easy*

INGREDIENTS
227 g tin pineapple slices (4 slices)
1 gammon steak per person

EQUIPMENT
Tin opener
Grill

METHOD
Open the tin of pineapple. Put the gammon on the grill pan. Cook for 5 to 10 minutes each side. Put it on a plate with a slice of pineapple on top.

ADDITIONS & ALTERNATIVES
Serve with salad and new potatoes.

Try a fresh peach or nectarine sliced up instead of the pineapple.

Eat any leftover pineapple chopped on breakfast cereal.

LAMB KEBABS

Serves 2–3   ① *Preparation 10 min plus 1–2 hours to marinade,*
Cooking 20 min – Easy

INGREDIENTS
500 g (1 lb) lean lamb
2 tablespoons olive oil
2 tablespoons lemon juice
1 teaspoon dried mint
1 teaspoon salt

EQUIPMENT
Sharp knife
Chopping board
Set of measuring spoons
Bowl
Wooden spoon
4 metal skewers
Grill

METHOD
Cut the lamb into 2 cm (1 inch) cubes. Put the oil, lemon juice, mint and salt in the bowl. Add the lamb and mix round. Cover and put in the fridge. If possible leave for at least an hour and up to 12 if you like.

Thread the meat on the skewers. Grill for about 20 minutes till well cooked. Turn it from time to time.

ADDITIONS & ALTERNATIVES
Serve with rice, salad, and wedges of lemon.

Cut a sweet pepper into squares and thread these on the skewers between the meat.

Try small onions or cherry tomatoes between the meat.

This can be cooked on a barbecue.

142

SAUSAGES

Serves 2   ⏱ *Preparation 1 min, Cooking 15 min – Easy*

INGREDIENTS
200 g (8 oz) sausages

EQUIPMENT
Grill
Fork

METHOD
Prick the skin of the sausages. This stops them bursting. Cook slowly under a moderate grill for 10 to 15 minutes, turning frequently.

ADDITIONS & ALTERNATIVES
Serve with eggs, bacon, baked beans, fried onions, mashed potato or grilled tomato.

The more meat in the sausages the better. There are few tastier foods than a herby, meaty sausage, and few worse than bland, mass-produced extruded stodge. Buy your sausages with care and attention. Supermarkets do various qualities of sausage and butchers often make their own.

Sausage sandwiches for two
Cook the sausages. Meanwhile, butter four slices of bread. Peel and chop a large onion. Put 2 tablespoons of oil in a frying-pan and heat over a moderate heat. Fry the onion for about five minutes till it is brown stirring to stop it sticking. Take off the heat. Cut the sausages in half lengthways. Put on the bread. Add the fried onions, and tomato sauce and/or mustard to taste.

STEAK IN CREAM

Serves 2 ⏱ *Preparation 2 min, Cooking 15 min – Easy*

INGREDIENTS

200 g (8 oz) button mushrooms, about 20–30
1 tablespoon butter
Freshly ground pepper to taste
2 beef steaks (sirloin, rump or fillet)
2 tablespoons Worcestershire sauce
1 tablespoon mushroom ketchup (not essential)
1 medium carton (284 ml or 10 fl oz) of single cream

EQUIPMENT

Sharp knife
Chopping board
Set of measuring spoons
Frying-pan
Wooden spoon

METHOD

Wipe the mushrooms clean. Discard any nasty ones. Chop the end off the stalks. Slice the mushrooms.

Heat the butter in the frying-pan. Grind pepper on top of the steaks. Sprinkle with a few drops Worcestershire sauce. Put in the pan, pepper side down. Cook on hot for a minute, moving them round so they don't stick. Grind more pepper on the top. Sprinkle with a few more drops Worcestershire sauce. Turn the steaks over. Cook for another minute. Turn the heat to medium and cook for a further 3 to 10 minutes, depending on how you like them. Take the steaks out and let them stand on a warm plate.

Put the mushrooms in and stir round to absorb the juices. Add a teaspoon of butter if it gets too dry. Add the rest of the Worcestershire sauce and the mushroom ketchup. Cook for a minute. Add the cream. Warm through (about 30 seconds). Pour over the steaks.

ADDITIONS & ALTERNATIVES

Serve with green salad.

Lea & Perrins make a well known Worcestershire sauce.

Mushroom ketchup is a thin brown liquid, which you may find in the supermarket.

You can grill the steaks with a little knob of butter, Worcestershire sauce and pepper.

If you bash the steak with a steak hammer or the end of a rolling pin before cooking it makes it more tender. Fillet steak will be tender anyway.

BEEF IN BEER

Serves 4   ① *Preparation 5 min, Cooking 2 hours – Easy*

INGREDIENTS
1 kg (2 lbs) beef, chuck steak or braising steak
200 g (8 oz) button mushrooms, about 20
2 large onions
2 carrots
1–2 tablespoons oil
1 bay leaf
1 tablespoon mixed herbs
2 tablespoons of tomato purée
500 ml tin brown ale
Salt and freshly ground pepper to taste

EQUIPMENT
Sharp knife
Chopping board
Frying-pan
Casserole with lid
Set of measuring spoons

METHOD
Cut the beef into 2 cm (1 inch) cubes. Wipe the mushrooms clean. Discard any nasty ones. Chop the end off the stalks. Peel the onions. Chop coarsely. Peel the carrots. Chop coarsely.

Put the oil in the frying-pan. Fry the beef chunks for about 2–3 minutes to brown. Stir. Put all the ingredients in the casserole. Stir round once. If the beer does not cover the ingredients either add more beer or a little water. Put the lid on the casserole. Cook for 2 hours at 140°C, 275°F, Gas mark 1.

ADDITIONS & ALTERNATIVES

Serve with potatoes or rice.

TIPS

Tomato purée comes in tubes. It keeps for four weeks in the fridge.

BRAISED BEEF

Serves 2–3　　　*① Preparation 15 min, Cooking 90 min – Easy*

INGREDIENTS

2 large onions
3 large carrots
500 g (1 lb) braising beef
1 tablespoon oil
1 glass of wine (optional)
Salt and freshly ground pepper to taste
2 beef stock cubes

EQUIPMENT

Sharp knife
Chopping board
Set of measuring spoons
Casserole dish with lid
Wooden spoon

METHOD

This is best cooked slowly in the oven, but it can be made in a saucepan on the top

Peel and slice the onions. Peel and slice the carrots. Cut the beef into large pieces.

Put the oil in the casserole. Put the beef, onion and carrot in and mix it round. Add a glass of wine if available. Season with salt and pepper. Crumble the stock cubes up into the casserole and stir round. Top up with water to cover the ingredients. Give it a stir. Put the lid on the casserole. Cook in a preheated oven at 150°C, 300°F, Gas mark 2 for an hour and a half.

TIPS

This can be cooked in a saucepan for 90 minutes on a low heat. Stir from time to time and top up with fluid if it looks dry.

This is one of the tenderest ways of cooking a very cheap cut of meat.

GREEK LAMB KLEFTIKOS

Serves 6   ⏱ *Preparation 10 min, Cooking 90 min – Easy*

INGREDIENTS
12 frozen lamb chump chops (1.5 kg or 3 lbs)
3 cloves garlic
2 tablespoons parsley
2 teaspoons dried rosemary
400 g tin tomatoes
1 stock cube
Salt and freshly ground pepper to taste

EQUIPMENT
Sharp knife
Chopping board
Casserole with lid
Wooden spoon
Tin opener
Set of measuring spoons

DEFROSTING

Make sure chops are thoroughly thawed. Thaw in a single layer for 3–4 hours at room temperature or overnight in a fridge.

METHOD

Trim off the excess fat. Put the chops in the casserole. Peel and chop the garlic. Add the garlic. Add the parsley and rosemary. Open the tin of tomatoes. Add to the casserole. Add stock cubes crumbled into 500 ml (1 pint) hot water. Season with salt and pepper. Cook in a preheated oven for two and a half hours at 150°C, 300°F, Gas mark 2.

ADDITIONS & ALTERNATIVES

Serve with rice and salad.

TIPS

Prepared garlic is sold in tubes and jars. Just read the tube or jar for the suggested equivalent amount. It keeps for six weeks in the fridge.

Packs of chump chops come from the freezer cabinet.

IRISH STEW

Serves 4   ① *Preparation 10 min, Cooking 90 min – Easy*

INGREDIENTS

3 large potatoes
2 large onions
2 large carrots
2 small turnips
500 g (1 lb) lamb or beef
2 tablespoons sunflower oil
Salt
Freshly ground black pepper
1 stock cube
$\frac{1}{2}$ cup frozen peas
Bread

EQUIPMENT

Sharp knife
Chopping board
Vegetable peeler
Large saucepan
Set of measuring spoons
Set of measuring cups
Wooden spoon

METHOD

Peel the potatoes, cutting away any nasty bits, and cutting out any eyes. Chop the potatoes into small dice. Peel and chop the onions. Peel the carrots, cutting off both ends. Chop into small cubes. Peel the turnips. Chop into small cubes. Chop the meat into 2.5 cm (1 inch) cubes.

Put the oil in the saucepan and heat over a moderate heat. Fry the onion for about three minutes till it is golden, stirring to stop it sticking. Add the meat and cook for about 5 minutes, till it is browned. Add the potatoes, carrots and turnips, salt and pepper, and cook for 5 minutes. Add stock cube and 750 ml (1½ pints) water. Bring to the boil, turn down the heat till it is just boiling (simmering). Put the lid on and cook for 1 hour.

Add the peas. Cook for 10 minutes.

Serve as it is with bread.

ADDITIONS & ALTERNATIVES

You can add sausages to the stew to make it go further.

PORK & CIDER

Serves 4   ① *Preparation 5 min, Cooking 2 hours – Easy*

INGREDIENTS
1 large onion
4 large pork chops, about 1 kg (2 lb) in total
1 large cooking apple
250 ml bottle of cider

EQUIPMENT
Sharp knife
Chopping board
Casserole with lid
Apple corer

METHOD
Peel and chop the onion. Put the onion in the bottom of the casserole. Put the chops on top. Peel the apple, discarding the seeds and core. Slice the apple and spread over the chops. Add the cider. Put the lid on the casserole.

Cook for two hours in a preheated oven at 150°C, 300°F, Gas mark 2.

ADDITIONS & ALTERNATIVES
Serve with rice and salad or potatoes and green vegetable.

SHEPHERD'S PIE

Serves 3–4   ⏱ *Preparation 15 min, Cooking 40 min – Easy*

INGREDIENTS
750 g (1½ lb) old potatoes (about 7 medium)
Salt and freshly ground pepper to taste
1 tablespoon butter
1 tablespoon milk
1 onion
2 carrots
1 tablespoon sunflower oil
500 g (1 lb) minced lamb or beef
1 stock cube

EQUIPMENT
Vegetable peeler
Sharp knife
Chopping board
Saucepan
Set of measuring spoons
Potato masher or fork
Grater
Frying-pan
Wooden spoon
Set of measuring cups
Ovenproof dish, at least 5 cm (2 inches) deep

METHOD
Peel the potatoes and chop in quarters. Boil in a saucepan with at least a pint of water and a teaspoon of salt for 20 to 25 minutes till soft. Drain and mash with the butter and milk. Add a quarter teaspoon of freshly ground pepper. Keep mashing the potatoes till they are smooth and lump free.

While the potatoes are cooking, peel and chop the onion. Peel and grate the carrots, cutting off the top and bottom. Put the oil in the frying-pan and fry the onions for a couple of minutes, stirring round. Add the meat and cook for another five minutes. Add the carrot, stock cube and 1 cup (280 ml or half pint) of water. Cook for another five minutes till most of the water has boiled off.

Put the meat mixture in the casserole. Level off the surface. Put the mashed potato on top. Spread to cover. Make artistic swirls, or whatever, in the mashed potato. Cook in a preheated oven at 180°C, 350°F, Gas mark 4 for 20 to 30 minutes till golden on top.

ADDITIONS & ALTERNATIVES

Sprinkle 50 g (2 oz or 1 cup) grated Cheddar cheese on the potato, or even in it while you are mashing.

Add 100 g (4 oz) chopped mushroom to the meat.

New potatoes make awful mashed potato. Only use old potatoes like King Edward's or Désirée Reds.

TOAD IN THE HOLE

Serves 3 to 4   ⏱ *Preparation 5 min, Cooking 35 min – Easy*

INGREDIENTS
1 packet batter mix
1½ tablespoons oil
8 chipolata sausages (225 g or 8 oz)
200 g (8 oz) pack streaky bacon (optional)

EQUIPMENT
Set of measuring spoons
Ovenproof dish
Wooden spoon
Bowl
Grill or frying-pan

METHOD
Make the batter mix according to the instructions on the packet, following directions for Yorkshire pudding.

Put the oil in the ovenproof dish and put in the oven at 200°C, 400°F, Gas mark 6.

Gently grill or fry the sausages for about 10 minutes, turning from time to time. You can wrap bacon round the sausage before cooking.

Take the dish out of the oven. Add the sausages and pour the batter mix on top. Return to the oven and cook for 20 to 25 minutes till golden. Follow the packet instructions for cooking Yorkshire pudding.

ADDITIONS & ALTERNATIVES
Serve with salad or green vegetables and apple sauce. There is a recipe for fresh apple sauce on page 162.

PORK CHOPS WITH ORANGE SAUCE

Serves 2   ① *Preparation 5 min, Cooking 20 min – Easy*

INGREDIENTS
1 tablespoon oil
2 pork chops, about 500g (1 lb)
1 orange
1 teaspoon of cornflour
Salt and freshly ground pepper to taste

EQUIPMENT
Set of measuring spoons
Frying-pan
Wooden spoon
Zester
Sharp knife
Chopping board
Juicer
Teacup

METHOD
Put the oil in the frying-pan on a medium heat. Fry the pork chops. Start by sealing the chops on both sides by cooking on medium to high heat for a minute or so a side. Turn down the heat and cook on low for about 20 minutes, turning from time to time.

Meanwhile scrape the rind off the orange with the zester. Juice the orange. Put the cornflour in the cup. Dissolve the cornflour by adding a teaspoon of water at a time and stirring.

Take the pan off the heat. Take the chops out of the pan. Add the orange rind to the pan. Stir. Add the orange juice and three tablespoons of water. Add the dissolved cornflour stirring all the time. Put the pan on a low heat and stir till the sauce goes thick.

Season with salt and pepper. Put the chops back in the pan and coat the chops in sauce.

ADDITIONS & ALTERNATIVES
Serve with rice or salad.

ROAST BEEF

Serves 4 ① Preparation 5 min, Cooking 45 mins per pound – Easy

INGREDIENTS
6 small onions
1 to 1.5 kg (2 to 3 lb) rib of beef
Salt and freshly ground pepper to taste

EQUIPMENT
Sharp knife
Roasting tin/ovenproof dish
or
Cast-iron casserole
Set of measuring cups

METHOD
Peel the onions. Season the beef well with salt and freshly ground black pepper. If you are using a roasting dish or ovenproof dish, just put the beef in with the onions and half a cup of water. Cover the top with foil.

If you have a cast-iron casserole (le Creuset or similar) put the beef in with the onions and half a cup of water and roast with the lid on.

Cook in a pre-heated oven at 170°C, 325°F, Gas mark 3 for 100 minutes per kilo (45 minutes a pound). Take the lid off for the last half hour.

When the beef is cooked, take it out of the oven and put it on a plate. Leave it for 10 minutes before carving it.

ADDITIONS & ALTERNATIVES

Traditional accompaniments are mustard, horseradish sauce and Yorkshire pudding.

Serve with roast potatoes and vegetables or mashed potatoes. Put the prepared vegetables in an ovenproof dish with half a cup of oil or so. Cook at the top of the oven for at least an hour. Full instructions are in the vegetarian section.

TIPS

There's a recipe for Gravy on page 111, if you need it.

Yorkshire pudding often fails, either burning, failing to rise or turning out stodgy. You can buy frozen Yorkshire puddings and really they are as good as you can make. If you are feeling brave there are packets of batter mixes. Just follow the instructions.

Cornish pasty, beef and tomato sandwiches and beef in gravy are all ways of using up left-over beef.

You can shred left-over beef and add it to a Chinese stir fry.

ROAST LAMB

Serves 4
⏱ *Preparation 5 min,*
Cooking 45 mins per pound – Easy

INGREDIENTS
6 small onions
Half leg of lamb or shoulder of lamb, about 1–1.5 kg (2–3 lb)
1 tablespoon of rosemary
Salt and freshly ground pepper to taste

EQUIPMENT
Sharp knife
Roasting tin/ovenproof dish
or
Cast-iron casserole
Set of measuring spoons
Set of measuring cups

METHOD
Peel the onions. Season the lamb with salt and pepper and sprinkle with rosemary. If you are using a roasting dish or ovenproof dish, just put the lamb in with the onions and half a cup of water. Cover the top with foil.

If you have a cast-iron casserole (le Creuset or similar) put the lamb in with the onions and half a cup of water and roast with the lid on.

Cook in a preheated oven at 170°C, 325°F, Gas mark 3 for 100 minutes per kilo (45 minutes a pound). Take the lid off for the last half hour.

When the lamb is cooked, take it out of the oven and put it on a plate. Leave it for 10 minutes before trying to carve it.

ADDITIONS & ALTERNATIVES

Serve with roast potatoes and vegetables or mashed potatoes. Put the prepared vegetables in an ovenproof dish with half a cup of oil or so. Cook at the top of the oven for at least an hour. Full instructions are in the vegetarian section.

Redcurrant jelly goes well with lamb.

Garlic Roast Lamb

Peel 4 cloves of garlic and cut in half. Make 8 stabs in the meat and push a piece of garlic in each before cooking.

Mint sauce

Put 1 teaspoon of mint sauce in a small jug with a teaspoon of sugar and 2 tablespoons of white wine vinegar.

TIPS

There's a recipe for gravy on page 111, if you need it.

Cornish Pasty and Shepherd's Pie can be made with left-over lamb. Recipes are included.

Sandwiches with pickle and salad are pretty good too.

ROAST PORK

Serves 4   ⏱ *Preparation 2 min, Cooking 45 mins*
per pound – Easy

INGREDIENTS
1 to 1.5 kg (2 to 3 lb) loin of pork
Salt and freshly ground pepper to taste

EQUIPMENT
Sharp knife
Roasting tin/ovenproof dish
or
Cast-iron casserole
Set of measuring cups

METHOD
Perhaps the most important thing about roast pork is the crackling. To get good crackling, just make cuts about 2 cm (1 inch) apart through the skin. Rub salt into skin.

If possible stand the pork on a metal rack to keep it out of the juices as it cooks. You will survive without the metal rack.

If you are using a roasting dish or ovenproof dish, put the pork in with half a cup of water. Do not cover.

If you have a cast-iron casserole (le Creuset or similar) put the pork in with half a cup of water.

Cook for 90 minutes per kilo (40 minutes a pound). When the pork is cooked, take it out of the oven and put it on a plate. Leave it for 10 minutes before carving.

ADDITIONS & ALTERNATIVES
Serve with roast potatoes and vegetables or mashed potatoes. Put the prepared vegetables in an ovenproof dish with half a cup of oil or so. Cook at the top of the oven for at least an hour. Full instructions are in the vegetarian section.

A traditional accompaniment is apple sauce. It's the next recipe.

TIPS

There's a recipe for gravy on page 111, if you need it.

Left-over pork can be cut into thin strips and made into a Chinese stir fry, or curried.

APPLE SAUCE

2 cups   ⏱ *Preparation 5 min, Cooking 10 min – Easy*

INGREDIENTS

4 large cooking apples (about 750 g or 1½ lbs)
2 tablespoons of brown sugar
1 tablespoon lemon juice
½ teaspoon of mixed spice, nutmeg or allspice (optional)

EQUIPMENT

Sharp knife
Chopping board
Set of measuring spoons
Saucepan
Wooden spoon

METHOD

Peel the apples. Cut out the core and seeds and discard. Slice the apples about 1 cm (half-inch) thick. Put the apples, sugar, lemon juice and spice in the pan and mix together. Cook over a low heat for about 10 minutes, to soften it. Let it cool down and serve.

GOULASH

Serves 6   ⓘ *Preparation 10 min, Cooking 90 min – Moderate*

INGREDIENTS
1 kg (2 lb) stewing beef
1 kg (2 lb) onions (about 4 large)
3 cloves garlic
1 kg (2 lb) potatoes (about 8 medium)
3 tablespoons sunflower oil
400 g tin chopped tomatoes
2 tablespoons paprika pepper
2 stock cubes
1 medium carton (284 ml or 10 fl oz) sour cream

EQUIPMENT
Sharp knife
Chopping board
Set of measuring spoons
Large saucepan
Wooden spoon
Tin opener

METHOD
Chop the meat into 2.5 cm (1 inch) cubes. Peel and slice the onions. Peel and slice the garlic. Peel and slice the potatoes.

Heat 2 tablespoons of oil in the saucepan. Add the onion and garlic and fry for a couple of minutes, stirring to stop it sticking. Add the meat and cook and stir for about 5 minutes. Add another tablespoon of oil and the potatoes and cook for another 5 minutes.

Open the tin of tomatoes and add to the mixture. Add the paprika. Add 500 ml water (1 pint) and the stock cubes. Cook for an hour on a low heat so it is just boiling (simmering). Stir from time to time to stop it sticking. If it looks like it is drying out add more fluid. The potato and onion should go to a thick gravy.

Just before serving, add the sour cream and stir round.

ADDITIONS & ALTERNATIVES

Serve with rice, green salad and bread.

Try pork or lamb instead of the beef.

STEAK & KIDNEY

Serves 4–6   ① *Preparation 15 min, Cooking 2 hours – Moderate*

INGREDIENTS

2 tablespoons flour
Salt and freshly ground pepper to taste
1 kg (2 lb) steak and kidney
200g (8 oz) button mushrooms (about 20 to 25)
1 large onion
1 tablespoon olive oil
1 bay leaf
1 tablespoon mixed herbs
1 stock cube

EQUIPMENT

Plastic bag
Set of measuring spoons
Sharp knife
Chopping board
Frying-pan
Wooden spoon
Casserole with lid

METHOD

Put the flour and some salt and pepper in the plastic bag. Chop the meat into 2.5 cm (1 inch) cubes. Put the steak and kidney in the bag, a few chunks at a time. Hold the bag shut and shake to cover in flour.

Wipe the mushrooms clean. Discard any nasty ones. Chop the end off the stalks. Peel and chop the onion.

Put the oil in the frying-pan and heat over a moderate heat. Fry the onion for about three minutes until golden, stirring to stop it sticking. Fish the onion out of the pan and put in the casserole dish. Fry the steak and kidney for a minute or so to seal it, stirring. It does not need to be cooked through. Put the meat in the casserole with the bay leaf and herbs and mushrooms.

Stir any of the remaining flour from the bag in the frying pan for 15 seconds with a tablespoon of water. Add to the casserole. Crumble the stock cube on top. Cover the meat with water. Put a lid on the casserole. Cook for 2 hours at 150°C, 300°F, Gas mark 2.

ADDITIONS & ALTERNATIVES

Serve with potatoes and vegetables.

You can use a glass of wine instead of some of the water.

TIPS

If you are using a cast-iron casserole, you can fry the onions and meat in it and dispense with the frying-pan.

STUFFED BREAST OF LAMB

Serves 2–3   ① *Preparation 5 min, Cooking 45 min*
– Moderate, messy

INGREDIENTS
1 boned breast of lamb about 500 g (1 lb)
170 g pack of stuffing mix

EQUIPMENT
Sharp knife
Chopping board
String or 2 metal skewers
Ovenproof dish

METHOD
Get the butcher to take the bones out of the breast of lamb. This is a fatty cut and benefits from having the stuffing mixture.

Lay down the breast of lamb skin side out. Cut five lengths of string longer than the breast of lamb and lay them under the breast of lamb. If you are using metal skewers forget this instruction.

Mix up the stuffing according to the instructions on the packet. This generally involves adding boiling water, stirring round and leaving to stand. Spoon the stuffing on to the breast of lamb along a line 5 cm (2 inches) from the shorter edge. Starting from this edge, roll the breast of lamb into a sausage. Secure it. Tie the strings round the breast of lamb or stick the metal skewers through to the middle.

Put the breast of lamb on the ovenproof dish. Cook in a preheated oven at 170°C, 325°F, Gas mark 3 for 45 minutes. Slice to serve.

ADDITIONS & ALTERNATIVES
This can be eaten hot with potatoes and vegetables, or cold with pickle and salad.

MINCE ROLL

Serves 3–4   ⏱ *Preparation 15 min, Cooking 30 min – Moderate*

INGREDIENTS

375 g pack pre-rolled puff pastry (chilled or frozen)
1 large onion
2 cloves garlic
2 slices of bread or 1–2 cups breadcrumbs
500 g (1 lb) mince
2 tablespoons freshly chopped parsley
Salt and freshly ground pepper to taste
1 egg

EQUIPMENT

Sharp knife
Chopping board
Baking tray
Wooden spoon
Bowl
Set of measuring spoons
Set of measuring cups

METHOD

Thaw the pastry according to the instructions on the packet. Four hours in the fridge seems typical.

Peel and chop the onion. Peel and chop the garlic. Crumble the bread into crumbs with your fingers.

Put the mince, onion, garlic, breadcrumbs, parsley, salt and pepper in the bowl. Break the egg into a cup. Fish out any bits of shell. Add the egg to the bowl. Mix it all together.

Open the pastry and spread it out flat. It should be oblong. The intention is to get the meat mixture on the pastry and seal it in to make a fat sausage shape. The pastry will stick together if it is moistened with some water or milk. If you don't seal it like this it will all fall apart. If it is too difficult to roll one large mince roll, cut the pastry in half and make two small ones.

Start from a short edge of the pastry. Put the meat mixture on the pastry in a thick sausage shape, leaving a gap at the edge. Pull the pastry over the top so it overlaps. Moisten the edges and gently press them together. Seal up the ends of the sausage shape by using water and pressing the pastry together.

Get the baking tray and rub with a little oil. Put the roll on the baking tray, turning it over as you do, so the join is on the bottom. Brush a little milk on top to give it a shine when it is cooked. Stab a few holes with a fork so the steam can get out as it cooks.

Cook in a pre-heated oven at 200°C, 400°F, Gas mark 6 for 30 minutes.

Slice and serve hot with vegetables or cold with salad.

ADDITIONS & ALTERNATIVES

Add 2 tablespoons mixed herbs.

There may be enough pastry left over to make a sweet mince pie roll (same principle, different filling) or jam roll (spread jam thickly on pastry leaving 2.5 cm (1 inch) margin, then roll like a Swiss roll).

TIPS

Prepared garlic is sold in tubes and jars. Just read the tube or jar for the suggested equivalent amount. It keeps for six weeks in the fridge.

CORNISH PASTY

Makes 2   ① *Preparation 10 min, Cooking 25 min*
*If you ever cook roast beef, this is an easy way of using
up the remains*

INGREDIENTS

375 g pack of pre-rolled puff pastry or shortcrust pastry
1 cup left-over beef
1 cup left-over potatoes
$\frac{1}{2}$ cup chopped carrot
Salt and freshly ground pepper to taste
1 teaspoon of milk

EQUIPMENT

Sharp knife
Chopping board
Set of measuring cups
Wooden spoon
Bowl
Baking sheet
Set of measuring spoons

METHOD

Thaw frozen pastry according to the instructions on the packet.
Four hours in the fridge seems typical.

Unfold the pastry. Cut the pastry into 15 cm (6 inch) squares.

Chop up the meat, potato and carrots and mix together in the
bowl with some salt and pepper. Put a couple of tablespoons of
mixture in the middle of each pastry square. Moisten the edge of
the pastry and pull the edges together over the top like a crest.
Pinch together. Use a fork to make a couple of holes. Lay on a
baking sheet. Brush the pastry with a little milk to gloss it up.

Cook in a preheated oven at 190°C, 375°F, Gas mark 3 for 20 to 25 minutes till golden brown.

ADDITIONS & ALTERNATIVES

You can use lamb, peas, or any cooked vegetables for the filling.

Use a block of prepared pastry and roll it yourself. Full instructions are in the 'How to' chapter.

GRILLED STEAK

Serves 1   ① *Preparation 3 min, Cooking 15 min – Moderate*

INGREDIENTS

150–200 g (6–8 oz) fillet, rump, or sirloin steak cut
    2.5 cm (1 inch) thick
1 tablespoon olive oil
Freshly ground pepper

EQUIPMENT

Sharp knife
Chopping board
Grill
Set of measuring spoons

METHOD

Cut through the fat every inch or so. If the meat is very lean, brush a tablespoon of olive oil on it. Season with fresh ground pepper.

Turn the grill on full and let it get really hot. Put the steak on the grill pan. Cook for one minute each side. Turn down the grill to medium and cook for 10 to 15 minutes depending on thickness. Turn the steak over every two minutes or so. This should give a medium done steak with a pink inside.

If you like your steak rare, cook for a shorter time, if you like it well done then give it longer. Also if it is a thinner cut it will take less time.

This is one recipe where practice and experience helps. If you want a reasonably foolproof right-first-time steak recipe try the Steak in Cream on page 144.

ADDITIONS & ALTERNATIVES

Serve with chips, salad, grilled tomato, fried onions or fried mushrooms.

Add a few drops of Worcestershire sauce to the steak during cooking.

Marinade for 24 hours in 3 tablespoons of soy sauce and 1 tablespoon of oil in a fridge.

TIPS

If you bash the steak with a steak hammer or the end of a rolling pin before cooking it makes it more tender. Fillet steak will be tender anyway.

BEEF STEW WITH WINE

Serves 4–6 ○ *Preparation 10 min, Cooking 2 hours – Moderate*
You have to keep adding things as it cooks

INGREDIENTS
1.5 kg (3 lbs) beef, chuck steak or braising steak
2 tablespoons flour
Salt and freshly ground pepper to taste
200 g (8 oz) button mushrooms (20 to 25)
200 g (8 oz) belly pork
12 small onions
1 tablespoon olive oil
1 bay leaf
1 teaspoon marjoram or oregano
1 bottle red wine
1 tablespoon parsley

EQUIPMENT
Sharp knife
Chopping board
Plastic bag
Set of measuring spoons
Frying-pan
Wooden spoon
Bowl
Casserole with lid

METHOD
Cut the beef into 2.5 cm (1 inch) cubes. Put the flour and some salt and pepper in the plastic bag. Put the beef in the bag, a few chunks at a time. Hold the bag shut and shake to cover in flour.

Wipe the mushrooms clean. Discard any nasty ones. Chop the end off the stalks. Cut the belly pork into thin slices then chop small. Peel the onions. Keep whole. Do not slice.

Put the oil in the frying-pan and heat over a moderate heat. Fry the mushrooms for a minute or so, stirring till they are coated. Lift the mushrooms out and put in the bowl.

Fry the belly pork and onions for about three minutes, stirring to stop it sticking. Lift out the pork and onions and put in the bowl.

Fry the beef chunks for a few minutes in the oil left from the belly pork to seal it. Put the beef in the casserole with the bay leaf and oregano. Cover the meat with a half and half mixture of wine and water. Cook for an hour at 150°C, 300°F, Gas mark 2.

Add the mushrooms, onions and pork. Cook for another hour. Add the parsley when ready to serve.

ADDITIONS & ALTERNATIVES

Serve with potatoes or rice.

Belly pork is what streaky bacon is made from and should have a lot of fat. If you can't find it try four rashers of bacon, chopped.

Try marinating the meat in the wine overnight in the fridge.

The better the wine, the better the dish tastes.

You can use just a glass of wine, using water and a stock cube to make up the rest of the fluid.

VEGETARIAN

MASHED POTATO

Serves 3–4   ① *Preparation 5 min, Cooking 25 min – Easy*

INGREDIENTS
750 g (1½ lb) old potatoes (about 7 medium)
1 tablespoon butter
Salt and freshly ground pepper to taste

EQUIPMENT
Sharp knife
Chopping board
Saucepan
Potato masher
Set of measuring spoons

METHOD
Peel potatoes and chop in quarters. Put in a saucepan and cover with water. Add a teaspoon of salt and boil for 20 to 25 minutes till soft. Drain and mash with the butter. Add a quarter teaspoon of fresh ground pepper. Keep mashing the potatoes till they are smooth and lump free. If you want them creamier add a little more butter or a splash of milk.

ADDITIONS & ALTERNATIVES
Sprinkle 50 g (2 oz or 1 cup) grated Cheddar cheese on the potato, or even in it while you are mashing.

TIPS

New potatoes make awful mashed potato. Only use old potatoes like King Edward's or Désirée Reds.

VEGETARIAN SAUSAGE & FRIED ONIONS

Serves 2   ⏱ *Preparation 5 min, Cooking 10 min – Easy*

INGREDIENTS

2 large onions
1 tablespoon olive oil
250 g pack of vegetarian sausages

EQUIPMENT

Sharp knife
Chopping board
Frying-pan
Set of measuring spoons
Grill

METHOD

Peel and chop the onion. Put the oil in the frying-pan and heat over a moderate heat. Fry the onion for about 8 to 10 minutes till it is well cooked, stirring to stop it sticking.

Grill the sausages for about 10 minutes, turning them from time to time.

ADDITIONS & ALTERNATIVES

Eat with mashed potato and apple sauce or in a bread roll.

BAKED POTATO & FILLINGS

Serves 1   ① *Preparation 5 min, Cooking 60 min – Easy*

INGREDIENTS
1 large potato
1 tablespoon butter
Salt and freshly ground pepper to taste

EQUIPMENT
Fork
Skewer
Aluminium foil
Oven glove
Set of measuring spoons

METHOD
Wash the potato. Prick the surface with a fork. Stick the skewer through the potato, it helps it to cook in the middle. Wrap the potato in aluminum foil.

Cook in a preheated oven on the top shelf at 230°C, 450°F, Gas mark 8 for an hour. It is ready when it gives when pressed. Remember to use oven gloves!

If you like your potato crisp on the outside, cook it for half an hour with the foil on, then take it off and cook for another half an hour.

Take out the skewer. Split the potato. Add butter, salt and pepper to taste with one of the suggested fillings:
Half a cup of grated Cheddar cheese
1 small tin baked beans
Left over (or a tin of) chilli con carne
1 small carton of sour cream and chopped fresh chives
Tuna mayonnaise (see p. 30)

ROAST POTATOES, CARROTS, PARSNIP & ONION

Serves 2 or vegetable for 4   ① *Preparation 10 min, Cooking 40 min – Easy*

INGREDIENTS
6 medium or 3 large potatoes
4 medium carrots
2 parsnips
8 small onions
2 tablespoons sunflower oil

EQUIPMENT
Sharp knife
Chopping board
Ovenproof dish
Vegetable peeler
Set of measuring spoons

METHOD
Peel the potatoes, cutting away any nasty bits, and cutting out any eyes. Chop the potatoes in half if medium sized or into quarters if large.

Peel the carrots, cutting off both ends. Chop the carrots lengthways into quarters. Peel the parsnips, cutting off both ends. Chop the parsnips lengthways into quarters. Peel the onions.

Put the potatoes, onions, carrots and parsnips in the ovenproof dish with the oil. Cook in the top of a preheated oven at 180°C, 350°F, Gas mark 4 for 40 to 60 minutes or longer if you like them really well done.

Turn over half-way through cooking.

177

TIPS

Heat the oil first by putting the dish with the oil in the oven for about 10 minutes before adding the vegetables. It helps to reduce sticking. You can cook this with any roast meat. If you are cooking the meat at a lower temperature just cook the vegetables for longer.

STUFFED TOMATO

Serves 4   ① *Preparation 5 min, Cooking 10 min – Easy*

INGREDIENTS

8 button mushrooms
$\frac{1}{2}$ tablespoon parsley
1 medium onion
$\frac{1}{2}$ tablespoon butter
4 large beef tomatoes
2 tablespoons grated cheese
1 egg
Salt and freshly ground pepper

EQUIPMENT

Sharp knife
Chopping board
Set of measuring spoons
Saucepan
Wooden spoon
Baking sheet

METHOD

Wipe the mushrooms clean. Discard any nasty ones. Cut the end of the stalks. Chop the mushrooms.

Wash, drain, dry and finely chop the parsley. Peel and chop the onion.

Put the butter in the saucepan and heat over a moderate heat. Fry the onion for about two minutes, stirring to stop it sticking. Take the pan off the heat.

Cut a 'lid' off the stalk end of the tomatoes. Scoop out the pulp from the tomato and add to the pan. Cook on a low heat for about three minutes. Take the pan off the heat. Add the mushrooms, parsley, cheese and egg. Mix together. Add salt and pepper to taste. Fill the tomato shells.

Put on the baking sheet and cook in a preheated oven at 200°C, 400°F, Gas mark 6 for 5 minutes.

BUTTER BEANS & TOMATO

Serves 2   ⏱ *Preparation 2 min, Cooking 10 min – Very Easy*

INGREDIENTS
2 cloves garlic
1 medium onion
1 tablespoon olive oil
140 g small tin tomato purée
1 teaspoon mixed herbs
1 vegetable stock cube
400 g tin butter beans

EQUIPMENT
Garlic crusher
Sharp knife
Chopping board
Set of measuring spoons
Saucepan
Wooden spoon
Set of measuring cups
Tin opener

METHOD

Peel and crush the garlic into the pan. Peel and chop the onion.

Put the oil in the pan and heat over a moderate heat. Fry the onion and garlic for about three minutes until golden, stirring to stop them sticking. Add the tomato purée, herbs and stock cube. Stir. Add half a cup of water. Heat up and stir.

Open the tin of butter beans and drain off the fluid. Add the butterbeans to the pan. Heat up for about three minutes.

ADDITIONS & ALTERNATIVES

Serve with rice and salad.

Try other beans like haricot.

Sprinkle the top with grated cheese.

Use half a tube of tomato purée instead of the tin.

TIPS

Prepared garlic is sold in tubes and jars. Just read the tube or jar for the suggested equivalent amount. It keeps for six weeks in the fridge.

AUBERGINE, CHICK PEA & TOMATO STEW

Serves 4   ① *Preparation 10 min, Cooking 50 min – Easy*

INGREDIENTS

2 large aubergines about 700 g ($1\frac{1}{2}$ lb)
2 onions
2 tablespoons of oil for frying
2 cloves garlic
1 teaspoon turmeric
$\frac{1}{2}$ teaspoon chilli powder
400 g tin tomatoes
2 x 400 g tins chick peas
Juice of 1 lemon
1 tablespoon parsley or coriander leaf
Pitta bread

EQUIPMENT

Sharp knife
Chopping board
Big pan or a wok
Set of measuring spoons
Garlic crusher
Wooden spoon
Tin opener
Cup

METHOD

Wash the aubergines and cut into slices, discarding the top and bottom. Soak the slices in water for a few minutes, then drain.

Peel and chop the onions. Put the oil in the pan. Peel and crush the garlic into the pan. Add the onion and cook on a medium heat for 5 minutes. Stir from time to time. Add the turmeric and chilli powder. Cook for another three minutes.

Add the aubergine slices and stir round until they start to cook and are golden, about ten minutes. Add the tin of tomatoes, mashing up if required.

Open the tins of chick peas. Pour the liquid off into a cup, you may need it later. Add the chick peas to the mixture. Stir it all together and cook on a medium heat (don't burn it) for about 35 minutes. If it starts to get too dry looking, add the chick pea liquid. If this runs out use water.

Just before serving, put in the lemon juice and parsley or coriander.

Serve with warm pitta bread (sprinkle them with water and grill for a minute, till they puff up).

ADDITIONS & ALTERNATIVES

Try eating this with Tabbouleh (page 83), an appropriate salad.

TIPS

Dutch Aubergines don't need soaking.

Prepared garlic is sold in tubes and jars. Just read the tube or jar for the suggested equivalent amount. It keeps for six weeks in the fridge.

WHITE SAUCE

Makes about 500 ml (1 pint) ⏱ *Preparation 2 min,*
Cooking 5 min – Easy

INGREDIENTS
4 tablespoons butter
6 tablespoons flour
500 ml (1 pt or 2 cups) milk
Salt and freshly ground pepper to taste

EQUIPMENT
Set of measuring spoons
Saucepan
Wooden spoon

METHOD
The secret of this sauce is to keep stirring.

Put the butter in the pan. Melt over moderate heat. Mix in the flour, and cook for a minute, stirring all the time. Take off the heat. Add the milk a bit at a time. Stir each time to make sure it is smooth. When all the milk is added put it back on the heat and bring to the boil. Keep stirring. Reduce the heat and simmer gently for 2 minutes, stirring. Season with salt and pepper.

TIPS
This is quite a thick sauce. If you want it thinner, just add a little more liquid.

CHEESE SAUCE

Makes about 500 ml (1 pint)

① *Preparation 2 min,
Cooking 5 min – Easy*

INGREDIENTS
2 tablespoons butter
2 tablespoons flour
500 ml (1 pt or 2 cups) milk
75 g (3 oz) mature Cheddar cheese (grated), about 1½ cups
Salt and freshly ground pepper to taste

EQUIPMENT
Saucepan
Wooden spoon
Grater for the cheese
Set of measuring spoons
Set of measuring cups

METHOD
The secret of this sauce is to keep stirring.

Put the butter in the pan. Melt over moderate heat. Mix in the flour and cook for a minute, stirring all the time. Take off the heat. Add the milk a bit at a time. Stir each time to make sure it is smooth. When all the milk is added put it back on the heat and bring it to the boil. Keep stirring. Reduce the heat and simmer gently for 2 minutes, stirring. Take off the heat.

Grate the cheese. Add the cheese to the sauce and mix. Continue to stir till the cheese has melted into the sauce. Season with salt and pepper.

ADDITIONS & ALTERNATIVES
Try other cheeses.
Add a teaspoon of whole grain mustard.
Use ready grated cheese.

CAULIFLOWER CHEESE

Serves 4 ⏲ *Preparation 10 min, Cooking 30 min – Easy*

INGREDIENTS

500 ml (1 pint) cheese sauce (previous recipe)
100 g (4 oz) mature Cheddar cheese, about 2 cups
1 medium cauliflower

EQUIPMENT

Grater for the cheese
Sharp knife
Chopping board
Saucepan
Wooden spoon
Ovenproof dish

METHOD

Make the cheese sauce. Add the extra cheese.

Break up the cauliflower. Throw away the leaves. Wash the cauliflower. Put the cauliflower in the pan with 2 cm (1 inch) water. Boil gently for 7 minutes. Drain and put into the ovenproof dish. Pour the cheese sauce over the cauliflower.

Cook in a preheated oven at 180°C, 350°F, Gas mark 4 for 15 minutes till golden brown.

ADDITIONS & ALTERNATIVES

Serve with boiled new potatoes.

Add grilled bacon or fake bacon (e.g. Protoveg 'Sizzles' or Betty Crocker 'Bac-Os').

COURGETTE & TOMATO BAKE

Serves 2   ① *Preparation 5 min, Cooking 20 min – Easy*

INGREDIENTS

3 large tomatoes (about 500 g or 1 lb)
6 courgettes (about 500 g or 1 lb)
2 tablespoons olive oil
1 tablespoon fresh basil or a teaspoon of dried
2 tablespoons fresh breadcrumbs
3 tablespoons grated Parmesan or Pecorino cheese
Freshly ground pepper

EQUIPMENT

Sharp knife
Chopping board
Set of measuring spoons
Frying-pan
Wooden spoon
Bowl
Casserole

METHOD

Wash and slice the tomatoes. Wash, trim and drain the courgettes. Cut the courgettes lengthways into 1 cm (half inch) slices.

Fry the slices of courgette in the oil over a medium heat until slightly softened. Cook enough at a time to cover the bottom of the pan. Scatter some of the basil on the courgettes.

Put a layer of courgettes in the bottom of the casserole. Add a layer of sliced tomato. Alternate layers of courgette and tomato.

Mix the breadcrumbs and cheese in the bowl. Spread the breadcrumbs and cheese over the top. Season with pepper.

Cook in a preheated oven at 200°C, 400°F, Gas mark 6 for 10 to 15 minutes till the top is browned.

POTATO PIE

Serves 4   ⏱ *Preparation 5 min, Cooking 45 min – Easy*

INGREDIENTS

1 kg (2 lbs) potatoes (about 8 medium)
1 egg
300 ml ($\frac{1}{2}$ pint) milk, about $1\frac{1}{4}$ cups
$\frac{1}{4}$ teaspoon ground nutmeg
Salt and freshly ground pepper to taste
1 tablespoon butter
1 tablespoon parsley

EQUIPMENT

Sharp knife
Chopping board
Bowl
Set of measuring cups
Ovenproof dish
Set of measuring spoons

METHOD

Peel the potatoes, cutting away any nasty bits, and cutting out any eyes. Cut into small pieces.

Break the egg into the bowl. Fish out any bits of shell. Add the milk, nutmeg, salt and pepper. Mix with a fork.

Arrange the bits of potato in the ovenproof dish. Pour the milk mix over the potatoes. Put little knobs of butter on top. Cook in a preheated oven at 200°C, 400°F, Gas mark 6 for about 45 minutes.

Take it out of the oven. Scatter the parsley on the top.

ADDITIONS & ALTERNATIVES

Serve with green salad.

Add grated cheese as you serve it.

MEATLESS CHILLI

Serves 2–3   ⏲ *Preparation 10 min, Cooking 20 min – Easy*

INGREDIENTS

150 g packet dried soya mince, Protoveg Burgamix or
   350 g pack Quorn mince
100 g (4 oz) or about 10 mushrooms (optional)
1 large onion
2 tablespoons oil
1 packet Mexican chilli seasoning
400 g tin tomatoes
400 g tin red kidney beans
1 cup rice
Salt to taste

EQUIPMENT

Bowl
Sharp knife
Chopping board
Set of measuring spoons
Frying-pan
Wooden spoon
Tin opener
Saucepan
Set of measuring cups

METHOD

Soak the soya mince in water according to instructions. This takes about 10 minutes. Or follow the instructions for the Burgamix.

If using mushrooms, wipe the dirt off and cut the end off the stalk. Slice roughly. Peel and chop the onion.

Put the oil in the frying-pan. Fry the onion over a medium heat for a couple of minutes to soften, stirring to stop it sticking. Add the Mexican chilli seasoning and salt and mix well.

Open the tin of tomatoes. Pour in the juice from the tin and then mash up the tomatoes in the tin with a wooden spoon. Add the mashed up tomatoes. Stir and bring to the boil. Turn down the heat so the mixture is just boiling.

Drain the mince and add to the pan. Open the tin of kidney beans and drain off the liquid. Add the beans to the pan. Add the mushrooms. Stir from time to time. If it looks like it is getting too dry then add some water. Cook for 5 minutes. Take off the heat.

You can let it cool and reheat when the rice is done. It seems that the flavour improves with reheating.

Serve with boiled rice, American long grain being the best for this. Look at the packet to see how long to cook it. There are full instructions on boiled rice in the 'How to' chapter.

ADDITIONS & ALTERNATIVES

Read what it says on the packet of seasoning to get the right amount. Try substituting half to one teaspoon chilli powder and 2 teaspoons ground cumin for the seasoning mix.

Try adding a small tin of sweet corn.

Add 1 chopped sweet pepper.

For 4–6 people double up the quantities.

VEGETARIAN SHEPHERD'S PIE

Serves 3–4   ① *Preparation 10 min, Cooking 30 min – Easy*

INGREDIENTS

150 g packet dried soya mince, or Protoveg Burgamix
750 g (1½ lb) old potatoes (about 7 medium)
Salt and freshly ground pepper to taste
1 tablespoon butter
1 tablespoon milk
1 onion
2 carrots
1 tablespoon sunflower oil
1 vegetable stock cube
2 teaspoons Marmite or yeast extract

EQUIPMENT

Bowl
Vegetable peeler
Sharp knife
Chopping board
Saucepan
Set of measuring spoons
Potato masher
Grater
Frying-pan
Wooden spoon
Set of measuring cups
Ovenproof baking dish, at least 5 cm (2 inches) deep

METHOD

Soak the soya mince for about 10 minutes while the potatoes are cooking, or follow the instructions for the Burgamix.

Peel the potatoes. Chop into quarters. Put them in a saucepan and cover with water. Add a teaspoon of salt and boil for 20 to 25 minutes till soft. Drain and mash the potatoes with the butter and milk. Add a quarter teaspoon of freshly ground pepper. Keep mashing the potatoes till they are smooth and lump free.

Meanwhile, peel and chop the onion. Peel and grate the carrots, cutting off the top and bottom. Put the oil in the frying-pan and fry the onions for a couple of minutes, stirring round.

Drain the soya mince. Add it, or the Protoveg mix, the carrot, stock cube, Marmite and 1 cup of water to the pan. Cook for another five minutes till most of the water has boiled off.

Put the meat mixture in the casserole. Level off the surface. Put the mashed potato on top. Spread to cover. Make artistic swirls or whatever in the mashed potato.

Cook in a preheated oven at 180°C, 350°F, Gas mark 4 for 15 to 20 minutes till golden on top.

ADDITIONS & ALTERNATIVES

Use broken up vegetarian hamburger instead of the soya mince. Sprinkle 1 cup (50 g or 2 oz) grated Cheddar cheese on the potato, or even in it while you are mashing.

Add 100 g (4 oz or about 10) chopped mushrooms to the meat substitute.

New potatoes make awful mashed potato. Only use old potatoes like King Edward's or Désirée Reds.

VEGETABLE LASAGNE

Serves 6   ① *Preparation 15 min, Cooking 60 min – Moderate*

INGREDIENTS

1 quantity of *Vegetarian Bolognese sauce*
3 cloves garlic
2 onions
1 tablespoon olive oil
400 g tin Italian plum tomatoes
2 teaspoons oregano, mixed herbs or mixed Mediterranean herbs
500 g (1 lb) minced Quorn or other mince substitute
Salt and freshly ground pepper to taste
White Sauce
4 tablespoons butter
6 tablespoons flour
2 cups milk (500 ml or 1 pint)
1–2 tablespoons grated Parmesan cheese
Salt and freshly ground pepper to taste

250 g packet of lasagne pasta (look for 'No pre-cooking required' on the packet)
1 tablespoon grated Parmesan cheese

EQUIPMENT

Garlic crusher
Sharp knife
Chopping board
Set of measuring spoons
Frying-pan
Tin opener
Wooden spoon
Saucepan
Set of measuring cups
Flat ovenproof dish (2 litre or 3½ pints)

METHOD

To make the Vegetarian Bolognese sauce

Peel and crush the garlic. Peel and chop the onion. Put the oil in the frying-pan and warm over a medium heat. Fry the garlic and chopped onion on a medium heat for about two minutes. Stir them every half a minute or so.

Open the tin of tomatoes. Pour the juice into the frying-pan. Use the wooden spoon to mash the tomatoes while they are still in the can (it's easier than chasing them round the pan). Pour the mashed tomatoes into the pan. Continue to cook, stirring as the mixture boils. Add your chosen herb. Cook for another five minutes or so until the fluid has reduced and the sauce is less sloppy.

The sauce can be improved by adding a glass of wine and cooking a bit longer. Take off the heat. Add the Quorn mince and stir. Season with salt and pepper.

To make the white sauce

Melt the butter in a saucepan over a low heat. Add flour and stir together to make a smooth paste. Take the pan off the heat. Continue to stir and add the milk a bit at a time. If you add it too quickly it will go lumpy. When all the milk has been added, put it back on the heat and add one or two tablespoons of Parmesan cheese. Stir until it thickens. Season with salt and pepper. Take off the heat.

Assemble the lasagne in the ovenproof dish. Start with a layer of Bolognese sauce. Cover with a layer of lasagne pasta. Then a layer of Bolognese sauce. Next a layer of white sauce. Then pasta, Bolognese, white sauce.

However many layers you do it must end up with white sauce on top. Sprinkle the top with Parmesan cheese. Cook in a preheated oven at 180°C, 350°F, Gas mark 4 for about 30 minutes. The top should be brown.

DESSERTS

BANANA CUSTARD

Serves 2   ① *Preparation 2 min, Cooking 3 min – Easy*

INGREDIENTS
2 ripe bananas
350 ml tub of Fresh Custard

EQUIPMENT
Sharp knife
Chopping board
Saucepan
Wooden spoon

METHOD
Peel the bananas and chop into slices. Put the custard in the pan and warm, stirring. When the custard is warm add the banana and stir round. Serve.

ADDITIONS & ALTERNATIVES
'Fresh Custard' can be found in the chiller cabinet at the supermarket.
   Use other ready-made custards in cartons or tins.

MARINADED ORANGES

Serves 2, easy to double up ① *Preparation 10 min; needs to stand for at least 2 hours – Easy*

INGREDIENTS
2 large oranges
2 tablespoons of Cointreau
1 tablespoon of sugar
1 small carton (142 ml or 5 fl oz) single cream or
    natural unsweetened yoghurt

EQUIPMENT
Sharp knife
Chopping board
Bowl
Set of measuring spoons

METHOD
Peel the oranges and cut off the pith (the bitter white stuff under the skin). Cut into 1 cm (half-inch) slices. Try and dig out the pips. Put the orange slices in the bowl with the Cointreau and the sugar. Put in the fridge for at least two hours.

   Arrange artistically on a plate and serve with the cream or yoghurt.

ADDITIONS & ALTERNATIVES
Try rum or brandy instead of the Cointreau.

BANANA SPLIT

Serves 2   ① *Preparation 5 min – Easy*

INGREDIENTS

2 bananas
1 tub vanilla ice-cream or other favourite flavour
Squirty raspberry sauce (comes in a plastic bottle)
Squirty cream (comes in a spray can)
2 cocktail cherries
Hundreds and thousands (from the baking section)

EQUIPMENT

Sharp knife
Chopping board
2 bowls

METHOD

Peel the bananas. Cut in half lengthways. Lay out in the bowls. Put a couple of scoops of ice-cream between the bananas. Put some raspberry sauce on top of the ice-cream. Do a couple of lines of squirty cream down the sides. Sprinkle the top with some hundreds and thousands. Serve with a cherry on top.

ADDITIONS & ALTERNATIVES

Use different sauces like strawberry or chocolate.
   Garnish with a sprig of mint.

ICE CREAM SUNDAES

Serves as far as it will go ① *Preparation 5 min – Easy*

INGREDIENTS
A matter of choice
At least 2 kinds of ice cream, preferably of different colours
  (vanilla, strawberry, pistachio, coffee)
Squirty sauces (raspberry, chocolate, butterscotch)
Glacé cherry
Chopped nuts

EQUIPMENT
Tall glasses
Long spoons

METHOD
It is a truth universally acknowledged that a restaurant in need of
a profit sells ice cream.

Assemble the ingredients of your choice, topping it off with
sauce, cream and chopped nuts and a glacé cherry.

Hire someone in braces and a striped shirt to sing as it comes
in.

Forget the sparklers.

ADDITIONS & ALTERNATIVES
Make it in bowls.

Put chopped fresh fruit in and go easy on the sauces.

TIPS
A magnificent stand-by dish if your latest creation fails.

FRUIT FOOLS

Serves 2 to 4 ① *Preparation 2 min, Cooling 1 hour or more – Easy*

INGREDIENTS
300 g tin raspberries
1 medium carton (284 ml or 10 fl oz) double cream

EQUIPMENT
Tin opener
Bowl
Whisk or fork

METHOD
Open tin of raspberries and drain juice into a cup. Mash up fruit. Pour the cream into the bowl. Whisk up or beat with a fork till it goes stiff. Mix in the mashed raspberries. Spoon into glasses or serving bowls. Keep in the fridge for at least an hour.

ADDITIONS & ALTERNATIVES
You can use almost any tinned fruit, just drain and lightly mash.
   Fresh raspberries, strawberries, blackcurrants lightly mashed.

BAKED BANANAS

Serves 4   ① *Preparation 10 min, Cooking 20 min – Easy*

INGREDIENTS
4 bananas
2 or 3 tablespoons of honey
2 tablespoons rum
2 tablespoons brown sugar
2 tablespoons water

EQUIPMENT
Sharp knife
Chopping board
Set of measuring spoons
Teacup
Baking dish

METHOD
Peel the bananas. Chop in half lengthways. Mix the honey, rum, water and sugar in a teacup. Coat the bananas in the mixture. Bake in a preheated oven at 170°C, 325°F, Gas mark 3 for about 20 minutes.

BAKED APPLES

Serves 1   ⏱ *Preparation 5 min, cooking 20–25 min – Easy*

INGREDIENTS
1 large baking apple
$\frac{1}{2}$ tablespoon sugar
1 tablespoon raisins
$\frac{1}{4}$ teaspoon mixed spice
1 teaspoon butter

EQUIPMENT
Apple corer
Bowl
Ovenproof dish
Set of measuring spoons

METHOD
Take the core out of the apple with the corer. Mix the sugar, raisins, mixed spice and butter in the bowl. Push the mixture into the hole left by the core. Put the apple in the ovenproof dish. Pour in a couple of tablespoons of water. Cook in a preheated oven at 170°C, 325°F, Gas mark 3 for 20 to 25 minutes.

ADDITIONS & ALTERNATIVES
Serve with custard, cream or yoghurt.

Try bought mincemeat (for mince pies) instead of the sugar and raisins.

RICH CHOCOLATE POT

Serves 4

① *Preparation 2 min,
Cooking 7 min – Easy*

INGREDIENTS
200 g dark chocolate
1 medium carton (284 ml or 10 fl oz) single cream
1 egg
1 drop vanilla essence
Pinch of salt

EQUIPMENT
Bowl
Saucepan
Wooden spoon
Fork

METHOD
Break the chocolate into pieces and put into the bowl. Warm the cream to boiling point. Pour over the chocolate and leave for 5 minutes for the chocolate to melt.

Add the egg, vanilla and salt. Mix with a fork until smooth. Pour into serving cups, ramekins or glasses. Cool in a refrigerator for three or four hours.

ADDITIONS & ALTERNATIVES
Serve with lightly whipped cream if required.

Put a teaspoon of Cointreau and some flaked chocolate on top.

FRUIT CRÊPES

Make one or two per person ① *Preparation 3 min, Cooking 10 min
if you want them warm – Easy*

INGREDIENTS
1 packet ready made crêpes
500 g jar fruit compôte
   or a 400 g tin or jar of fruit pie filling
1 tablespoon butter
1 tablespoon sugar
Small carton (142 ml or 5 fl oz) of single cream

EQUIPMENT
Tin opener
Ovenproof dish (if you want them warmed)
Set of measuring spoons

METHOD
Put a couple of spoons of fruit filling on each crêpe. Roll it up. This can be eaten cold, with a little cream.

To warm up: put the rolled up crêpes in an ovenproof dish. Put a couple of dabs of butter on each crêpe and sprinkle with sugar. Warm in the oven for 10 minutes at 150°C, 300°F, Gas mark 2.

ADDITIONS & ALTERNATIVES
Use a tin of fruit instead of the compôte. Open the tin, Drain off the fluid. Mash the fruit a bit then spoon on to the crêpes.

Use fresh fruit. Try a peach sliced and then left to stand with a tablespoon of brandy or rum and a tablespoon of sugar. When you serve the crêpe pour the juice over the top.

Use natural unsweetened Greek yoghurt or vanilla ice-cream instead of the cream.

APPLE CRUMBLE

Serves 4   ① *Preparation 12 min, Cooking 35 min – Easy*

INGREDIENTS

700 g (1½ lbs) cooking apples, about 3
2 tablespoons brown sugar
1 teaspoon mixed spice

For the crumble
6 tablespoons flour
3 tablespoons butter
3 tablespoons brown sugar

EQUIPMENT

Apple peeler and corer
Sharp knife
Chopping board
Saucepan
Wooden spoon
Ovenproof dish. Should be at least 5 cm (2 inches) deep
Bowl
Set of measuring spoons

METHOD

Peel, core and chop the apples. Put them in the pan with the sugar, spice and about 3 tablespoons of water. Cook over a low heat for about 10 minutes, stirring. Allow to cool down and put in ovenproof dish.

Rub the flour and butter together in a bowl with your fingertips till it makes crumbs. Stir in the sugar. Spread on the top.

Cook in a preheated oven at 200°C, 400°F, Gas mark 6 for 25 minutes.

ADDITIONS & ALTERNATIVES

Serve with yoghurt or ice-cream.

Use tinned cherry pie filling instead of the apple or substitute rhubarb.

APPLE FRITTERS

Serves 4   ⏱ *Preparation 10 min, Cooking 10 min – Moderate*

INGREDIENTS

1 pack batter mixture
2 big cooking apples or 4 Granny Smiths
Sunflower oil for frying
1 tablespoon sugar to sprinkle on top (optional)
Lemon (optional)

EQUIPMENT

Bowl
Wooden spoon
Apple peeler and corer
Sharp knife
Chopping board
Frying-pan
Slotted spoon for fishing the fritters out of the oil
Kitchen roll
Set of measuring spoons

METHOD

Mix the batter in the bowl according to the instructions on the packet. Peel and core the apples, then slice into circles. If you don't have the corer tool then peel and cut the apple in half, cut out the core, and cut into segments. Put all the apple slices in the batter mix.

Pour oil in the frying-pan to about 1 cm (half-inch) deep and put on the heat. After a couple of minutes, drip a bit of batter into the oil. If it sizzles and puffs up the oil is hot enough. If not wait. When the oil is hot enough, put some of the rings in the oil, one at a time. Don't put too many in at a time or they will stick together. After a minute or so, depending on how hot the oil is, turn them over. They are ready when they are golden brown on both sides and the batter looks crisp.

Fish the fritters out with the slotted spoon and put on a plate covered in kitchen paper. It helps absorb the oil. If you have an oven you can put them in it to keep warm at 140°C, 275°F, Gas mark 1.

Serve them on a plate with sugar and a slice of lemon to squeeze on top.

ADDITIONS & ALTERNATIVES
Use bananas instead of apples.

CRÈME FRAÎCHE BRÛLÉE

Serves 2 to 4   ⏱ *Preparation 5 min, Cooking 5 min – Easy*

INGREDIENTS

Some fruit, e.g. grapes, raspberries, strawberries, peach slices, nectarine slices, apple slices
400 ml tub of crème fraîche
2 tablespoons brown sugar

EQUIPMENT

Sharp knife
Chopping board
2 ramekins (small ovenproof bowls) or 1 small ovenproof dish
Set of measuring spoons
Fork
Grill

METHOD

Prepare the fruit (wash, peel, slice as appropriate). Put the fruit in the bottom of the ramekins or ovenproof dish. There should be enough to half fill them.

Whip the crème fraîche with a fork till it is smooth. Put the crème fraîche on the fruit and smooth the top. Put them in the fridge till ready to serve. Then sprinkle the top with a layer of sugar up to half a centimetre (quarter inch) thick.

Heat the grill. Toast them until the sugar bubbles. Allow to cool slightly and serve.

ADDITIONS & ALTERNATIVES

Pour a teaspoon of brandy or kirsch on the fruit.

Use whipped double cream instead of the crème fraîche.

QUICK CRÈME BRÛLÉE

Serves 2   ⏲ *Preparation 2 min, Cooking 3 min*
                                              – A cheat classic

INGREDIENTS

100 g (4 oz) fruit e.g. raspberries, strawberries or blueberries
350 ml tub fresh custard
4 tablespoons brown sugar

EQUIPMENT

Sharp knife
Chopping board
2 ramekins (small ovenproof bowls) or 1 small ovenproof dish
Set of measuring spoons
Grill

METHOD

Prepare the fruit (wash, peel, slice as appropriate). Put the fruit in the bottom of the ramekins. There should be enough to make a layer. Cover with the custard and flatten. Leave enough room to put the sugar on later. Put the ramekins in the fridge till ready to serve.

Sprinkle the top with a layer of sugar up to half a centimetre (quarter inch) thick. Heat the grill. Toast the ramekins until the sugar bubbles.

Allow to cool slightly and serve.

ADDITIONS & ALTERNATIVES

'Fresh Custard' can be found in the chiller cabinet at the supermarket.

Use other ready made custard
Pour a teaspoon of brandy or kirsch on the fruit.

SHERRY TRIFLE

Serves 6 ⏲ *Preparation 5 min, Cooking 5 min*
– The ideal party food for children

INGREDIENTS

150 g packet sponge fingers
200 g tin mixed fruit
2 tablespoons sweet sherry
135 g packet jelly
350 ml pot Fresh Custard
1 can squirty cream
Hundreds and thousands or chocolate vermicelli
(cake decoration)

EQUIPMENT

Bowl
Tin opener
Set of measuring spoons
Cup
Saucepan
Wooden spoon

METHOD

Get a bowl and put a layer of sponge fingers at the bottom. Open the tin of mixed fruit. Put the sherry in a cup together with a tablespoon of the syrup from the tinned fruit. Pour over the sponge fingers.

Read the instructions on the jelly packet. It probably says use half the jelly with about 300 ml (half pint or 1¼ cups) boiling water. Cut up the jelly into pieces. Put them in the boiling water and stir till they dissolve. Add the drained mixed fruit. Pour on to the sponges and leave to set, about half an hour.

Open the pot of custard. Pour on to the jelly. Keep in the fridge.

Before serving squirt a layer of squirty cream on the top. Scatter 'hundreds and thousands' on the cream.

TIPS

This is about the only use for sweet sherry except for soaking fruit.

Fresh fruit is better though more work.

RICE PUDDING

Serves 4   ⏱ *Preparation 2 min, Cooking 120 min – Easy*

INGREDIENTS

3 tablespoons pudding rice
500 ml (1 pint or 2 cups) milk
1 tablespoon sugar
1 tablespoon butter
$\frac{1}{2}$ teaspoon ground nutmeg

EQUIPMENT

Ovenproof dish
Set of measuring spoons

METHOD

Wash the rice. Put the rice, milk and sugar in the ovenproof dish. Break up the butter into little blobs and drop them on top. Sprinkle the nutmeg on the top.

Cook in a preheated oven at 150°C, 300°F, Gas mark 2 for two hours.

TIPS

This method gives great skin.

The creamiest rice comes from cooking at 140°C, 275°F, Gas mark 1 for two and a half hours and stirring it a couple of times during cooking.

CHEAT'S APPLE STRUDEL

Serves 4   ① *Preparation 15 min, Cooking 30 min – Moderate*

INGREDIENTS

2 cooking apples or 4 eating apples
½ cup raisins
Juice and rind of unwaxed lemon
1 tablespoon sugar
½ teaspoon cinnamon
1 tablespoon butter
375 g pack frozen puff pastry
½ cup milk

EQUIPMENT

Sharp knife
Chopping board
Vegetable peeler (optional)
Zester (optional)
Set of measuring spoons
Bowl
Set of measuring cups
Wooden spoon
Baking tray

METHOD

Thaw the pastry according to the instructions on the packet. Four hours in the fridge seems typical.

Peel the apples. Take out the core and pips. Slice it up. Put the apple into the bowl with the raisins, lemon, sugar and cinnamon.

Wipe the baking tray with a little butter or sunflower oil to stop the strudel sticking. Open the pack of pre-rolled puff pastry. Unfold it and put it on the baking tray. Spoon the apple mixture in a line up the middle of the pastry. Put little dots of butter on top of the mixture. Fold the edges of the pastry over the top. Use a little of the milk to wet the edges to help it stick together. Cut three or four slits through the top of the pastry. If you get to the mixture, stop. Brush some of the milk on the top. Sprinkle a teaspoon of sugar on top.

Cook in a preheated oven at 180°C, 350°F, Gas mark 4 for about half an hour. When it is cooked it will be golden brown.

ADDITIONS & ALTERNATIVES

Try adding sultanas or candied peel.

Get a rolling pin and roll your own bought puff pastry. There are full instructions on rolling pastry in the 'How to' chapter.

TIPS

On lemon peel. A lot of fruit has been 'treated' with various things including wax to make it shiny. It is better to look out for lemons which are marked as 'unwaxed' or even 'organic'. Leave out the lemon peel if you like.

APPLE PIE

Serves 6   ⏲ *Preparation 10 min, Cooking 30 min – Easy*

INGREDIENTS
Butter for greasing
450 g pack ready rolled shortcrust pastry
4 large cooking apples (about 750 g or 1½ lbs)
2 tablespoons brown sugar
1 tablespoon lemon juice
½ teaspoon of 'apple pie spice', nutmeg or mixed spice (optional)
milk for glazing

EQUIPMENT
Pie dish
Sharp knife
Chopping board
Set of measuring spoons
Saucepan
Wooden spoon
Fork

METHOD
Rub the inside of the pie dish with a little butter or margarine.

If the pastry is frozen make sure it is thawed properly (read the instructions on the packet). Unfold the pastry. Lay the pastry over the pie dish and push it gently into place. Check there is enough pastry for the lid. Leave a margin of 2 cm (1 inch) above the lip of the dish.

Peel the apples. Cut out the core and seeds and discard. Slice the apples about 1 cm (half inch) thick. Put the apples, sugar, lemon juice and spice in the pan and mix together. Cook over a low heat for about 10 minutes, to soften it up a bit. Let it cool down a bit.

Pour the mixture into the pastry case and even out with the spoon. Wipe round the edge with a little water. Put the pastry lid on top and push the edges down to seal them. Prick some holes in the lid with a fork. Brush the top with a little milk, which makes it shiny. Cook in a preheated oven at 200°C, 400°F, Gas mark 6 for 20 to 25 minutes. The pastry will have gone golden.

ADDITIONS & ALTERNATIVES

Serve with custard, cream, ice-cream or yoghurt.

Use a block of prepared pastry and roll it yourself. There are full instructions on rolling pastry in the 'How to' chapter.

Try different fillings like apple and blackberry, or even canned pie filling.

LEMON PIE

Serves 6 ⏱ *Preparation 15 min, Cooking 45 min*
Cooking the pastry in two stages is a bit of a fiddle,
but otherwise no problem

INGREDIENTS

450 g pack frozen shortcrust pastry
Butter for greasing
2 lemons
4 tablespoons sugar
2 eggs
200 g (8 oz) Mascarpone cheese

EQUIPMENT

Round ovenproof dish about 20–25 cm (8–10 inch) across and
    about 1 to 2 cm (½ to 1 inch) deep
Fork
Greaseproof paper
1 pack of dried beans to hold the pastry down
Grater
Sharp knife
Chopping board
Juicer
Bowl
Set of measuring spoons
Wooden spoon

METHOD

Make sure the pastry is thawed, about four hours in the fridge.
Unroll the pastry.

Grease the dish and then put the pastry in the dish. Pastry is
fairly flexible so you can push it into place. If it tears patch it with
a spare bit, moistening with a bit of water to make sure it sticks.

Pastry shrinks when it cooks so trim it above the top of the rim. Prick the bottom of the pastry with a fork at least five times to let steam out.

Cut a piece of greaseproof paper and press gently on to the pastry. Fill the bottom with a layer of cheap dried beans, for instance butter beans.

Cook the pastry case at 200°C, 400°F, Gas mark 6 for 15 minutes until the top edges go golden. Take the pastry case out of the oven.

Meanwhile make the filling. Grate the skin off the lemons and put in the bowl. Squeeze the juice into the bowl. Fish out any stray pips and discard. Add the sugar and eggs. Beat together. Add the Mascarpone and beat some more. It will take a couple of minutes to get the Mascarpone incorporated and the mixture smooth.

Take the beans and the greaseproof paper out of the pastry case. Put the lemon filling in. Cook in a preheated oven at 150°C, 300°F, Gas mark 2 for about 35 minutes till puffed up gently and brown on the top.

ADDITIONS & ALTERNATIVES

Serve on its own or with a dollop of natural set yoghurt.

Substitute 3 limes or 2 oranges for the 2 lemons.

MINCE TART

Serves 6   ⏱ *Preparation 10 min, Cooking 30 min – Moderate*

INGREDIENTS

450 g pack pre-rolled shortcrust pastry (frozen or chilled)
Butter for greasing
450 g jar mincemeat

EQUIPMENT
Round ovenproof dish about 25 cm (10 inch) across and about 1 to
2 cm ($\frac{1}{2}$ to 1 inch) deep.
Sharp knife

METHOD
Thaw the pastry. Rub a bit of butter or margarine on the inside of
the dish. Line the dish with pastry. Cut around the edge, trimming
the extra pastry off. Don't cut it too close to the edge, cut it a bit
big because the pastry will shrink.

Fill the pie with the mincemeat. Cook in an oven at 180°C,
350°F, Gas mark 4 for about 30 minutes.

Take it out and cool. It is better not to eat it hot as the
mincemeat retains heat. Cut into slices.

ADDITIONS & ALTERNATIVES
Serve with yogurt, custard or cream.

As an option, get the rest of the pastry and lay it out flat on the
board. Cut into 1 cm (half inch) strips. Lay some of these across the
top, weaving them over and under.

Make small tarts.

Make turnovers with puff pastry. Cut circles round a saucer, put
on a tablespoon of mincemeat and fold over the edge, sealing with
a little water. Pierce with a fork to let out any steam.

Make a roll. Use pre-rolled puff pastry. Spread it with the
mincemeat and roll up. Cook and slice.

TIPS
Jars of mincemeat vary a lot in price. The cheapest are mainly
sugar. Improve the taste with alcohol and extra dried fruit.

Ready made custard is as good as that made from powder, it
just costs more.

TREACLE TART

Serves 6 ① *Preparation 10 min, Cooking 30 min – Moderate*

INGREDIENTS
450 g pack frozen pre-rolled shortcrust pastry
Rind of a lemon
100 g (4 oz) breadcrumbs (this is about 4 slices of wholemeal bread)
6 tablespoons golden syrup
2 tablespoons treacle

EQUIPMENT
Round ovenproof dish about 25 cm (10 inch) across and about 1 to 2 cm (½ to 1 inch) deep.
Grater or zester for the lemon
Set of measuring spoons

METHOD
Thaw the pastry according to the instructions on the packet, probably about four hours in the fridge. Line the flan dish with the pastry.

Take the zest off the lemon with the grater or zester. Mix the breadcrumbs with the golden syrup, treacle and lemon zest.

Pour the mixture into the pastry and cook in a preheated oven at 200°C, 400°F, Gas mark 6 for 30 minutes or so until golden.

Allow to cool before trying to get it out of the dish.

ADDITIONS & ALTERNATIVES
Serve with cream, yoghurt or ice-cream
Try all golden syrup.

MILLE FEUILLE

Serves 6   ⓘ *Preparation 15 min, cooking 10 to 15 min*
– Moderate

INGREDIENTS
375 g pack ready rolled puff pastry
3 tablespoons raspberry jam or other favourite jam
Squirty cream in a can
Icing sugar

EQUIPMENT
Sharp knife
Chopping board
Baking tray
Set of measuring spoons
Wire cooling rack

METHOD
Thaw the pastry according to the instructions on the packet, probably about four hours in the fridge. Open the pack of puff pastry and unfold. Cut into three equal pieces. Put the puff pastry on the baking tray and bake in a preheated oven at 200°C, 400°F, Gas mark 6 for 10 to 15 minutes, until it has puffed and gone golden. Put the puff pastry on the cooling rack and leave for at least 20 minutes.

Put the bottom layer of pastry on a plate. Spread half the jam on it and then squirt a layer of cream. Put jam on the next piece of puff pastry. Put the piece of puff pastry on the first layer. Squirt cream on the jam layer. Put the last piece of puff pastry on top. Sprinkle icing sugar on the top.

The final mille feuille should be from the bottom up, pastry, jam, cream, pastry, jam, cream, pastry and icing sugar.

ADDITIONS & ALTERNATIVES

Try putting a layer of some soft fruit like strawberries, blackberries, blueberries between the jam and the cream layer.

Try thick custard instead of the cream. Tinned or carton will not do. Make up powdered instant custard according to the instructions on the packet, but increase the amount of powder by half, so if it says use two tablespoons, use three. Let the custard cool down and go fairly solid, then spread on the jam.

Use double cream instead of squirty cream. Beat a medium carton (284 ml or 10 fl oz) of double cream with a fork or whisk till it goes stiff then spread it.

BREAD PUDDING

Serves at least 4   ① *Preparation 5 min but needs to be left overnight, Cooking 90 min – Moderate*

INGREDIENTS

Half a large loaf of bread (can be stale but NOT mouldy!)
1 egg
1 cup dried fruit, sultanas, raisins, etc.
3 tablespoons brown sugar
2 tablespoons butter
1 teaspoon nutmeg

EQUIPMENT

Bowl
Wooden spoon
Ovenproof dish about 5 cm (2 inches) deep
Set of measuring spoons
Set of measuring cups

METHOD

Break up the bread, put it in the bowl, cover with water and leave it overnight or at least 2 hours. Squeeze out the water and put the bread in clean bowl.

Wipe the inside of the ovenproof dish with a little butter.

Mix the egg up in a cup. Add the egg, dried fruit, sugar, butter broken into little blobs and nutmeg to the squeezed out bread. Mix together. Put into the ovenproof dish, press down the mixture with the back of a spoon and sprinkle a little sugar on top.

Put into the oven at 150°C, 300°F, Gas mark 2 for 90 minutes. When you think it is cooked, stick a knife or skewer in. If it comes out clean it is cooked. If it comes out sticky, it needs more cooking. Take out of the oven, cut into squares whilst still in tin and allow to cool. You can eat it hot with custard if you like.

BREAD & BUTTER PUDDING

Serves 4, depending on amount   ⏱ *Preparation 10 min,*
                                    Cooking 60 min – Moderate

INGREDIENTS
Half to a whole loaf of bread (can be stale but NOT mouldy)
Butter
1 cup of dried fruit (sultanas, raisins, etc.)
4 tablespoons of sugar
2 eggs
4 tablespoons milk

EQUIPMENT
Ovenproof dish. Should be at least 5 cm (2 inches) deep
Set of measuring spoons
Set of measuring cups

METHOD
Slice the bread. Butter each slice. Wipe butter on the inside of the dish. Put in a layer of bread. Sprinkle with dried fruit and sugar. Put another layer of bread, then fruit and sugar. Finish up with a layer of bread.

Mix the eggs with the milk and pour over the top. Sprinkle with a final bit of sugar.

Put in the oven 170°C, 325°F, Gas mark 3 for an hour. Check it is cooked by sticking a knife in. If it comes out clean, it is cooked.

ADDITIONS & ALTERNATIVES
This can be eaten hot or cold, with or without custard.

Use mincemeat instead of the fruit and sugar mix.

CHINESE & FAR EASTERN

STIR FRY PORK WITH BLACK BEAN SAUCE

Serves 4   ① *Preparation 5 min, Cooking 5 min – Easy*

INGREDIENTS

500 g (1 lb) pork fillet
1 bunch spring onions
227 g tin bamboo shoots
2 tablespoons oil
150 g jar Chinese black bean sauce

EQUIPMENT

Sharp knife
Chopping board
Tin opener
Set of measuring spoons
Wok or big frying-pan
Wooden spoon

METHOD

Cut the pork fillet into very thin slices. Clean and prepare the spring onions. Cut the root end off, trim the leaves. Peel off and discard any dried up or slimy ones. Cut into 1 cm (half inch) pieces. Open the tin of bamboo shoots and drain.

Heat the oil in the wok. Stir fry the pork till cooked, about three minutes. Add the spring onions and stir fry for another minute. Add the bamboo shoots. Add the jar of black bean sauce. Heat up and stir (about a minute).

ADDITIONS & ALTERNATIVES

Serve with rice or noodles.

Thin sliced beef can be substituted for the pork.

STIR FRY VEGETABLES

Serves 3–4   ① *Preparation 10 min, Cooking 5 min – Easy*

INGREDIENTS
1 bunch spring onions
1 red sweet pepper
100 g (4 oz) mange tout
1 pack 250 g bean sprouts
1 clove garlic
2 tablespoons oil
1 teaspoon ground five spice powder (optional)
2 tablespoons soy sauce
1 tablespoon sherry (optional)
Rice or noodles

EQUIPMENT
Sharp knife
Chopping board
Garlic crusher
Set of measuring spoons
Wok or big frying-pan
Wooden spatula

METHOD
The vegetables should be hot on the outside but still retain their crispness. Prepare everything before hand.

Clean the spring onions, chopping the root end off, trimming the leaves and throwing away any slimy bits. Wash, shake dry and shred. Wash the sweet pepper. Cut out the seeds and the stalk end. Slice the sweet pepper. Wash the mange tout peas. Wash and drain the bean sprouts. Peel the garlic.

Put the oil in the wok or deep frying-pan. Put the pan on a moderate heat. Crush the garlic into the hot oil. Add the five spice powder if you have any. Stir round. Add the spring onion, sweet pepper and mange tout. Stir and fry for about 30 seconds. Keep it all moving so that everything gets coated in oil. Add the bean sprouts. Stir for 10 seconds. Add the soy sauce and sherry. Stir fry for a couple of minutes.

Serve with boiled rice or noodles.

ADDITIONS & ALTERNATIVES

In general, broccoli, cauliflower, baby sweet corn and carrots need to be cooked for about 3 minutes. Everything else takes about 2 minutes.

All of the following are particularly suitable

100 g (4 oz) mushrooms (button, oyster, or shitake)
1 carrot peeled and cut into matchsticks
1 broccoli head
1 pack baby sweet corn
5 chopped lettuce or cabbage leaves
227 g tin water chestnut
227 g tin bamboo shoots

TIPS

Supermarkets and health food shops sell ready to cook bean sprouts.

If you are having rice or noodles, read the packet for the cooking time. Rice will take much longer to cook than the stir fry, so put it on when you have the rest of the ingredients together, but before you start cooking.

This is the quickest Chinese dish. It is very flexible. You can use almost any vegetable that you happen to have around. The secret is to prepare all the vegetables beforehand. Put them on side plates or bowls so they can go in the wok in order.

SWEET & SOUR SAUCE

Add to stir fry   ① *Preparation 1 min, Cooking 5 min – Easy*

INGREDIENTS
1 $\frac{1}{2}$ tablespoons cornflour
2 tablespoons water
5 tablespoons orange juice
3 tablespoons vinegar
2 tablespoons soy sauce
2 tablespoons sherry
1 tablespoon tomato purée
1 tablespoon sugar

EQUIPMENT
Set of measuring spoons
Cup
Saucepan
Wooden spoon

METHOD
Mix the cornflour with the water in a cup. It will form a smooth paste if you add the water a bit at a time.

Put all the other ingredients in a small pan. Heat gently. Add the cornflour mix. Heat, stirring all the time, to stop it sticking and going lumpy. As it heats up it will thicken. Take off the heat.

ADDITIONS & ALTERNATIVES
You can adjust this to your taste with more vinegar for the sour taste, or sugar for the sweet.

Substitute lemon juice for some of the orange

TIPS
This sauce can be made in quantity and frozen.

SWEET & SOUR CHICKEN

Serves 3–4   ① *Preparation 2 min, Cooking 5 min – Easy*

INGREDIENTS
500 g (1 lb) chicken off the bone
2 tablespoons oil
1 quantity of sweet and sour sauce (previous recipe)
    or a jar of sweet and sour sauce (about 200 g)

EQUIPMENT
Sharp knife
Chopping board
Wok or frying-pan
Set of measuring spoons
Wooden spoon

METHOD
Cut the chicken into thin slices. Put the oil in the pan. Heat up. Add the chicken and stir fry until the chicken is cooked (about three to five minutes). Add the sweet and sour sauce. Stir for another minute.

ADDITIONS & ALTERNATIVES
Serve with noodles.
    Add half a sliced sweet red pepper with the seeds thrown away.
    Add a packet of bean shoots (250 g).
    Add a small tin of pineapple chunks, drained.
    Try thin sliced pork fillet instead of chicken.
    Try prawns instead of chicken.

TERIYAKI BEEF

Serves 3 ⓘ *Preparation 10 min, Cooking 7 min – Easy*

INGREDIENTS
1 bunch spring onions
500 g (1 lb) lean frying steak
227 g (8 oz) tin water chestnuts
2 tablespoons sunflower or groundnut oil
150 g jar Teriyaki sauce

EQUIPMENT
Sharp knife
Chopping board
Tin opener
Set of measuring spoons
Frying-pan or wok
Wooden spoon

METHOD
If you are having rice or noodles, read the packet for the cooking time. Rice will take longer to cook than the stir fry.

Clean and prepare the spring onions. Cut the root end off, trim the leaves. Peel off and discard any dried up or slimy leaves. Chop into thin slices.

Cut the beef into thin strips. Open the tin of water chestnuts and drain off the fluid.

Heat the oil in the frying-pan. Fry the beef, stirring all the time. It will be cooked in about 3–5 minutes. Add the spring onions and water chestnuts. Stir fry for a minute or so. Add the Teriyaki Sauce. Stir and heat.

ADDITIONS & ALTERNATIVES
Serve with rice or noodles.

TIPS
There are full instructions on cooking rice and noodles in the
'How to' chapter. Teriyaki is Japanese, but the technique is similar
to Chinese.

CHINESE PORK & GINGER

Serves 4   ① *Preparation 10 min, Cooking 6 min – Moderate*

INGREDIENTS
500 g (1 lb) pork fillet
3 cloves garlic
1 cm ($\frac{1}{2}$ inch) root ginger or $\frac{1}{2}$ teaspoon dried ginger
4 spring onions
2 tablespoons oil
1 teaspoon Chinese five spice powder
2 tablespoons soy sauce

EQUIPMENT
Sharp knife
Chopping board
Set of measuring spoons
Frying-pan or wok
Wooden spoon

METHOD
Prepare everything beforehand. There is just not time while it is
cooking.

   Trim any fat off the pork and cut into thin strips. Peel and crush
the garlic. Peel the ginger and cut into small cubes. Clean and
prepare the spring onions. Cut the root end off, trim the leaves.
Peel off and discard any dried up or slimy leaves. Chop into thin
slices.

Put the oil in the frying-pan or wok. Heat up. Stir fry the garlic and ginger for 2 minutes. Add the pork and five spice powder and stir fry for a couple of minutes. Add the soy sauce. Heat for two more minutes.

ADDITIONS & ALTERNATIVES

Serve with rice or noodles.

TIPS

There are full instructions on cooking rice and noodles in the 'How to' chapter. You can buy prepared chopped ginger root in jars. It will keep for six weeks in the fridge.

LEMON CHICKEN

Serves 4   ⓘ *Preparation 15 min, Cooking 10 min – Moderate*

INGREDIENTS

4 chicken quarters
1 teaspoon salt
4 tablespoons sunflower or groundnut oil
1 cm (½ inch) root ginger or ½ teaspoon dried ginger
4 spring onions
1 red pepper
100 g pack Chinese shitake or oyster mushrooms
1 lemon
1 teaspoon cornflour
1 tablespoon soy sauce
2 tablespoons dry sherry
1 teaspoon sugar

EQUIPMENT

Sharp knife
Chopping board
Zester
Juicer
2 cups and some plates or bowls for putting ingredients in
Frying-pan or wok
Set of measuring spoons
Wooden spoon

METHOD

Prepare everything beforehand. There is just not time while it is cooking.

Take the chicken off the bone and cut into bite-sized chunks. Mix the pieces in the bowl with the salt and 2 tablespoons of oil.

Peel the ginger and cut into small cubes. Clean and prepare the spring onions. Cut the root end off, trim the leaves. Peel off and discard any dried up or slimy leaves. Chop into thin slices.

Wash the red pepper. Cut out the seeds and discard. Cut into thin slices. Cut the mushrooms into thin slices. Take the peel off the lemon with the zester or grate it off. If you have neither zester nor grater, peel finely with a sharp knife. Cut the peel into fine strips. Make sure you don't get any pith. Extract the lemon juice and put it in a cup. Mix the cornflour with about a tablespoon of water in a cup.

Put 2 tablespoons of oil in the frying-pan or wok. Heat up. Stir fry the chicken for five minutes. Take the chicken out of the pan. Add another tablespoon of oil to the pan if needed. Stir fry the ginger, spring onions, red pepper, mushrooms and lemon peel for 2 minutes. Add the soy sauce, sherry and sugar. Stir and add the cornflour mixture. Keep stirring as it thickens. Put the chicken back in the pan and cook for a minute. Add the lemon juice and serve.

ADDITIONS & ALTERNATIVES

Use the equivalent amount of other chicken pieces off the bone. Serve with rice or noodles. There are full instructions on cooking rice and noodles in the 'How to' chapter.

TIPS

Now you have made this any stir fry will seem simple. You can buy prepared chopped ginger root in jars. It will keep for six weeks in the fridge.

SATAY CHICKEN

Serves 2   ① *Preparation 60 min, Cooking 15 min – Easy*

INGREDIENTS
1 medium onion
2 cloves garlic
2 chicken breasts
1 tablespoon lemon juice
1 tablespoon sunflower oil
2 tablespoons soy sauce
1 teaspoon ginger powder (optional)
½ teaspoon cumin powder (optional)
1 tablespoon sesame oil (optional)
190 g jar satay sauce (peanut and chilli)

EQUIPMENT
Sharp knife
Chopping board
Bowl
Set of measuring spoons
Bamboo skewers
Saucepan
Wooden spoon
Grill

METHOD
Peel and chop the onion finely. Peel and chop the garlic. Cut the chicken into bite-sized chunks. Put in the bowl with the lemon juice, sunflower oil, soy sauce, ginger, cumin and sesame oil. Mix round so the chicken is coated. Leave for at least an hour to soak into the chicken.

Soak the bamboo skewers in cold water.

Make the satay sauce according to the instructions on the jar.

233

Thread the chicken pieces on to the skewers. Grill for 10 to 15 minutes, turning to make sure they are cooked on all sides.

ADDITIONS & ALTERNATIVES

Serve with rice and chopped cucumber.

Some shops sell satay marinade. Just follow the instructions.

TIPS

Satay sauce is only spiced up peanut butter. Get half a jar of unsweetened crunchy peanut butter, a cup of water, 2 tablespoons coconut powder, 2 tablespoons of soy sauce, half a teaspoon of chilli powder. Heat it in a small saucepan and stir. Cook for about five minutes.

THAI CHICKEN CURRY

Serves 2   ① *Preparation 10 min, Cooking 15–20 min – Easy*

INGREDIENTS

3 cloves of garlic
4 medium/large chicken thighs (boneless)
2½ cm (1 inch) root ginger or 1 teaspoon powdered ginger
1 lime
2 tablespoons sunflower oil
1 cup coconut milk (either powder and water or tinned)

1 *pack Thai curry herbs from the supermarket or*
2 red and 2 green very small chilli peppers or ½ to
   1 teaspoon chilli powder
Small bunch fresh coriander
2 or 3 lemon grass stems
2 lime leaves

2 sheets of noodles from a packet of medium noodles
1 tablespoon sesame oil

EQUIPMENT

Garlic crusher
Sharp knife
Chopping board
Zester or grater
Juicer
Saucepan
Set of measuring spoons
Wok or frying-pan
Wooden spoon
Set of measuring cups

METHOD

Peel and crush the garlic. Chop the chicken into bite-sized pieces. De-seed and chop the chilli peppers. Wash, dry and chop the coriander leaves. Peel, slice and chop the ginger. Zest the lime and juice it. Use a grater or a sharp knife if you don't have a zester. Hit the lemon grass so the stems begin to separate but do not fall apart.

Fill the saucepan with water and bring to the boil.

Meantime, put the sunflower oil into the frying-pan. Add the garlic, ginger, lime zest, lime leaves, chopped chillies, the lemon grass and stir for 2–3 minutes. Add the chopped chicken and stir so that it is evenly coated and the flavours are spread equally. Cook for approximately 7 minutes.

Add the lime juice and stir and cook for 1–2 minutes. Add the coconut milk. When the coconut milk has reduced by about half add the noodles to the boiling water, turn off the heat and cover the saucepan.

Meantime continue to stir the chicken and the coconut milk.

Check how long the noodles take on the packet. They will probably need about 4 or 5 minutes. When the noodles are cooked, drain and then return them to the saucepan, add the sesame oil and toss the noodles so that they get coated. Pick out the lemon grass stems and lime leaves, and add the coriander leaves. Pile the noodles on to the plates and pile the chicken on top.

ADDITIONS & ALTERNATIVES

Serve with soy sauce and sliced spring onion if desired.

Instead of chicken use bite-sized pieces of pork or beef or white fish.

Serve with rice instead of noodles.

TIPS

Prepared garlic is sold in tubes and jars. Just read the tube or jar for the suggested equivalent amount. It keeps for six weeks in the fridge.

Prepared lemon grass is available dried or in jars. It will keep in the fridge for six weeks.

Chillies are available in jars or tubes. It keeps for six weeks in the fridge.

SPECIAL FRIED RICE

Serves 2 to 3 ① *Preparation 5 min, Cooking 5 min – Moderate, it helps if someone can put the rice in the wok while you beat the eggs*

INGREDIENTS

2 or 3 cups cooked rice
$\frac{1}{2}$ cup frozen peas
$\frac{1}{2}$ cup frozen sweet corn (optional)
$\frac{1}{2}$ cup or more frozen prawns (optional)
100 to 200 g (4 to 8 oz) cooked chicken, or cup of left-over chicken
4 spring onions
2 eggs
2 tablespoons oil

EQUIPMENT

Saucepan
Set of measuring cups
Sharp knife
Chopping board

Bowl
Fork
Set of measuring spoons
Frying-pan or wok
Wooden spoon

METHOD

If you are cooking the rice, follow the instructions on the packet. There are full instructions on cooking rice in the 'How to' chapter.

Thaw the frozen ingredients in cold water and drain them.

Shred the cooked chicken. Clean and prepare the spring onions. Cut the root end off, trim the leaves. Peel off and discard any dried up or slimy leaves. Chop roughly. Break the eggs into a bowl. Fish out any bits of shell then whisk the eggs with a fork.

Heat the oil in a wok. Pour the eggs in the wok and stir round for 30 seconds. This is the bit where an assistant may help. Keep stirring and put in the rice. Stir fry, breaking up the rice with the spoon. Stir until the rice grains separate (less than 5 minutes). Add the other ingredients and stir for a couple of minutes until they are warmed through then serve.

ADDITIONS & ALTERNATIVES

This is a meal on its own. Serve with soy sauce.

Add chopped sweet pepper.

Use chopped cooked left-over beef or pork instead of the chicken or leave out the meat altogether.

CHINESE SPARE RIBS

Serves 3 to 4   ⏱ *Preparation 5 min, Cooking 90 min – Moderate*

INGREDIENTS
1 kg (2 lbs) spare ribs, separated
$\frac{1}{2}$ bottle (150 ml) Hoi Sin sauce

EQUIPMENT
Bowl
Ovenproof dish
Aluminium foil

METHOD
Put the Hoi Sin sauce in a bowl then add the ribs. Stir them round so they are coated. Put the ribs in the ovenproof dish and cover with foil. Cook in a preheated oven for 90 minutes at 180°C, 350°F, Gas mark 4.

ADDITIONS & ALTERNATIVES
Serve with rice
Grill the ribs for 25 minutes, turning them often.

TIPS
You can use this recipe for a barbecue.

ITALIAN

ANTIPASTI

Serves 2 or 4   ① *Preparation 3 min – Easy but expensive*

INGREDIENTS
Jars of antipasti
Sun-dried tomatoes
Mushrooms
Italian mixed vegetables
Artichoke hearts
Aubergines
Courgettes
Olives
Bread

EQUIPMENT
Plate

METHOD
Open the jars and fish out the vegetables. Arrange tastefully on a
plate. Serve with crusty bread or Italian bread.

TOASTED ROASTED PEPPERS

A plate full   ① *Preparation 5 min, Cooking 15 min – Easy*

INGREDIENTS
2 or 3 large ripe red peppers
1 tablespoon olive oil

EQUIPMENT
Sharp knife
Chopping board
Grill
Set of measuring spoons

METHOD
What you are aiming for are soft, sweet, cooked, peeled, red pepper.

Wash and dry the peppers. Cut the peppers in half. Remove the seeds and the central white bit under the stalk.

Turn the grill on full. Put the pepper on the grill tray skin side down and cook for a couple of minutes. Turn them over and cook for another couple of minutes. The skins will go brown and start to bubble up.

Take the peppers from under the grill and allow to cool. Slide the burnt skin off. Put the peppers on a plate and pour the oil over them.

ADDITIONS & ALTERNATIVES
Serve as a starter or as a snack with other bits like cheese, olives, salami and chorizo (spiced, sliced sausage).

GRILLED COURGETTES

Starter for 4   ① *Preparation 5 min, Cooking 15 min – Easy*

INGREDIENTS
4 courgettes
4 cloves garlic
1 dried chilli
4 tablespoons olive oil
1 tablespoon of white wine vinegar

EQUIPMENT
Sharp knife
Chopping board
Grill
Bowl
Set of measuring spoons
Wooden spoon

METHOD
Wash the courgettes and cut off the top and bottom. Cut into four slices lengthways. Cook under a hot grill for about ten minutes each side. When they are brown turn them over. It is OK if they go quite black in places.

Meanwhile peel and cut the garlic into small pieces. Carefully chop the dried whole chilli. Put the courgette in the bowl. Add the garlic, chilli, oil and vinegar. Stir and refrigerate.

ADDITIONS & ALTERNATIVES
Serve with Italian bread and other antipasti.

ITALIAN ROAST CHICKEN

Serves 4   ① *Preparation 10 min, Cooking 35 min*
(can increase quantities)   *– Easy and impressive*

INGREDIENTS

8–12 chicken thighs
3 tablespoons of olive oil
1 bunch fresh rosemary or 3 tablespoons dried
Salt and freshly ground pepper to taste
3 cloves garlic
1 kg (2 lbs) small new potatoes
Lettuce, tomato, spring onion, olives, etc. for salad
Italian bread (optional). There is a recipe for Focaccia on page 261.

EQUIPMENT

Set of measuring spoons
2 roasting tins or ovenproof dishes
Sharp knife
Chopping board
1 wooden spoon
Potato peeler

METHOD

Make sure frozen chicken is completely thawed before use. This means leaving it in the fridge overnight, or out of the fridge, covered, for six hours.

Turn the oven on at 200°C, 400°F, Gas mark 6. Put half the oil in each roasting tin. Break the rosemary leaves off the stem (or open the jar). Put the chicken pieces in one of the roasting dishes. Add half the rosemary. Mix with the spoon so that the chicken is coated in oil and rosemary. Add a little salt (half a teaspoon) and pepper. Peel and chop the garlic. Put in the dish with the chicken.

243

Wash the potatoes. Peel them if you have to. Cut off any nasty bits and sprouts. Cut the potatoes into 1 cm (half-inch) slices. Put the potatoes into the other roasting dish. Add the rest of the rosemary and mix so the potatoes are covered in oil and rosemary. Add a little (half a teaspoon) fresh ground salt.

Put both roasting dishes in the oven for 30–35 minutes, until the potatoes are golden and the chicken is golden and cooked.

ADDITIONS & ALTERNATIVES

Serve with salad and Italian bread.

Use chicken breasts or legs instead of thighs. Add 5–10 minutes to the cooking time if you are using larger pieces.

Roast fresh baby sweet corn or small onions in with the chicken.

ITALIAN ROAST LAMB

*Serves 4 (can
increase quantities)*

*① Preparation 10 min,
Cooking 35 min – Easy and impressive*

INGREDIENTS

8–12 mini lamb chops instead of chicken pieces in the previous recipe

METHOD

Substitute the mini lamb chops for the chicken pieces in the recipe above.

ADDITIONS & ALTERNATIVES

Mini lamb chops come from the supermarket freezer cabinet.

244

TOMATO SAUCE

Enough for spaghetti for 2

① *Preparation 5 min,*
Cooking 10 min – Easy

INGREDIENTS

2 medium onions
2 tablespoons olive oil
3 cloves garlic
400 g tin Italian plum tomatoes
1–2 teaspoons oregano, mixed herbs or mixed Mediterranean
herbs
Salt and freshly ground pepper to taste

EQUIPMENT

Sharp knife
Chopping board
Set of measuring spoons
Frying-pan
Wooden spoon
Tin opener

METHOD

Peel the onion and cut into thin slices, then chop across so you end up with small bits.

Put the oil in the frying-pan and put on a medium heat. Peel and crush the garlic into the pan. Fry the garlic and the onion on a medium heat for about two minutes. Stir them every half a minute or so.

Open the tin of tomatoes. Pour the juice into the frying-pan. Use the wooden spoon to mash the tomatoes while they are still in the can (it's easier than chasing them round the pan). Pour the mashed tomatoes into the pan. Continue to cook, stirring as the mixture boils. Add your chosen herb, oregano being most authentic. Season with salt and pepper. Cook for another five minutes and serve.

ADDITIONS & ALTERNATIVES

The sauce can be made even better by adding a glass of wine and cooking a bit longer.

TIPS

This sauce is the basis of a whole load of Italian food. It is great on spaghetti with Parmesan cheese.

It is the basis of the sauce for Bolognese and the meat sauce for Lasagne, and their vegetarian versions.

It is a tomato sauce for pizza.

BOLOGNESE SAUCE

Enough for spaghetti for 2 ⏱ *Preparation 5 min, Cooking 12 min – Easy*

INGREDIENTS

2 medium onions
1 tablespoon olive oil
3 cloves garlic
500 g (1 lb) beef mince
400 g tin Italian plum tomatoes
1 beef stock cube
1–2 teaspoons oregano, mixed herbs or mixed Mediterranean herbs
Salt and freshly ground pepper to taste

EQUIPMENT

Sharp knife
Chopping board
Set of measuring spoons
Frying-pan

Wooden spoon
Tin opener

METHOD

Peel the onion and cut into thin slices, then chop across so you end up with small bits. Put the oil in the frying-pan and put on a medium heat. Peel and crush the garlic into the pan. Fry the garlic and the onion on a medium heat for about two minutes. Stir them every half a minute or so.

Put the meat in the frying-pan and fry for two or three minutes, stirring all the time. By this time it should have broken up and be an even colour, with no pink bits.

Open the tin of tomatoes. Pour the juice into the frying-pan. Crumble the stock cube into the pan. Use the wooden spoon to mash the tomatoes while they are still in the can (it's easier than chasing them round the pan). Pour the mashed tomatoes into the pan. Continue to cook, stirring as the mixture boils. Add your chosen herb, oregano being authentic. Season with salt and pepper. Cook for another five minutes or so until the fluid has reduced and the sauce is less sloppy.

ADDITIONS & ALTERNATIVES

Serve with spaghetti or other pasta. Just follow the cooking time on the packet. There are full instructions on cooking pasta in the 'How to' chapter. The sauce can be improved by adding a glass of wine and cooking a bit longer. The vegetarian version of this uses soya mince instead of the meat. Read the pack instructions, but in general it tastes as good, and is quicker to cook.

TIPS

Mince quality and price are related. The cheaper the mince the more fat, the less meat, the more colouring, and odd bits you may not consider as actual 'meat'. The best stuff is made by buying a cheap cut of beef and getting the butcher to mince it up. That way you know what you're getting.

TUNA MAYONNAISE PASTA

Serves 2   ⏲ *Preparation 5 min, Cooking 5 to 15 min – Easy*

INGREDIENTS

200 g tin tuna
2 or 3 spring onions
2 tablespoons mayonnaise
Freshly ground pepper
250 g (half a packet) pasta shapes
1 or 2 tablespoons grated Parmesan cheese

EQUIPMENT

Tin opener
Bowl
Fork
Sharp knife
Chopping board
Set of measuring spoons
Saucepan

METHOD

Open the tin of tuna. Drain the liquid from the tin. Put the tuna in the bowl and mash it up with the fork.

Get the spring onions and take off the outer leaves. Cut off the root end and trim off the green leaves and any other unsavoury bits. Wash the spring onions and dry. Shred the onions into thin rings with the knife. Put the onions and the mayonnaise in with the tuna and mix up. Add pepper, if you wish.

Read the pasta packet to give you the cooking time (somewhere between 5 and 15 minutes). Put at least a pint of water and a teaspoon of salt in the saucepan. Bring to the boil and add the pasta. Stir once. When the pasta is cooked, drain it and put it in the bowl. Add the tuna mayonnaise and mix round.

ADDITIONS & ALTERNATIVES

Serve sprinkled with grated Parmesan cheese and freshly ground pepper, and with fresh warm bread and salad.

TIPS

There are full instructions on cooking pasta in the 'How to' chapter.

PASTA & BACON

Serves 2   ⏱ *Preparation 3 min, cooking 10 min – Easy*

INGREDIENTS

Half pack of pasta shells (250 g)

2 or more cloves garlic

1 or 2 medium onions

1 pack streaky bacon (about 6 to 8 rashers)

1 tablespoon olive oil

10 mushrooms (100 g or 4 oz) (optional)

Salt and freshly ground pepper to taste

2 tablespoons Parmesan cheese

EQUIPMENT

Saucepan

Sharp knife

Chopping board

Set of measuring spoons

Frying-pan

Wooden spoon

METHOD

Put at least a pint of water and a teaspoon of salt in the saucepan. Bring to the boil. Put in the pasta, cooking according to the instructions on the packet. Stir it once to stop it sticking to the pan.

Peel and chop the garlic and the onions. Chop the bacon. Put the oil in the frying-pan. Fry the bacon for about 3 minutes, stirring from time to time. Add the onions and garlic. Fry for another couple of minutes. Keep on stirring. Add the mushrooms if you like and cook for another minute or so. Season with salt and pepper. Strain the pasta and put it together with the bacon mixture in a bowl. Serve with Parmesan cheese.

TIPS

Work out the timing so it is all ready at about the same time. Read the cooking instructions on the packet of pasta shapes. They will need boiling for between 5 and 15 minutes. The bacon takes about 5 minutes. If the bacon is cooked too soon, just take it off the heat and warm it up when the pasta is cooked.

Serve with salad.

PASTA WITH BROCCOLI & CHILLI

Serves 2   ① *Preparation 5 min, Cooking 6 to 15 min – Easy*

INGREDIENTS

250 g (half a packet) of pasta shapes, orchetti, shells or similar
Medium head of broccoli (300 g or 10 oz)
2 cloves garlic
2 tablespoons olive oil
$^1/_2$ teaspoon hot chilli powder
2 tablespoons grated Parmesan cheese

EQUIPMENT

Saucepan
Sharp knife

Chopping board
Set of measuring spoons
Frying-pan
Wooden spoon
Bowl

METHOD

Read the pasta packet to get the cooking time (anything between 5 and 15 minutes). Put at least a pint of water with a teaspoon of salt in the saucepan, bring to the boil. Put the pasta in the water. Stir once to stop it sticking to the pan. Bring back to the boil.

Break the broccoli into little bits (florets). Peel and chop the garlic.

Meanwhile, put the oil in the frying-pan and fry the garlic and chilli powder for a minute or so. Add the broccoli and stir round so that the broccoli is covered in the garlic, chilli and oil. Keep stirring and frying till it is cooked, about three to five minutes. Take off the heat.

Drain the pasta. Stir the pasta and broccoli together in a bowl. Put two tablespoons of grated Parmesan on top.

ADDITIONS & ALTERNATIVES

Serve with salad

Substitute Pecorino cheese for Parmesan.

Add chopped tinned anchovies sprinkled on the top when serving.

Substitute mange tout, French beans or cauliflower for the broccoli.

CARBONARA HAM PASTA SAUCE

Serves 2   ① *Preparation 5 min, Cooking 5 min – Easy*

INGREDIENTS
2 cloves garlic
1 medium onion
10 mushrooms (about 100 g or 4 oz)
3 slices of cooked ham
1 tablespoon olive oil
1 tablespoon flour
Small carton (142 ml or 5 fl oz) single cream
1 teaspoon of mixed Mediterranean herbs
Salt and freshly ground pepper to taste
250 g packet tagliatelli

EQUIPMENT
Sharp knife
Chopping board
Frying-pan
Saucepan
Wooden spoon
Garlic crusher
Set of measuring spoons

METHOD
Peel and crush the garlic. Peel the onion and slice thinly. Wipe the mushrooms to get any dirt off and then slice them. Cut the ham up into 1 cm (half-inch) squares.

Heat oil in frying-pan. Add the onion and garlic. Cook till the onion has gone soft, about a couple of minutes, stirring so they cook evenly. Add the mushrooms, stir and cook for a couple of minutes more. Add the ham. Add the flour and stir round until it has absorbed the oil and juices in the pan. Add the cream, the herbs and some salt and pepper. Stir round and cook for about a minute until it has made a smooth sauce and serve with pasta (see below for cooking instructions).

ADDITIONS & ALTERNATIVES

Try bacon instead of ham. Chop the bacon up and fry it with the onions. This adds a couple of minutes to the cooking time. You can buy this sauce ready made.

TIPS

Prepared garlic is sold in tubes and jars. Just read the tube or jar for the suggested equivalent amount. It keeps for six weeks in the fridge.

The best pasta for this is tagliatelli, which takes about three to five minutes to cook. Read the packet for the correct time. Anyway this works out quite well, just boil the water for the tagliatelli while you are chopping up the onion and the rest. Then throw the pasta in the water when you have cooked the onions. The sauce will be cooked before you need to drain the pasta, just take it off the heat, check the pasta is cooked, drain it and serve.

PASTA WITH PESTO

Serves 2   ⓘ *Preparation 1 min, Cooking 5 to 15 min – Easy*

INGREDIENTS
250 g (half a packet) pasta shapes
2 tablespoons pesto
1 tablespoon olive oil

EQUIPMENT
Saucepan
Bowl
Set of measuring spoons

METHOD
Read the pasta packet to give you the cooking time (somewhere between 5 and 15 minutes). Put at least a pint of water and a teaspoon of salt in the saucepan. Bring to the boil and add the pasta. When the pasta is cooked, drain it and put it in the bowl. Add the pesto and olive oil and mix round.

ADDITIONS & ALTERNATIVES
Serve immediately, with salad and bread.
    Pesto is a sauce made from basil among other things, available in green and red.

TIPS
There are full instructions on cooking pasta in the 'How to' chapter.

LEMON SEAFOOD & ANGEL'S HAIR PASTA

2 generous portions   ① *Preparation 20 min, Cooking 15 min*
– Moderate

INGREDIENTS
6 mushrooms
1 small/medium broccoli head
2 courgettes
1 lemon
4–6 small ready prepared squid tubes
2 tablespoons sunflower oil
1 tablespoon olive oil
3 cloves garlic
$\frac{1}{3}$ × 500 g packet dried Angel's Hair (or other fine pasta)
10–16 large cooked and shelled prawns (can use frozen ones)
Salt and black pepper to taste

EQUIPMENT
Sharp knife
Chopping board
Lemon zester or grater
Lemon juicer
Large saucepan
Set of measuring spoons
Large frying-pan
Garlic crusher
Wooden spoon or spatula
Sieve to drain pasta

METHOD
Wipe and slice mushrooms. Rinse the broccoli and break it into florets. Slice the florets up. Rinse and slice the courgettes. Peel the skin off the lemon in thin strips with the zester or a knife. Juice

the lemon. Slice the squid into 1 cm (half-inch) rings. Cut the tentacles in half. Fill the saucepan with water and put on to boil.

Put the oil into the frying-pan, and put on a medium heat. When the oil is warm crush the garlic into the frying-pan, add the lemon zest, and cook gently for 2 minutes. Add the squid rings and cook for 5 minutes. Add the broccoli and courgettes.

Put the pasta into the saucepan and bring the water back to the boil. Once boiled it will take 3 minutes to cook.

Add the sliced mushrooms, prawns and lemon juice to the frying-pan. Reduce the heat, stir occasionally, and cook for 3 minutes.

Drain the water from the pasta. Combine the pasta with the seafood and vegetables and serve.

ADDITIONS & ALTERNATIVES

Serve with white wine, Italian bread and mixed salad leaves.

Use other vegetables instead of courgettes and broccoli, like French beans, asparagus, cauliflower or sliced green pepper.

Use other seafood, such as scallops, clams or mussels, small pieces of fish or even small fish like whitebait, fresh anchovies or fresh sardines.

Use other fine pasta like tagliattellini, or fine spaghetti. These will take longer to cook so check the time on the packet and adjust when you put them on to boil.

TIPS

Squid tubes are stocked by supermarkets and some fishmongers. Don't buy unprepared squid unless you like slimy things and know how to take the quill out. But check the prepared ones, as you chop them, for a strip of clear plastic like stuff. If you find it, throw it away. It is the quill.

Prepared garlic is sold in tubes and jars. Just read the tube or jar for the suggested equivalent amount. It keeps for six weeks in the fridge.

LASAGNE

Serves 6   ① *Preparation 15 min, cooking 60 min – Moderate*

INGREDIENTS

1 *quantity of Bolognese sauce*
1 tablespoon olive oil
3 cloves of garlic
2 medium onions
500 g (1 lb) beef mince
400 g tin Italian plum tomatoes
1 beef stock cube
1–2 teaspoons oregano, mixed herbs or mixed Mediterranean
    herbs
Salt and freshly ground pepper to taste

250 g packet of lasagne pasta (look for 'no pre-cooking required'
    on the packet)
Parmesan cheese

White sauce
4 tablespoons butter
6 tablespoons flour
2 cups milk (500 ml or 1 pint)
1–2 tablespoons grated Parmesan cheese
Salt and freshly ground pepper to taste

EQUIPMENT

Sharp knife
Chopping board
Large ovenproof dish (2 litre or 3 ½ pints)
Frying-pan
Saucepan
Wooden spoon

257

Tin opener
Set of measuring spoons
Set of measuring cups

METHOD

To make the Bolognese sauce

Put the oil in the frying-pan. Peel and crush the garlic. Peel and chop the onions. Fry the garlic and chopped onion on a medium heat for about two minutes. Stir them every half a minute or so.

Put the meat in the frying-pan and fry for two or three minutes, stirring all the time. By this time it should have broken up and be an even colour, with no pink bits.

Open the tin of tomatoes. Pour the juice into the frying-pan. Crumble stock cube into pan. Use the wooden spoon to mash the tomatoes while they are still in the can (it's easier than chasing them round the pan). Pour the mashed tomatoes into the pan. Continue to cook, stirring as the mixture boils. Add your chosen herb, oregano being authentic. Season with salt and pepper. Cook for another five minutes or so until the fluid has reduced and the sauce is less sloppy.

The sauce can be improved by adding a glass of wine and cooking a bit longer.

To make the white sauce

Melt the butter in a saucepan over a low heat. Add flour and stir together to make a smooth paste. Take the pan off the heat. Continue to stir and add the milk a bit at a time. If you add it too quickly it will go lumpy. When all the milk has been added, put it back on the heat and gently bring to the boil, stirring all the time, until thickened. Add one or two tablespoons of Parmesan cheese. Season with salt and pepper.

Assemble the lasagne in the ovenproof dish
Start with a layer of Bolognese sauce. Cover with a layer of lasagne pasta. Then a layer of Bolognese sauce. Next a layer of white sauce. Then pasta, Bolognese, white sauce.

However many layers you do, it must end up with white sauce on top. Sprinkle the top with Parmesan cheese.

Cook in a preheated oven at 180°C, 350°F, Gas mark 4 for about 30 minutes. The top should be golden brown.

ADDITIONS & ALTERNATIVES
Use prepared Bolognese sauce from the supermarket.

TIPS
Prepared garlic is sold in tubes and jars. Just read the tube or jar for the suggested equivalent amount. It keeps for six weeks in the fridge.

RISOTTO

Serves 4 ① *Preparation 5 min, Cooking 20 to 25 min*
Needs an eye keeping on it all the time

INGREDIENTS
1 medium onion
3–4 cloves garlic
3 tablespoons olive oil
400–500 g (about 1 lb) of one of the following:
    minced beef, chopped chicken, frozen vegetables, prawns
1 cup risotto rice
227 g tin chopped tomatoes
2 tablespoons parsley
$\frac{1}{2}$ cup of wine
$1\frac{1}{2}$ cups water or stock
Salt

EQUIPMENT
Sharp knife
Chopping board
Large saucepan
Set of measuring spoons
Wooden spoon
Set of measuring cups
Tin opener

METHOD
Peel and chop the onion and the garlic. Put the oil in a large saucepan. Fry the onion a minute or so then add the mince, chicken, vegetables or prawns and fry for a further three minutes or so.

Add the rice and fry for another couple of minutes. Add the garlic, tomatoes, parsley, wine, stock and salt to taste. Simmer for 20–25 minutes, until the fluid is absorbed and the rice is cooked. If it looks like it is getting dry, add some more water or wine and give it a stir.

ADDITIONS & ALTERNATIVES
This dish needs watching to make sure it cooks but stays moist.

FOCACCIA BREAD

Serves 4   ① *Preparation 15 min plus 20 and 30 minutes to rise,*
          Cooking 25 min – Moderately strenuous, but worth it

INGREDIENTS

2 cups (250 g or half a small bag) plain white flour
Coarse sea salt
2 teaspoons easy blend dried yeast
3 tablespoons olive oil
150 ml (10 tablespoons) warm water
and, if you like, one or more of the following:
A few leaves of fresh rosemary
6 cloves of garlic
10 olives
3 sun dried tomatoes

EQUIPMENT

Sieve
Mixing bowl
Set of measuring spoons
Wooden spoon
1 clean tea towel or some cling film
Baking tray

METHOD

Sieve the flour and 1 teaspoon of salt into the mixing bowl. If there is no sieve, break up any lumps with a fork. Add the easy blend yeast. Mix again. Make a well in the middle of the flour.

Mix a tablespoon of olive oil and the warm water, and pour it into the flour mixture. Use the wooden spoon to mix the dough. Try to get rid of any lumps of dry flour and keep at it till the dough becomes less sticky and comes away from the side of the bowl.

Now knead the dough. This is a process of stretching the dough and then folding it back on itself, rather than hitting it. It makes the gluten in the flour develop, and makes the springy texture which lets the bubbles of gas make the bread rise. Form the dough into a ball. Sprinkle some flour on a firm, clean, dry surface, like a bread board or kitchen surface. Alternatively, knead it in the bowl. Use the heel of the hand to push half the dough away. Fold it over, turn it round a bit and repeat until the dough is springy and smooth. This is much easier to do than to describe. Knead for about ten minutes.

Put the dough back in the bowl. Cover the bowl with something clean and damp, like a tea towel. Failing being able to locate a tea towel, use cling film. Put the bowl somewhere warm for about twenty minutes. The dough should have doubled in size. Take the towel/cling film off. Hit the top of the dough. It should collapse as you knock the air out of it.

Wipe the baking tray with a little oil. Stretch out the dough using your fingers so it ends up about half to one centimetre (quarter to half an inch) thick. Cover the dough with that damp tea towel or cling film again and leave for half an hour. It will have expanded a bit.

Gently push your fingertip into the surface in several places, so it becomes deeply dimpled. Brush or dribble the olive oil on the top. Sprinkle 2 teaspoons of coarse (unground) sea salt on top.

Rosemary is the standard garnish, but olives, garlic or sun-dried tomatoes are very good.

Cook in a preheated oven at 220°C, 425°F, Gas mark 7 for about 20 to 25 minutes. Allow to cool but eat while warm if possible.

ADDITIONS & ALTERNATIVES
This looks a bit like pizza, and the dough is exactly the same. It is also the dough for Calzoni, a kind of inside-out pizza, great for packed meals.

TIPS

There are three kinds of yeast. Fresh yeast comes from health food shops. It will keep in the fridge for a few days but will eventually die.

Dried yeast comes in tubs from the supermarket. It, like fresh yeast, needs to be 'activated' before use, by adding it to warm water, often with a teaspoon of sugar. There are generally instructions on the packet.

Easy to blend yeast comes in packets from the supermarket. It can be mixed straight in with the flour.

PIZZA

Makes 2 pizzas   ① *Preparation 5 min for bought pizza bases,*
(8 to 12 slices)   *15 minutes otherwise, Cooking 20 min*
   – Easy if you use bought bases, moderate if you make your own

INGREDIENTS

1 quantity Focaccia dough (see previous recipe)
   or bought pizza bases
400 g tin Italian plum tomatoes
150 g Mozzarella cheese
1–2 teaspoons oregano
Choose toppings from:
salami, tuna, sliced tomatoes, anchovies, olives, capers, mushrooms, red sweet pepper slices, sweet corn, ham and pineapple,
sardines.

EQUIPMENT

Baking tray
Tin opener
Wooden spoon
Sharp knife
Chopping board

METHOD

Make the Focaccia dough, just like in the last recipe, except divide
it in two, and roll it out into circles on the baking sheet. Or buy
pizza bases. If you are using bought bases read the packet carefully
and cook according to their instructions. The cooking times here
are for pizza made with fresh dough.

    Drain the tomatoes. Squeeze two tomatoes through your
fingers on to each pizza. Spread the layer with a spoon. Sprinkle
with oregano. Put your chosen topping on top. Cover with slices

of mozzarella cheese. Cook in a preheated oven at 240°C, 475°F, Gas mark 9 for 10 to 15 minutes.

ADDITIONS & ALTERNATIVES

Use the tomato sauce on page 245, bought tomato pizza sauce or even tomato paste instead of the tomato sauce.

Use Cheddar cheese instead of Mozzarella.

TIPS

Shops sell ready shredded Mozzarella cheese.

Great party food. Double quantities will make 4 pizzas for 16 to 24 slices.

MEAT CALZONI

Serves 4   ⏱ *Preparation 15 min plus 40 minutes rising time,*
Cooking 15 to 20 min – Moderate

INGREDIENTS
1 quantity Focaccia dough (page 261)
1 medium onion
1 tablespoon olive oil
2 tinned plum tomatoes
50 g (2 oz) Italian sausage or salami
2 slices of cooked ham
1 tablespoon chopped parsley
100 g Mozzarella cheese

EQUIPMENT
Sharp knife
Chopping board
Set of measuring spoons
Frying-pan
Tin opener
Rolling pin

METHOD
Make the Focaccia dough from the previous recipe, mixing, kneading and allowing it to rise for about 20 minutes till it has doubled in size. While waiting for the dough to rise, make the filling.

Meat filling: peel and chop the onion. Put the oil in the frying-pan. Gently fry the onion for about three to five minutes, until it goes soft. Take the frying-pan off the heat. Open the tin of tomatoes. Drain the tomatoes. Put them into the frying-pan, and mash them up. Chop the sausage and the ham. Put them into the pan with the parsley.

Knock the dough down and give it another brief knead. Divide the dough into four pieces. Roll it out or flatten it to about the size of a small plate about 15 cm (6 inches) across. Divide up the filling into 4 and put it into the middle of each circle. Chop the Mozzarella into cubes and divide it up between the Calzonis. Fold over the dough sealing the edge with a little water. Brush each Calzoni with a little olive oil. Smear some oil on a baking sheet. Put the Calzoni on the baking sheet. Wait about 15 minutes for the dough to rise a little. Cook in a preheated oven at 220°C, 425°F, Gas mark 7 for about 15 to 20 minutes.

VEGETABLE CALZONI

Serves 4   ① *Preparation 15 min plus 40 minutes rising time,*
Cooking 15 to 20 min – Moderate

INGREDIENTS
1 quantity Focaccia dough

Vegetable filling
4 cloves of garlic
1 medium onion
1 red sweet pepper
1 tablespoon olive oil
400 g tin of artichoke hearts
tinned plum tomatoes
2 tablespoons Parmesan cheese
2 tablespoons parsley
100 g Mozzarella cheese

EQUIPMENT
Sharp knife
Chopping board
Garlic crusher
Set of measuring spoons
Frying-pan
Tin opener
Rolling pin

METHOD
Follow the instructions in the previous recipe for dough and preparation but use vegetable filling instead of meat.

Vegetable filling: Peel and crush the garlic. Peel and chop the onion. Chop the red pepper, throwing away the core and seeds.

Put the oil in the frying-pan. Gently fry the garlic, onion and sweet pepper for about three to five minutes, until the onion goes soft. Take the frying pan off the heat.

Open the tins of artichoke hearts and tomatoes. Drain the tomatoes. Put them into the frying-pan, and mash them up. Mix in the Parmesan cheese. Chop the artichoke hearts and put them into the pan. Add the parsley. Put the mixture on to the dough. Chop the Mozzarella into cubes and divide it up between the Calzonis.

FISH CALZONI

Serves 4   ① *Preparation 15 min plus 40 minutes rising time, Cooking 15 to 20 min – Moderate*

INGREDIENTS
1 quantity Focaccia dough
3–4 cloves garlic

1 medium onion
1 tablespoon olive oil
200 g tin tuna
2 tinned plum tomatoes
100 g tin clams (optional)
2 tablespoons fresh parsley
100 g Mozzarella cheese

EQUIPMENT

Sharp knife
Chopping board
Garlic crusher
Set of measuring spoons
Frying-pan
Tin opener
Rolling pin

METHOD

Follow the instructions in the previous recipe for the dough and preparation but use fish filling instead of meat or vegetables.

Peel and crush the garlic. Peel and chop the onion. Put the oil in the frying-pan. Gently fry the garlic and onion for about three to five minutes, until the onion goes soft. Take the frying-pan off the heat.

Open the tins of tuna, tomatoes and clams. Drain the tomatoes. Put them into the frying- pan, and mash them up. Put the tuna, parsley and clams into the pan. Put the mixture on to the dough. Chop the Mozzarella into cubes and divide it up between the Calzonis.

TEX-MEX

GUACAMOLE

Serves 2   ① *Preparation 5 min – Easy*

INGREDIENTS
2 ripe avocados
1 large ripe tomato
1 tablespoon lemon juice
$\frac{1}{2}$ to 1 teaspoon chilli powder
    or 1 or 2 fresh shredded chillies with the seeds removed
Salt and freshly ground pepper to taste

EQUIPMENT
Sharp knife
Chopping board
Bowl
Fork for mashing
Set of measuring spoons

METHOD
Ripe avocados mash easily. Cut the avocados in half, peel and remove the stone. Mash the avocado with a fork.

Peel the tomato, chop in half, take out the seeds and chop up small. *To peel tomatoes*: make a cut in the shape of a cross in the base and top of the tomato. Drop into a saucepan of boiling water for 30 seconds. Pour the boiling water away and cover with cold water. When it's cool enough to touch, the skin should slide off easily.

Mash all the ingredients together. Serve as a dip for crisps, taco chips, nachos, or with other salads.

TIPS

FRESH CHILLI – A WARNING! When you chop up the chillies be careful and avoid getting juice on your hands. If you touch your eyes, mouth or other sensitive areas even an hour after chopping them they will smart and burn. So wash your hands or wear rubber gloves.

Prepared chilli is sold in tubes and jars. Just read the tube or jar for the suggested equivalent amount. It keeps for six weeks in the fridge.

BARBECUE SAUCE

For barbecues or meat ⏱ *Preparation 2 min,*
Cooking 2 min – Easy

INGREDIENTS
2 tablespoons butter
1 tablespoon sugar
3 tablespoons tomato ketchup
2 tablespoons HP sauce
1 tablespoon Worcestershire sauce (Lea and Perrins)
1 tablespoon mushroom ketchup (if you can find it)
2 drops Tabasco

EQUIPMENT
Saucepan
Wooden spoon
Set of measuring spoons

METHOD
Melt the butter with the sugar in the pan over a low heat. Take the pan off the heat. Add the ketchup, HP sauce, Worcestershire sauce, mushroom ketchup and the Tabasco. Mix it all together. Ready to serve.

ADDITIONS & ALTERNATIVES
Try fruity brown sauces, whatever you have, instead of the brown sauce.

TIPS
This is a multipurpose sauce. You can cook with it, or use it as a sauce with barbecue burgers or sausages.

This will keep in the fridge for 48 hours.

Use this as a marinade and sauce for spare ribs (recipe below).

TEXAN BARBECUED SPARE RIBS

Serves 3 to 4   ① *Preparation 5 min, Cooking 25 min – Easy*

INGREDIENTS
1 kg (2 lbs) spare ribs, separated
1 quantity barbecue sauce (as above)

EQUIPMENT
Bowl
Wooden spoon
Grill
Cooking tongs

METHOD
Put two-thirds of the barbecue sauce in a bowl then add the ribs. Stir them round so they are coated. Preferably leave for a couple of hours.

Turn on the grill. Put the ribs on the grill on edge. As you will notice the meat on a rib is at the edges and the knobbly end. This is the bit that needs cooking. The hassle of this is that you need to keep an eye on them, turning them over and moving the cooked ones to the edge. Think of it as a barbecue.

ADDITIONS & ALTERNATIVES
You can serve this without anything other than the remaining barbecue sauce, or serve with boiled rice and salad.

There is not much meat on a spare rib.

Use this recipe for a barbecue.

FRESH COOKED POTATO SKINS

Starter for 4   ⏱ *Preparation 5 min, Cooking 20 min – Easy*

INGREDIENTS
3 large potatoes
Sunflower oil
1 medium carton (284 ml or 10 fl oz) sour cream
1 pack fresh chives

EQUIPMENT
Sharp knife
Chopping board
Frying-pan
Wooden spoon
Bowl

METHOD
Take a potato and wash it. Cut it into quarters or eighths (a bit like following the seams on a rugby ball). Cut away half the potato flesh.

Fry skins in sunflower oil for about 5 to 10 minutes until done. Lift out the skins and drain on kitchen roll. You can keep them warm in the oven while you cook the rest.

Wash, dry and chop the chives. Put the sour cream in the bowl. Add the chives. Stir. Serve with the fried potato skins.

ADDITIONS & ALTERNATIVES
Try with other dips like Guacamole (page 270) or Fresh Mexican Salsa (page 276). You can buy a wide range of sauces and dips in jars.

BOUGHT POTATO SKINS

Starter for 4   ⏱ *Preparation 3 min, Cooking 15 min – Easy*

INGREDIENTS
250 g pack frozen potato skins
1 medium carton (284 ml or 10 fl oz) sour cream
1 pack fresh chives

EQUIPMENT
Baking sheet
Sharp knife
Chopping board
Bowl
Wooden spoon

METHOD
Read the instructions on the frozen potato skins. Generally, they can be cooked from frozen and cooked for about 10 to 15 minutes at 200°C, 400°F, Gas mark 6. They can be grilled as well.

Wash, dry and chop the chives. Put the sour cream in the bowl. Add the chives. Stir round. Serve with the hot potato skins.

ADDITIONS & ALTERNATIVES
Try with other dressings like Guacamole (page 270) or Fresh Mexican Salsa (see page 276).

FRESH MEXICAN SALSA

Enough for a large packet of taco chips   ① *Preparation 5 min*
                                                 – Moderate

INGREDIENTS
1 green pepper
Bunch coriander
1 or 2 green chillies or $\frac{1}{2}$ teaspoon chilli powder
1 medium onion
Clove garlic
1 large ripe tomato
Pinch salt
1 teaspoon sugar

EQUIPMENT
Sharp knife
Chopping board
Set of measuring spoons
Food processor liquidiser (optional)

METHOD
Wash the green pepper. Take the seeds out. Wash the coriander and cut off the stalks. Carefully take the seeds out of the chillies. Peel the onion and the garlic. Put all the ingredients in a food processor or liquidiser and blend together for about 10 seconds.

If no food processor, chop everything up really small then mix in a bowl.

ADDITIONS & ALTERNATIVES
Serve with tortilla chips, or with enchiladas, tacos or tortillas.

FRESH CHILLI – A WARNING! When you chop up the chillies be careful and avoid getting juice on your hands. It will sting. If you touch your eyes, mouth or other sensitive areas even an hour after chopping them they will smart and burn. So wash your hands or wear rubber gloves.

276

CHEESE SALSA

Enough for a large packet　　　① *Preparation 2 min – Easy*
of tortillo chips

INGREDIENTS

Half a 300 g jar Taco relish, or ½ quantity Fresh Mexican Salsa
　　(recipe above)
200 g pack processed cheese spread
1 small carton (142 ml or 5 fl oz) sour cream

EQUIPMENT

Spoon
Bowl

METHOD

Mix all the ingredients together.

ADDITIONS & ALTERNATIVES

Use chopped vegetables like carrot, cauliflower or celery to dip in
the salsa.

　Use as an accompaniment to burgers or ribs.

REFRIED BEANS

Serves 2 to 4   ⏱ *Preparation 2 min, Cooking 10 min – Easy*

INGREDIENTS
420 g tin baked beans
440 g red kidney beans
1 tablespoon butter
$\frac{1}{2}$ teaspoon paprika pepper
$\frac{1}{2}$ teaspoon chilli powder

EQUIPMENT
Tin opener
Set of measuring spoons
Saucepan
Wooden spoon

METHOD
Open the tins. Drain the kidney beans.

Put the butter, paprika and chilli powder in the pan. Put on a low heat and melt the butter. Add the baked beans and red kidney beans. Cook over a low heat for 5 minutes. Leave to cool.

Can be reheated later or eaten immediately.

ADDITIONS & ALTERNATIVES
You can add some grated Cheddar cheese.

Serve with green salad or with other Tex-Mex dishes.

CHILLI CON CARNE

Serves 2–3   ⏲ *Preparation 5 min, Cooking 45 min – Easy*

INGREDIENTS

100 g (4 oz) mushrooms (about 10) (optional)
1 large onion
2 tablespoons oil
500 g (1 lb) mince
1 packet Mexican chilli seasoning
1 teaspoon salt
400 g tin plum tomatoes
440 g tin red kidney beans

EQUIPMENT

Sharp knife
Chopping board
Set of measuring spoons
Frying-pan
Wooden spoon
Tin opener

METHOD

If using mushrooms, wipe the dirt off and cut the end off the stalk. Slice roughly. Peel and chop the onion.

Put the oil in the frying-pan. Fry the onion over a medium heat for a couple of minutes to soften, stirring to stop it sticking. Add the mince and continue to fry, breaking up the meat with the spoon so that it browns. This should take about five minutes. Add the seasoning and salt and mix well.

Open the tin of tomatoes. Pour in the juice from the tin and then mash up the tomatoes in the tin with a wooden spoon. Add the mashed up tomatoes. Stir and bring to the boil. Turn down the heat so the mixture is just boiling.

Open the tin of kidney beans and drain off the liquid. Add the beans to the pan. Add the mushrooms. Stir from time to time. If it looks like it is getting too dry then add some water. Cook for at least 15 minutes.

You can let it cool and reheat when the rice is done. It seems that the flavour improves with reheating.

ADDITIONS & ALTERNATIVES

Serve this with boiled rice, American long grain being the best for this. Look at the packet to see how long to cook it. There are full instructions on boiled rice in the 'How to' chapter.

Read what it says on the packet of seasoning to get the right amount. Try substituting half to one teaspoon chilli powder and 2 teaspoons ground cumin for the seasoning mix.

Leave out the onions and mushrooms.

Try adding a small tin of sweet corn.

Add 1 chopped sweet pepper.

It's easy to double up the quantities.

MEXICAN CHICKEN TORTILLAS

Makes enough for 8 tortillas　　　　① *Preparation 10 min,*
　　　　　　　　　　　　　　　　　　　Cooking 15 min – Easy

INGREDIENTS

100 g (4 oz) grated Cheddar cheese (about 2 cups)
Iceberg or other crisp lettuce
2 large ripe tomatoes
500 g frozen small chicken breasts or chicken breasts chopped
　　into bite-sized pieces
1 red pepper
1 large onion
3 cloves garlic
2 tablespoons oil
1 teaspoon ground cumin
1 teaspoon paprika pepper
1 teaspoon chilli pepper
1 pack ready made soft tortillas
300 g jar taco salsa or Mexican Salsa on page 276

EQUIPMENT

Set of measuring cups
Grater
3 small bowls or plates
Sharp knife
Chopping board
Set of measuring spoons
Frying-pan
Wooden spoon

METHOD

Grate the cheese and put in a bowl. Wash and drain the lettuce. Shred it and put in a bowl. Chop the tomatoes into 1 cm (half-inch) chunks. Put them in the last bowl.

Make sure the chicken is defrosted (follow the instructions on the pack), but at least 6 hours at room temperature. Chop the chicken into bite-sized bits.

Wash and chop the red pepper. Discard the central white lump and the seeds. Peel and chop the onion and garlic.

Put the oil in the frying pan. Heat the oil over a medium heat. Add the onion and garlic and fry for a couple of minutes to soften them up. Add the ground cumin, paprika and chilli. Stir round. Add the chicken and cook for five minutes, stirring to make sure the chicken is cooked on all sides. Add the sweet pepper and stir and cook for two minutes. Add two tablespoons of water. Stir round. Cook for three minutes.

Warm the tortillas either by putting under a grill for 10 seconds each or by putting in a warm oven for a couple of minutes. Look at packet for details.

This is a simple construction job. Put a tablespoon or so of the cooked chicken mix on the tortilla, add shredded lettuce, chopped tomato and grated cheese with salsa. Fold up the tortilla and eat with your hands.

ADDITIONS & ALTERNATIVES

You can use Chilli con Carne (page 279) or taco meat mixture (page 286) instead of the chicken.

ENCHILADA SAUCE

Enough for 8 tortillas ① *Preparation 3 min, Cooking 5 min – Easy*

INGREDIENTS

2 tablespoons sunflower oil
1 clove garlic
1 medium onion
1 teaspoon cumin powder
1 teaspoon chilli powder
1 teaspoon paprika
Half 500 g carton creamed tomato
Salt and freshly ground pepper to taste

EQUIPMENT

Set of measuring spoons
Frying-pan
Garlic crusher
Sharp knife
Chopping board
Wooden spoon

METHOD

Put the oil in the frying-pan. Peel and crush the garlic into the pan.
Peel and chop the onion. Fry the garlic and onion for a couple of
minutes till golden. Add the cumin, chilli and paprika and stir
round for 30 seconds. Add the tomato. Season with salt and
pepper. Bring to the boil. Take off the heat.

ADDITIONS & ALTERNATIVES

You can buy jars of enchilada sauce.

Garlic purée is available in tubes and jars. It keeps for six weeks
in the fridge. Check the pack for equivalent amounts.

CHEESE ENCHILADAS

Serves 4   ① *Preparation 10 min, Cooking 25 min – Easy*

INGREDIENTS
1 large onion
2 cups grated Mozzarella cheese
1 packet 8 flour tortillas
1 jar enchilada sauce (250 g) or recipe on previous page
1 medium carton (284 ml 10 fl oz) sour cream
Salt and freshly ground pepper

EQUIPMENT
Sharp knife
Chopping board
Grater
Set of measuring cups
Bowl
Ovenproof dish

METHOD
The filling is equal parts of cheese and onion. Peel and chop the onion finely. Chop or grate the cheese. Keep a bit of the cheese to sprinkle on the top. Mix the onion and cheese together in the bowl.

Get a tortilla. Put an eighth of the mixture on the tortilla. Roll it up like a pancake. Put it in an ovenproof baking dish. Repeat for the other seven tortillas. Pour the enchilada sauce over the top. Sprinkle the top with cheese and season with salt and pepper.

Cook in a preheated oven at 180°C, 350°F, Gas mark 4 for 25 minutes. Put a tablespoon of sour cream on each enchilada when serving.

ADDITIONS & ALTERNATIVES

Serve with sour cream, guacamole (page 270), and a bit of salad.

Instead of the cheese filling use Chilli con Carne (page 279), or the Chicken Tortilla filling (page 281).

Substitute Cheddar cheese for the Mozzarella.

Supermarkets sell bags of grated cheese.

NACHOS

Serves 2   ⏲ *Preparation 3 min, Cooking 5 min – Easy*

INGREDIENTS

Half bunch (4–6) spring onions
100 g (4 oz) Cheddar cheese (2 cups)
1 bag (200 g or 8 oz) tortilla chips
300 g jar taco relish, or ½ quantity Fresh Mexican Salsa (page 276)

EQUIPMENT

Sharp knife
Chopping board
Grater for the cheese
Set of measuring cups
Ovenproof dish

METHOD

Clean and prepare the spring onions. Cut the root end off, trim the leaves. Peel off and discard any dried up or slimy leaves. Chop roughly. Grate the cheese.

Put the tortilla chips in the ovenproof dish. Sprinkle with spring onions and cheese. Cook in an oven at 180°C, 350°F, Gas mark 4 for 5 minutes, till the cheese is runny. Take out and pour the relish on top.

ADDITIONS & ALTERNATIVES
Serve with sour cream, guacamole (page 270) and salad.

TACOS

Serves 2–3   ⏱ *Preparation 5 min, Cooking 20 min – Easy*

INGREDIENTS
100 g (4 oz) grated Cheddar cheese (2 cups)
Iceberg or other crisp lettuce
2 large ripe tomatoes
500 g (1 lb) mince
1 packet Mexican taco seasoning
1 packet of 12 taco shells
300 g jar taco salsa or Mexican Salsa (page 276)

EQUIPMENT
Grater
Set of measuring cups
3 bowls
Sharp knife
Chopping board
Frying-pan
Wooden spoon

METHOD
Grate the cheese and put in a bowl. Wash and drain the lettuce. Shred it and put in a bowl. Chop the tomatoes into 1 cm (half-inch) chunks. Put them in the last bowl.

Add the mince to the frying-pan on a medium heat, and fry, breaking up the meat with the spoon so that it browns. This should take about five minutes. Add the seasoning mix and stir round. Add half a cup (quarter pint) of water. Cook on a medium heat till the fluid is reduced, about 15 minutes.

Warm the taco shells according to the instructions on the packet.

This dish is a construction job. Put two tablespoons or so of the cooked meat mix in the taco, add shredded lettuce, chopped tomato and grated cheese with salsa. Eat with your hands.

ADDITIONS & ALTERNATIVES

Read what it says on the packet of seasoning to get the right amount. Try substituting half to one teaspoon chilli powder and 2 teaspoons ground cumin for the seasoning mix.

Try adding a small tin of sweet corn to the meat mixture as it is cooking.

Add 1 chopped sweet pepper to the meat mixture.

HAMBURGERS

4 quarter pounders ① *Preparation 10 min, Cooking 10 min – Easy*

INGREDIENTS
Lettuce leaves
1 large (beef) tomato
1 large onion (optional)
4 burger buns
500 g (1 lb) chuck steak or minced steak
2 tablespoons mayonnaise (optional)
Relishes
Ketchup
Salt and freshly ground pepper to taste

EQUIPMENT
Sharp knife
Chopping board
Food processor or mincer, or friendly butcher if mincing specially
Set of measuring spoons
Hamburger patty press (optional)

METHOD
Wash and drain the lettuce. Wash and slice the tomato. Peel and slice the onion. Separate the burger bun halves and grill them.

Grind up the meat if not already minced. Put a quarter of it in the hamburger press and push. Take out and repeat for each one.

If you don't have a hamburger press, you will have to use something to bind the meat together. Put the mince in a bowl with an egg and beat round. If it looks too wet add a tablespoon of breadcrumbs. Then use your hands to press the mixture into flat disks. Make them fairly chunky.

Grill the burgers for about 5 minutes a side. If the meat was very lean (had no fat) put a teaspoon of butter on each burger.

Get the bun. If you like put some mayonnaise on the bottom half. Then put some lettuce leaves on the bun, followed by the onion, burger, tomato and top of the bun.

Serve with the relish and ketchup.

ADDITIONS & ALTERNATIVES

Serve with a bit more salad or oven chips.

To make the meat go further peel and grate and add 1 medium carrot.

Vegetarian version. Buy vegetarian burgers. Some supermarkets sometimes make their own. Go for ones that say 'chargrilled' as they taste better.

TIPS

You can use mince for this, but grinding chuck steak is much better. You know what you're getting. Chuck steak is a cut of beef, with not too much fat, and reasonably cheap. Any steak type can be ground up into mince. The cheaper the mince the more fat and the less 'meat'.

The hamburger press is a steel contraption which you fill with minced meat and press. It gives uniform size and thickness to your burgers. Handmade burgers tend to fall apart, and have thin edges which cook too quickly.

INDIAN

APPLE & TAMARIND SAMBAL

A fresh chutney   ① *Preparation 10 min – Easy*

INGREDIENTS
Half a pack tamarind
2 cups water
1 medium cooking apple
½ teaspoon ground pepper
½ teaspoon chilli powder
2 teaspoons sugar

EQUIPMENT
Bowl
Set of measuring cups
Vegetable peeler
Apple corer
Grater
Set of measuring spoons

METHOD
Break up the tamarind and put in the bowl with the water. Squeeze the tamarind so the flesh comes away from the pips. Mush it all up. Throw away the pulp and keep the water.

Peel the apple, take the core out. Grate up the apple. Put in the bowl with the tamarind water, pepper, chilli and sugar.

That's all there is to it.

ADDITIONS & ALTERNATIVES
Dried tamarind comes in blocks with seeds or tubs without.

CUCUMBER, ONION OR MINT RAITA

Eat with curry   ⏱ *Preparation 3 min – Easy*

INGREDIENTS
250 g set, natural yoghurt
one of the following:
$\frac{1}{4}$ cucumber
1 small onion
1 teaspoon mint sauce

EQUIPMENT
Bowl
Fork
Sharp knife
Chopping board
Set of measuring spoons

METHOD
Put the yoghurt in the bowl. Whip it up with a fork. It should go creamy in about ten seconds. Peel the cucumber, if using, and cut into small cubes, about 5 mm (quarter inch). Mix together.

ADDITIONS & ALTERNATIVES
Substitute a small onion, peeled and diced, for the cucumber.

Substitute or add a teaspoon of mint sauce.

PLAIN RICE

Serves 2 or 3   ① *Preparation 1 min, Cooking 10–15 min – Easy*

INGREDIENTS
1 cup basmati or long grain rice
2 cups of water
½ teaspoon of salt

EQUIPMENT
Saucepan with lid
Set of measuring cups

METHOD
Read the packet to get the correct cooking time. Put the water and the rice in the saucepan with the salt. Bring to the boil. Turn down the heat to low. Stir once to stop it sticking to the pan. Put the lid on the pan. Cook for the correct time until the fluid is absorbed (10–15 minutes for long grain or basmati rice). Do not stir until the time is up.

Leave it to stand for a couple of minutes. Free up the grains of rice by flicking with a fork.

ADDITIONS & ALTERNATIVES
The cup referred to is a standard measuring cup of 250 ml. It is approximately the same as a mug.

Generally use twice as much water as rice.

Brown rice takes longer to cook. Read the packet.

Basmati is more fragrant than long grain, and also more forgiving, because it holds together well.

TANDOORI QUICK FRY

Serves 2 ⏱ *Preparation 5 min, Cooking 15 min – Easy*

INGREDIENTS
2 boneless chicken breasts
2 tablespoons sunflower oil
1 tablespoon lemon or lime juice
4 tablespoons Tandoori powder
1 large onion
2 tablespoons sunflower oil for frying
4 cloves garlic

EQUIPMENT
Sharp knife
Chopping board
Set of measuring spoons
Bowl
Frying-pan
Garlic crusher
Wooden spoon

DEFROSTING
Make sure frozen chicken is completely thawed before use. This means leaving it in the fridge overnight, or out of the fridge, covered, for six hours.

METHOD
Cut the chicken into bite-sized pieces.

Put the oil, lemon or lime juice and the Tandoori powder in the bowl. Mix. Add the chicken and stir to coat with the mixture. Leave to stand for anything between 30 minutes and 24 hours in a fridge.

Peel and chop the onion. Put the oil in the frying-pan and heat over a moderate heat. Peel and crush the garlic into the pan. Fry

293

the onion for about three minutes till it is golden, stirring to stop it sticking. Add the chicken and fry till chicken is done, about 10 minutes.

ADDITIONS & ALTERNATIVES
Serve with chutney, naan bread and rice.
Substitute other boneless chicken bits.

COURGETTE & CUMIN

Serves 2–4 as side dish① Preparation 2 min, Cooking 5 min – Easy

INGREDIENTS
3 courgettes
2 tablespoons butter
1 to 2 teaspoons cumin seed

EQUIPMENT
Sharp knife
Chopping board
Set of measuring spoons
Frying-pan
Wooden spoon

METHOD
Wash the courgettes. Cut off the top and bottom ends. Slice lengthways. The slices should be about half a centimetre (quarter inch) thick.

Put the butter and the cumin seed in the frying-pan. Put on a medium heat and melt the butter. Gently fry the courgettes for about five minutes, turning occasionally.

TIPS
Makes a good accompaniment to other curries.

TANDOORI CHICKEN

Serves 4   ① *Preparation 15 min, Cooking 45 min – Easy*

INGREDIENTS
4 large chicken quarters or 8–12 pieces
2 medium onions
2 cloves garlic
3 tablespoons Greek unsweetened yoghurt
4 tablespoons Tandoori mix (check amount on pack)
1 lemon

EQUIPMENT
Sharp knife
Chopping board
Set of measuring spoons
Bowl
Wooden spoon
Casserole, roasting dish or Tandoori pot
Aluminium foil if the dish has no lid

DEFROSTING
Make sure frozen chicken is completely thawed before use. This means leaving it in the fridge overnight, or out of the fridge, covered, for six hours.

METHOD
Peel and chop the onion and garlic. Mix the yoghurt, Tandoori mix, onion and garlic in the bowl.

Slash the chicken pieces through to the bone on the legs, thighs and breast. Rub the Tandoori mix over the chicken pieces so it is well coated. Leave for at least an hour to soak in. It is better to leave it for twelve to twenty-four hours.

Put the chicken in the casserole, roasting dish or Tandoori oven. Put a lid on, or cover the top in aluminium foil. Cook in a preheated oven for 200°C, 400°F, Gas mark 6 for about 35 minutes. Take off the lid or foil, turn the chicken bits over and cook for another ten minutes or so till it is golden and cooked through.

Chicken is cooked if the juices run clear when it is pierced by a fork.

Cut the lemon into quarters and serve with the chicken.

ADDITIONS & ALTERNATIVES
Serve with rice, salad, naan bread.

TIPS
Prepared garlic is sold in tubes and jars. Just read the tube or jar for the suggested equivalent amount. It keeps for six weeks in the fridge.

CHICKEN TIKKA

Serves 2 or 3   ① *Preparation 10 min, Cooking 20 min – Easy*

INGREDIENTS
750 g (1½ lbs) boneless chicken pieces
3 tablespoons Tikka mix
3 tablespoons Greek unsweetened yoghurt
2 tablespoons lemon or lime juice, or juice of a lemon or lime
2 or 3 tablespoons sunflower oil

EQUIPMENT
Sharp knife
Chopping board
Set of measuring spoons
Wooden spoon
Bowl

Bamboo skewers
Grill

DEFROSTING

Make sure frozen chicken is completely thawed before use. This means leaving it in the fridge overnight, or out of the fridge, covered, for six hours.

METHOD

Cut chicken into 2 cm (1 inch) chunks. Combine the Tikka mix with the lemon and oil in the bowl and then add the yoghurt. Add the chicken pieces and stir round. Leave covered preferably in a fridge for at least an hour.

Thread the chicken on the skewers, about four or five chunks each. This is a slippery but satisfying job. Grill for 15 to 20 minutes, turning frequently so all sides get cooked.

ADDITIONS & ALTERNATIVES

Serve with salad, naan bread or boiled rice.

CHICKEN TIKKA MASSALA

Serves 2   ⏱ *Preparation 15 min, Cooking 25 min – Easy*

INGREDIENTS

750 g (1½ lbs) boneless chicken pieces
3 tablespoons Tikka mix
3 tablespoons Greek unsweetened yoghurt
2 tablespoons lemon or lime juice, or juice of a lemon or lime
2 tablespoons sunflower oil
For sauce
3 tablespoons of chopped fresh coriander
200 ml (½ pint) single cream
1 tablespoon Tikka Mix

EQUIPMENT
Sharp knife
Chopping board
Set of measuring spoons
Bowl
Wooden spoon
Bamboo skewers
Grill
Frying-pan

DEFROSTING
Make sure frozen chicken is completely thawed before use. This means leaving it in the fridge overnight, or out of the fridge, covered, for six hours.

METHOD
Cut chicken into 2 cm (1 inch) chunks. Combine the Tikka mix with the lemon and oil in the bowl and then add the yoghurt. Add the chicken pieces and stir. Leave covered preferably in a fridge for at least an hour.

Thread the chicken on the skewers, about four or five chunks each. This is a slippery but satisfying job. Grill for 15 to 20 minutes, turning frequently so all sides get cooked.

Pick the dead leaves off the coriander. Wash and chop the leaves and throw away the stalks. Put the cream, Tikka mix and half the coriander in the frying-pan. Warm up. Take the chicken off the bamboo skewers, and put in the frying-pan. Stir round. Just before serving, sprinkle the rest of the coriander on top.

ADDITIONS & ALTERNATIVES
Serve with salad, naan bread or boiled rice.

Use firm white fish (cod, hake, haddock) instead of the chicken. It works well.

BELPOORI

Serves 4 to 6   ⏲ *Preparation 10 min, Cooking 15 min*
– Easy curry accompaniment

INGREDIENTS

2 cold boiled medium-sized potatoes
2 tablespoons fresh coriander
1 medium onion
1 or 2 tablespoons oil
2 or 3 puffed rice wafers or 1 cup of puffed rice
Half a packet of 'Punjab Pooris'
1 teaspoon tamarind paste

EQUIPMENT

Sharp knife
Chopping board
Saucepan
Bowl
Wooden spoon
Set of measuring spoons
Cup

METHOD

If you need to cook the potatoes, new ones are best. Peel the potatoes, cutting away any nasty bits, and cutting out any eyes. Chop the potatoes into quarters. Cook for 10 to 15 minutes in boiling water till just cooked. Drain and allow to cool. Cut into small pieces.

Wash, drain and chop the coriander leaves. Peel and chop the onion. Put the oil in the bowl with the potato, onion and coriander. Stir round. All this can be made in advance.

Break the puffed rice wafers into individual bits of puffed rice. Add the puffed rice to the bowl and stir round. Put a couple of

299

tablespoons of the potato mixture on to plates. Break up the Pooris, or eat the whole ones and use the bits. Sprinkle some broken pooris on top. Mix the teaspoon of tamarind paste in a cup of cold water. Add a tablespoon of tamarind water and serve.

TIPS

Tamarind paste comes from Indian supermarkets or some larger supermarkets stock it.

HOT CHICKEN JALFREZI

Serves 4   ⏲ *Preparation 5 min, Cooking 25 min – Easy*

INGREDIENTS

500 g (1 lb) chicken
1 large onion
1 tablespoon of oil
3 tablespoons Hot Curry Paste
1 small tin tomatoes (about 200 g)
1 red pepper
1 green pepper

EQUIPMENT

Sharp knife
Chopping board
Saucepan with lid
Wooden spoon
Set of measuring spoons
Tin opener

DEFROSTING

Make sure frozen chicken is completely thawed before use. This means leaving it in the fridge overnight, or out of the fridge, covered, for six hours.

METHOD

Cut chicken into 2 cm (1 inch) chunks. Peel and chop the onion. Put the oil in the saucepan and fry the onion for about three minutes till it is golden, stirring to stop it sticking. Add the chicken. Fry and stir for a couple of minutes. Add the curry paste. Stir and fry for another couple of minutes. Add the tomatoes. Stir. Bring to the boil, then turn the heat down so it is just boiling (simmering). Put a lid on the pan and cook for about 20 minutes. Stir a couple of times. If it gets too dry add a bit of water (a couple of tablespoons).

Meanwhile, wash the red and green peppers. Cut the top bits off and remove the seeds. Slice up. Add the peppers about half-way through the cooking.

ADDITIONS & ALTERNATIVES

Serve with rice.

Use 2 tablespoons of hot curry powder instead of the Hot Curry Paste.

ROGAN JOSH, A MEDIUM CURRY

Serves 4   ① *Preparation 10 min, Cooking 2½ hours – Easy*

INGREDIENTS

500 g (1 lb) boneless lamb
1 large onion
1 tablespoon sunflower oil
1 sachet Rogan Josh curry powder
400 g tin of tomatoes

EQUIPMENT

Sharp knife
Chopping board

Set of measuring spoons
Saucepan
Casserole with lid
Wooden spoon
Tin opener

METHOD

The lamb should be lean, that is not have too much fat on it. Chops are therefore not a good idea.

Cut the lamb in cubes. Peel and chop the onion. Put the oil in the saucepan and heat over a moderate heat. Fry the onion for about three minutes till it is golden, stirring to stop it sticking. Fry the lamb for 5 minutes, stirring to keep it from sticking. The outside should be browned. Add the contents of the packet of Rogan Josh curry powder. Stir round. Put the lot in the casserole.

Open the tin of tomatoes. Pour the juice into the casserole. Use the wooden spoon to mash the tomatoes while they are still in the can. Pour the mashed tomatoes into the casserole. Stir it round. Put a lid on the casserole.

Cook in an oven at 180°C, 350°F, Gas mark 4 for 2 hours.

ADDITIONS & ALTERNATIVES

Serve with rice and pickles.

There are full instructions on cooking plain rice on page 292 and pilau rice on page 310.

POTATO & CAULIFLOWER CURRY

Serves 2–4 ① *Preparation 10 min, Cooking 25 min – Easy*

INGREDIENTS
1 medium onion
2 cloves garlic

1 large tomato

4 medium potatoes (about 500 g or 1 lb)

4 tablespoons oil

1 medium cauliflower

1 tablespoon lemon juice

Salt and pepper to taste

1 tablespoon of mild or medium curry powder

or try this mixture instead

1 teaspoon paprika

$\frac{1}{2}$ teaspoon turmeric

$\frac{1}{2}$ teaspoon cumin powder

$\frac{1}{2}$ teaspoon cinnamon

$\frac{1}{2}$ teaspoon chilli powder

$\frac{1}{2}$ teaspoon cardamom powder (optional)

$\frac{1}{2}$ teaspoon clove powder (optional)

EQUIPMENT

Sharp knife

Chopping board

Saucepan

Deep frying-pan, balti dish or wok

Wooden spoon

Set of measuring spoons

METHOD

Peel and chop the onion. Peel and chop the garlic. Chop the tomato. Peel and boil the potatoes for 10 minutes. Drain and chop them into 1 cm (half-inch) cubes.

Heat the oil in the frying-pan. Add the onions and fry for three minuets till golden. Add the garlic and all the spices or the curry powder. Stir round. Add the potatoes and fry for 5 minutes. Stir to stop it sticking and burning. Add the cauliflower and cook and stir for 5 minutes. Add the chopped tomato and lemon. Season with salt and pepper. Cook for 5 minutes.

ADDITIONS & ALTERNATIVES

Serve with rice. There are full instructions on cooking plain rice on page 292 and Pilau rice on page 310.

TIPS

Prepared garlic is sold in tubes and jars. Just read the tube or jar for the suggested equivalent amount. It keeps for six weeks in the fridge.

LAMB KORMA, A MILD CURRY

Serves 4   ① *Preparation 10 min, Cooking 40 min – Easy*

INGREDIENTS

500 g (1 lb) lamb steak
1 large onion
1 tablespoon oil
3 tablespoons mild curry paste
2 tablespoons dried coconut milk powder
3 tablespoons Greek yoghurt

EQUIPMENT

Sharp knife
Chopping board
Saucepan
Wooden spoon
Set of measuring spoons
Set of measuring cups

DEFROSTING

Defrost lamb in a single layer for four hours at room temperature or overnight in the fridge.

METHOD

The lamb should be lean. Chops are therefore not a good idea unless you can hand pick them.

Cut the lamb in cubes. Peel and chop the onion. Put the oil in the saucepan and heat over a moderate heat. Fry the onion for about three minutes till it is golden, stirring to stop it sticking. Add the lamb and fry for 5 minutes, stirring to keep it from sticking. The outside should be browned. Add the mild curry paste and half a cup (120 ml or $\frac{1}{4}$ pint) water.

Mix the coconut milk with a couple of tablespoons of water. Add to the curry. If you add it to the curry directly it may not dissolve property. Bring back to the boil, then turn the heat down so it is just boiling (simmering). Put a lid on the pan and cook for about 30 minutes. Stir a couple of times. If it gets too dry add a bit of water (a couple of tablespoons at a time).

Just before serving stir in the yoghurt.

ADDITIONS & ALTERNATIVES

Serve with plain rice (page 292).

Use 2 tablespoons of mild curry powder instead of the mild curry paste.

MIXED VEGETABLE CURRY

Serves 4　　　　*① Preparation 10 min, Cooking 25 min – Easy*

INGREDIENTS

2 large potatoes
1 large carrot
1 handful (100g or 4 oz) French beans, runner beans or mange tout
1 courgette

$^1\!/_2$ cauliflower head
3 tablespoons oil
2 teaspoons cumin
2 teaspoons turmeric
Salt
400 g tin plum tomatoes
$^1\!/_2$ teaspoon chilli powder

EQUIPMENT
Sharp knife
Chopping board
Large frying-pan or Wok
Set of measuring spoons
Wooden spoon
Tin opener

METHOD
Peel and dice the potatoes. Peel and slice the carrot. Wash all the other vegetables. Break the cauliflower into 1 cm (half-inch) bits. Cut up the other vegetables.

Heat the oil in the frying-pan. Add the potatoes, carrot, cumin, turmeric and salt, and fry for 5 minutes. Stir to stop it sticking and to coat the potato and carrot evenly. Add the tomatoes and chilli powder and stir for a couple of minutes. Add the rest of the vegetables and stir round. Add enough water to cover the vegetables. Bring to the boil and simmer for 15–20 minutes until potatoes are cooked.

ADDITIONS & ALTERNATIVES
Serve with rice.

Use mild curry powder instead of the spices above.

Use any fresh vegetables that are available. Leave out any you find loathsome, increase the amount of any you particularly like.

DAAL

Serves 2   ⏱ *Preparation 5 min, Cooking 30 mins – Easy*

INGREDIENTS

250 g red split lentils, about $1\frac{1}{2}$ cups
1 teaspoon turmeric
1 teaspoon salt
1 large onion
2 cloves garlic
1 tablespoon oil
1 tablespoon garam masala

EQUIPMENT

Saucepan
Set of measuring spoons
Set of measuring cups
Wooden spoon
Sharp knife
Chopping board
Frying-pan

METHOD

Wash the lentils. Put the lentils in the pan with about 500 ml (1 pint) water and the turmeric and salt. Bring to the boil. Turn down the heat so that the water is just boiling (simmering). Stir from time to time. The object is to get the lentils to a smooth paste. This takes about 30 minutes. It may need more water to stop it sticking.

Peel and slice the onion and garlic. Put the oil in the frying-pan. Fry the onion and the garlic until they are caramelised and dark brown.

When the lentils are smooth, stir in the garam masala, put into a bowl and put the onion and garlic on top.

TIPS

Prepared garlic is sold in tubes and jars. Just read the tube or jar for the suggested equivalent amount. It keeps for six weeks in the fridge.

LAMB OR CHICKEN MADRAS

Serves 4   ① *Preparation 5 min, Cooking 55 min – Moderate (you have to keep an eye on it while it is cooking)*

INGREDIENTS

1 kg (2 lbs) of lamb steak or chicken pieces
1 large onion
2 cloves garlic
3 tablespoons oil
About 2 tablespoons Madras powder or paste (see below)
400 g tin tomatoes
Salt
1–2 tablespoons lemon juice

EQUIPMENT

Sharp knife
Chopping board
Frying-pan
Set of measuring spoons
Wooden spoon
Tin opener

DEFROSTING

Make sure frozen chicken is completely thawed before use. This means leaving it in the fridge overnight, or out of the fridge, covered, for six hours.

METHOD

Cut the lamb or chicken into 2 cm (1 inch) cubes. Peel and chop the onion and the garlic.

Put the oil in a pan. Cook the onion and garlic, stirring so they don't stick. Add the Madras curry powder. Cook for three minutes. Add the chopped lamb pieces or chicken pieces. Fry for five minutes, stirring. Add the mashed-up tinned tomatoes and juice and some salt to taste. Stir and bring to the boil. Turn down the heat and cook gently, stirring from time to time, till the oil comes to the top and the meat is tender. If it gets too dry add a little water, to make thick gravy. Cook for 45 minutes. Add the lemon juice.

ADDITIONS & ALTERNATIVES

Serve with boiled rice and chutney, and Cucumber, Onion or Mint Raita (see page 291).

There are several brands of Madras powder or paste. The exact quantity of these vary but are in the region of 2 tablespoons per kg (2 lb) of meat. Read the packet. There are also cook-in sauces, both in tins and jars. They are OK as a last resort.

TIPS

Madras curry is fairly hot. Keep to the quantity of any powder suggested on the packet the first time you cook it. If it isn't hot enough either increase the amount of Madras powder or add extra chilli. A BAD mistake is to try the taste before it is cooked and add more chilli. As it cooks it gets hotter.

Prepared garlic is sold in tubes and jars. Just read the tube or jar for the suggested equivalent amount. It keeps for six weeks in the fridge.

PILAU RICE

Serves 4   ① *Preparation 10 min, Cooking 30 min – Moderate*

INGREDIENTS
$\frac{1}{2}$ cup almonds
3 tablespoons sunflower oil
3 cups long grain rice
2 medium onions
1 teaspoon ground turmeric
$\frac{1}{4}$ teaspoon saffron
5 cups chicken stock (or water and stock cubes)
1 teaspoon salt
$\frac{1}{4}$ teaspoon of peppercorns
$\frac{1}{4}$ cup sultanas
1 cup cooked peas

EQUIPMENT
Frying-pan
Set of measuring spoons
Sieve
Sharp knife
Chopping board
Set of measuring cups
Large thick-bottomed saucepan with a lid
Wooden spoon
Fork

METHOD
Fry the almonds gently in 1 tablespoon of oil till golden brown.
Take out of the pan. Take the pan off the heat.

Wash and drain the rice. Peel and chop the onions. Heat the
rest of the oil, preferably in a thick-bottomed pan. Fry the onions,
stirring, until golden brown. Add the turmeric, saffron and rice

and stir well. Fry for about five minutes until the rice is golden and coated. Add the stock to the pan and bring to the boil. Add about 1 teaspoon salt and the peppercorns. Stir well. Put a lid on the pan. Turn the heat down so it is just boiling (simmering) and cook for 20 minutes. Don't stir, and if you can handle the stress, don't take the lid off.

Turn off the heat. Take the lid off. Leave to stand for ten minutes, to let the steam out. Loosen the grains with a fork. Add the sultanas, almonds and peas and serve.

ADDITIONS & ALTERNATIVES

Try adding 3 whole cardamom pods and/or a 2 cm (1 inch) cinnamon stick when the stock is added to the rice.

TIKKA BARBECUE

Serves 4   ① *Preparation 5 min, up to a day to stand,*
Cooking 25 min – Easy

INGREDIENTS
8 chicken legs
2 tablespoons oil
1 tablespoon lemon juice (half a lemon)
2 tablespoons Tikka mix powder

EQUIPMENT
Sharp knife
Chopping board
Wooden spoon
Bowl
Set of measuring spoons

METHOD
Slash the chicken legs through to the bone.

Mix the oil, lemon juice and Tikka mix in a bowl. Put the chicken legs in the bowl and stir round till they are covered. It is best to leave this in a fridge overnight, though half an hour will do.

Barbecue or grill for about 25 minutes, turning from time to time.

ADDITIONS & ALTERNATIVES

Serve with French bread and salad.

Use a plastic box with a lid to mix the powder, lemon and oil. Shake it to make sure the legs are covered.

Other chicken bits will do.

SALADS FOR BARBECUES

Recipes for all the following are in the salad chapter. They are all easy, and can be made in quantity. The least trouble and most unusual is the watermelon.

Watermelon & Feta Cheese Salad (page 69)
Greek Salad (page 72)
Coleslaw (page 77)
Chick Pea Salad (page 70)
Pasta Salad (page 79)

MEATS FOR BARBECUES

Burgers (page 288)
Sausages (page 144)
Spare Ribs with Barbecue Sauce (page 273)

FISH FOR BARBECUES

Salmon Steaks wrapped in tin foil
Trout
Sardines

VEGETARIAN OPTIONS

Vegetarian burgers or sausages
Whole Sweet Corn

SAUCES

Fresh Mexican Salsa (page 276)
Barbecue Sauce (page 272)

EASY BULK PARTY FOOD

Make food that is quick and easy.

Recipes for all of the following can be found in the book
Hummus & pitta bread (page 49)
Prawn Dip and crisps (page 47)
Taco chips and Fresh Mexican Salsa (page 276)
Potato Salad (page 82)
Greek Salad (page 72)
Pasta Salad (page 79)
Mini Pizza (page 58)

There are no recipes for the following which require no preparation
French bread and Brie cheese
Grapes
Apples

DRINKS

General

We drink water with most meals. It is also reasonable to offer anyone a non-alcoholic drink, particularly if they are driving. Anyway, a broad exposition on alcohol is well beyond the scope of this book. If you need any instruction, please write to the publishers demanding they commission 'Drinking for Blokes'.

Lager

Lager makes a refreshing drink with curry, Chinese, Italian and Tex-Mex.

Red Wine

Lots of red wines are available. It is traditionally the accompaniment for meat. Some supermarkets are grading wine A to E for how full-bodied they are. A robust Cabernet Sauvignon or Shiraz (Syrah) would be C or D.

Red wine should not be chilled, but served at room temperature.

White Wine

White wine comes from sharp and fruity through creamy or buttery to sweet. It is better served chilled. There are some very good Australian or New Zealand wines. Supermarkets are keen to get your business and often describe the wine well on the label of the bottle.

Some off-licence chains (particularly Oddbins) can be very helpful.

Some supermarkets are grading white wine from 1 (dry) to 6 (sweet). Number 2 is a good place to start with an Australian Chardonay or Semillion. White wine is good with fish and chicken.

Try to avoid the sweetish German wines. Although it is none of our business what you choose to drink, they are probably the most consistently bland and mediocre to poor wines on the market.

Rosé or Rosada

Rosé or Rosada are pink wines. There are several good ones around and a good supermarket or off-licence will know which.

The label often says serve chilled but try it at room temperature, because some have a delicate strawberry or raspberry flavour and chilling kills it dead.

They are thought of as summer wines and are great for picnics or barbecues. They are also good with chicken or salads. They are not very strong so do not go well with highly spiced food like curry.

COLD PUNCH

Serves 15–20   ① *Preparation 5 min – Easy*

INGREDIENTS
1 bunch mint
3 oranges
2 apples
3 lemons
2 litres orange juice
1 litre pineapple juice
1 bottle rum
1 litre fizzy water
1 bag ice

EQUIPMENT
Sharp knife
Chopping board
Juicer for the lemon
Bowl

METHOD
Keep all the ingredients in the fridge till you are ready to make the punch.

Wash and drain the mint. Pull off some leaves. Wash and cut the oranges and apples into slices. Discard the apple core and pips. Extract the juice from the lemon and pour into the bowl. Add the orange juice, fruit, pineapple juice and rum. Stir. Add the mint, fizzy water and ice.

ADDITIONS & ALTERNATIVES
Any carton of fruit juice, such as mango or five fruits can be substituted for the orange or pineapple.

HOT PUNCH OR MULLED WINE

Serves 10   ① *Preparation 10 min, Cooling 10 min – Moderate*

INGREDIENTS
1 whole nutmeg
1 cup sugar
3 sticks cinnamon
3 tablespoons whole cloves
4 lemons
3 oranges
2 bottles red wine

EQUIPMENT
Nutcracker or hammer
Sharp knife
Chopping board
Set of measuring spoons
Set of measuring cups
Large saucepan
Wooden spoon
Sieve
Zester
Juicer
Corkscrew

METHOD
Crush the nutmeg with the nut cracker or hammer – it's easier than it looks. Heat the sugar, nutmeg, cinnamon and cloves in the pan with a cup of water. Boil for about 5 minutes, stirring. Take the pan off the heat. Strain the liquid and throw away the cinnamon, nutmeg and cloves. Put the liquid back in the pan.

Use the zester to take the skin off 2 lemons and 2 oranges. Add to the pan. Extract the juice from the oranges and lemons and add

to the pan. Put the pan back on the heat and heat up. Add the two
bottles of wine. Heat and serve.

ADDITIONS & ALTERNATIVES

This is a drink that is good from Halloween through New Year to
early spring.

Add half a bottle of brandy.

Take it easy.

ALCOHOL FREE PUNCH

Serves 15   ⏱ *Preparation 10 min – Easy*

INGREDIENTS
2 litres (3 pints) strong tea
1 cup sugar
6 lemons
Bunch mint
1 litre (2 pints) dry ginger ale
Bag ice

EQUIPMENT
Kettle
Teapot
Sieve
Large bowl
Set of measuring cups
Sharp knife
Juicer

METHOD
Keep all the ingredients in the fridge till needed. Make the tea. Strain out the leaves. Dissolve the sugar in the tea. Allow the tea to cool, and put in the fridge.

Cut the lemons in half and extract the juice. Wash the mint and pull off some leaves.

Just before serving put all the ingredients in the bowl. Stir. Add the ice and serve.

ADDITIONS & ALTERNATIVES
Use lemonade instead of the ginger ale.

Add some, strawberries, washed and cut in half.

This can be made into an alcoholic punch by adding a bottle of vodka or rum.

INDEX

Flash Cooking For Blokes

**Thanks to all the friends
who have given us recipes
and to our editor, Barbara Boote.**

We use standard measuring cups and spoons in the recipes. The cups are 250 ml, the tablespoons 15 ml and the teaspoons 5ml. Unless otherwise stated they are level measures.

CONTENTS

INTRODUCTION

What makes cooking flash? Well, if you believe a recent survey when more than one person in three put making a sandwich as their top culinary accomplishment, then anything that gets above room temperature must be pretty flash. The next highest achievements were toast, which I suppose fits the bill, and cereal. And this was among people who said they knew how to cook. Now we are not knocking making a sandwich, and some can be pretty elaborate, (we even included recipes for sandwiches in our first book) but we think you can take a step beyond that. When I started out, one of the first things I learnt to make was profiteroles; the little pastry balls with chocolate sauce. They're not difficult to do and if you can cook them it doesn't matter what else you do, because when you say you made them yourself you'll be up there with Superman. It doesn't matter that it's the only thing you can make because it's so flash. But don't stop at just one recipe, there are lots like that in this book. By now it has become obvious that one thing we are talking about is cooking to impress. Think about someone's birthday, or cooking something to make up for forgetting their birthday, a big date, or any other special occasion. You could make some of these recipes every day and every one of them is beyond a bowl of cereal.

There is still no need to panic. We have kept true to our principles and you need never have cooked anything before to use this book. There are sections on 'how to' basics, ingredients and tools. They are at the back of the book.

Just like DIY there is a point where you progress into the purchase of power tools, sometimes because you like the power tools
and sometimes because they help. We have only included them
because they help. We have avoided them before, but now a few of
the dishes are much easier to make if you have a food processor or
liquidiser.

So just what is flash? Some of the recipes in this book are more
unusual and exotic; some take a little more effort, some are easy
but seem, because of their ingredients, to be exotic. We've included
some Balti and Japanese dishes and that show-stopper, Black
Forest Gateau. We have responded to your letters and put in some
requests. We've included cakes and biscuits and extra chocolate
recipes. Because everyone loves chocolate, don't they? You will find
liquid food, both with and without alcohol. Like the other 'Cooking
for Blokes' books there are some things which do not even need
cooking, we make use of packets, tins and you still do not need a set
of scales. To get you started we have broken all the rules and put the
desserts at the front of the book, but to encourage you to stay the
course we have put the drinks at the end.

Remember what we said, it may be special food but it is so easy
anyone can make it. Have a go at one of the dishes. Practice makes
perfect. Don't get obsessive and fussy like one person we heard
about who was following a recipe (not one of ours) that said cut
something into 1 cm chunks and who used a ruler to help with the
accuracy. This is cooking, not brain surgery. Cook, eat and enjoy.

HOW HOT IS YOUR OVEN?

OVENS AND TEMPERATURES

Although every recipe that needs an oven has got the correct cooking time and oven temperature in it, it has become somewhat of a tradition to start a cookbook with the equivalent temperatures for different kinds of oven and to tell the reader that all cooking appliances like people are individual and variable and therefore the following temperature equivalents are approximate only. We hope you enjoy this piece of tradition, and that you find the rest of the book even more relevant to your life. Approximate equivalent temperatures are shown below for different ovens.

140° C, 275° F, Gas mark 1
150° C, 300° F, Gas mark 2
170° C, 325° F, Gas mark 3
180° C, 350° F, Gas mark 4
190° C, 375° F, Gas mark 5
200° C, 400° F, Gas mark 6
220° C, 425° F, Gas mark 7
230° C, 450° F, Gas mark 8
240° C, 475° F, Gas mark 9

Gas ovens and fan-assisted ovens get hotter quicker than standard electric ones.

In most ovens the top is hotter than the bottom. Most things are best cooked in the middle. Roast potatoes and vegetables are best cooked at the top if you like them crispy.

Fan-assisted ovens have less of a difference between top and bottom and need different cooking times. Please refer to your instruction book.

DEVILISH DESSERTS

Are you ready for a baptism of fire? Actually, the things that are on fire are in the middle of the chapter, but we have started off with probably the three most difficult recipes in the chapter. If you can do them you will be able to cook anything else in this entire book. If you cannot, skip them for now and come back when you are ready. Mostly these are dishes for special occasions. A lot can be made in advance. This means that if it all goes horribly wrong you will still be able to go out and buy some ice cream. You can make the chocolate sauce (see page 9) to pour on top.

TARTE TATIN

Serves 4   ① *Preparation 15 min, Cooking 35 min – Easy*

This French apple tart is cooked upside down with the pastry on top. You turn it over and get these neatly arranged apple pieces in a solid glossy sauce. One of the best things is that you can make this beforehand, so you can relax and not spend all your time stressed out in the kitchen.

INGREDIENTS
1 lemon
5 eating apples, not cookers

3 rounded tablespoons butter (75 g, 3 oz)
6 level tablespoons sugar (75 g, 3 oz)
$1/2 \times 450$ g pack ready-rolled puff pastry

EQUIPMENT
Lemon juicer
Sharp knife
Chopping board
Vegetable peeler
Apple corer
Set of measuring spoons
20 cm (8 in) frying-pan. You need a frying-pan that can go in the oven, so not one with a wooden or plastic handle. A cast iron one is best.
Wooden spoon
Palette knife
Fork

DEFROSTING
Thaw frozen pastry according to the instructions on the packet. 4 hours in the fridge seems typical.

METHOD
Preheat the oven to 190° C, 375° F, Gas mark 5. Juice the lemon. Peel, core and cut the apples into quarters. Melt the butter in the pan on a moderate heat. Add the sugar and fry gently until the sugar has melted. Add the apples, arranging them in circles with rounded sides up, and fry for 5 minutes. Turn the apple pieces over once, until golden and covered in caramel. Add the lemon juice and cook for another 3 minutes.

Take off the heat and rearrange the apples so that the rounded sides are facing down and the pointed edges upwards.

Meanwhile, unroll the pastry. Cover the apples with the pastry,

2

and then trim and carefully tuck the edges down the inside of the pan with a palette knife and not your fingers because it will be hot. Prick holes in the pastry with a fork. Cook in the preheated oven for 25 minutes until the pastry is cooked.

Let it cool for a few minutes then loosen the edges with a palette knife. Turn it out by putting a plate on top and turning the whole thing over. Push any rebellious bits of apple back into place. Do not let it cool completely or it will not come out.

ADDITIONS & ALTERNATIVES
Serve with cream, yoghurt or ice cream.

Use a block of prepared pastry and roll it yourself. Full instructions are in the 'How to' chapter (see page 336).

BLACK FOREST GATEAU

Serves 4 to 6
① Preparation 25 min, Cooking 20 min – Moderate

One of the classic desserts. Although it looks daunting it is mostly simple steps and easy assembly. This recipe bears little resemblance to the ones you can buy. For a start it uses no flour in the sponge so it is unbelievably light. It can be made some time before you eat it but leave the cream topping to the last minute.

INGREDIENTS
1 teaspoon sunflower oil
6 large eggs
11 level tablespoons caster sugar (just less than 3/4 cup)
4 tablespoons cocoa powder
1 medium carton (284 ml, 10 fl oz) double cream
400 g tin morello cherries

3

2 tablespoons rum
50 g bar dark chocolate

EQUIPMENT
2 × 20 cm (8 in) sponge tins
Greaseproof paper
Oil or pastry brush (or screwed up kitchen paper)
2 cups
2 bowls
Egg separator
Tablespoon
Set of measuring spoons
Whisk or hand mixer
Sieve
Tin opener
Cherry stoner (optional)
Plate
Cake rack
Grater

METHOD
Preheat the oven to 180° C, 350° F, Gas mark 4. Line the bottom of each sponge tin with a circle of greaseproof paper and brush the tin and paper lightly with oil.

Separate the eggs. It is important not to get any yolk in with the whites as they will not whisk up properly. Break the eggs one at a time into a cup and pick out any bits of shell. Hold the egg separator over a bowl. Put the eggs one at a time into the egg separator and let the white fall away into the bowl beneath. Put the yolks into a bowl. Or break the eggs one at a time into a cup and then lift out the yolk with a large spoon and put it in a small bowl. Empty the egg white out and repeat until all the eggs are done. Add 10 tablespoons of caster sugar to the yolks. Whisk until they start to go pale and thicken. Put the cocoa into a sieve and shake it through into the mixture then fold in with a metal spoon.

Whisk the egg whites until stiff. Add to the cocoa and yolks. Add a spoonful first and fold in, then fold in the rest. Put the mixture in the cake tins and gently smooth the tops flat. Bake in the preheated oven for 15 to 20 minutes until the tops are firm and springy to the touch. Turn out the cakes onto a rack to cool. When only slightly warm peel off the greaseproof paper.

When ready to serve, whip the cream and the remaining tablespoon of sugar in a clean bowl until floppy (firmer than when you started but not solid).

Open the tin of morello cherries and drain, keeping 3 tablespoons of juice in a cup. Add the rum to the juice. Take the stones out of the cherries. Some garlic crushers have a device on the handle for getting the stones out of olives and this will do. Keep 12 of the least mangled to put on top. Slice the rest.

Put one of the cakes on a plate. Sprinkle the juice on. Add about $1/3$ of the cream followed by the sliced cherries. Put the other cake on top. Spread the rest of the cream over the cake, arrange the cherries round the top and grate the chocolate on top.

TIPS
You can separate the yolks by cracking the egg in half and then juggling the egg from one eggshell half to the other but this takes practice. The downside is that the yolk can get popped on the shell, and of course your fingers tend to get covered with egg white.

'Folding in' is using a spoon or palette knife to gently combine. Not to be confused with whisking which gets lots of air in to the mixture by beating, which is vigorous. Folding in stops you losing the little bubbles you have spent all the effort trying to incorporate into the mixture beforehand.

PROFITEROLES

Serves 4 (4 profiteroles each)
① Preparation 30 min, Cooking 20 min – Easy

What seems like a very difficult dish is easy if you take it a step at a time. These are as good as almost any restaurant can provide. For a big show arrange them in a pile for serving.

METHOD
Make the choux pastry balls. Make the vanilla cream while they are cooking. When cool put about a teaspoon of cream inside each ball. Make the chocolate sauce and pour over the top just before serving. All the recipes are below.

CHOUX PASTRY

INGREDIENTS
$^1/_2$ cup plain flour (75 g, 3 oz)
$^1/_4$ teaspoon salt
$^1/_2$ cup water (125 ml)
4 level tablespoons unsalted butter (60 g, 2 oz)
2 eggs

EQUIPMENT
Sieve
Greaseproof paper
Set of measuring cups
Set of measuring spoons
Saucepan
Wooden spoon

6

Cup
Baking sheet
Cake rack

METHOD
Preheat the oven to 190° C, 375° F, Gas mark 5. Sift the flour and
salt on to the greaseproof paper. Put the water and butter in the
saucepan on a low heat until the butter has melted. Bring the water
to the boil. Take off the heat, and shoot all the flour off the paper
into the pan. Stir the mixture vigorously over a medium heat until
it forms a ball that comes away cleanly from the sides of the pan.
Take off the heat and leave to cool for a few minutes.

Break an egg into a cup and pick out any bits of shell. Add to
the pan, beating with a spoon to incorporate the egg thoroughly.
Repeat with the other egg.

Put 16 teaspoonfuls of the pastry on an ungreased baking sheet.
Leave a decent gap between them as they will end up about 3 to 4
times bigger across. Bake in the preheated oven for 20 minutes.
Cool on a rack.

VANILLA CREAM

Enough for 16 profiteroles
① *Preparation 25 min, Cooking 4 min – Easy*

INGREDIENTS
6 eggs
$^1/_2$ cup sugar (125 g, 4 oz)
5 level tablespoons flour (40 g, $1^1/_2$ oz)
$^1/_4$ teaspoon salt
2 cups milk (500 ml, 1 pint)
5 drops vanilla essence

EQUIPMENT

Egg separator
2 cups
2 bowls
Tablespoon
Fork
Set of measuring cups
Set of measuring spoons
Saucepan
Wooden spoon
Whisk

METHOD

Separate the eggs. Break the eggs one at a time into a cup and pick out any bits of shell. Hold the egg separator over a cup. Put the eggs one at a time into the egg separator and let the white fall away into the cup beneath. Put the yolks into the bowl. Keep about 2 egg whites in another bowl. Or break the eggs one at a time into a cup and then lift out the yolk with a large spoon and put it in a small bowl. Empty the egg white out and repeat until all the eggs are done.

Mix the sugar and egg yolks together with a spoon, beating until the mixture is thick and cream-coloured. Gradually work in the flour, and season with a pinch of salt.

Heat the milk with the vanilla essence to boiling point, stirring constantly. Slowly pour the milk into the egg mixture, stirring. Put the mixture back into the saucepan. Stir vigorously and bring to the boil, then turn down the heat until it is just boiling (simmering). Cook for 2 minutes then remove from the heat. Leave the mixture to cool, stirring from time to time. Whisk the egg whites until stiff and fold into the cream before it cools.

8

TIPS

You can separate the yolks by cracking the egg in half and then juggling the egg from one eggshell half to the other but this takes practice. The downside is that the yolk can get popped on the shell, and of course your fingers tend to get covered with egg white.

You can use a medium carton (284 ml, 10 fl oz) of double cream whipped until stiff with 2 tablespoons of caster sugar instead of the vanilla cream.

CHOCOLATE SAUCE

Enough for 16 profiteroles
① Preparation 5 min, Cooking 5 min – Easy

Although this sauce is for the profiteroles it can transform ice cream and shop-bought chocolate sponge cake.

INGREDIENTS
1 teaspoon cornflour
$^1/_2$ cup water (125 ml, 4 fl oz)
150 g bar plain chocolate
1 rounded tablespoon butter (25 g, 1 oz)

EQUIPMENT
Cup
Set of measuring spoons
Spoon
Heat resistant glass bowl (e.g. Pyrex)
Saucepan
Set of measuring cups
Wooden spoon

METHOD
Mix the cornflour in 1 tablespoon of the water in the cup to make a thin paste. Put the bowl on top of the saucepan of hot water (not boiling) over a low heat. This stops the mixture from getting too hot, but steam-heats it through the bowl. Add the chocolate and butter and then the water. Leave until melted, then add the cornflour mixture and stir to thicken.

RICH CHOCOLATE POT

Serves 4   ① *Preparation 2 min, Cooking 7 min – Easy*

Think ahead. This needs to stand in the fridge for 3 or 4 hours before serving.

The fastest, richest chocolate dessert around. Just do not be tempted to make or eat too much.

INGREDIENTS
200 g dark chocolate
1 medium carton (284 ml, 10 fl oz) single cream
1 egg
1 drop vanilla essence
Pinch of salt

EQUIPMENT
Bowl
Saucepan
Wooden spoon

METHOD

Break the chocolate into pieces and put into the bowl. Warm the cream to boiling point. Pour over the chocolate and leave for 5 minutes for the chocolate to melt.

Break the egg into a cup and pick out any pieces of shell. Lightly beat the egg with a fork. Add the egg, vanilla and salt to the chocolate and cream in the bowl. Mix with a fork until smooth. Pour into serving cups, or glasses and leave to cool in the fridge for 3 or 4 hours.

ADDITIONS & ALTERNATIVES

Put a teaspoon of Cointreau, rum or whisky and some flaked chocolate on top.

Serve with lightly whipped cream if required.

You can make a version with white chocolate instead of the dark chocolate. The white chocolate version will be a little different in texture. It makes a really delicious and very impressive dessert if you mix the two kinds of chocolate in a glass in layers.

For the best results with the dark chocolate version buy the best cooking chocolate (with a minimum of 70% cocoa solids).

CHOCOLATE MOUSSE

Serves 2 to 4
⏱ Preparation 15 min, Melting 10 min — Moderate

Think ahead. This needs to stand in the fridge for 4 hours before serving.

A classic of our time and utterly smooth, delicious and chocolatey with no artificial additives. What more can you ask from a chocolate mousse. Just make sure you let it cool enough before you add the eggs.

INGREDIENTS

150 g plain chocolate
1 tablespoon butter
2 tablespoons black coffee
1 teaspoon rum
3 eggs

EQUIPMENT

2 bowls
Egg separator
2 cups
Saucepan
Wooden spoon
Set of measuring cups
Set of measuring spoons
Egg whisk
4 ramekins or serving bowl

METHOD

The secret of this recipe is to make sure the mixture never gets too hot so that the eggs cook. Otherwise you will end up with chocolate scrambled egg. What you do is use a heatproof glass bowl which can sit on top of a saucepan of boiling water. Break up the chocolate and put it in the bowl with the butter. Leave to melt, then add the coffee and rum and stir in. Take the melted chocolate off the heat.

Break the eggs one at a time into a cup and pick out any bits of shell. Hold the egg separator over another cup and let the white fall into the cup beneath. Put the yolks into the bowl with the chocolate and gently but thoroughly mix in.

Put the egg whites in the other bowl and whisk until stiff while the chocolate mixture is cooling down. Add a tablespoon of whisked egg white to the chocolate and stir in. This helps break up the mixture so that the rest of the egg whites go in easily. Fold the egg whites into the chocolate mixture. Put the mixture into ramekins or a serving bowl and chill in the fridge for at least 4 hours.

ADDITIONS & ALTERNATIVES

Serve with a little cream.

Try brandy or whisky instead of rum.

TIPS

A ramekin is a small circular pot roughly 5 cm (2 in) tall, and 8 cm (3 in) across. They are good for making individual desserts such as chocolate mousse or cream caramel.

You can separate the yolks by cracking the egg in half and then juggling the egg from one eggshell half to the other, but this takes practice. The downside is that the yolk can get popped on the shell, and of course your fingers tend to get covered with egg white. Another method is to break the egg into a cup and then try to lift the yolk out with a tablespoon.

CHESTNUT MOUSSE

Serves 4   ① *Preparation 10 min – Easy*

Think ahead: this needs to chill for 6 hours.

You can prepare this well ahead of the time you need it. One of the mistakes people make when they are starting to cook is doing things which need to be timed to the nearest minute and then seeing the timings going wrong, leading to kitchen distress.

INGREDIENTS

400 g tin unsweetened chestnut purée
$^1/_2$ cup caster sugar (100 g, 4 oz)
2 tablespoons rum
$^1/_2$ teaspoon dried ginger
250 g tub thick Greek yoghurt

EQUIPMENT

Tin opener
Fork
Food processor or liquidiser (optional) or whisk or electric hand
blender and bowl
Set of measuring cups
Set of measuring spoons
4 serving bowls

METHOD

Open the tin of chestnut purée and empty it into the processor,
liquidiser or mixing bowl. Add the sugar, rum and ginger and
blend in the processor or with the whisk. Add the yoghurt and mix
in thoroughly.

Divide between the bowls. Chill for 6 hours.

ADDITIONS & ALTERNATIVES

Serve with brandy snaps
Try cinnamon instead of ginger.

FLAMING CHESTNUT PANCAKES

Serves 4   ① *Preparation 10 min, Cooking 10 min – Easy*

Baby you can light my fire. A lot of the effect is lost if this is served in daylight, but of course, it does not affect the taste.

INGREDIENTS
500 g carton crème fraîche
$^1/_2$ x 400 g tin chestnut purée
4 tablespoons caster sugar
1 teaspoon vanilla extract or essence
1 pack 12 to 16 small, ready-made crêpes or pancakes
3 tablespoons rum (an option for the brave)

EQUIPMENT
Bowl
Whisk
Tin opener
Set of measuring spoons
Heatproof dish
Sieve
Box of matches

METHOD
Beat the crème fraîche in the bowl. Open the tin of chestnut purée and add half of it to the mixture. Mix in 2 tablespoons of the sugar and the vanilla essence.

Spread 1 to 2 tablespoons of the mixture on each pancake. Fold in quarters. Either arrange on individual heatproof plates or one large dish. Sieve the remaining sugar over the top and then cook under the grill until browned. Heat the rum, set it alight and pour onto the pancakes. It will not light if you pour it on the pancakes first.

ADDITIONS & ALTERNATIVES

Eyebrow watch. People of a nervous disposition can leave out the rum or just not set light to it.

Substitute 3 tablespoons of Kahlua (coffee liqueur) for the rum, though this will not burn.

Try making your own pancakes. Use a bought batter mix and add a couple of tablespoons of sugar and a beaten egg. Either cook in a small 15 cm (6 in) frying-pan smeared with a little butter or use an ordinary sized one and cut into halves. I mean, who really has a 15 cm frying-pan just for crêpes?

FLAMBÉ RUM OMELETTE

Serves 4   ① *Preparation 15 min, Cooking 5 min – Easy*

Another exciting ignite-and-stand-back recipe for all those who wish to be ultra, ultra flash. But remember to watch out for those eyebrows.

INGREDIENTS
6 eggs
$^1/_4$ teaspoon salt
2 tablespoons butter
4 tablespoons heated apricot jam
3 tablespoons caster sugar
4 tablespoons heated rum

EQUIPMENT
Bowl
Set of measuring spoons
Whisk
Wooden spoon

Small saucepan
Small frying-pan or omelette pan
Fork
Box of matches

METHOD

Break the eggs into a bowl and pick out any bits of shell. Add the salt and 2 tablespoons sugar and beat the eggs with a whisk. Melt the jam in the saucepan stirring with the wooden spoon.

Put the butter in the frying-pan and heat until sizzling. Add the eggs. Shake the pan to stop it sticking and stir round the surface with the back of a fork. Cook for 3 to 5 minutes until just set. Do not turn over. You only cook one side. Spread the jam on top and then slide the omelette onto a plate. Fold in half. Sprinkle the sugar on. Warm the rum, light it and pour on top.

ADDITIONS & ALTERNATIVES

Try marmalade and Cointreau instead of the apricot jam and rum.

Try Nutella instead of the jam, but stick to the rum for the flames.

SWEET APPLE OMELETTE

Serves 4   ① *Preparation 10 min, Cooking 10 min – Easy*

A simple and fluffy apple dessert which can be done in a hurry.

INGREDIENTS

6 eggs
$^1/_4$ teaspoon salt
5 tablespoons caster sugar
2 apples

5 tablespoons butter
3 tablespoons brandy
3 tablespoons crème fraîche

EQUIPMENT
Bowl
Set of measuring spoons
Whisk
Vegetable peeler
Apple corer
Sharp knife
Chopping board
Saucepan
Wooden spoon
Small frying-pan or omelette pan
Fork

METHOD
Break the eggs into a bowl and pick out any bits of shell. Add the salt and 2 tablespoons of the sugar and beat the eggs with a whisk. Peel, core and slice the apples.

Put 2 tablespoons of butter in the saucepan. Heat until sizzling. Add the apples and fry for about 3 minutes on each side until browned. Add 2 tablespoons of the sugar, the brandy and crème fraîche and stir with the wooden spoon.

Put the rest of the butter in the frying-pan. Heat until sizzling. Add the eggs. Shake the pan to stop it sticking and stir round the surface with the back of a fork. Cook for 3 to 5 minutes until just set. Do not turn over. You only cook one side. Slide the omelette onto a plate. Spread the apple mixture on top. Fold in half. Sprinkle with the remaining tablespoon of sugar and serve.

ADDITIONS & ALTERNATIVES

Serve with crème fraîche.

Try blueberries instead of apples. Just heat them briefly in 1 tablespoon of butter then continue as before.

Try pears instead of apples and treat them in exactly the same way as the apples.

IRISH APPLES

Serves 4   ⏲ *Preparation 15 min, Cooking 25 min – Easy*

This is baked apples in a pastry coat with whiskey at its core. A sophisticated baked apple for consenting adults.

INGREDIENTS
1 lemon
3 rounded tablespoons butter
2 tablespoons honey
3 tablespoons Irish whiskey
4 apples
450 g pack ready-rolled puff pastry

EQUIPMENT
Zester or grater
Sharp knife
Chopping board
Set of measuring spoons
Mixing bowl
Vegetable peeler
Apple corer
Spoon
Oven-proof dish

DEFROSTING
Thaw frozen pastry according to the instructions on the packet.
4 hours in the fridge seems typical.

METHOD
Preheat the oven to 180° C, 350° F, Gas mark 4. Zest or grate
the lemon peel, or peel and cut into thin little strips. Mix the peel,
butter, honey and whiskey in a bowl. Peel and core the apples. Fill
the apples with the mixture.

Unroll the pastry and cut into 4 pieces. Wrap each apple in the
pastry. Pastry is fairly flexible so you can push it into place. If it
tears, patch it with a spare bit, moistening with water to make sure
it sticks.

Put the apples in the oven-proof dish and cook for 25 minutes.

ADDITIONS & ALTERNATIVES
Use a block of prepared pastry and roll it yourself. Full instructions
are in the 'How to' chapter (see page 336).

APPLE TART

Serves 4   ① *Preparation 25 min, Cooking 40 min – Easy*

A really classic dish jazzed up with a puffy base and a crunchy
almond top.

INGREDIENTS
6 eating apples
2 tablespoons lemon juice
$^1/_2 \times$ 250 g pack butter
1 cup flour (100 g, 4 oz)
1 cup caster sugar (225 g, 8 oz)

100 g pack chopped almonds
2 drops vanilla extract or essence
2 teaspoons ground cinnamon
450 g pack ready-rolled puff pastry

EQUIPMENT

Vegetable peeler
Apple corer
Sharp knife
Chopping board
Bowl
Set of measuring spoons
Set of measuring cups
Mixing bowl
25 cm (10 in) pie dish

DEFROSTING

Thaw frozen pastry according to the instructions on the packet. 4 hours in the fridge seems typical.

METHOD

Preheat the oven to 200° C, 400° F, Gas mark 6. Peel, core and thinly slice the apples and put in a bowl. Sprinkle with the lemon juice. Cut the butter in small pieces. Put the butter in the mixing bowl with the flour, sugar, almonds, vanilla essence and cinnamon. Use your fingers to mix together until the mixture looks like breadcrumbs.

Unroll the pastry. Grease the pie dish and then line with the pastry. Pastry is fairly flexible so you can push it into place. If it tears, patch it with a spare bit, moistening with water to make sure it sticks. Pastry shrinks when it cooks so trim it 1 cm ($^1/_2$ in) above the top of the rim.

Next put the apples in the dish followed by the flour and sugar

21

mixture. Bake in the preheated oven for 40 minutes, until the apples and pastry are cooked and the flour mixture is golden and a little crunchy.

ADDITIONS & ALTERNATIVES

Serve with cream, yoghurt, ice cream or custard.

Use a block of prepared pastry and roll it yourself. Full instructions are in the 'How to' chapter (see page 336).

ORANGE TART

Serves 4   ① *Preparation 15 min, Cooking 25 min – Easy*

A simple and unusual tart. The effect is enhanced by the attractive arrangement of the oranges.

INGREDIENTS

4 unwaxed oranges, preferably organic
About $1/_2$ jar apricot jam (250 g, 8 oz)
Blob of butter or margarine to grease the tart tin
$1/_2$ × 450 g pack ready-rolled shortcrust pastry

EQUIPMENT

Sharp knife
Chopping board
Small saucepan
Set of measuring spoons
25 cm (10 in) tart tin
Brush

DEFROSTING

Thaw frozen pastry according to the instructions on the packet. 4 hours in the fridge seems typical.

METHOD

Preheat the oven to 200° C, 400° F, Gas mark 6. Wash and thinly slice the oranges. Dig out the pips. Put the jam in the saucepan and melt over a low heat.

Unroll the pastry. Grease the tart tin and then line with the pastry. Pastry is fairly flexible so you can push it into place. If it tears, patch it with a spare bit, moistening with water to make sure it sticks. Pastry shrinks when it cooks so trim it 1 cm ($^1/_2$ in) above the top of the rim.

Pour half the warmed jam into the uncooked pastry case and spread with the back of a spoon. Lay the orange slices evenly on top of the jam, so they overlap. Brush with the rest of the jam. Bake in the preheated oven for 25 minutes.

ADDITIONS & ALTERNATIVES

Serve with custard, ice cream, crème fraîche or cream.

Use a block of prepared pastry and roll it yourself. Full instructions are in the 'How to' chapter (see page 336).

TIPS

A tart tin has low sides and is generally metal, sometimes with fluted edges. Get one with a base that lifts out and straight sides if you can.

FIGS IN BRANDY

Serves 4   ① *Preparation 5 min, Cooking 25 min – Easy*

It is hard to believe that something so easy could be so good. It is almost wicked to take the credit for it, but you will just have to.

INGREDIENTS
8 ripe fresh figs
8 tablespoons brandy
2 tablespoons brown sugar
$^1/_2$ teaspoon grated nutmeg

EQUIPMENT
Sharp knife
Chopping board
Set of measuring spoons
Oven-proof dish
Aluminium foil

METHOD
Preheat the oven to 180° C, 350° F, Gas mark 4. Rinse the figs and cut a cross in the top. Put in the oven-proof dish. Add the brandy and sprinkle with the sugar and nutmeg, preferably grated fresh. Cover the dish with foil and cook in the preheated oven for 25 minutes. Serve with some of the cooking juice spooned over the figs.

ADDITIONS & ALTERNATIVES
Serve with yoghurt, crème fraîche or cream.
   Try cooking the figs in port or Cointreau instead of brandy.

LEMON SPONGE PUDDING

Serves 4   ① *Preparation 25 min, Cooking 25 min – Easy*

What should happen is that the sponge rises to the top and the lemon sauce ends up underneath. Somehow they pass each other in the oven. If you have a glass-fronted oven and you make this in a Pyrex bowl you could watch it and tell us how it is done.

INGREDIENTS

1 lemon
2 eggs
2 rounded tablespoons soft margarine, plus extra for greasing
8 level tablespoons caster sugar (100 g)
6 level tablespoons self-raising flour (50 g)
$^1/_2$ cup water

EQUIPMENT

1 litre oven-proof bowl
Zester or grater
Sharp knife
Chopping board
Juicer
Egg separator or a cup and a spoon
2 cups
Set of measuring spoons
2 bowls
Whisk or hand mixer
Spoon

METHOD

Preheat the oven to 180° C, 350° F, Gas mark 4. Grease the bowl. Zest or grate the lemon, or peel and cut into little strips. Juice the lemon. Separate the eggs. Break the eggs one at a time into a cup and pick out any bits of shell. Hold the egg separator over a cup. Put the eggs one at a time into the egg separator and let the white fall away into the cup beneath. Put the yolks into the bowl. If you do not have the luxury of an egg separator break the eggs one at a time into a cup and then lift out the yolk with a large spoon. Add the lemon juice and rind, margarine, sugar, flour and water. Whisk until smooth, about 3 minutes.

Put the egg whites in another bowl and whisk until fairly stiff. Add a tablespoonful to the lemon mixture and fold in, then fold in the rest. Put in the greased bowl and cook in the preheated oven for 25 minutes.

ADDITIONS & ALTERNATIVES
Serve with custard.

You can separate the yolks by cracking the egg in half and then juggling the egg from one eggshell half to the other but this takes practice. The downside is that the yolk can get popped on the shell, and of course your fingers tend to get covered with egg white. Another method is to break the egg into a cup and then to lift the yolks out with a tablespoon.

PAPAYA PUDDING

Serves 4   ⏱ *Preparation 10 min, Cooking 5 min – Easy*

Needs to cool for 3 hours.

This is an exotic fruit dessert that would go well after a heavy main course or after anything Asian.

INGREDIENTS

3 oranges
1 lime
1 very large or two medium papaya
$^1/_2$ cup sugar
3 tablespoons cornflour
$^1/_4$ teaspoon salt
4 strawberries
4 mint leaves

EQUIPMENT

Sharp knife
Chopping board
Juicer
Spoon
Food processor or liquidiser (optional)
Bowl
Fork
Sieve
Set of measuring cups
Set of measuring spoons
Saucepan
Wooden spoon
Bowl
Individual serving bowls or glasses

METHOD

Juice the oranges and lime. Cut the papaya in half and scoop out the seeds with a spoon. Peel and chop roughly. Put the papaya in the liquidiser or food processor and blend until it is smooth. If you do not have a processor press it through a sieve with the back of a spoon after mixing it well in a bowl with a fork. Mix the sugar, cornflour and salt in the saucepan. Gradually add the juice. Add the papaya. Bring to the boil, stirring constantly, then turn down the heat until it is just boiling (simmering) and cook for 3 minutes, stirring.

Allow to cool and then put in a covered bowl in the fridge for 3 hours. Stir round and put into individual glasses. Before serving put a strawberry and a mint leaf on top of each one.

STUPENDOUS SALADS

Some of these salads are meals in themselves and some only accompaniments. If you are going for the Black Forest Gateau as your dessert then think light, think salad. Again, you can make a lot of these in advance. So you could have done all your cooking long before you have to eat, and be able to give your full attention to your guest or guests.

CHILLED AVOCADO & MELON SALAD

Serves 4 to 6   ① *Preparation 10 min, Chilling 1 hr – Easy*

This is a cool, fresh salad combining the firm sweetness of the melon with the soft yielding flesh of the avocado. The bite of the dressing with its hint of chilli is the final touch. I think I will have to go and lie down just thinking about it.

INGREDIENTS
2 avocado pears
2 oranges
$^1/_2$ ripe honeydew melon
1 spring onion
2 tablespoons olive oil
1 tablespoon wine vinegar

$^{1}/_{4}$ teaspoon chilli powder
$^{1}/_{2}$ teaspoon salt
Freshly ground black pepper

EQUIPMENT
Sharp knife
Chopping board
Set of measuring spoons
Bowl
Small bowl and whisk or jam jar with tight-fitting lid

METHOD
Peel and slice the avocados. Peel and thinly slice the oranges. Scrape the seeds from the melon. Peel and cut into chunks. Clean and prepare the spring onion. Cut the root end off, trim the leaves. Peel off and discard any dried up or slimy leaves. Chop into thin slices.

Mix the spring onion, oil, vinegar, chilli, salt and pepper. You can whisk them together in a bowl or put them all together in a jam jar with a tight-fitting lid and shake until mixed. Mix the fruit and dressing in a bowl and preferably put in the fridge for an hour before serving.

ADDITIONS & ALTERNATIVES
This goes well with grilled or barbecued chicken or meat and can be made in bulk.

You can increase the amount of chilli to about $^{1}/_{2}$ teaspoon if you prefer.

GREEN PEPPER & TOMATO SALAD

Serves 4   ① *Preparation 10 min, Cooking 35 min – Easy*

A Basque-style salad combining the tastes of sweet roasted peppers and slightly bitter olives. Great as a side salad or a starter.

INGREDIENTS
3 medium green peppers
4 small tomatoes
10 large green olives
1 teaspoon salt
4 tablespoons olive oil
2 tablespoons red wine vinegar

EQUIPMENT
Oven-proof dish
Sharp knife
Chopping board
Set of measuring cups
Set of measuring spoons

METHOD
Put the peppers in an oven-proof dish. Roast for 35 minutes at 190° C, 375° F, Gas mark 5, turning them halfway through. Cut out the core and seeds and discard. Skin and finely slice the peppers. Cube the tomatoes. Stone and chop the olives.

Put the pepper strips on a plate and sprinkle with salt. Arrange the tomatoes on top and then the chopped olives. Add a little more salt. Drizzle with the oil and vinegar when ready to serve.

DATE & APPLE SALAD

Serves 4   ① *Preparation 10 min – Easy*

This salad combines different textures and tastes. The crunchy apple and lettuce go really well with the nuts.

INGREDIENTS
15 fresh dates
1 heaped tablespoon walnut pieces, about 25 to 50 g (1 to 2 oz)
$^1/_2$ iceberg lettuce
2 red-skinned eating apples
Juice of $^1/_2$ lemon
$^1/_2$ cup mayonnaise (page 284)
2 tablespoons yoghurt

EQUIPMENT
Sharp knife
Chopping board
Apple corer
Lemon juicer
Small bowls or plates
Bowl
Set of measuring spoons
Spoon

METHOD
Stone and chop the dates. Chop the walnuts. Wash and shred the lettuce. Core and slice the apples. Juice the lemon. Coat the apples in the lemon juice. Mix the mayonnaise and yoghurt together in a large bowl. Add the dates, walnuts, and apples and stir until coated with the mayonnaise. Serve on a pile of shredded lettuce.

ADDITIONS & ALTERNATIVES
Use ready-made mayonnaise.

ORANGE & OLIVE SALAD

Serves 4   ① *Preparation 15 min, Chilling 2 hours – Easy*

A mildly alcoholic salad for hot weather.

INGREDIENTS
4 large oranges
8 tablespoons ($^1/_2$ cup) olive oil
4 tablespoons dry sherry
15 g pack mint
Salt and freshly ground black pepper
100 g (4 oz) pitted black olives
1 tablespoon raisins

EQUIPMENT
Sharp knife
Juicer
Chopping board
Set of measuring cups
Set of measuring spoons
Bowl
Small bowl and whisk or jam jar with tight-fitting lid

METHOD
Thinly slice the rind from 1 orange and cut the peel into matchstick strips. Juice the orange. Wash, shake dry and finely chop enough mint to make about 1 tablespoonful. Keep the rest for garnish. Mix the oil, orange juice, sherry, strips of orange peel, chopped mint,

salt and pepper in a bowl and whisk, or put them all together in a jam jar with a tight-fitting lid and shake until mixed.

Peel the remaining 3 oranges and slice. Put the orange slices in overlapping rings on a serving plate. Scatter the olives and raisins over them. Add about $^1/_2$ the prepared dressing. Cover and chill for 2 hours. Add the remaining dressing. Garnish with a few mint sprigs just before serving.

COURGETTE SALAD

Serves 4   ① *Preparation 15 min, Cooking 20 min – Easy*

This salad uses cooked garlic which gives a sweet mild taste to the vegetables. Do not worry that you will reek of garlic for days – the cooking removes those odours.

INGREDIENTS
3 medium courgettes
2 sticks celery
2 tablespoons parsley
8 large cloves garlic
2 cups water
4 tablespoons olive oil
1 tablespoon lemon juice
Salt and freshly ground black pepper

EQUIPMENT
Sharp knife
Chopping board
Grater
Small saucepan
Set of measuring cups

Set of measuring spoons
Small bowl and whisk or jam jar with tight-fitting lid
Bowl
Wooden spoon

METHOD

Cut the ends off the courgettes and grate coarsely. Trim, wash and finely slice the celery. Wash, shake dry and finely chop the parsley.

Put the garlic into a saucepan with the water. Bring to the boil, then turn down the heat until it is just boiling (simmering). Put a lid on and cook for 20 minutes. Check the water level from time to time and top it up if needed.

Drain the garlic and let cool. Remove the skins, then press the garlic through a sieve with a wooden spoon or mash in a small bowl with a fork. Mix the garlic, oil, lemon juice, salt and pepper. You can whisk them together in a bowl or put them all together in a jam jar with a tight-fitting lid and shake until mixed.

Combine the vegetables and dressing in a bowl and serve.

ROAST AUBERGINE SALAD

Serves 4 to 6   ① *Preparation 10 min, Cooking 35 min – Easy*

This salad comes from the Catalan region of Spain, the home of the late artist Salvador Dali. We have heard it was one of his favourite dishes and he would insist on a plate of it before getting his brushes out.

INGREDIENTS

4 to 6 tiny onions, about 100 g (4 oz)
1 large aubergine
2 red peppers

2 medium ripe tomatoes
1 clove garlic
15 g pack fresh parsley
2 tablespoons olive oil
1 tablespoon red wine vinegar
$^1/_4$ teaspoon Dijon style mustard
Salt
Freshly ground pepper
$^1/_4$ teaspoon sugar

EQUIPMENT
Sharp knife
Chopping board
Oven-proof dish
Bowl
Wooden spoon
Small bowl and whisk or jam jar with tight-fitting lid
Set of measuring spoons

METHOD
Preheat the oven to 190° C, 375° F, Gas mark 5. Peel the onions.
Cut the aubergine in half lengthways and discard the stem. Chop
the end off the peppers and cut out the core and seeds. Put the
onions, aubergine halves (skin-side up), and red peppers in an oven-
proof dish. Roast for 35 minutes in the preheated oven, turning
them halfway through. When cooked take them out of the oven
and cool.

Peel the garlic and chop it into tiny pieces. Put it in the bowl.
Wash, shake dry and finely chop about 1 tablespoon of the parsley
and add to the bowl.

When cool enough to handle, peel the peppers and aubergine.
Chop the peppers, aubergine, onions, and tomatoes roughly into
1 cm ($^1/_2$ in) pieces. Add to the bowl and gently stir round.

Mix the oil, vinegar, mustard, salt, pepper, and sugar. You can whisk them together in a small bowl or put them all together in a jam jar with a tight-fitting lid and shake until mixed. Add to the vegetables and stir gently. Cool and serve.

TIPS

You can prepare this all in advance and then combine the vegetables and the dressing just before serving.

BEAN SPROUT SALAD

Serves 2 to 4   ① *Preparation 5 min, Cooking 12 min – Easy*

This salad requires brief cooking of the vegetables, only enough to soften them, not cook them to destruction. These subtle flavours would work with simple Chinese food or fish dishes, or would make a crunchy salad for two people.

INGREDIENTS

225 g pack bean sprouts
2 medium carrots
3 small green peppers
3 cups water
$1/4$ teaspoon salt
3 tablespoons soy sauce
2 tablespoons rice vinegar
1 tablespoon sunflower oil
$1/2$ tablespoon sesame oil

EQUIPMENT
Colander or sieve
Vegetable peeler
Sharp knife
Chopping board
Saucepan
Set of measuring spoons
Whisk
Small bowl or jam jar with tight-fitting lid

METHOD
Rinse the bean sprouts in the colander under cold running water, then drain. Peel the carrots, cutting off both ends. Chop into matchsticks about 2 cm (1 in) long. Chop the end off the green peppers and cut out the core and seeds. Cut the pepper into thin rings, then cut the rings into quarters. Everything should end up the same sort of size and thickness.

Boil the water and salt in a saucepan. Add the carrots and cook for 1 minute. Add the bean sprouts and green peppers and bring back to the boil. Drain the vegetables and cool. Squeeze slightly to remove excess water.

Mix the soy sauce, vinegar, sunflower and sesame oils. You can whisk them together in a bowl or put them all together in a jam jar with a tight-fitting lid and shake until mixed.

Keep the dressing and the vegetables in the fridge until just before serving then mix the two together.

SPINACH SALAD

Serves 4   ① *Preparation 10 min, Cooking 20 min– Easy*

A substantial meal of a salad, which would go well with the Orange & olive salad (see page 33) on the side.

INGREDIENTS

4 eggs
1 large lettuce
225 g pack (8 oz) small leaf spinach
10 charlotte potatoes or small new potatoes (about 500 g, 1 lb)
225 g pack smoked streaky bacon
5 tablespoons mayonnaise
2 teaspoons lemon juice
1 tablespoon wholegrain mustard
1 teaspoon sugar

EQUIPMENT

Saucepan
Sharp knife
Chopping board
Set of measuring spoons
Bowl
Cup

METHOD

To hard boil the eggs, put it in a small saucepan nearly full of water. Bring to the boil, and boil for 10 minutes. Cool the eggs by putting in cold water. When cold, take off the shells. Wash and break up the lettuce. Wash the spinach and shake dry. Wash the potatoes, cutting away any nasty bits. Boil the potatoes in salted water for 20 minutes. Drain, cover and keep warm. Grill the bacon until crisp.

Put the lettuce and spinach on four plates. Mix the mayonnaise, lemon juice, mustard and sugar in a cup. Cut the potatoes in half and the eggs in quarters. Chop the bacon. Divide between the plates and dribble or dollop the dressing on top.

BACON & GREEN BEAN SALAD

Serves 2 or 4   ① *Preparation 5 min, Cooking 15 min – Easy*

This can be a main course for two people, or a side salad for four.

INGREDIENTS
2 chicken stock cubes
2 cups boiling water
3 tablespoons rice
400 g tin green flageolet beans in brine
1 small to medium onion
225 g pack unsmoked back bacon
1 tablespoon butter
1 clove garlic
3 tablespoons olive oil
2 tablespoons lemon juice
1 teaspoon Dijon mustard
Salt and freshly ground black pepper
1 teaspoon sugar

EQUIPMENT
Jug
Set of measuring cups
Bowl
2 saucepans
Wooden spoon

40

Tin opener
Sharp knife
Chopping board
Frying-pan
Heatproof dish
Set of measuring spoons
Garlic crusher
Small bowl and whisk or jam jar with tight-fitting lid

METHOD

Dissolve the stock cube in the water in the jug. Put the stock and rice into the saucepan and cook for the time it says on the pack (probably about 10 minutes). Stir from time to time to stop it sticking. Open the tin of beans, drain and rinse. Peel and chop the onion. Cut the bacon into strips. Fry the bacon strips for 3 or 4 minutes, transfer to a heatproof dish and keep warm in the oven at 150° C, 300° F, Gas mark 2.

Meanwhile, put the butter in a large saucepan over a moderate heat. Peel and crush the garlic into the pan. Add the onion and fry for about 3 minutes until it is golden, stirring to stop it sticking.

Mix the oil, lemon juice, mustard, salt, pepper and sugar. You can whisk them together in a bowl or put them all together in a jam jar with a tight-fitting lid and shake until mixed. Add to the onion pan and bring to the boil. Add the drained rice and beans and stir carefully until it is warmed through. Add the bacon and serve.

FANCY CHICKEN SALAD WITH WALNUT DRESSING

Serves 4   ⏲ *Preparation 10 min, Cooking 10 min – Easy*

This is a salad without any vegetables, but an abundance of fruit, but it is a main course salad, not a fruit salad.

INGREDIENTS
2 cooked chicken breasts
2 eggs
2 ripe avocados
2 or 3 tablespoons lemon juice
2 sweet grapefruit
100 g pack (1 cup) whole walnuts

Walnut dressing
$^1/_2$ cup walnut oil
1 tablespoon white wine vinegar
1 teaspoon mild French mustard
1 teaspoon salt
1 tablespoon sugar

EQUIPMENT
Saucepan
Sharp knife
Chopping board
Set of measuring spoons
Set of measuring cups
Bowl
Wooden spoon
Small bowl and whisk or jam jar with tight-fitting lid

METHOD

If you need to cook the chicken, make sure frozen chicken is completely thawed before use. This means leaving it in the fridge overnight, or out of the fridge for 6 hours. Then just brush with oil, wrap in aluminium foil and cook in an oven-proof dish in the oven for 30 minutes at 200° C, 400° F, Gas mark 6.

To hard boil the eggs, put in a small saucepan nearly full of water. Bring to the boil, and boil for 10 minutes. Cool by putting in cold water. When cold, take off the shells. Chop the eggs into quarters.

Peel the avocado and chop into chunks. Stir with the lemon juice to stop it going brown. Peel the grapefruit and divide into segments.

Cut the chicken into chunks and put in a bowl with the eggs, avocado and grapefruit. Add half the walnuts. Chop the remaining walnuts and keep to sprinkle on the salad before serving.

Mix the oil, vinegar, mustard, salt and sugar. You can whisk them together in a bowl or put them all together in a jam jar with a tight-fitting lid and shake until mixed.

Pour the dressing over the salad, and sprinkle with the chopped nuts.

ADDITIONS & ALTERNATIVES

Use pecan nuts instead of walnuts.

Serve as a starter for 6 to 8.

TIPS

Great party food. Double up the quantities and it will do about 10 people (or maybe a few more) as part of a buffet.

CHILLED THAI CHICKEN SALAD

Serves 4   ① *Preparation 20 min, Cooking 2 min – Easy*

This Thai salad uses chicken mince in a way that you will probably not have had before. This is an easy and exotic tasting recipe using easy to find ingredients.

INGREDIENTS

6 cups (1.5 litres, $2^1/_2$ pints) water
$^1/_2$ teaspoon salt
200 g pack minced chicken
1 bunch spring onions (about 6 to 8)
15 g pack coriander leaves
1 cup bean sprouts

Festival dressing
1 large lemon or 5 tablespoons lemon juice
1 clove garlic
4 teaspoons fish sauce or soy sauce
1 teaspoon salt
$^1/_4$ teaspoon of chilli powder

Few iceberg lettuce leaves
4 cherry tomatoes

EQUIPMENT

Set of measuring cups
Saucepan
Set of measuring spoons
Sieve
Sharp knife

Chopping board
Lemon juicer
Garlic crusher
Small bowl and whisk or jam jar with tight-fitting lid
Bowl
Wooden spoon

METHOD
Boil the water and salt. Add the chicken, stirring to break it up. Boil for 2 minutes or until chicken is white and cooked through. Drain and leave to cool.

Clean and prepare the spring onions. Cut the root end off, trim the leaves. Peel off and discard any dried up or slimy leaves. Keep 4 whole for serving and chop the others into thin slices. Wash and shake dry the coriander. Wash and drain the beansprouts.

Juice the lemon. Peel and crush the garlic. Mix the lemon juice, fish sauce, garlic, salt and chilli. You can whisk them together in a bowl or put them all together in a jam jar with a tight-fitting lid and shake until mixed.

Put the chicken in a bowl. Add the dressing, chopped spring onions and coriander. Stir to coat the chicken in the dressing. Cover and refrigerate until chilled.

Line serving bowls or plates with lettuce leaves. Add the chicken mixture. Garnish with the remaining spring onions, cherry tomatoes and beansprouts, chopping if you like.

CHICKEN & MANGO SALAD

Serves 4   ① *Preparation 5 min, Cooking 15 min – Easy*

Exotic, fragrant and creamy. This is a light summer meal to remember.

INGREDIENTS

1 kg (2 lb) cooked chicken
1 small onion
1 tablespoon sunflower oil
1 tablespoon curry paste
1 tablespoon tomato purée
$^1/_2$ cup (125 ml, 4 fl oz) red wine
1 tablespoon red wine vinegar
2 tablespoons mango chutney
500 g tub fromage frais
50 g pack toasted flaked almonds

EQUIPMENT

Sharp knife
Chopping board
Set of measuring spoons
Set of measuring cups
Food processor or liquidiser (optional)
Wooden spoon

METHOD

If you need to cook the chicken, make sure frozen chicken is completely thawed before use. This means leaving it in the fridge overnight, or out of the fridge for 6 hours. Then just brush with oil, wrap in aluminium foil and cook in an oven-proof dish in the oven for 40 minutes at 200° C, 400° F, Gas mark 6. Chop the chicken into bite-sized chunks.

Peel and finely chop the onion. Put the oil in the frying-pan over a moderate heat. Fry the onion for about 3 minutes until it is golden, stirring to stop it sticking.

Add the curry paste, tomato purée, red wine and red wine vinegar. Bring to the boil, then turn down the heat until it is just boiling (simmering). Cook gently for about 10 minutes. Take off

46

the heat, stir in the mango chutney and leave to cool. Put the sauce in the liquidiser or food processor and blend briefly until it is smooth. If you do not have a processor press it through a sieve with the back of a spoon or have it lumpy. You might like to chop up the chutney a bit before you put it in.

Stir in the chicken pieces.

ADDITIONS & ALTERNATIVES
Serve with salad and pitta bread.

Use lime pickle or chutney instead of the mango chutney.

WARM SPICY CHICKEN & ORANGE SALAD

Serves 4
⏲ *Preparation 25 min plus 1 hour to marinate, Cooking 10 min – Easy*

This is an exception to the idea that salad should be served cold. The chicken is added to the salad whilst still warm, so choose lettuce varieties that do not wilt too easily, such as Cos or Lollo Rosso. The marinade doubles as the dressing in this recipe.

INGREDIENTS
4 large boneless, skinless chicken breasts
2 lettuces (e.g. Lollo Rosso or Cos)
2 teaspoons sherry vinegar

The marinade
3 oranges
1 clove garlic
3 tablespoons virgin olive oil

47

1 teaspoon Mediterranean dried herbs
$^1/_2$ teaspoon paprika
$^1/_8$ teaspoon chilli powder
Salt and freshly ground black pepper to taste

EQUIPMENT
Zester
Bowl
Sharp knife
Chopping board
Garlic crusher
Set of measuring spoons
Frying-pan
Wooden spoon
Slotted spoon

METHOD
Scrape the skin off an orange with the zester, or thinly peel and then chop the peel. You will need about 1 teaspoon of zest. Place in a bowl. Peel and crush the garlic into the bowl. Add the oil, herbs, paprika, chilli powder, salt and pepper. Mix together.

Cut the chicken into thin strips and mix into the marinade. Leave to stand for 1 hour in the fridge. Wash the chopping board and knife before preparing the orange. Peel the oranges and scrape away the pith. Cut the oranges into segments. Add any orange juice to the chicken. Wash and shake dry the lettuce leaves, tear them into manageable pieces and put into a large serving bowl with the orange segments.

Put a frying-pan on a moderate heat. Add the chicken and marinade and cook for about 10 minutes, stirring, until the chicken is cooked. Take off the heat and lift out with a slotted spoon onto a plate and cool for 2 minutes. Add the sherry vinegar to the juices in the pan and stir. Put the chicken in the bowl and pour the hot dressing on top. Serve.

ORANGE & SMOKED SALMON SALAD

Serves 4   ⏱ *Preparation 20 min – Easy*

The light taste of the orange and dressing compliments the richness of the smoked salmon and the avocado. This makes a substantial meal.

INGREDIENTS

2 oranges
2 avocados
2 or 3 tablespoons of lemon juice
8 thin slices smoked salmon
2 spring onions
5 tablespoons olive oil
1 tablespoon orange juice
1 tablespoon red wine vinegar
$1/8$ teaspoon mild French mustard
Salt and freshly ground pepper to taste
1 teaspoon brown sugar
4 lettuce leaves

Orange chive butter
2 heaped tablespoons soft butter
15 g pack fresh parsley
15 g pack fresh chives
$1/4$ teaspoon salt
The merest sprinkling of ground mace
Brown bread

49

EQUIPMENT
Lemon zester
Sharp knife
Chopping board
Set of measuring spoons
Set of measuring cups
Bowl
Wooden spoon
Small bowl and whisk or jam jar with tight-fitting lid
Knife

METHOD
Scrape the skin off an orange with the zester or thinly peel and then chop the peel. You will need about 2 teaspoons of it. Peel and chop the avocado into quarters. Stir with the lemon juice to stop it going brown. Wrap each piece of avocado in a slice of smoked salmon. Peel the oranges and divide into segments. Clean and prepare the spring onions. Cut the root end off, trim the leaves. Peel off and discard any dried up or slimy leaves. Chop into long thin strips. Put in cold water and they should curl up.

Mix 1 teaspoon of the orange zest with the oil, orange juice, vinegar, mustard, salt, pepper and sugar. You can whisk them together in a bowl or put them all together in a jam jar with a tight-fitting lid and shake until mixed.

Put a lettuce leaf on each of four plates then put 2 pieces of avocado on top. Garnish with the orange segments and drained strips of spring onion. Sprinkle more of the dressing on top. Put in the fridge.

To make the orange herb butter, wash, shake dry and finely chop the parsley and chives to make 1 tablespoon of each. Mix the butter, parsley, chives, remaining orange zest, mace and salt with a knife. Spread on thin slices of brown bread and serve with the salad.

FISH SALAD WITH WALNUTS

Serves 4 to 6   ⏲ *Preparation 15 min, Cooking 10 min – Easy*

This salad is full of flavours and textures that are rare in just one dish. Really impressive for fish lovers.

INGREDIENTS
1 kg (2 lb) mussels in their shells or 2 × 500 g packs ready-cooked mussels in shells
1 pink grapefruit
Few lettuce leaves
200 g tin tuna in oil
$^1/_2$ × 200 g tin salmon
$^3/_4$ cup cooked, peeled small prawns
$^1/_2$ cup mayonnaise (see page 284)
$1^1/_2$ tablespoons Dijon mustard
$^1/_2$ tablespoon brandy
$^1/_8$ teaspoon paprika
100 g pack whole walnuts
Salt and freshly ground black pepper to taste

EQUIPMENT
Sharp knife
Frying-pan
Chopping board
Set of measuring cups
Set of measuring spoons
Bowl
Tin opener
Wooden spoon

METHOD

Try to buy mussels that have been cleaned up. Wash the mussels thoroughly in running water and scrape them to get any mud or wildlife off them. Throw away any cracked or open ones they could make you ill. Scrape off the beard (the bit that sticks out from the edge of the shell) and give them a final rinse. Heat the mussels briefly in the frying-pan over a high heat to open, then remove from their shells. Discard any that did not open. If using the ready-cooked mussels warm them through, then remove from the shells.

Peel the grapefruit and remove the segments carefully from their thin inner membrane. Cut the skinned segments in half lengthways. Wash and dry the lettuce and use to line a salad bowl. Break up the tuna and salmon with a fork and mix with the mussels, prawns and grapefruit pieces. Put in the bowl. Keep a few whole walnuts for garnish and crush the others. Mix the mayonnaise with the mustard, brandy and paprika. Sprinkle the crushed walnuts over the salad. Add a little freshly ground pepper. Sprinkle with the mayonnaise just before serving and decorate with the remaining whole walnut halves.

ADDITIONS & ALTERNATIVES

Use 500 g (1 lb) of cooked mussels instead of the mussels in the shell.

With fresh uncooked mussels the most important thing to remember is to throw away any mussels that are not closed when you wash them as they are dead and any that do not open during cooking.

Try using some chopped grilled monkfish.

Serve with chunky or French bread as a main course salad for the summer.

RUSSIAN TUNA SALAD

Serves 4 to 6   ⏱ *Preparation 15 min, Cooking 25 min – Easy*

This Russian salad passed down from the Romanovs is one of Europe's most popular. You can find it anywhere from the Balkans to the Tapas bars of Madrid.

INGREDIENTS
2 spring onions
1 clove garlic
15 g pack parsley
200 g tin tuna
1 teaspoon capers
2 dill or cornichon pickled gherkins
4 medium Desiree red potatoes, about 500 g (1 lb)
3 tablespoons peas (fresh, frozen or tinned)
1 carrot
2 eggs
1^1/$_2$ teaspoons red wine vinegar
Salt to taste
^{1}/$_2$ cup mayonnaise (see page 284)

EQUIPMENT
Sharp knife
Chopping board
Garlic crusher
Tin opener
Saucepan
Set of measuring spoons
Bowl
Set of measuring cups
Wooden spoon

53

METHOD

Peel and chop the spring onions. Peel and crush the garlic. Wash the parsley, shake dry and finely chop 1 to 2 tablespoons. Open the tin of tuna and drain. Break up the tuna up into flakes. Drain and chop the capers and the gherkins. Peel the potatoes, cut in half and boil in a saucepan of salted water until they are tender, about 20 minutes. Cool slightly, then peel and dice. Cook the peas for about 5 minutes and the peeled diced carrot for 10 minutes.

To hard boil the eggs, put in a small saucepan nearly full of water. Bring to the boil, and boil for 10 minutes. Cool by putting in cold water. When cold, take off the shells. Chop the egg up. It is easier to chop the white separately then lightly mash the yolk.

Mix the tuna, vinegar, onion, garlic, parsley, capers and gherkin in a bowl. Add the potatoes, eggs, peas, and carrots. Add salt to taste and leave to sit for about 30 minutes. Gently mix the mayonnaise into the potato mixture. Serve at room temperature.

SPECIAL SOUPS

Soups are much more versatile than you may at first think. They are not just a small bowl, first course, option. With a bit of bread or a delicately fried crouton these can make fantastic meals.

We have started with a couple that do not even need cooking, and one of us has driven miles for a decent bowl of gazpacho. Some soups are wonderful served chunky, but we have to say that some of these are a lot easier to make if you have taken the power tool path and invested in a liquidiser.

GAZPACHO

Serves 4   ① *Preparation 15 min – Easy*

A cooling, soothing soup for a hot summer day. Best taken beneath the shade of a tree outside a Spanish bar with a glass of Spanish beer. But if you cannot get a Spanish person to make this for you, here is how to make it yourself. There is nothing like it. No cooking.

INGREDIENTS
3 or 4 spring onions
$^1/_4$ cucumber
1 small green or red pepper

3 medium tomatoes, about 200 g (8 oz)
1 clove garlic
$^1/_2$ × 50 g pack parsley
1 cup tomato juice
$^1/_2$ cup water
1 tablespoon tomato purée
Salt and freshly ground black pepper to taste

For serving
1 tomato
1 spring onion
half a green pepper
2 or 3 slices bread cut into cubes
3 tablespoons sunflower oil

EQUIPMENT
Sharp knife
Chopping board
Vegetable peeler
Food processor or liquidiser (essential)
Bowl
Set of measuring cups
Set of measuring spoons
Wooden spoon
Frying-pan

METHOD
Clean and prepare the spring onions. Cut the root end off, trim the leaves. Peel off and discard any dried up or slimy leaves. Peel the cucumber. Chop the end off the pepper and cut out the core and seeds. Roughly chop all the vegetables. Peel the garlic. Wash, shake dry and chop the parsley.

Blend all the solid ingredients together with a little of the water in small quantities in a liquidiser or food processor until smooth. Put them in the bowl. Then stir in the tomato juice, remaining water, tomato purée, salt and pepper. Chill thoroughly.

Chop up the tomato, spring onion, and half pepper really small.

Cut the bread into 1 cm ($^1/_2$ in) cubes. Put the oil in the frying-pan on a medium heat. Wait until the oil gets hot and then fry the bread until it is brown, stirring often. Fish out the croutons and keep to serve with the soup. Serve the Gazpacho with ice cubes in it if you can and the chopped vegetables and croutons separately by the side. It should be really cold.

CHILLED AVOCADO SOUP

Serves 4   ① *Preparation 15 min – Easy*

This cool soup does not need any cooking at any stage. Like all chilled soup it is surprising just because it is cold. This one is creamy too. Great in the middle of summer when the weather is hot and the avocados are cheaper.

INGREDIENTS
1 lemon or 4 tablespoons lemon juice
2 vegetable stock cubes
4 ripe avocado pears
Medium carton (284 ml, 10 fl oz) single cream
1 teaspoon chilli sauce or a few drops of Tabasco
Salt and freshly ground black pepper

EQUIPMENT
Set of measuring cups
Bowl
Sharp knife
Chopping board
Food processor or liquidiser (optional)
Set of measuring spoons
Lemon juicer

METHOD
Juice the lemon. Dissolve the stock cubes in the bowl with about $^1/_2$ a cup of boiling water then add 2 cups of cold water. Peel the avocado pears and discard the stones. Chop one into chunks and stir round with 2 tablespoons of lemon juice. Process the other avocado pears in the food processor or liquidiser with the rest of the lemon juice, or mash to make a smooth purée.

Mix in the stock and cream in the processor or in a bowl with a whisk, adding chilli sauce or Tabasco to taste.

Chill. Before serving add the cubes of avocado pear.

ADDITIONS & ALTERNATIVES
If cold soup is just too weird for you, you can warm this up before adding the cubes. Do it gently or it will go a sort of off-green brown colour. You could serve it cold but add some hot croutons.

CARROT & CUMIN SOUP

Serves 4   ℗ *Preparation 15 min, Cooking 40 min – Easy*

This soup is flash not just because of its flavour but because of its colour which is 'bright and beautiful'. This is a rich orange soup with cumin flavour, and it is substantial enough for a meal.

SPECIAL SOUPS

INGREDIENTS
1 chicken or vegetable stock cube
3 cups boiling water
1 potato, about 125 g (4 oz)
6 carrots, about 350 g (12 oz)
2 celery sticks
1 large onion
2 cloves garlic
3 tablespoons butter
1 teaspoon ground cumin
Salt and freshly ground black pepper to taste
2 teaspoons tomato purée
2 teaspoons lemon juice
2 fresh or dried bay leaves
1 cup milk

EQUIPMENT
Set of measuring cups
Bowl
Vegetable peeler
Sharp knife
Chopping board
Garlic crusher
Set of measuring spoons
Large saucepan with lid
Wooden spoon
Food processor or liquidiser or sieve or Mouli

METHOD
Dissolve the stock cube in the water. Peel the potato, cutting away any nasty bits, and cutting out any eyes. Chop the potatoes into dice. Peel and slice the carrots, cutting off both ends. Wash, trim and slice the celery sticks. Peel and chop the onion. Peel and crush the garlic.

Melt the butter in a large saucepan. Add the onion and garlic and fry over a low heat for a couple of minutes until the onion begins to soften. Add the carrots and continue to fry gently for a further 5 minutes, stirring frequently and taking care they do not burn. Add the stock, potato, celery, cumin, salt and pepper, tomato purée, lemon juice and bay leaves and bring to the boil. Cover and simmer gently for about 30 minutes until all the vegetables are very tender.

Remove the bay leaves, let the soup cool a little and then blend in a food processor or liquidiser until smooth or press it through a sieve (a time-consuming and potentially messy job unless you have a Mouli).

Put the soup into a clean pan, add the milk and bring slowly to the boil. Taste and adjust the seasoning.

TIPS

You can buy ready-made stock in cartons from most supermarkets. You can also buy Swiss vegetable bouillon powder (vegetable stock), if you are worried about the stuff that goes into chicken stock cubes.

CHICKEN & CHESTNUT SOUP

Serves 4   ① *Preparation 20 min, Cooking 35 min – Easy*

This is a rich soup with pieces of chicken and chopped chestnuts which add to its interesting flavour and texture.

INGREDIENTS
2 chicken stock cubes
5 cups water
2 onions

2 chicken breasts
1 bouquet garni (looks like a herb tea bag)
2 medium carrots
175 g tin of whole chestnuts
3 tablespoons butter
3 tablespoons plain flour
$^1/_2$ cup milk
$^1/_2$ teaspoon ground coriander
Salt and pepper to taste
1 tablespoon chopped fresh parsley

EQUIPMENT
Saucepan
Set of measuring cups
Sharp knife
Chopping board
Slotted spoon
Bowl
Vegetable peeler
Grater
Tin opener
Set of measuring spoons
Wooden spoon

METHOD
Dissolve the stock cubes in the water in a saucepan. Peel the onions. Chop one of them into quarters and put in the pan with the bouquet garni. Chop the chicken breasts into quarters and put in the pan. Bring to the boil and cook gently for 20 minutes. Take off the heat. Fish out the bouquet garni and the onion and throw away. Fish out the chicken with the slotted spoon and carefully shred. Pour the chicken stock into a bowl and keep to one side. Wash out the pan and dry.

Peel and chop the carrots, cutting off both ends, then grate them. Open the tin of chestnuts and drain. Chop the chestnuts finely. Chop the remaining onion.

Melt the butter in the saucepan, add the onion and fry gently for about 3 minutes until soft. Stir in the flour and cook for a minute. Gradually stir in the chicken stock and bring to the boil, stirring. Boil gently for 2 minutes, then add the milk, chopped chicken, carrots, chestnuts, coriander, salt and pepper.

Cook for a final 10 minutes, then stir in the parsley, if using. Adjust the seasoning and serve.

TIPS

You can buy ready-made stock in cartons from most supermarkets. You can also buy Swiss vegetable bouillon powder (vegetable stock), if you are worried about the stuff that goes into stock cubes. Bouquet garni has a mixture of herbs in it, so you can substitute a teaspoon of mixed Mediterranean herbs. It means you get little specks of herb in the soup, but so what.

HOT CHICKEN & COCONUT SOUP

Serves 4 ① *Preparation 15 min, Cooking 10 min – Easy*

Hot and spicy and not like anything you have ever had before. If you thought soups were wet you were wrong.

INGREDIENTS
1 chicken breast (cooked)
2 chicken stock cubes
4 cups boiling water
1 bunch fresh coriander
1 lemon

1 tablespoon cornflour
3 bird's eye chillies
1 small onion
1 clove garlic
5 cm (2 in) piece fresh galangal or root ginger
1 tablespoon oil
75 g (3 oz) creamed coconut, dissolved in $^1/_2$ cup boiling water
3 tablespoons crème fraîche
Salt and freshly ground black pepper

EQUIPMENT
Set of measuring cups
Bowl
Sharp knife
Chopping board
Lemon zester
Lemon squeezer
Set of measuring spoons
Cup
Grater
Vegetable peeler
Garlic crusher
Saucepan
Wooden spoon

METHOD
If you need to cook the chicken, make sure frozen chicken is completely thawed before use. This means leaving it in the fridge overnight, or out of the fridge for 6 hours. Then just brush with oil and cook in an oven-proof dish in the oven for 30 minutes at 200° C, 400° F, Gas mark 6. When it is cool cut it into small pieces.

Dissolve the stock cubes in the water. Wash, shake dry and finely chop the coriander. Put a bit on one side to sprinkle on the soup when you serve it. Use the zester to scrape the skin off the lemon. Juice the lemon. Mix the cornflour with the lemon juice in a cup to make a smooth paste. Chop the ends off the chillies, split in half, and scrape out the seeds. Cut the chilli into tiny bits. Hold them down with a fork to stop the juice getting on your fingers.

Peel and chop the onion. Peel and crush the garlic. Peel the galangal and grate it. Put the oil in the frying-pan over a moderate heat. Fry the chillies, onion, garlic and galangal for about 3 minutes until it is golden, stirring to stop it sticking.

Add the stock, the creamed coconut, the lemon zest, most of the coriander and the blended cornflour and lemon. Bring to the boil and cook gently for 3 minutes. Add the chicken, 1 tablespoon of crème fraîche and salt and pepper and stir round.

Serve with a dollop of crème fraîche and a sprinkling of corriander on top.

TIPS

You can buy ready-made stock in cartons from most supermarkets. You can also buy Swiss vegetable bouillon powder (vegetable stock), if you are worried about the stuff that goes into stock cubes.

You can use dried galangal or fresh ginger instead of the fresh galangal.

TOMATO & COCONUT SOUP

Serves 4
⏱ Preparation 10 min, Cooking 10 min – Easy but do not let it boil

It is important that this soup is not allowed to boil, because the creamed coconut will curdle at high temperatures. This is a kind of curry soup with a subtle chilli flavour.

INGREDIENTS
2 fresh green chillies
2 tablespoons sunflower oil
$^1/_2$ teaspoon black mustard seeds
1 tablespoon curry leaves
1 cup (300 ml, $^1/_2$ pint) passata
75 g (3 oz) creamed coconut, cut into small pieces
2 cups warm water
1 teaspoon salt or to taste
1 tablespoon sugar

EQUIPMENT
Sharp knife
Chopping board
Set of measuring spoons
Set of measuring cups
Wooden spoon
Food processor or liquidiser or sieve or Mouli

METHOD
Chop the end off the chillies, split in half, and scrape out the seeds. Hold the chilli down with a fork and cut into thin strips.

Heat the oil in the saucepan over a medium heat. Add the mustard seeds. They will pop. Then add the curry leaves and fry for 15 seconds.

Add the chillies, passata, coconut and water. Heat until it is almost boiling then stir until the coconut is dissolved. Remove from the heat and allow to cool slightly. Put the soup in the liquidiser or food processor and blend until it is smooth or use a Mouli. If you do not have a processor press it through a sieve with the back of a spoon.

Put it back in the pan, add the salt and sugar and heat. Simmer for 5 minutes. Remove from the heat and serve.

ADDITIONS & ALTERNATIVES
Serve with new potatoes, green vegetable or salad.

TIPS
Passata is a sort of thick tomato sauce used in pastas and is easily available in supermarkets.

LENTIL & HAM SOUP

Serves 4   ⏲ *Preparation 10 min plus 2 hr soaking time for lentils, Cooking 30 min or 1 hr 20 min – Easy*

Ideal for a cold winter's day, rich and chunky. This soup is based on a stock originally made from a ham knuckle, but we use bacon instead. The vegetables and red lentils thicken it and add flavour.

INGREDIENTS
175 g pack lean bacon
$^1/_2$ × 500 g pack (1 cup) red lentils or $1^1/_2$ × 400 g tins lentils
2 vegetable stock cubes
6 cups water
2 onions
2 large carrots
4 large tomatoes
1 clove garlic
2 bay leaves
2 to 3 medium potatoes (about 250 g, 8 oz)
1 tablespoon white wine vinegar
$^1/_4$ teaspoon ground allspice
Salt and freshly ground black pepper to taste
2 spring onions

SPECIAL SOUPS

EQUIPMENT
Sharp knife
Chopping board
Set of measuring cups
Saucepan with lid
Vegetable peeler
Garlic crusher
Set of measuring spoons
Wooden spoon
Food processor or liquidiser (optional)

METHOD
Chop the bacon. Put the lentils, stock cubes and water in a saucepan and leave to soak for 2 hours. Peel and chop the onions. Peel and chop the carrots, cutting off both ends. Skin and chop the tomatoes. Peel and crush the garlic into the pan. Add the onions, carrots, bacon, tomatoes, bay leaves, salt and pepper.

Bring to the boil, cover and boil gently (simmer) for about 1 hour until the lentils are tender. If using tinned lentils remember to drain them before use. There is no need to cook them – add to the pan when the potatoes are cooked and simmer for another 10 minutes.

Peel the potatoes, cutting away any nasty bits, and cutting out any eyes. Chop the potatoes into smallish bits. Add them and cook for 20 minutes more until tender.

Fish out the bay leaves. You can leave the soup lumpy or process about half of it. Add the vinegar and allspice. Cook gently for a further 5 minutes (15 if using tinned lentils). Clean and prepare the spring onions. Cut the root end off, trim the leaves. Peel off and discard any dried up or slimy leaves. Chop into thin slices. Sprinkle on top of the soup when you serve it.

LENTIL SOUP

Serves 4   ① *Preparation 10 min, Cooking 40 min – Easy*

Subtle in taste and comforting in texture and very easy on the pocket. A real good all rounder then.

INGREDIENTS

2 tinned peeled plum tomatoes
1 carrot
2 medium onions
25 g pack parsley
$^1/_2$ × 500 g pack (1 cup) red or yellow split lentils
4 cups (1 litre, 2 pints) water
Salt and freshly ground pepper to taste
2 tablespoons sunflower oil
Juice of $^1/_2$ lemon

EQUIPMENT

Sharp knife
Chopping board
Vegetable peeler
Set of measuring cups
Saucepan
Food processor or liquidiser (optional) or sieve and wooden
spoon or Mouli
Wooden spoon
Set of measuring spoons
Frying-pan
Tin opener

METHOD

Chop the tomatoes. Peel and chop the carrots, cutting off and discarding both ends. Peel and chop the onions. Wash, shake dry and finely chop the parsley.

Put the lentils, the tomato, carrot and half the onion in a large saucepan and pour in the water. Boil vigorously for 10 minutes, then turn the heat down and cook gently for 20 to 30 minutes until the lentils are soft. Give it the odd stir to stop it sticking. If it starts to dry out add more water. Put the soup in the liquidiser or food processor and blend until it is smooth. If you do not have a processor press it through a sieve with the back of a spoon or have it lumpy or put through a Mouli. Add salt and pepper.

Heat the oil in a frying-pan and fry the remaining onion for about 5 minutes until golden brown. Reheat the soup and add the fried onion and lemon juice.

Serve with the chopped parsley sprinkled on top.

ADDITIONS & ALTERNATIVES

Serve with warm pitta bread or a crusty loaf.

SHRIMP GUMBO

Serves 4   ℚ *Preparation 10 min, Cooking 50 min – Easy*

You know the song, well we did jambalaya in the last book, and you just cannot get the crawfish for the pie so we have gone for the gumbo. This soup is really thick with onions, red peppers, rice, prawns and okra. Authentic New Orleans.

INGREDIENTS

1 or 2 vegetable stock cubes
4 cups (1 litre, 2 pints) boiling water

1 large red pepper
15 g pack fresh parsley
Approximately 18 okra, 2 handfuls or 150 g (6 oz)
1 large onion
2 rashers lean bacon
2 tablespoons olive oil
2 cloves garlic
1 bay leaf
$^1/_4$ teaspoon ground allspice
1 blade mace
1 tablespoon white wine vinegar
3 tablespoons long-grain rice
Salt and pepper
125 g pack peeled prawns
1 tablespoon anchovy paste
2 teaspoons tomato purée

EQUIPMENT
Sharp knife
Chopping board
Set of measuring cups
Set of measuring spoons
Bowl
Wooden spoon
Spoon
Garlic crusher
Frying-pan
Saucepan
Saucepan with lid
Fork for mashing
Small bowls or plates

METHOD

Dissolve the stock cube in the water. Chop the end off the red peppers and cut out the core and seeds. Cut the pepper into little bits. Wash, shake dry and chop the parsley. Cut the ends off the okra and slice very thinly. Peel and finely chop the onion. Chop the bacon.

Put the oil in a large saucepan on a medium heat. Peel and crush the garlic into the pan. Add the onion and bacon and fry gently for 3 minutes until golden. Add the pepper to the pan and continue to fry gently for a couple of minutes.

Add the stock, bay leaf, allspice, mace, vinegar, rice, salt and pepper. Bring to the boil, then turn down the heat until it is just boiling (simmering). Put a lid on and cook for 20 minutes. Stir occasionally.

Keep a few prawns to put on the gumbo when finished. Add the rest of the prawns, the okra, anchovy paste and tomato purée . Put the lid back on and simmer gently for 15 minutes until the okra is tender and the mixture slightly thickened.

Fish the bay leaf and mace from the soup and adjust the seasoning. Add the parsley and serve each portion garnished with a whole prawn.

TIPS

You can buy tubes of anchovy paste. You can use any of the stuff you have left over on pizza. It keeps for about 6 weeks in the fridge.

FRENCH MUSSEL SOUP (MOULES MARINIERE)

Serves 4   ① *Preparation 20 min, Cooking 15 min – Easy*

This is simple country food which has been hijacked by expensive restaurants. This is the best back to basics version we know. You want a really big pan to do this in. Although it may seem a dreadful undertaking this is one the best dishes in the world. Just make sure you buy the mussels fresh, clean them thoroughly and do not cook them for too long.

Most important is to throw away any mussels that are not closed when you wash them and any that do not open during cooking.

INGREDIENTS

2 kg (4 lb) fresh mussels
25 g pack parsley
4 shallots or 2 medium onions
1 tablespoon of butter
1 cup (250 ml, 8 fl oz) dry white wine
1 bouquet garni (looks like a herb tea bag)
Freshly ground black pepper to taste

EQUIPMENT

Sharp knife
Chopping board
Set of measuring cups
Set of measuring spoons
Wooden spoon
Spoon
Big saucepan with lid
Slotted spoon

METHOD

Try to buy mussels that have been cleaned up. Wash the mussels thoroughly in running water and scrape them to get any mud or wildlife off them. Throw away any cracked or open ones, they could make you ill. Scrape off the beard (the bit that sticks out from the edge of the shell) off and give them a final rinse.

Wash, shake dry and finely chop the parsley. Peel and finely chop the shallots or onions. Put the butter in the pan over a moderate heat. Fry the onions for about two minutes until it is transparent, stirring to stop it sticking. Add the wine, 2 tablespoons parsley, bouquet garni and pepper, and boil gently for 5 minutes. Add the mussels. Put the lid on the pan and cook for about 5 minutes, shaking the pan often until the mussel shells open.

Discard the bouquet garni. With a slotted spoon transfer the mussels to a warm serving dish, and then boil the liquid vigorously to reduce it while you remove and discard the empty half shells.

Pour the cooking liquid over the mussels and sprinkle some of the remaining parsley on top.

ADDITIONS & ALTERNATIVES

Eat with fresh crusty bread.

You can serve it up in individual bowls.

To make the sauce thicker you can mix a tablespoon of flour with two tablespoons of butter and then whisk it into the juice.

You can make the sauce richer by gradually adding 4 tablespoons single or double cream to the juice after you have lifted out the mussels.

Bouquet garni has a mixture of herbs in it, so you can substitute a teaspoon of mixed herbs. Or try a bay leaf, and $1/2$ a teaspoon of dried thyme.

FRENCH ONION SOUP

Serves 4   ① *Preparation 10 min, Cooking 1 hour – Easy*

This is the authentic taste of France and it is delicious. It has one slightly difficult technique: you have to cook the onions really, really slowly until they are dark brown without burning them.

INGREDIENTS

2 beef or vegetable stock cubes
4 cups (1 litre, 1³/₄ pints) boiling water
3 medium onions, sliced thinly
2 tablespoon butter
2 tablespoons oil
1 clove garlic
¹/₂ × 50 g pack parsley
1 tablespoon brown sugar
1 tablespoon white wine vinegar
2 bay leaves
¹/₄ teaspoon ground allspice
Salt and pepper to taste
1 loaf of French bread
¹/₂ cup grated Gruyère, Emmental or Cheddar cheese

EQUIPMENT

Set of measuring cups
Bowl
Sharp knife
Chopping board
Set of measuring spoons
Saucepan with lid
Garlic crusher
Grater

METHOD

Dissolve the stock cubes in the water. Peel and finely slice the onion. Put the butter and oil in the saucepan and heat over a gentle heat. Peel and crush the garlic into the pan. Add the onion. Fry very gently for 25 minutes, stirring frequently, until the onions turn a golden brown and become caramelised. Meanwhile wash, shake dry and finely chop the parsley.

Add the sugar, vinegar, bay leaves, allspice, salt and pepper. Add the stock and bring to the boil. Cover the pan and simmer gently for about 30 minutes. Fish out the bay leaves and adjust the seasoning.

Cut 8 thin slices of French bread. Toast one side. Turn them over and sprinkle grated cheese on top. Grill until the cheese is bubbling.

Put 2 slices of toasted bread on each bowl of soup. Sprinkle with chopped parsley. Serve.

TIPS

You can buy ready-made stock in cartons from most supermarkets. You can also buy Swiss vegetable bouillon powder (vegetable stock), if you are worried about the stuff that goes into stock cubes.

This soup keeps for 24 hours in the fridge. Just reheat and then do the toasted cheese.

MUSHROOM SOUP

Serves 4 ① *Preparation 10 min, Cooking 25 min – Easy*

Fresh ingredients and easy preparation make for a simple soup that actually tastes of mushroom.

INGREDIENTS

20 button mushrooms (about 250 g, 8 oz)
1 small potato
1 medium onion
15 g pack parsley
4 level tablespoons butter or margarine
1 pint plus $^1/_2$ a cup of milk
1 teaspoon dried thyme
Salt and freshly ground black pepper to taste

EQUIPMENT

Sharp knife
Chopping board
Vegetable peeler
Set of measuring spoons
Set of measuring cups
Wooden spoon
Saucepan
Food processor or liquidiser (optional) or sieve and wooden
spoon or Mouli

METHOD

Wipe the mushrooms clean. Discard any nasty ones. Chop the
end off the stalks. Peel the potato, cutting away any nasty bits, and
cutting out any eyes. Chop the potato and the mushrooms. Peel
and chop the onion. Wash, shake dry and finely chop the parsley.

Put the butter in the pan over a moderate heat. Fry the onion for
about 2 minutes until it is transparent, stirring to stop it sticking.
Add the potato and mushrooms and cook, stirring, for 2 minutes.
Add the milk and herbs. Bring to the boil, then turn down the
heat until it is just boiling (simmering). Put a lid on and cook for
20 minutes.

Put the soup in the liquidiser or food processor and blend until it is smooth. If you do not have a processor press it through a sieve with the back of a spoon or use a Mouli, or have it lumpy. Add salt and pepper, reheat and serve.

ADDITIONS & ALTERNATIVES
You can use oregano instead of thyme.

CREAMY PARSNIP & TARRAGON SOUP

Serves 4   ① *Preparation 15 min, Cooking 45 min – Easy*

Parsnip soup will surprise you. The taste seems to be so much better than the vegetable could hope to achieve.

INGREDIENTS
2 slices bread
3 tablespoons sunflower oil
15 g pack fresh tarragon, 2 or 3 sprigs of fresh tarragon, or 2 teaspoons dried tarragon
1 or 2 chicken stock cubes
4 cups boiling water
1 carrot
2 or 3 medium parsnips, about 500 g (1 lb)
1 large onion
3 tablespoons butter
1 clove garlic (optional)
2 tablespoons lemon juice
$^1/_2$ pint (1 cup) milk
$^1/_2 \times 250$ g tub fromage frais
Salt and freshly ground black pepper to taste

EQUIPMENT
Sharp knife
Chopping board
Frying-pan
Set of measuring spoons
Set of measuring cups
Bowl
Vegetable peeler
Garlic crusher
Wooden spoon
Saucepan with lid
Food processor, liquidiser, sieve or Mouli

METHOD
Cut the bread into cubes. Put the oil in the frying-pan on a medium heat. Wait until the oil gets hot and then fry the bread until it is brown, stirring often. Fish out the croutons and keep to serve with the soup.

Wash and shake dry the tarragon. Keep about half to add during cooking and finely chop the rest to add near the end. Dissolve the stock cubes in the water in the bowl. Peel and slice the carrot, cutting off both ends. Peel the parsnips and cut into chunks. Peel and chop the onion.

Put the butter in the large saucepan over a moderate heat. Peel and crush the garlic into the pan. Add the onion and cook for about 2 minutes until soft, stirring to stop it sticking. Add the carrot and parsnips and cook for 3 minutes, stirring frequently. Add the stock, unchopped tarragon and lemon juice. Bring to the boil, then turn down the heat until it is just boiling (simmering). Put a lid on and cook for 30 minutes until the carrots and parsnips are soft.

Fish out the unchopped tarragon. Put the soup in the liquidiser or food processor and blend until it is smooth. If you do not have a processor press it through a sieve with the back of a spoon or use a Mouli.

Rinse out the saucepan. Put the soup back in the pan and add the milk. Bring slowly to the boil. Mix the fromage frais with a fork and add to the soup and reheat again gently, but do not allow to boil.

Adjust the seasoning and stir in half the chopped tarragon. Serve the soup with the fried croutons and the remaining tarragon sprinkled on top.

ADDITIONS & ALTERNATIVES

You can use dried tarragon in the cooking but not to sprinkle on top before serving.

You can substitute a medium carton (284 ml, 10 fl oz) single cream for the fromage frais.

TIPS

You can buy ready-made stock in cartons from most supermarkets. You can also use vegetable stock cubes or buy Swiss vegetable bouillon powder (vegetable stock), if you are worried about the stuff that goes into stock cubes.

PUMPKIN SOUP

Serves 4   ① *Preparation 15 min, Cooking 30 min – Easy*

This American classic cannot help being impressive with its subtle flavour and orange colour.

INGREDIENTS

1 or 2 chicken stock cubes
4 cups boiling water
About 1 kg (2 lb) pumpkin
1 onion
3 tablespoons butter
1 clove garlic
Salt and pepper to taste
$^1/_2$ teaspoon ground ginger
1 tablespoon lemon juice
1 bouquet garni (looks like a herb tea bag)
$^1/_2$ pint (1 cup) milk
$^1/_2$ small carton (142 ml, 5 fl oz) single cream

EQUIPMENT

Set of measuring cups
Bowl
Sharp knife
Chopping board
Set of measuring spoons
Saucepan with lid
Garlic crusher
Wooden spoon
Frying-pan
Food processor or liquidiser or sieve or Mouli

METHOD

Dissolve the stock cubes in the water in the bowl. Peel the pumpkin and remove the seeds. Cut the flesh into 2 cm (1 in) cubes. Peel and thinly slice the onion.

Melt the butter in a large saucepan. Peel and crush the garlic into the pan. Add the onion and fry gently for 2 minutes until soft but not coloured. Add the pumpkin and cook and stir for about 3 minutes.

Add the stock and bring to the boil. Add the seasoning, ginger, lemon juice and bouquet garni. Bring to the boil, then turn down the heat until it is just boiling (simmering). Put a lid on and cook gently for 20 minutes until the pumpkin is soft.

Remove the bouquet garni. Cool the soup and then put the soup in the liquidiser or food processor and blend until it is smooth. If you do not have a processor press it through a sieve with the back of a spoon or use a Mouli.

Rinse out the saucepan. Put the soup back in the pan and add the milk. Bring slowly to the boil. Mix the fromage frais with a fork and add to the soup and reheat again gently, but do not allow to boil. Adjust the seasoning. Garnish with a swirl of cream, natural yoghurt or fromage frais and serve.

ADDITIONS & ALTERNATIVES

Sprinkle a couple of teaspoons of chopped parsley or chives on top. Bouquet garni has a mixture of herbs in it, so you can substitute a teaspoon of mixed Mediterranean herbs. It means you get little specks of herb in the dish, but so what.

Substitute natural yoghurt or fromage frais for the cream.

TIPS

You can buy ready-made stock in cartons from most supermarkets. You can also buy Swiss vegetable bouillon powder (vegetable stock), if you are worried about the stuff that goes into stock cubes.

BEAN SOUP

Serves 6   ① *Preparation 10 min, Cooking 15 min – Easy*

INTRODUCTION

This is a soup that is truly hearty, and if you are worried about the consequences of over-consumption of beans the parsley should help with that as well as add to the flavour.

INGREDIENTS

$1^1/_2$ × 400 g tins of white haricot beans
2 cups chicken stock or 1 chicken stock cube and 2 cups water
Salt and freshly ground pepper
2 tablespoons olive oil, plus extra to garnish
2 cloves garlic
3 tablespoons chopped parsley

EQUIPMENT

Tin opener
Food processor or liquidiser (optional)
Saucepan
Sharp knife
Chopping board
Set of measuring cups
Set of measuring spoons
Frying-pan
Garlic crusher

METHOD

Open the tins of beans and drain. Put half in the food processor or liquidiser with 1 cup of chicken stock. If you do not have a processor mash it up with a fork.

Put all the beans (whole and mashed) in the saucepan with the rest of the chicken stock. Add salt and pepper to taste. Warm gently for about 10 minutes.

Heat the olive oil in a small frying-pan. Peel and crush the garlic into the pan. Fry gently until soft. Stir in the parsley, then add to the soup. Pour the hot soup into bowls, pour over a little olive oil and serve.

ADDITIONS & ALTERNATIVES
Serve with crunchy white bread.

You can cook your own beans but it must be said it is a lot more time-consuming. Wash 1 cup dried white haricot beans. Put the beans in the bowl. Pour boiling water on top of them, and cover with about 5 cm (2 in) of water. Leave overnight to swell up. Then wash the haricot beans and put in the saucepan with at least 4 cups of fresh water. Bring to the boil and boil vigorously for 10 minutes. Turn down the heat and simmer until they are soft. This should take about $2^1/_2$ hours, unless you have a pressure cooker and then they will cook in 10 to 15 minutes once they have reached pressure. Add more water if it runs low. Let the haricot beans cool down.

VIBRANT VEGETABLES

These are mainly vegetarian meals, and you could adopt a pick and mix attitude with the curries for variety. We have chosen all these dishes so they will appeal to vegetarians and carnivores alike.

There are also a couple of recipes for side dishes for meat or fish at the end of the chapter. If you just want to know how to cook vegetables as in meat and two veg it is all in the 'How to' chapter (see page 326).

CHILLI BROCCOLI CURRY

Serves 4   *① Preparation 15 min, Cooking 15 min – Easy*

This broccoli dish is not a meal unless it is all eaten by 1 or 2 people (maximum) with some rice. It is a side dish and could accompany meat or other vegetables if it is to feed 4.

INGREDIENTS
250 g (8 oz) head of broccoli (about the size of a grapefruit)
2 fresh green chillies
1 small onion
3 tablespoons sunflower oil
4 cloves garlic
1 teaspoon cumin seeds

Salt to taste
1 tablespoon water

EQUIPMENT
Sharp knife
Chopping board
Fork
Set of measuring spoons
Garlic crusher
Saucepan with lid
Wooden spoon

METHOD
Wash the broccoli. Trim off the end of the stem. Cut or break into small florets. Chop the end off the chillies, split in half, and scrape out the seeds. Hold the chilli down with a fork and wash your hands afterwards. Chilli juice really stings if you get it anywhere sensitive. Cut the chilli into tiny bits. Peel and chop the onion.

Put the oil in the saucepan on a moderate heat. Peel and crush the garlic into the pan. Add the chilli and cumin. Cook for 2 minutes. Add the onion and fry for about 3 minutes until it is golden, stirring to stop it sticking.

Add the broccoli and salt. Stir round. Add the water. Turn the heat low and put the lid on. Cook very gently for about 10 minutes, shaking the pan from time to time.

ADDITIONS & ALTERNATIVES
Serve with any meat curries.

Try cauliflower, Savoy cabbage or sprouting broccoli instead of broccoli.

COCONUT MUSHROOM CURRY

Serves 2 to 4　　　　*① Preparation 10 min, Cooking 10 min – Easy*

This is a creamy Thai curry which will impress anybody.

INGREDIENTS
40 button mushrooms, about 500 g (1 lb)
400 ml tin coconut milk
1 tablespoon Thai Green Curry Paste
1 tablespoon fish sauce or soy sauce
1 teaspoon lemon juice
$^1/_2$ teaspoon salt
250 g packet frozen green peas, thawed

EQUIPMENT
Sharp knife
Chopping board
Tin opener
Set of measuring spoons
Saucepan with lid

METHOD
Wipe the mushrooms clean. Discard any nasty ones. Chop the end off the stalks. Put the coconut milk, curry paste, fish sauce, lemon juice and salt in a large saucepan. Bring to a boil. Add the mushrooms and peas. Bring to the boil, then turn down the heat until it is just boiling (simmering). Put a lid on and cook for 5 minutes.

ADDITIONS & ALTERNATIVES
Serve with rice or naan bread and other curries or meat dishes. This is very versatile and can be used for other vegetables such as

cauliflower or courgettes. You can also do chicken, steak or pork but you will need either to cook it first, or to slice it finely and cook for a little longer.

TIPS
You can buy Thai fish sauce in bottles.

AUBERGINE CURRY

Serves 4
⏱ Preparation 30 min, Cooking 45 min – Moderate

Loads of flavours here with lashings of tomato-based sauce.

INGREDIENTS
1 medium aubergine
1 large onion
3 cloves garlic
1 cm ($^1/_2$ in) fresh root ginger
400 g tin tomatoes
3 medium potatoes
1 tablespoon poppy seeds
1 tablespoon sesame seeds
3 tablespoons desiccated coconut
3 tablespoons sunflower oil
4 teaspoons fenugreek seeds
1 teaspoon ground cumin
1 teaspoon ground coriander
$^1/_2$ teaspoon chilli powder
1 teaspoon paprika
1 teaspoon ground turmeric
$1^1/_2$ cups warm water

1 teaspoon salt or to taste
1 tablespoon white wine vinegar

EQUIPMENT
Sharp knife
Chopping board
Tin opener
Set of measuring spoons
Garlic crusher
Vegetable peeler
Saucepan
Frying-pan
Wooden spoon
Saucepan with lid
Set of measuring cups
Coffee grinder, pestle and mortar or back of spoon

METHOD
Cut the ends off the aubergine, and cut into 5 cm (2 in) cubes. Peel and chop the onion. Peel and crush the garlic. Peel the ginger and cut into tiny cubes. Drain the tomatoes and keep the juice to use later. Mash the tomatoes in a cup. Peel the potatoes, cutting away any nasty bits, and cutting out any eyes. Boil the potatoes in the saucepan until tender, about 20 minutes. Drain, allow to cool, and cut into 5 cm (2 in) cubes.

Toast the poppy seeds, sesame seeds and desiccated coconut in a frying-pan with no oil in it over a very low heat, stirring all the time. When browned leave to cool, then crush them either in a clean coffee grinder or in a pestle and mortar. You can do a pretty good job with the back of a spoon in the pan.

Put the oil in a saucepan on a moderate heat. Fry the onion and fenugreek seeds for about 3 minutes until golden, stirring to stop it sticking. Add the garlic, ginger, cumin and coriander and fry for 2 minutes. Add the ground-up roasted seed and coconut mixture, chilli powder, paprika and turmeric. Cook for 1 minute. Add the aubergines and stir round, then carefully add the tomato juice, water, tomatoes and salt. Bring to the boil, then turn down the heat until it is just boiling (simmering). Put a lid on and cook for 10 minutes. Add the potatoes and vinegar and cook for 5 minutes.

ADDITIONS & ALTERNATIVES
Serve with naan bread or rice and other curries.

TIPS
Potatoes are cooked when a fork will go into them without pushing hard. If you push too hard they will fall apart.

PUMPKIN & COCONUT MILK CURRY

Serves 4   ① *Preparation 20 min, Cooking 30 min – Easy*

Pumpkin is a bit neglected here. There is more to this vegetable than Halloween lanterns. It is sweeter than you would expect and picks up curry flavour well, while keeping its own subtle flavour. Also it is brightly coloured.

INGREDIENTS
500 g (1 lb) piece pumpkin
2 onions
2 cloves garlic
1 cm ($^1/_2$ in) fresh root ginger
15 g pack fresh coriander
4 tablespoons sunflower oil

$^1/_2$ teaspoon onion seeds
4 curry leaves
1 small carton (142 ml, 5 fl oz) natural yoghurt
100 g pack ground almonds
$^1/_2$ teaspoon ground turmeric
$^1/_2$ teaspoon chilli powder
1 teaspoon garam masala
1 teaspoon salt
$^1/_2$ × 400 g tin coconut milk
1 tablespoon chopped toasted almonds

EQUIPMENT
Sharp knife
Chopping board
Set of measuring cups
Deep frying-pan, balti dish or wok
Set of measuring spoons
Bowl
Wooden spoon
Tin opener
Vegetable peeler

METHOD
Peel and deseed the pumpkin and cut into 2 cm (1 in) cubes. Peel and chop the onions. Peel and crush the garlic. Peel the ginger and cut into tiny cubes. Wash, shake dry and chop enough coriander to make about 2 tablespoons.

Put the oil in the pan or wok on a moderate heat. Add the onion seeds and curry leaves and fry until the seeds start popping. Add the onions and fry for 3 minutes until golden. Add the pumpkin and fry for about 5 minutes until golden brown. Gradually stir in the yoghurt to prevent it curdling. Add the garlic, ginger, ground almonds, turmeric, chilli powder, garam masala, salt, coconut milk and 1 tablespoon of fresh coriander. Bring to the boil, then turn down the heat until it is just boiling (simmering). Cook gently for 10 to 15 minutes until the pumpkin is tender.

Serve garnished with toasted almonds and the other tablespoon of chopped coriander.

ADDITIONS & ALTERNATIVES

Serve with rice, naan bread and pickles, or with other curries.

Try substituting another squash such as butternut or acorn for the pumpkin. It may cook more quickly, so check sooner.

VEG BALTI

Serves 4   ① *Preparation 30 min, Cooking 60 min – Easy*

Any combination of vegetables or pulses can be used in this recipe. It is a good dish to serve to your vegetarian friends, but you could also cook it as one curry to be served with a meat or fish dish.

INGREDIENTS

$^1/_2$ × 500 g pack (1 cup) yellow split peas
Salt
2 fresh green chillies
1 small aubergine
1 medium potato, cut into 1 cm ($^1/_2$ in) cubes
2 medium carrots
1 medium courgette
2 medium tomatoes
2 onions
3 cloves garlic

15 g pack fresh coriander
3 tablespoons sunflower oil
1 teaspoon onion seeds
1 teaspoon ground cumin
1 teaspoon ground coriander
1 teaspoon salt
1 teaspoon garam masala
1 cup water

EQUIPMENT
Set of measuring cups
Saucepan with lid
Vegetable peeler
Sharp knife
Chopping board
Set of measuring spoons
Deep frying-pan, balti dish or wok
Wooden spoon
Garlic crusher

METHOD
Check the split peas for stones and wash in a sieve. Put the split peas and salt into a saucepan of water. Bring to the boil, then turn down the heat until it is just boiling (simmering). Put a lid on and cook for 30 minutes. Check the water level from time to time and top it up if needed. Drain the peas and keep warm.

Get everything chopped while the split peas are cooking. Chop the end off the chillies, split in half, and scrape out the seeds. Hold the chilli down with a fork and wash your hands afterwards. Chilli juice really stings if you get it anywhere sensitive. Cut the chilli into thin strips.

Cut the ends off the aubergine, and cut into slices. Peel the potatoes, cutting away any nasty bits, and cut out any eyes. Chop the potatoes into 1 cm ($^1/_2$ in) cubes. Peel and slice the carrots, discarding both ends. Slice the courgettes, discarding both ends. Chop the tomatoes. Peel and slice the onions. Peel and crush the garlic. Wash, shake dry and finely chop the coriander, making about 2 tablespoons.

Put the oil in the frying-pan over a moderate heat. Fry the onion seeds until they start to pop, about 30 seconds. Add the onion and fry for about 3 minutes until it is golden, stirring to stop it sticking. Add the aubergine, potatoes, carrots and courgettes to the pan and stir-fry for 2 minutes.

Add the split peas, chillies, tomatoes, garlic, cumin, ground coriander, salt, garam masala and water. Bring to the boil, then turn down the heat until it is just boiling (simmering). Cook gently for 15 minutes or until all the vegetables are tender.

Add the fresh coriander just before serving.

ADDITIONS & ALTERNATIVES
Serve with rice or naan bread and pickles.

FALAFEL

Serves 4 to 6
① *Preparation 30 min, Cooking 15 min – Fiddly but fun*

Needs soaking for 2 hours if you use dried chickpeas.

An authentic Middle Eastern dish, familiar to festival goers and great for parties as you can make them in bulk.

INGREDIENTS
500 g pack chickpeas or 3 × 400 g tins
15 g pack fresh parsley
$^{1}/_{2}$ × 15 g pack fresh coriander
1 medium onion
4 spring onions
3 cloves garlic
2 teaspoons ground cumin
2 teaspoons ground coriander
$^{1}/_{2}$ teaspoon baking powder
2 cups sunflower oil for frying

EQUIPMENT
Sieve
Bowl
Tin opener
Sharp knife
Chopping board
Food processor or liquidiser (optional)
Garlic crusher
Set of measuring spoons
Deep frying-pan, balti dish or wok
Set of measuring cups
Kitchen paper

METHOD
Check the chickpeas for stones and wash in a sieve. Put the chickpeas in a bowl, cover well with boiling water and leave for at least 2 hours. Drain. Take their skins off by rubbing in a clean tea towel. Put the chickpeas in the food processor and grind, leaving them there. If using tins of chickpeas, open and drain the liquid off, then grind in the food processor.

Wash, shake dry and chop the parsley and coriander. Peel and chop the onion. Clean and prepare the spring onions. Cut the root end off and trim the leaves. Peel off and discard any dried up or slimy leaves. Chop into slices. Peel and crush the garlic into the food processor. Add the herbs, onion, spring onion, ground cumin, coriander and baking powder. Process until it becomes a smooth paste. Leave for an hour for the flavour to combine.

Wet your hands then shape the falafel into flat cakes about 4 cm (1¹/₂ in) across. Heat the oil in the deep frying-pan or wok and fry a few at a time until golden (about 3 minutes). Drain on kitchen paper and keep warm.

ADDITIONS & ALTERNATIVES
Serve with pitta bread and salad with some humus and chilli sauce. Tahini dip (see page 283) and Aubergine dip (see page 281) go well with this.

IBIZAN POTATO & AUBERGINE BAKE

Serves 4   ① *Preparation 30 min, Cooking 60 min – Easy*

If you have been to Ibiza you may not have got around to eating this dish – but then you were probably there in the heat of summer and not in the depths of a Balearic winter.

INGREDIENTS
1 onion
1 yellow pepper
³/₄ cup olive oil
2 cloves garlic
400 g tin tomatoes

2 teaspoons fresh oregano
$^1/_4$ teaspoon sugar
Salt and freshly ground pepper to taste
2 medium or 1 large aubergine (about 500 g, 1 lb)
3 medium potatoes (about 500 g, 1 lb)

EQUIPMENT
Sharp knife
Chopping board
Garlic crusher
Set of measuring cups
Set of measuring spoons
Saucepan with lid
Wooden spoon
Tin opener
Vegetable peeler
Frying-pan
Oven-proof dish
Aluminium foil

METHOD
Peel and finely chop the onion. Chop the end off the yellow pepper and cut out the core and seeds. Finely chop the pepper.

Put 3 tablespoons of the oil in the saucepan over a moderate heat. Peel and crush the garlic into the pan. Add the onion and yellow pepper and fry for about 5 minutes until soft, stirring to stop the mixture sticking.

Pour the juice from the tomatoes into the saucepan. Use the wooden spoon to mash the tomatoes while they are suntil in the tin. Pour the mashed tomatoes into the pan. Add the oregano, sugar, salt and pepper. Bring to the boil, then turn down the heat until it is just boiling (simmering). Cook gently for 20 to 30 minutes until it is thick.

Meanwhile, peel the potatoes, cutting away any nasty bits, and cut out any eyes. Slice the potatoes. Cut the ends off the aubergines, and cut into 1 cm ($^1/_2$ in) slices.

Fry the aubergines in 4 tablespoons olive oil until golden and cooked on both sides. Put to one side. Next fry the potatoes in 4 tablespoons olive oil until golden brown. Put the tomato sauce in the oven-proof dish. Put the aubergines and then potatoes on top. Dribble the rest of the olive oil on top. Cover the dish with foil and bake in an oven at 200° C, 400° F, Gas mark 6 for 20 minutes. Remove the foil and cook for 20 minutes more. Serve.

ADDITIONS & ALTERNATIVES
Serve with chunky bread and green salad.

POTATO & CHEESE FRY-UP

Serves 2 ① *Preparation 10 min, Cooking 40 min – Easy*

Not strictly vegetarian as it contains bacon, but almost, and you could always leave it out.

INGREDIENTS
1 large onion
4 rashers smoked back bacon
2 or 3 medium potatoes
100 g (4 oz) Cheshire cheese
$^1/_2$ teaspoon salt
1 tablespoon olive oil
Salt and freshly ground pepper
1 teaspoon chopped fresh sage

EQUIPMENT

Saucepan
Set of measuring spoons
Sharp knife
Chopping board
Set of measuring cups
Frying-pan
Wooden spoon

METHOD

Peel and slice the onion. Chop the bacon. Scrub the potatoes, cutting away any nasty bits, and cut out any eyes. Chop the potatoes into 1 cm ($^1/_2$ in) dice. Break up the cheese into bits.

Put the potatoes in a saucepan of cold water with the salt. Bring to the boil, then turn down the heat until it is just boiling (simmering) and cook for 2 minutes only. Drain.

Put the oil in the frying-pan on a moderate heat. Add the onion and bacon and fry gently for about 5 minutes, stirring to stop it sticking. Add the potatoes and stir round. Add the salt and pepper and the sage. Stir round, cover the pan with a lid and cook gently over a low heat for 15 minutes, or until the potatoes are tender.

Stir in the cheese, and heat with the lid off for 5 minutes.

ADDITIONS & ALTERNATIVES

Serve with green salad or sliced tomato.

Substitute Lancashire or mature Cheddar cheese.

SWEET POTATO & SPINACH

Serves 4   ① *Preparation 15 min, Cooking 15 min – Easy*

You eat this as a meal or use it as an exotic vegetable.

VIBRANT VEGETABLES

INGREDIENTS

2 onions
100 g pack pine nuts
2 medium sweet potatoes (about 500 g, 1 lb)
1 teaspoon salt
4 tablespoons sunflower or olive oil
1 clove garlic
500 g (1 lb) fresh spinach
1 tablespoon garam masala
2 chopped dried red chillies
2 teaspoons water
Fresh nutmeg

EQUIPMENT

Sharp knife
Chopping board
Vegetable peeler
Aluminium foil or oven-proof dish
Saucepan
Sieve
Deep frying-pan, balti dish or wok
Set of measuring spoons
Wooden spoon
Garlic crusher
Bowl
Grater

METHOD

Peel and slice the onion. Toast the pine nuts either on the foil under the grill or in the oven-proof dish at 220° C, 425° F, Gas mark 7 for 5 minutes.

Peel the sweet potatoes, cutting away any nasty bits, and chop into 2 cm (1 in) cubes. Put the sweet potatoes in a saucepan of water with the salt. Bring to the boil and cook for 5 minutes. Drain.

Put the oil in the frying-pan over a moderate heat. Fry the onion for about three minutes until it is golden, stirring to stop it sticking. Peel and crush the garlic into the pan. Add the sweet potatoes and pine nuts and fry for 2 minutes until the sweet potatoes have absorbed the oil.

Rinse the spinach, cut off any stems and shake dry. Crush the dried chillies in the bowl with a spoon. Add the spinach, garam masala and chilli to the frying-pan and stir-fry for 2 minutes. Add the water and stir-fry for 4 minutes until the sweet potatoes and spinach are cooked. Grate some nutmeg on top before serving.

ADDITIONS & ALTERNATIVES
Serve with rice and other curries or salad.

This goes well with roast or grilled chicken.

POTATO PANCAKE

Serves 2 to 4   ⏲ *Preparation 10 min, Cooking 10 min – Easy*

You can serve this with bacon or sausages or just eat alone with a little pickle, or follow the alternatives below.

INGREDIENTS
3 medium potatoes (about 500 g, 1 lb)
1 small onion
2 eggs
4 heaped tablespoons plain flour
1 teaspoon salt
$^1/_2$ teaspoon baking powder
2 tablespoons sunflower oil

EQUIPMENT
Vegetable peeler
Sharp knife
Chopping board
Kitchen paper
Bowl
Food processor or liquidiser (optional)
Set of measuring cups
Set of measuring spoons
Frying-pan or griddle

METHOD
Peel the potatoes, cutting away any nasty bits, and cutting out any eyes. Chop the potatoes into little bits. Peel and roughly chop the onion. Break the eggs into a bowl and pick out any bits of shell.

Put everything in the liquidiser or food processor and blend until it is well chopped and mixed. Scrape the sides down if you need to. Wipe some oil on a griddle or thick frying-pan and put on a high heat. Pour large dollops of the mixture into the heated pan and brown on each side. Repeat (if necessary) until you have used up all the mixture. Keep warm.

ADDITIONS & ALTERNATIVES
Good with a dollop of crème fraîche and a teaspoon of lumpfish roe or bits of chopped smoked salmon.

PEPPER & TOMATO STEW

Serves 4   ⏱ *Preparation 15 min, Cooking 35 min – Easy*

This is a really good accompaniment to simple meat dishes like steak or roast chicken. Make sure it gets to be rich and thick and not watery and runny.

INGREDIENTS
1 large onion
6 red peppers
6 large ripe tomatoes, about 750 g ($1^1/_2$ lb) or 2 × 400 g tins
5 tablespoons olive oil
2 cloves garlic
15 g pack fresh parsley
Salt and freshly ground black pepper to taste

EQUIPMENT
Sharp knife
Chopping board
Set of measuring spoons
Frying-pan or wok with lid
Wooden spoon
Garlic crusher

METHOD
Peel and finely slice the onion. Chop the end off the red peppers and cut out the core and seeds. Cut the pepper into strips. If using the tinned tomatoes drain and roughly chop. If using fresh tomatoes cut a small cross in the bottom of each one. Bring a small saucepan of water to the boil. Put the tomatoes in for about 30 seconds then lift them out with a slotted spoon and put in cold water. When cooled pull the skin off starting at the cut in the base.

Skin and roughly chop the tomatoes. Wash, shake dry and finely chop about 1 tablespoon of parsley.

Put the oil in the frying-pan over a moderate heat. Fry the onion for about 3 minutes until it is golden, stirring to stop it sticking. Peel and crush the garlic into the pan. Add the peppers and cook on a low heat for about 3 minutes. Add the tomatoes, parsley and salt and pepper to taste. Cover and cook very gently for 30 minutes until the mixture is pretty dry. Check about 10 minutes before the end of cooking and take off the lid to allow the liquid to evaporate. Taste and adjust seasoning before serving either hot or cold.

ADDITIONS & ALTERNATIVES
Serve with roast meat or steak.
Serve cold with thick slices of crusty bread as a starter.

SPINACH & PINE NUTS

Serves 4   ① *Preparation 15 min, Cooking 12 min – Easy*

This classy little Italian number will liven up your meat a treat. Keep the cooking to a minimum for the spinach otherwise you will end up with green sludge, particularly if you are using the frozen stuff.

INGREDIENTS
2 tablespoons sultanas
1 kg (2 lb) fresh spinach or 500 g (1 lb) frozen spinach
1 rounded tablespoon butter
2 tablespoons olive oil
1 clove garlic
1 heaped tablespoon pine nuts
Salt and freshly ground pepper to taste

EQUIPMENT
Bowl
Saucepan
Sieve
Wooden spoon
Sharp knife
Chopping board
Garlic crusher
Set of measuring spoons

METHOD
Put the sultanas in a bowl and cover with hot water for 15 minutes until they swell up.

Wash the spinach (if fresh). Put in the saucepan without any water. Cook gently for about 5 minutes, or until thawed if using frozen spinach. Drain the spinach, allow to cool and squeeze out as much moisture as possible in a sieve with a spoon.

Put the butter and oil in the frying-pan over a moderate heat. Peel and crush the garlic into the pan. Cook gently for 2 minutes. Add the spinach and stir until coated and completely heated through, about 2 to 3 minutes. Drain the sultanas. Add the sultanas, pine nuts and salt and pepper to taste to the spinach. Heat through for about 1 minute, then serve immediately.

ADDITIONS & ALTERNATIVES
Serve as a vegetable with any meat or fish dish.

FENNEL AU GRATIN

Serves 4   ① *Preparation 10 min, Cooking 25 min – Easy*

A good vegetable with grilled fish or steak.

INGREDIENTS
4 small fennel bulbs
1 teaspoon salt
4 tablespoons butter
4 tablespoons olive oil
50 g ($^1/_2$ cup) Fontina cheese, grated
3 tablespoons freshly grated Parmesan cheese
Salt and freshly ground pepper to taste

EQUIPMENT
Sharp knife
Chopping board
Large saucepan
Set of measuring spoons
Grater
Set of measuring cups
Flame-proof gratin dish
Wooden spoon

METHOD
Wash and trim the fennel. Cut each bulb into quarters lengthways.
Put the fennel into a large pan of boiling salted water. Cook for 20
minutes until tender. Drain.

Put the flame-proof gratin dish on a low heat and melt the butter
with the oil. Add the fennel and stir to coat in the oil and butter.
Take off the heat. Arrange the fennel quarters in the dish. Cover
with the two cheeses, salt and pepper.

Grill under a hot grill for about 5 minutes, until the cheeses are
melted, bubbling and slightly brown.

ADDITIONS & ALTERNATIVES
Use Gruyère or Emmental instead of the Fontina.

FLASH FISH

This is not fish and chips. You can get that at the chippy. These are fish dishes from all round the world with wonderful spices and flavours. Although the flavours are exotic the fish are easy to find, and fish is surprisingly easy and quick to cook. And although the recipes are all flash you can do any of them any day of the week and not be disappointed.

BAKED HAKE

Serves 4   ① *Preparation 15 min, Cooking 30 min – Easy*

This is a meal in a dish. It needs nothing more than a bit of salad to complement it.

INGREDIENTS
3 medium potatoes
1 clove garlic
1 medium onion
1 bay leaf
400 g tin tomatoes
1 teaspoon salt
500 g (1 lb) hake fillets
3 tablespoons flour

$^1/_2$ cup (8 tablespoons) oil
1 cup frozen peas
$^1/_2$ cup pitted green olives
3 or 4 anchovy fillets from a 50 g tin

EQUIPMENT

Saucepan
Sharp knife
Chopping board
Tin opener
Sieve
Wooden spoon
Set of measuring cups
Plastic bag
Frying-pan
Oven-proof dish

METHOD

Wash and peel the potatoes, boil for 10 minutes, drain, and slice. Peel the garlic and onion. Chop the onion in half. Put the garlic, onion and bay leaf in the saucepan. Open the tin of tomatoes. Pour the juice from the tomatoes into the saucepan. Use the wooden spoon to mash the tomatoes while they are still in the tin, then pour the mashed tomatoes into the pan. Bring to the boil, then turn down the heat until it is just boiling (simmering). Cook for 20 minutes. Remove the garlic, onion and bay leaf and discard.

Rinse and dry the hake. Cut the hake into big bite-sized pieces. Put the flour in the plastic bag with a little salt and pepper. Put a few lumps of hake in the bag and holding the top tight closed shake them up. They will get coated in flour. Pick them out. Repeat until all the hake is coated. Fry the hake in 4 tablespoons of oil until pale golden, about 3 to 5 minutes.

Put the other 4 tablespoons of oil in the oven-proof dish. Put in the potatoes followed by the hake, tomato sauce, peas, and olives. Chop the anchovies into small bits and scatter on top. Cook for 15 to 20 minutes at 200° C, 400° F, Gas mark 6, and then serve

ADDITIONS & ALTERNATIVES
Serve with salad.
  Use cod or other white fish instead of the hake.
  Use passata (sieved tomatoes) instead of the tinned ones.

CAN GAT SQUID

Serves 2   ① *Preparation 20 min, Cooking 20 min – Easy*

Another recipe from Ibiza. This is very much like a sautéed squid dish from a restaurant called Can Gat in St Vincent. It is great on hot summer's days for lunch or dinner and pretty good in cold weather too.

INGREDIENTS
1 red and 1 yellow pepper
1 onion
8 cloves garlic
2 fresh red chillies
15 g pack fresh parsley
500 g (1 lb) prepared small squid tubes
4 tablespoons olive oil
1 to 2 teaspoons paprika
2 tablespoons brandy
Salt

EQUIPMENT
Sharp knife
Chopping board
Frying-pan
Wooden spoon
Set of measuring cups

METHOD
Chop the end off the red and yellow peppers and cut out the core and seeds. Cut the pepper into small pieces. Peel and chop the onion. Peel the garlic and cut in half. Wash and stab the chillies with a fork in several places. Wash, shake dry and finely chop the parsley.

Check the squid. Throw the squid tentacles away. Cut the squid open and wash. Now would be a good time to check for the clear plastic-like quill. If it is there take it out and throw away. Cut the squid into strips.

Put the oil in the frying-pan over a low heat. Fry the garlic and chilli gently for about 5 minutes. Add the peppers, onion and paprika and cook gently for 10 minutes. Add the squid strips and cook for 2 minutes. Add the brandy and cook for 4 minutes.

ADDITIONS & ALTERNATIVES
Serve with crusty bread and green salad.

Use squid rings.

You can cook almost anything in this oil mixture including fine slices of chicken, pork or beef, prawns or scallops.

TIPS
Squid tubes are stocked by supermarkets and some fishmongers. Don't buy unprepared squid unless you like slimy things and know how to take the quill out. But check the prepared ones as you chop

them for a strip of clear plastic-like stuff. If you find it, throw it away. It is the quill.

CRUSTY SALMON

Serves 4   ① *Preparation 20 min, Cooking 25 min – Easy*

You get a thick crunchy crust on top of the fish with a lot of flavour. It improves the taste of the salmon without overwhelming it. You can pre-prepare the crust.

INGREDIENTS
3 heaped tablespoons fresh white breadcrumbs
12 pitted black olives
15 g pack fresh tarragon
4 spring onions
4 boneless and skinless salmon fillets, about 175 g (6 oz) each
1 clove garlic
2 tablespoons olive oil
1 level tablespoon butter, melted, plus extra for greasing
Juice of $1/2$ lemon
$1/4$ teaspoon wholegrain mustard
Salt and freshly ground black pepper to taste
$1/8$ teaspoon sugar

EQUIPMENT
Grater
Sharp knife
Chopping board
Oven-proof dish
Garlic crusher
Bowl

Lemon juicer
Set of measuring cups
Set of measuring spoons
Small bowl/whisk or jam jar with tight-fitting lid
Wooden spoon

METHOD
Grate the bread into crumbs. Chop the olives. Wash, shake dry and
finely chop the tarragon. Clean and prepare the spring onions. Cut
the root end off and trim the leaves. Peel off and discard any dried
up or slimy leaves. Chop into thin slices.

Lay the salmon fillets on a lightly greased oven-proof dish. Peel
and crush the garlic into the bowl. Add the breadcrumbs, olives,
tarragon, 1 tablespoon of oil, the butter and spring onions and mix
well. Spread the mixture on the salmon fillets. Cook for 25 minutes
at 190° C, 375° F, Gas mark 5.

Mix the remaining oil with the lemon, mustard, salt, pepper and
sugar. You can whisk them together in a bowl or put them all
together in a jam jar with a tight-fitting lid and shake until mixed.
Pour on the salmon before serving.

ADDITIONS & ALTERNATIVES
Serve with tomato salad.

Use parsley instead of tarragon.

You can buy ready-made breadcrumbs from a supermarket or
baker if you are feeling lazy.

APPLE MACKEREL

Serves 4   ⏲ *Preparation 10 min, Cooking 20 min – Easy*

This is a fish that is just so under-rated. Just make sure you buy it firm and fresh. The apples and lemon add a bit of a tart taste.

INGREDIENTS

4 fresh mackerel
15 g pack fresh parsley
4 tablespoons butter, plus extra for greasing
$^1/_2$ teaspoon dried thyme
Salt and freshly ground black pepper
2 large cooking apples
2 tablespoons olive oil
1 tablespoon brandy
2 tablespoons lemon juice

EQUIPMENT

Sharp knife
Chopping board
Set of measuring spoons
Bowl
Oven-proof dish
Aluminium foil
Vegetable peeler
Apple corer
Frying-pan
Wooden spoon

METHOD

Preheat the oven to 220° C, 425° F, Gas mark 7.
  Buy cleaned fish with the heads off.

Wash, shake dry and finely chop the parsley to make about 2 tablespoons. Mix the parsley with half the butter and the thyme. Put the fish in a well buttered oven-proof dish. Spread bits of the butter mixture over the fish and season with salt and pepper. Cover the dish with aluminium foil. Bake in the preheated oven for 20 to 25 minutes.

Peel, core and slice the apples. Put the oil and the remaining butter in the frying-pan. Add the apple slices and fry for about 5 minutes until soft. Add the brandy 30 seconds before taking it off the heat. Drain the apples on kitchen paper and keep warm.

Serve the mackerel with the apple slices.

ADDITIONS & ALTERNATIVES
Serve with salad.

MARINATED SWORDFISH

Serves 2 ① *Preparation 15 min, Cooking 10 min – Easy*

Needs to marinate for 1 hour.

This is a regular favourite with us. It is quick to cook and tastes really fresh. The griddle pan can make a bit of smoke while the fish is cooking and can set off the smoke alarm, so open a window.

INGREDIENTS
2 cm (1 in) fresh root ginger
2 cloves garlic
2 limes or 1 lemon (or 4 tablespoons lime or lemon juice)
2 swordfish steaks, 1 to 2 cm ($^1/_2$ to $^3/_4$ in) thick, about 250 to 400 g (8 to 12 oz) together
1 tablespoon sunflower oil

EQUIPMENT
Sharp knife
Chopping board
Lemon juicer
Set of measuring spoons
Bowl
Wooden spoon
Griddle pan (or grill)

METHOD
Peel and thinly slice the ginger and garlic. Juice the limes or lemon. Put the swordfish in the bowl with the lime juice, ginger and garlic. Leave for at least 1 hour, turning over once.

Cook the steaks for 5 minutes each side on a hot griddle pan with the oil. If you do not have a griddle pan then grill them. They will not get the pleasing brown griddle lines on them though, and will need about another 5 minutes to cook through.

ADDITIONS & ALTERNATIVES
Serve with salad, couscous or sauté potatoes.

MUSSELS AU GRATIN

Serves 4   ① *Preparation 30 min, Cooking 15 min – Easy*

The most important thing to remember about mussels is to throw away any that are not closed when you wash them and any that do not open during cooking.

INGREDIENTS
1 kg (2 lb) fresh mussels in shell
15 g pack fresh parsley

15 g pack fresh chives
$^{1}/_{2}$ Spanish onion
$^{1}/_{2}$ cup (125 ml, 4 fl oz) dry white wine
4 tablespoons butter
2 slices bread

EQUIPMENT
Sharp knife
Chopping board
Set of measuring cups
Set of measuring spoons
Wooden spoon
Saucepan with lid
Oven-proof dish
Grater

METHOD
Try to buy mussels that have been cleaned up. Wash the mussels thoroughly in running water and scrape them to get any mud or wildlife off them. Throw away any cracked or open ones they could make you ill. Scrape off the beard (the bit that sticks out from the edge of the shell) and give them a final rinse.

Wash, shake dry and finely chop the parsley and chives separately. Peel and finely chop the onion. Put the onion, 2 tablespoons of parsley, the mussels and the wine in the pan over a moderate heat. Put the lid on the pan and cook for about 5 minutes, shaking the pan often until the mussel shells open. Lift out the mussels and keep the juice. Remove and discard the empty half shells.

Arrange the mussels in an oven-proof dish or 4 individual gratin dishes. Add the butter to the mussel liquid and cook for 5 minutes or until reduced by half. Meanwhile, grate the bread to make breadcrumbs. Pour the butter mixture over the mussels and top off with the breadcrumbs, chives and remaining parsley. Grill for 2 minutes until slightly crispy.

ADDITIONS & ALTERNATIVES
Serve as a starter.

TIPS
Always buy fresh mussels on the day you intend to eat them. You should deal with them as soon as you can after getting home, but if this is not possible, put them to soak in a large bowl of cold water until you are ready. Discard the water and rinse the mussels when you are ready to prepare them.

You can buy ready-made breadcrumbs from a supermarket or baker.

MUSTARD TUNA

Serves 4   ⏱ *Preparation 10 min, Cooking 10 min – Easy*

Plus 30 minutes to marinate.

Fresh tuna is not like tinned tuna. It is quite meaty for a fish and there are no little fish bones to deal with. This is really quick and flash.

INGREDIENTS
$^1/_2$ cup Dijon mustard
1 tablespoon flour
Salt and freshly ground pepper to taste
4 tuna steaks, about 250 g (8 oz) each

EQUIPMENT
Set of measuring cups
Set of measuring spoons
Bowl
Wooden spoon
Spoon

METHOD
Mix the mustard, flour, salt and pepper to a smooth paste. Spread on both sides of the tuna steaks and leave to stand for 30 minutes so the flavours sink in.

Grill for 5 to 10 minutes or until done, turning once and spreading any spare mustard mixture on the second side. Serve at once.

ADDITIONS & ALTERNATIVES
This works well on a barbecue.

Serve with new potatoes, or couscous and salad.

PRAWN CRÊPES

Serves 4   ⏱ *Preparation 15 min, Cooking 25 min – Easy*

This has a creamy prawn filling and by using shop bought crêpes we think we have taken the pain out of the preparation of this dish.

INGREDIENTS
250 g pack cooked peeled prawns
1 tablespoon fresh parsley
1 tablespoon fresh fennel leaves
$^1/_2$ onion, chopped
125 g (4 oz) button mushrooms, sliced
2 rounded tablespoons butter

2 tablespoons flour
$^1/_2$ cup milk
1 small carton (142 ml, 5 fl oz) single cream
Salt and freshly ground pepper to taste
1 tablespoon grated Parmesan cheese
1 pack of pre-cooked crêpes

EQUIPMENT
Frying-pan
Sharp knife
Chopping board
Set of measuring spoons
Set of measuring cups
Oven-proof dish
Wooden spoon
Saucepan

METHOD
Preheat the oven to 190° C, 375° F, Gas mark 5. Let the prawns thaw. Wash, shake dry and finely chop the parsley and fennel. Peel and chop the onion. Wipe the mushrooms clean. Discard any nasty ones. Chop the end off the stalks. Slice the mushrooms.

Put 1 tablespoon of butter in the frying-pan over a moderate heat. Fry the onion for about 3 minutes until it is golden, stirring to stop it sticking. Add the mushrooms and cook for 1 minute. Add the flour and stir round. Gradually add the milk and then the cream. Cook until it thickens, 3 to 5 minutes. Add the prawns, parsley, fennel, and salt and pepper to taste and stir round.

Divide the filling between the pancakes, roll them up and put in a greased oven-proof dish. Dot the remaining butter and cheese on top. Cook in the preheated oven for 15 minutes.

ADDITIONS & ALTERNATIVES

Serve with salad.

If you want to make your own crêpes just follow this recipe. It
will add about 15 minutes to the cooking times.

1 egg
1 cup milk
1 cup (125 g, 4 oz) plain flour
1 tablespoon oil
Pinch of salt

EQUIPMENT

Food processor or liquidiser or bowl and whisk
15 cm (6 in) omelette pan

Break the egg into a bowl and pick out any bits of shell. Put it
and all the other ingredients in the liquidiser or food processor and
blend until smooth. Or put all the ingredients in the bowl and
whisk until smooth.

Heat the omelette pan and add a few drops of oil. Add 1 tablespoon of the batter and tilt the pan to let it spread over the pan
evenly. Cook until the underside is brown, about 20 seconds, then
turn and cook for 10 seconds. Repeat with the remaining batter.

SALMON CURRY

Serves 4 ⏱ *Preparation 25 min, Cooking 20 min – Easy*

This is more spicy than hot, being somewhere between Indian and
Mediterranean cooking.

INGREDIENTS

4 salmon steaks with skin on, about 200 g (7 oz) each
1 teaspoon salt
5 cloves garlic
1 medium onion
4 tablespoons vegetable oil
4 teaspoons ground coriander
1 teaspoon chilli powder
1 teaspoon ground turmeric
$1/2 \times 400$ ml tin coconut milk
2 tablespoons lime juice
Few bits of coriander to garnish (optional)

EQUIPMENT

Plate
Sharp knife
Chopping board
Garlic crusher
Set of measuring cups
Set of measuring spoons
Large frying-pan with lid or wide wok
Bowl
Wooden spoon
Tin opener

METHOD

Scrape the scales from the fish. Halve the steaks lengthways discarding the bone and lay them on a large plate in a single layer. Sprinkle the salt on the steaks and leave for 20 minutes. Peel and crush the garlic. Peel and chop the onion.

Put the oil in the frying-pan over a moderate heat. Fry the onion for about 5 minutes until it is golden, stirring to stop it sticking.

Add the garlic and fry for 30 seconds. Add the coriander, chilli and turmeric and fry for 1 minute, stirring constantly. Add the coconut milk to the pan. Add the lime juice and cook gently for 2 minutes. Arrange the fish in the pan in a single layer. Bring to the boil, then turn down the heat until it is just boiling (simmering). Put a lid on and cook for 5 minutes. Turn the fish over and cook for 5 minutes more. Serve garnished with the coriander.

ADDITIONS & ALTERNATIVES

Serve with rice and salad.

Try shark instead of salmon.

Substitute tamarind concentrate for the lime juice.

SAVOURY HAKE

Serves 4   ① *Preparation 25 min, Cooking 45 min – Easy*

This is a kind of exotic fish and potato pie with a hint of chilli and a heap of flavour.

INGREDIENTS

500 g (1 lb) hake fillets

1 lemon

15 g pack fresh parsley

3 fresh sage leaves

1 red chilli

2 cloves garlic

4 or 5 medium waxy potatoes, about 500 g (1 lb) (Desiree, Charlotte, large new Jersey, Egyptian or Cyprus)

2 tablespoons butter

$^1/_2$ teaspoon dried rosemary

Salt and freshly ground pepper to taste
3 tablespoons olive oil
1 cup dry white wine

EQUIPMENT
Sharp knife
Chopping board
Lemon juicer
Set of measuring cups
Set of measuring spoons
Saucepan
Bowl
Wooden spoon
Spoon
Ovenproof dish

METHOD
You can cook the fish from frozen. Juice the lemon. Wash, shake
dry and finely chop the parsley. Chop the sage. Chop the end off
the chilli, split in half, and scrape out the seeds. Hold the
chilli down with a fork and wash your hands afterwards. Chilli
juice really stings if you get it anywhere sensitive. Cut the chilli
into tiny bits. Peel the garlic then chop it into tiny pieces.

Wash the potatoes and boil in their skins for 15 minutes. If they
are new, drain, and cut into medium slices. If they are Desiree or
Charlotte, peel before slicing.

Rub the inside of the oven-proof dish with the butter. Arrange
the fish and potatoes in layers, starting with the potatoes. Sprinkle
each layer with lemon juice, parsley, sage, chilli, garlic, rosemary,
salt and pepper and oil. End with a layer of potato on top. Add the
wine and cook at 180° C, 350° F, Gas mark 4 for 30 minutes.

TIPS
You can buy 600 g packs of frozen white fish fillets (cod, hake, or haddock).

SPICED SOLE

Serves 4 ⏱ *Preparation 15 min, Cooking 20 min – Easy*

This needs to marinate for about an hour.

Dover sole is a prince among fish and this recipe elevates it to the level of king among fish.

INGREDIENTS
4 Dover soles or lemon soles, each about 250 g (8 oz)
1 onion
1 spring onion
2 cloves garlic
2 cm (1 in) fresh root ginger
1 red chilli
1 tablespoon fresh coriander leaves
1 teaspoon ground coriander
1 tablespoon ground cumin
1 teaspoon turmeric
$1/2$ teaspoon salt
6 tablespoons sunflower oil

EQUIPMENT
Sharp knife
Chopping board
Grater

Garlic crusher
Bowl
Wooden spoon
Set of measuring spoons
Large frying-pan

METHOD

Buy prepared fish with the heads off and skinned if possible. If not skin it yourself. Score criss-cross lines down to the bone on both sides of the fish. Peel and finely chop the onion. Clean and prepare the spring onion. Cut the root end off, trim the leaves. Peel off and discard any dried up or slimy leaves. Chop into thin slices. Peel and crush the garlic into the bowl. Peel and grate the ginger. Chop the end off the chillies, split in half, and scrape out the seeds. Hold the chilli down with a fork and wash your hands afterwards. Chilli juice really stings if you get anywhere sensitive. Cut the chilli into tiny bits. Wash, shake dry and finely chop 1 tablespoon of the fresh coriander. Keep a few bits to put on the fish before serving.

Put the ground coriander, cumin and turmeric in the bowl with the onion, ginger and salt. Mix with a few tablespoons of water to make a thin paste. Add the spring onion, chilli and fresh coriander.

Spread the mixture over the fish, pressing it into the cuts. Leave to stand for an hour.

Put the oil in the large frying-pan over a moderate heat. Cook the fish a couple at a time for about 5 to 7 minutes on each side until golden brown. The fish are large and should lie flat when cooking.

ADDITIONS & ALTERNATIVES

Serve with salad, rice salad or couscous.

Try buying skinless fillets. Allow 2 per person and score only one side lightly before spreading on the marinade. Since the fish is only half as thick it will take about half as long to cook.

SPICY TROUT

Serves 4   ① *Preparation 30 min, Cooking 20 min – Easy*

It needs to marinate for about 30 minutes.

Forget your trout and almonds and go for this spicy Indian trout recipe instead.

INGREDIENTS

4 prepared trout, headless and gutted, each about 200 g (7 oz)
15 g pack fresh coriander
4 tablespoons lemon juice
1 teaspoon ground cumin
$^1/_2$ teaspoon salt
$^1/_2$ teaspoon fresh ground pepper
3 tablespoons sunflower oil
1 teaspoon fennel seeds
1 teaspoon onion seeds
1 clove garlic
$^1/_2$ × 400 ml tin coconut milk
3 tablespoons tomato purée
$^1/_3$ cup (50 g, 2 oz) sultanas
1 teaspoon garam masala (see page 347)
$^1/_4$ cup (25 g, 1 oz) chopped cashew nuts
1 lemon

EQUIPMENT

Sharp knife
Chopping board
Deep frying-pan, balti dish or wok
Set of measuring spoons
Lemon juicer

Set of measuring cups
Bowl
Wooden spoon
Garlic crusher
Tin opener

METHOD

Wash the trout and scrape the skin with a knife. Make some deep cuts in the trout to help the marinade to flavour the fish. Wash, shake dry and finely chop 2 tablespoons of coriander. Keep a few sprigs for garnish. Mix the coriander, lemon juice, cumin and salt. Pour over the trout. Turn the fish over in the marinade to coat evenly, then leave to marinate for 30 minutes.

Put the oil in the frying-pan on a moderate heat. Fry the fennel seeds and onion seeds until they start popping, about 30 seconds. Peel and crush the garlic into the pan. Add the coconut milk and tomato purée. Bring to the boil, then turn down the heat until it is just boiling. Add the trout, sultanas and garam masala. Cover the pan and cook gently for 5 minutes. Turn the trout over and simmer for 10 minutes. Sprinkle the cashew nuts and coriander sprigs on top before serving. Cut the lemon into wedges and serve with the trout.

ADDITIONS & ALTERNATIVES

Serve with rice or salad.

Use bought fish stock, or 1 stock cube dissolved in 1 cup (250 ml, 8 fl oz) of boiling water instead of the coconut milk. Or use a 4 cm (2 in) cube of creamed coconut and 1 cup of water.

TROUT & BACON

Serves 4   ① *Preparation 5 min, Cooking 25 min – Easy*

This recipe is almost too good to be true. Really, really simple and with an unusual and delicious flavour.

INGREDIENTS
8 trout fillets with the skin on
Small bunch fresh parsley
8 slices bacon
Salt and freshly ground black pepper to taste
2 tablespoons melted butter

EQUIPMENT
Sharp knife
Chopping board
Oven-proof dish
Set of measuring cups
Set of measuring spoons

METHOD
Preheat the oven to 180° C, 350° F, Gas mark 4.

Rinse the fish.

Wash, shake dry and finely chop 2 tablespoons of parsley. Put the bacon in the bottom of the oven-proof dish. Put the trout on the bacon, skin-side up. Sprinkle with salt, pepper and parsley. Put dabs of butter on top and cook in the preheated oven for about 25 minutes.

ADDITIONS & ALTERNATIVES
Serve with crusty bread, new potatoes and salad. Be sure to serve it with the bacon from the oven.

TUNA WITH BEANS

Serves 3 or 4   ① *Preparation 10 min, Cooking 5 min – Easy*

If you can open tins you will do all right with this Italian dish.

INGREDIENTS
1 small onion
Small bunch fresh parsley
15 g pack fresh coriander
200 g tin tuna fish in oil
400 g tin cannellini or white haricot beans
2 cups water
3 tablespoons olive oil
1 tablespoon white wine vinegar
Salt and freshly ground pepper to taste

EQUIPMENT
Sharp knife
Chopping board
Tin opener
Set of measuring cups
Set of measuring spoons
Saucepan
Bowl
Wooden spoon
Spoon

METHOD
Peel and thinly slice the onion. Wash, shake dry and finely chop 1 tablespoon of parsley. Wash, shake dry and finely chop 2 tablespoons of coriander. Drain the tuna and break it up with a fork.

Open the tin of beans and drain. Put in the pan with the water and bring to the boil and cook for 5 minutes.

Put the oil, vinegar, salt and pepper in a bowl and whisk, or put in a jam jar with a tight-fitting lid and shake until mixed. Add to the hot beans. Add the coriander. Add the onion and the tuna and gently stir.

Sprinkle the parsley on top before serving.

ADDITIONS & ALTERNATIVES
Serve with crusty bread and salad.

Cook your own beans. Rinse 1 cup of beans. Put the beans in the bowl. Pour enough boiling water on top of them to cover. Leave them for 1 to 2 hours to swell up. Then rinse the beans and put in the saucepan with at least 2 cups (500 ml) of fresh water. Bring to the boil and boil vigorously for 10 minutes. Turn down the heat and simmer until they are soft. This should take about $1^1/_2$ hours. Add more water if it runs low. Let the beans cool down.

BRILLIANT BIRDS

These recipes are flash AND easy. What more could you ask for?
We start off with some chicken recipes for familiarity and end up
with the exotic duck.

CHICKEN & LEEKS

Serves 4   ① *Preparation 15 min, Cooking 90 min – Easy*

Particularly good for cool or cold weather and just what you want if
you do not want to have to get a lot of individual timings right. Pull
off the lid and VOILA!

INGREDIENTS
4 small leeks
4 chicken quarters (skinned if possible)
1 rounded tablespoon butter
2 cups (chicken or vegetable) stock or 1 stock cube and 2 cups
water
$^1/_2$ cup long-grain rice
Freshly ground black pepper to taste

EQUIPMENT
Sharp knife
Chopping board
Set of measuring spoons
Set of measuring cups
500 ml (1 pint) Pyrex jug
Wooden spoon
Frying-pan if casserole is ceramic or glass
Casserole with lid.
Aluminium foil if the casserole has no lid.

METHOD
Clean the leeks. First take off the outer leaves, cut the roots off and trim the top. Split the leeks in half lengthways. Hold the leeks under running water and wash any grit out. Shake them dry. Cut into 2 cm (1 in) slices. Take the skin off the chicken pieces if not skinless.

Melt the butter in the casserole (if you can use it on the top of the cooker) or frying-pan. Add the chopped leeks and cook for 5 to 10 minutes to soften – don't let them start to brown. Put the stock cube into the Pyrex jug, add boiling water and stir.

Put the leeks and butter in the casserole. Add the chicken and the rice and mix all the ingredients together. Add a little freshly ground black pepper. Add the stock. Cover with a lid or tin foil and cook in a slow oven at 150° C, 300° F, Gas mark 2 for 1^1/$_2$ hours.

ADDITIONS & ALTERNATIVES
If your casserole is big enough you can add some peeled and halved medium-sized potatoes, or some peeled sliced carrots.

We have not used any salt in this recipe because some stock cubes or powder are salty enough not to need to add more.

CHICKEN IN BEER

Serves 4   ① *Preparation 10 min, Cooking 15 min – Easy*

Think ahead – this needs to marinate for several hours.

This chicken has a subtle lemony flavour, even though you would expect it to taste of beer.

INGREDIENTS
12 chicken wings, or boneless thighs
$1^1/_2$ cups beer (350 ml, just over $^1/_2$ pint)
Salt and freshly ground black pepper to taste
$1^1/_4$ teaspoons dried thyme
1 bay leaf
2 tablespoons olive oil

EQUIPMENT
Sharp knife
Chopping board
Set of measuring spoons
Cup or small bowl
Large shallow dish
Wooden spoon
Bowl
Kitchen paper
Grill
Spoon

METHOD
If using wings chop them into three parts and throw way the bony tip piece. If using thighs cut them in half or three (depending on

size) through the length. Take 1 tablespoon of beer from the bottle and put into a cup and save until later. In a shallow dish which will hold the chicken (preferably in one layer) put the beer, salt, pepper, 1 teaspoon thyme and the bay leaf. Put the chicken pieces in the dish with the marinade and turn them in the mixture to coat evenly. Leave for several hours in the marinade.

Put the tablespoon of beer in a bowl and add the remaining thyme and the olive oil.

Remove the chicken from the marinade and shake off any excess liquid. Blot the chicken on kitchen paper. Arrange the chicken on a grill tray and spoon on half the beer and oil mixture, smoothing it over with the back of the spoon. Sprinkle with salt and pepper. Grill the chicken for about 7 minutes. Turn and add the remaining mixture. Sprinkle with salt and pepper, and continue grilling until the chicken is golden but suntil juicy, about 8 minutes more. Check that it is done by piercing with a fork. The juices should run clear.

ADDITIONS & ALTERNATIVES

You can cook this chicken on a barbecue. If you have neither a grill nor a barbecue then cook it in the oven for about 25 minutes at 180° C, 350° F, Gas mark 4, turning and recoating with the cooking sauce halfway through.

HOT CHICKEN STIR-FRY

Serves 4   ① *Preparation 20 min, Cooking 25 min – Easy*

This sweet and sour flavoured recipe is both Chinese and Indian. So if you are caught between take-aways this is for you.

INGREDIENTS
2 fresh green chillies
3 cloves garlic
4 cm ($1^1/_2$ in) fresh root ginger
1 lemon or 4 tablespoons lemon juice
Small bunch fresh coriander
$^1/_2$ cup chicken stock or $^1/_2$ cup boiling water and $^1/_2$ stock cube.
4 to 6 skinless and boneless chicken breasts (750 g, $1^1/_2$ lb or $1^1/_2 \times 500$ g) packs stir-fry chicken pieces
3 tablespoons sunflower oil
$^1/_2$ teaspoon crushed pomegranate seeds (optional)
$^1/_2$ teaspoon ground turmeric
1 teaspoon garam masala
$^1/_2$ teaspoon salt

EQUIPMENT
Sharp knife
Chopping board
Fork
Set of measuring cups
Garlic crusher
Lemon zester or grater
Lemon juicer
Set of measuring spoons
Small bowls
Deep frying-pan, balti dish or wok
Wooden spoon

METHOD
Chop the end off the chillies, split in half, and scrape out the seeds.
Cut the chillies into thin strips. Hold the chilli down with a fork
and wash your hands afterwards. Chilli juice really stings if you get

it anywhere sensitive. Peel and crush the garlic. Peel and thinly slice the ginger. Grate or zest the rind of the lemon, then juice it. Wash the coriander and shake the excess water off. Cut off the stalks and throw them away. Chop the leaves quite finely. Put the $^1/_2$ stock cube in a cup (if using) and add $^1/_2$ cupof boiling water. Cut the chicken into strips about 5 × 1 cm (2 by $^1/_2$ in).

Heat the oil in the frying-pan over moderate heat and fry the garlic, ginger and pomegranate seeds for 1 minute. Stir in the turmeric, garam masala and chillies and fry for 30 seconds. Add the chicken and stir-fry until it is golden brown on both sides, about 5 minutes.

Add the salt, lemon juice, lemon rind, coriander and stock. Stir the chicken to ensure it is evenly coated. Bring to the boil, then lower the heat and simmer for 10 to 15 minutes, until the chicken is cooked and tender. The chicken juices should run clear if pierced in the thickest part with a sharp knife when it is cooked.

ADDITIONS & ALTERNATIVES

Serve with naan bread or aromatic Basmati rice.

This dish can be served cold in the summer with a spicy rice salad or a mixed lettuce salad.

LEMON CHICKEN

Serves 4   ① *Preparation 20 min, Cooking 60 min – Easy*

Think ahead – the chicken should be marinated for 2 to 6 hours.

This is an unusual way to roast chicken and give it a fresh flavour.

INGREDIENTS

1 clove garlic
1 lemon or 4 tablespoons lemon juice
2 tablespoons finely chopped parsley
4 chicken quarters
4 tablespoons olive oil
4 teaspoons dried thyme
Salt and freshly ground black pepper to taste
2 rounded tablespoons butter

EQUIPMENT

Sharp knife
Chopping board
Grater or zester
Lemon juicer
Set of measuring spoons
Bowl
Spoon
Large oven-proof dish

METHOD

Peel and finely chop the garlic. Grate or zest the lemon rind and then juice the lemon. Wash the parsley, shake off the excess water and cut off the stems and throw them away. Finely chop the parsley leaves. Cut chicken quarters into serving pieces (2 or 3 pieces each) and put in a shallow bowl. Sprinkle with olive oil, garlic, lemon rind and juice, thyme, salt and pepper.

Marinate the chicken pieces for 2 hours, turning the pieces from time to time. You can leave in the marinade for 5 to 6 hours if you like.

Butter the oven-proof baking dish generously. Put the chicken pieces and marinade in the oven-proof dish and dot with the remaining butter. Cook at 170° C, 325° F, Gas mark 3 for 50 to 60 minutes, until tender, basting frequently. Remove from the oven, sprinkle with the finely chopped parsley and serve immediately.

ADDITIONS & ALTERNATIVES

Use 8 to 12 chicken thighs or small breasts.

Serve with boiled rice (see page 334) or mashed potatoes or something that will absorb some of the juices.

LIME & CORIANDER CHICKEN

Serves 4   ⏱ *Preparation 15 min, Cooking 25 min – Easy*

Think ahead – the chicken should be marinated for 2 hours.

This has a strong Thai influence to it and would go well with plain rice.

INGREDIENTS

2 × 15 g bunches of coriander or one large bunch
3 limes
2 small chillies
4 to 6 cloves garlic
2 to 4 cm (1 to 2 in) fresh root ginger
1 sachet of creamed coconut (or a piece the size of a matchbox cut from a slab)
4 large boneless chicken breasts
2 tablespoons sunflower oil

EQUIPMENT
Sharp knife
Chopping board
Food processor or liquidiser (optional)
Grater or zester
Lemon juicer
Fork
Bowl
Deep frying-pan, balti dish or wok
Small bowls or plates

METHOD
Wash the coriander, chop roughly, and put the whole lot, including stalks, in a food processor or liquidiser. Zest and juice the limes and add to the food processor. Chop the end off the chillies, split in half and scrape out the seeds. Hold the chilli down with a fork and wash your hands afterwards. Chilli juice really stings if you get it anywhere sensitive. Peel and roughly chop the garlic and ginger. Add the chillies, garlic and ginger to the processor.

Add the creamed coconut and whiz together until all are combined. If you do not have a processor or liquidiser then chop everything up as small as you can and mash together for a minute or two in a bowl. Your marinade will be more lumpy but the flavours should suntil be pretty good. Marinate chicken in the mixture in a bowl for 2 hours. Put the oil in the frying-pan on a moderate heat. Add the chicken and fry for 5 minutes, then add the marinade and cook for 20 minutes more.

ADDITIONS & ALTERNATIVES
Could add lemon grass (comes in jars now as well as by the stalk). If using a stalk add to all ingredients in the pan. Crush the lemon grass but do not break up. Then you can remove it and throw it

away as it is not a pleasant texture when used whole. This way you get the benefit of flavour and not texture. The stuff in jars is finely chopped and it will soften in the marinade and the cooking.

ORANGE HONEY CHICKEN

Serves 4   ① *Preparation 20 min, Cooking 1¹/₂ hours – Easy*

Just like the title suggests this has a sweet orange flavour. Roast chicken is easy and this version is easy too.

INGREDIENTS
1¹/₂ kg (3¹/₂ lb) chicken
Salt and freshly ground black pepper to taste
2 onions
4 tablespoons honey
2 tablespoons sunflower oil
¹/₂ cup (150 ml, ¹/₄ pint) orange juice
1 orange

EQUIPMENT
Sharp knife
Chopping board
Oven-proof dish
Saucepan
Set of measuring cups
Set of measuring spoons

METHOD
Preheat the oven to 200° C, 400° F, Gas mark 6.

Rub the skin and inside of the chicken with salt. Peel and slice the onions. Put the onions in an oven-proof dish and put the chicken on top. In a saucepan heat the honey, oil and orange juice until the honey dissolves. Season with pepper. Spoon some sauce inside the chicken, and pour the rest over the top. Bake in the preheated oven for $1^1/_4$ to $1^1/_2$ hours, basting from time to time with the juice. Test the chicken is done by pricking with a fork in between the leg and the body or in the thickest part of the thigh. If the juices run clear, then it is done. Slice the orange. Serve garnished with the orange slices.

ADDITIONS & ALTERNATIVES
Serve with couscous for a Middle Eastern flavour, or with new potatoes, green vegetable or salad.

POMEGRANATE CHICKEN

Serves 4   ① *Preparation 20 min, Cooking 25 min – Easy*

Keeping up the fruit theme we have gone for something exotic here, though widely available.

INGREDIENTS
1 clove garlic
2 medium onions
2 pomegranates
4 tablespoons sunflower oil
4 chicken breasts, skinned
Salt and freshly ground black pepper to taste
$1/_2$ × 100 g packet flaked almonds
Sprigs of parsley

EQUIPMENT
Garlic crusher
Sharp knife
Chopping board
Bowl
Lemon juicer
Cup
Frying-pan with lid or shallow saucepan with a lid
Set of measuring spoons
Slotted spoon

METHOD
Crush the garlic and peel and slice the onions. Cut one of the pomegranates in half, scoop out the red seeds and put in a bowl until later. Discard any of the yellow pith. Juice the other pomegranate and reserve the juice in a cup or bowl. Heat the oil in a frying-pan over moderate heat and fry the onion rings and garlic until just beginning to brown. Remove them, add the chicken and carefully fry for 7 to 8 minutes each side. Take care that the chicken does not stick to the pan. Remove the chicken and keep warm. Stir the pomegranate seeds and 2 tablespoons of the reserved pomegranate juice into the pan. Return the onions and garlic to the pan and enough water to make a thin sauce. Place the chicken in the sauce, season to taste, cover and simmer for 15 to 20 minutes. Serve hot, sprinkled with flaked almonds and garnished with parsley.

ADDITIONS & ALTERNATIVES
You can juice a pomegranate just like an orange, or substitute 2 tablespoons lemon juice mixed with 1 teaspoon tomato purée and 1 teaspoon brown sugar.

POMEGRANATE & WALNUT CHICKEN

Serves 4   ① *Preparation 10 min, Cooking 50 min – Easy*

Just when you thought you were safe from the pomegranate chicken here comes another one. The sauce for this one is much thicker than the first.

INGREDIENTS
1 onion
3 tablespoons sunflower oil
4 chicken breasts, skinned
2 × 100 g packs ground walnuts
1 pomegranate
1 cup water
Salt and freshly ground black pepper to taste

EQUIPMENT
Sharp knife
Chopping board
Set of measuring cups
Set of measuring spoons
Plate
Food slice
Wooden spoon
Lemon juicer
Deep frying-pan with lid or shallow saucepan with lid

METHOD
Peel and finely chop the onion. Heat the oil in a frying-pan, and fry the chicken breasts for 4 to 5 minutes on each side until lightly golden brown. Take care that the chicken does not stick to the pan.

Remove the chicken and keep warm. In the same pan, fry the onion for 3 minutes until it just begins to brown. Stir in the ground walnuts, and continue cooking for 2 to 3 minutes. Cut the pomegranate in half and juice like an orange. Add the juice to the pan with the water, salt and pepper.

Put the chicken back in the pan then cover and simmer for 35 to 40 minutes until the chicken is cooked.

ADDITIONS & ALTERNATIVES
Serve hot with plain rice.

If the sauce is too thick add a small dollop of yoghurt or cream just before serving.

Substitute 2 tablespoons lemon juice, 1 teaspoon tomato purée and 1 teaspoon brown sugar for the pomegranate juice.

SWEET STUFFED CHICKEN

Serves 4 to 6 ① *Preparation 30 min, Cooking 2 hours – Easy*

This is a Persian delicacy and it suntil would be if Persia existed today.

INGREDIENTS
1¹/₂ kg (3¹/₂ lb) chicken
Oil or butter for greasing
1 teaspoon salt
¹/₂ cup long-grain rice (100 g, 4 oz)
1 cup water
¹/₂ × 100 g pack flaked almonds
1 rounded tablespoon butter
¹/₂ cup sultanas (75 g, 3 oz)
Juice of ¹/₂ lemon or 2 tablespoons lemon juice

Salt and freshly ground black pepper to taste
3 tablespoons tomato purée
$^1/_2$ cup water

EQUIPMENT
Set of measuring spoons
Oven-proof dish or casserole with lid
Aluminium foil if the dish or casserole has no lid
Set of measuring cups
Saucepan
Sieve
Lemon juicer
Frying-pan
Bowl
Fork for mixing
Small bowls

METHOD
Rub the skin and inside of the chicken with the salt. Oil or butter the oven-proof dish.

To make the stuffing, put the rice in a saucepan with 1 cup of water, bring to the boil, cover and simmer for 10 minutes. The rice should have absorbed the water; if there is any surplus, drain. Juice the lemon. Fry the almonds in the butter for 3 to 4 minutes until golden. In a bowl mix together the rice, butter and almonds, sultanas, lemon juice, salt and pepper.

Push as much of the stuffing as possible into the chicken. If there is any extra, place it under the chicken in the oiled oven-proof dish. Mix together the tomato purée and water in a cup and pour over the chicken. Cover with foil or a lid and cook at 200°C, 400°F, Gas mark 6 for $1^1/_2$ to 2 hours, until the chicken is cooked. Baste after the first 40 minutes and again after 80 minutes. When the chicken is cooked uncover for a final 10 minutes to brown the skin. The chicken is cooked when the juices run clear if pricked with a fork in the thickest bit of the thigh or between the leg and the body.

ADDITIONS & ALTERNATIVES
Serve hot with couscous or salad and the rice mixture.

SPICED TURKEY & BASIL

Serves 4   ⏱ *Preparation 20 min, Cooking 8 min – Easy*

This is an oriental type of dish, but the basil makes it seem almost Italian. When you need a quick, easy dish that is economic, try this. To vary the flavour, use beef or pork instead of turkey. Fresh basil is essential to this dish.

INGREDIENTS
3 large cloves garlic
1 fresh green chilli
1 tablespoon sunflower oil
350 g (3/4 lb) pack turkey mince
2 tablespoons soy sauce or fish sauce
1 teaspoon sugar
2 × 15 g packs fresh basil leaves (1 cup)

EQUIPMENT
Sharp knife
Chopping board
Set of measuring cups
Set of measuring spoons
Wooden spoon
Garlic crusher

Frying-pan
Small bowls or plates

METHOD
Peel and finely chop the garlic. Chop the end off the chilli, split in half, and scrape out the seeds. Hold the chilli down with a fork and wash your hands afterwards. Chilli juice really stings if you get it anywhere sensitive. Chop the chilli into small pieces.

Heat the oil in a medium frying-pan. Add the garlic and chilli and cook for 30 seconds. Add the turkey mince and cook for 3 minutes until browned, stirring to break it up. Add the soy sauce or fish sauce and sugar and cook for 2 minutes more. Add the basil and cook while stirring for another 2 minutes more.

Spoon into a heated serving bowl.

ADDITIONS & ALTERNATIVES
Serve with noodles (see page 335) or egg pasta.

TURKEY & BLUE CHEESE

Serves 4 ① *Preparation 20 min, Cooking 40 min – Easy*

An unusual combination of tastes for the sophisticated palate, and you, dear reader, have that sophisticated palate.

INGREDIENTS
10 small new potatoes, 500 g (1 lb)
2 cloves garlic
125 g pack of blue cheese (Stilton, Danish blue, or Roquefort)
1 rounded tablespoon butter
4 turkey breast fillets

5 tablespoons dry white wine
$^1/_2$ cup chicken stock or $^1/_2$ cup boiling water and $^1/_2$ stock cube.
1 level teaspoon dried herbes de Provence
2 tablespoons double cream

EQUIPMENT
Sharp knife
Chopping board
Garlic crusher
Bowl
Large frying-pan with a lid or shallow saucepan with lid
Plate
Wooden spoon
Slotted spoon
Set of measuring spoons
Set of measuring cups
Bowl or dish for serving

METHOD
Scrub the new potatoes. Peel and crush the garlic. Crumble the cheese into small pieces. Melt the butter in a large frying-pan (use one that has a lid), add the turkey fillets and fry for about 5 minutes until golden brown on both sides. Lift from the pan on to a large plate.

Stir the potatoes into the hot butter in the pan and cook for 5 minutes, stirring once or twice, until they are just beginning to brown. With a slotted spoon, lift out the potatoes and add to the turkey fillets.

Add the white wine to the hot pan drippings and stir to pick up the flavouring bits. Add the chicken stock, garlic and the herbes de Provence. Bring to the boil. Return the potatoes to the pan and arrange the turkey fillets on top. Cover and simmer gently for 20 to 25 minutes, or until the turkey is tender and the potatoes cooked.

With a slotted spoon, lift the potatoes and turkey fillets onto a warm serving dish. Add the cheese to the pan juices with the cream. Heat together gently, stirring, until the cheese has melted. Season with pepper to taste and pour the sauce over the turkey and potatoes.

FIVE-SPICE DUCK

Serves 4   ① *Preparation 10 min, Cooking 50 min – Easy*

Think ahead – it needs to stand for about an hour.

This is a very rich-tasting recipe because duck is such a rich meat. The stem ginger makes it really exciting.

INGREDIENTS
4 duck breasts
2 teaspoons five-spice powder
2 teaspoons caster sugar
3 tablespoons diced stem ginger from a jar
2 tablespoons red wine vinegar
1 cup orange juice (250 ml, $^1/_2$ pint)
2 tablespoons ginger syrup from the stem ginger jar
3 clementines or small oranges
Salt and freshly ground black pepper to taste

EQUIPMENT
Sharp knife
Chopping board
Set of measuring cups
Set of measuring spoons
Bowl

Plate
Large frying-pan or sauté pan
Wooden spoon
Spoon
Slotted spoon
Serving plate

METHOD

Cut the skin on each duck breast with about 4 to 6 shallow neat lines. Mix the five-spice powder and the sugar in a small bowl and rub well into the duck skin. Put the breasts on a plate and leave for 30 to 60 minutes. Dice the stem ginger.

Heat a large dry frying-pan. Do not add any fat. Put the duck breasts in, skin-side down, and fry over a moderate heat until they are well browned, about 8 to 10 minutes. Then turn and brown the other side. Quite a lot of fat will have come out of the duck. Take the duck pieces out of the pan with a slotted spoon. Pour off the fat but keep the darker bits that have been left behind from the frying. Add the red wine vinegar to the pan and stir well. Add the orange juice, diced stem ginger and ginger syrup to the pan. Bring gently to the boil. Put the duck pieces back into the pan, the skin-side upwards. This will help the skin stay crisp. Try to keep it out of the liquid. Simmer gently for 30 to 40 minutes.

Cut the clementines into quarters and add to the pan 20 to 25 minutes after you have started to simmer the duck. When cooked and tender put the duck breasts and clementines on a serving dish and keep hot. Bring the remaining sauce to the boil and simmer for up to 5 minutes to thicken. Pour the thickened sauce over the duck and clementines and serve.

ADDITIONS & ALTERNATIVES

Serve with boiled rice (see page 334) or with Chinese pancakes and some shredded Chinese leaves or white cabbage.

DEVILLED DUCK

Serves 6
⏲ Preparation 10 min, Cooking 10 to 20 min – Easy

Leftovers like you have never had them before. This is so good it is
worth cooking the duck specially, and of course that is the only way
you could have so much pre-cooked meat on hand!

INGREDIENTS
6 portions cold roast duck, chicken or turkey
$^1/_2 \times 250$ g pack softened butter
1 tablespoon Dijon mustard
1 teaspoon English mustard
1 tablespoon chutney
1 level teaspoon curry powder
1 to 2 tablespoons lemon juice
Salt and cayenne pepper

EQUIPMENT
Sharp knife
Chopping board
Set of measuring spoons
Bowl
Wooden spoon
Fork for mashing

METHOD
Score the pre-cooked duck, chicken or turkey pieces with a sharp
knife. In a bowl mix together the butter, mustards, chutney, curry
powder and lemon juice. Use a fork or wooden spoon to mash the
ingredients together to make a smoothish paste. Season to taste
with salt and cayenne pepper. Spread the mixture on the duck

150

pieces and grill until sizzling hot. Or place in an oven-proof dish and cook in the oven for 20 minutes at 190° C, 375° F, Gas mark 5.

SLOW POT-ROAST DUCK

Serves 4 ① *Preparation 15 min, Cooking 1 hr 50 min –*
Easy

Think ahead – it needs 2 hours to marinate.

It is worth remembering that duck is a very rich and strongly flavoured meat. This is very rich and needs to be eaten at a leisurely pace and not hurried.

INGREDIENTS
1 stick celery
2 carrots
2 large onions
6 rashers streaky bacon
20 button mushrooms, about 200 g (8 oz)
1 clove garlic
1 tender duck or 4 ready-cut duck portions
Salt and freshly ground black pepper
8 tablespoons brandy
1^1/$_2$ cups dry red wine (375 ml, ^{3}/$_4$ pint)
1 tablespoon olive oil
1 bouquet garni

EQUIPMENT
Sharp knife
Chopping board
Set of measuring cups

Set of measuring spoons
Bowl
Vegetable peeler
Garlic crusher
Frying-pan
Slotted spoon
Heatproof casserole with lid or heavy bottomed saucepan with lid.
Fork for mashing

METHOD

Wash and chop the celery. Wash and slice the carrots. Peel and slice the onions. Chop the bacon into small cubes, and rinse and slice the mushrooms. Peel and thinly slice the garlic. Cut the duck into serving pieces and place in a bowl. Add salt and freshly ground black pepper, the celery, carrots, sliced onions, brandy and red wine. Marinate the duck in this mixture for at least 2 hours.

Remove the duck pieces from the marinade, reserving the marinade. Drain and dry on kitchen paper. Heat the oil in a frying-pan, add the diced bacon and cook slowly until the bacon is golden. Remove the bacon bits with a slotted spoon and brown the duck in the pan. Place the bacon bits, duck pieces and the juices from the pan in a large heatproof casserole. Cover and simmer gently for 20 minutes.

Add the marinade, bouquet garni, garlic and mushrooms. Simmer over a very low heat for $1^1/_2$ hours, until the duck is tender. Remove the bouquet garni and skim off the fat. Taste and adjust the seasoning and serve.

MAGIC MEAT

A lot of people do not feel as if they have had a meal unless they have had some meat. We obviously do not think that way, but we have put in lots of recipes for people who do. We start off with steak which is really easy to cook so long as you do not the leave the room, and move onto some dishes that need no supervision at all. The oven-cooked ones are great because you put them in the oven and take them out and the time in between is your own.

PEPPER STEAK SAUTÉ

Serves 3 to 4   ① *Preparation 10 min, Cooking 30 min – Easy*

This cooks on the top of the cooker and makes lots of sauce. Mmm.

INGREDIENTS
1 beef stock cube
1 cup boiling water
500 g (1 lb) sirloin steak
1 tablespoon paprika
1 bunch spring onions
2 green peppers
2 large tomatoes
2 tablespoons butter

2 cloves garlic
2 tablespoons soy sauce
4 tablespoons water
1 tablespoon cornflour

EQUIPMENT

Set of measuring cups
Bowl
Sharp knife
Chopping board
Set of measuring spoons
Plate
Garlic crusher
Saucepan with lid
Small bowl or cup

METHOD

Dissolve the stock cube in the water. Cut the steak into 5 mm ($^1/_4$ in) strips. Put the steak on the plate and sprinkle with paprika. Clean and prepare the spring onions. Cut the root end off and trim the leaves. Peel off and discard any dried up or slimy leaves. Chop roughly. Chop the end off the green peppers and cut out the core and seeds. Cut the pepper into strips. Chop the tomatoes.

Put the butter in the saucepan over a moderate heat. Peel and crush the garlic into the pan. Add the steak and stir round until it is browned, about 5 minutes.

Add the spring onions, peppers, tomatoes and stock. Bring to the boil, then turn down the heat until it is just boiling (simmering). Put a lid on and cook for 15 minutes.

Mix the soy sauce, water and cornflour in a cup or small bowl. Add to the pan and simmer for a few minutes to thicken the sauce.

ADDITIONS & ALTERNATIVES
Serve with rice and salad or mashed potatoes or boiled new potatoes.

TIPS
You can buy ready-made stock in cartons from most supermarkets. You can also buy Swiss vegetable bouillon powder (vegetable stock), if you are worried about the stuff that goes into stock cubes.

GREEN PEPPER STEAK IN CREAM SAUCE

Serves 2   ⏱ *Preparation 5 min, Cooking 15 min – Easy*

A really quick luxury dish with a cream brandy sauce. You cannot fail if you are cooking to impress with this foolproof recipe.

INGREDIENTS
$^1/_2$ tablespoon green peppercorns
2 sirloin steaks, about 350 g ($^3/_4$ lb)
Salt to taste
2 tablespoons sunflower or olive oil
2 tablespoons butter
2 tablespoons brandy
Small carton (142 ml, 5 fl oz) double cream

EQUIPMENT
Sharp knife
Chopping board
Frying-pan
Set of measuring spoons
Spoon

155

METHOD

Crush the peppercorns. (These are the soft ones not the dried ones). Rub the steaks with salt and the peppercorns.

Put the oil and butter in the frying-pan over a moderate heat. Fry the steaks on both sides until done to taste, about 5 to 10 minutes. Take out of the pan and keep warm. Pour the fat out. Add the brandy to the pan and stir to lift off the brown bits. Set the brandy alight. Add the cream and bring to the boil, then turn down the heat until it is just boiling (simmering). Cook gently for 3 minutes. Pour the sauce over the steaks and serve.

ADDITIONS & ALTERNATIVES

Serve with oven chips, tomato and salad.

TIPS

Green peppercorns are available in jars or tins, packed either in water or vinegar. Drain the peppercorns before crushing.

STEAK SATAY

Serves 4   ① *Preparation 10 min, Cooking 20 min – Easy*

Think ahead – it needs to stand for 3 hours.

Elegant steak on a stick.

INGREDIENTS

750 g (1¹/₂ lb) rump steak
1 clove garlic
¹/₂ mild onion
6 tablespoons olive oil
2 tablespoons soy sauce

2 tablespoons lemon juice
1 tablespoon powdered cumin
Freshly ground black pepper

EQUIPMENT
Sharp knife
Chopping board
Garlic crusher
Bowl
Set of measuring spoons
Bamboo skewers

METHOD
Cut the steak into 1 cm ($^1/_2$ in strips) about 5 cm (2 in) long. Peel and crush the garlic into the bowl. Peel and finely chop the onion.

Add the steak, onion, oil, soy sauce, lemon juice, cumin and pepper to the bowl and stir round. Leave to stand for 3 hours.

Soak the skewers in water. Thread the meat on the skewers and grill until cooked, about 5 to 10 minutes on each side.

ADDITIONS & ALTERNATIVES
Serve with rice and salad or noodles tossed in sesame oil.

You can buy a peanut satay sauce or a mild chilli sauce to go with this.

GREEK POTATO CASSEROLE

Serves 4   ① *Preparation 10 min, Cooking 60 min – Easy*

When is a casserole not a casserole? When it is cooked in a saucepan. Gently does it with this recipe so it does not dry out.

INGREDIENTS
1 beef or chicken stock cube
1 cup water
2 onions
2 tomatoes
8 medium potatoes
4 tablespoons butter
$^1/_4$ teaspoon dried thyme
$^1/_4$ teaspoon dried oregano
Salt and freshly ground pepper to taste
500 g (1 lb) minced beef

EQUIPMENT
Set of measuring cups
Bowl
Sharp knife
Chopping board
Vegetable peeler
Set of measuring spoons
Frying-pan
Wooden spoon
Saucepan with lid or flame-proof casserole

METHOD
Dissolve the stock cube in the water. Peel and finely slice the onions. Slice the tomatoes. Peel the potatoes, cutting away any nasty bits, and cutting out any eyes. Chop the potatoes into 1 cm ($^1/_2$ in) slices.

Put 2 tablespoon of butter in the frying-pan over a moderate heat. Fry the potatoes for about a minute on both sides. Put the potatoes in the saucepan. Put 2 tablespoon of butter in the frying-pan over a moderate heat. Fry the onion for about 3 minutes until it is golden, stirring to stop it sticking. Add the mince and fry, stirring until it is well browned and broken up, about 7 minutes. Add the meat and onions to the potatoes. Put the tomato slices on top, then add the thyme, oregano and salt and pepper. Add the stock. Put the lid on tightly and cook very gently for about 45 minutes. If it goes too dry add some more stock.

ADDITIONS & ALTERNATIVES
Use turkey mince instead of the beef.

TIPS
You can buy ready-made stock in cartons from most supermarkets. You can also buy Swiss vegetable bouillon powder (vegetable stock), if you are worried about the stuff that goes into stock cubes.

BEEF & MUSHROOM PIE

Serves 3 to 4   ① Preparation 20 min, Cooking 2 hr 35 min – Easy

This has got beer in it. The beer makes rich gravy and all the difference.

INGREDIENTS
500 g (1 lb) stewing beef
1 large onion
3 tablespoons sunflower oil
1 tablespoon wholemeal flour
$^1/_2$ pint (300 ml) beer
Salt and freshly ground pepper to taste
1 egg
15 button mushrooms

2 tablespoons chopped parsley
450 g pack ready-rolled shortcrust pastry

EQUIPMENT
Sharp knife
Chopping board
Saucepan with lid
Set of measuring spoons
Wooden spoon
900 ml ($1^{1}/_{2}$ pint) pie dish

DEFROSTING
Thaw frozen pastry according to the instructions on the packet. 4 hours in the fridge seems typical.

METHOD
Chop the beef into 2 cm (1 in) cubes. Peel and chop the onion. Put the oil in the saucepan over a moderate heat. Fry the beef for 2 minutes, stirring, to brown. Lift out. Add the onion and cook for about three minutes until it is golden, stirring to stop it sticking. Add the flour and stir round. Add the beer, salt and pepper. Bring to the boil, then turn down the heat until it is just boiling (simmering). Add the meat. Put a lid on and cook very gently for 2 hours. Check the beer level from time to time and top it up if it starts to dry out.

Break the egg into a bowl and pick out any bits of shell. Mix the egg with a fork. Wipe the mushrooms clean. Discard any nasty ones. Chop the end off the stalks. Chop into quarters. Wash, shake dry and finely chop 2 tablespoons parsley. Add the mushrooms and parsley to the pan. Mix and pour into the pie dish.

Unroll the pastry. Cut a strip off and place on the moistened rim of the pie dish. Moisten the strip. Cover the dish with the pastry, pressing the edges down firmly.

Trim the edges and make a hole in the centre. Brush with egg so it comes out of the oven shiny. Cook at 200° C, 400° F, Gas mark 6 for 30 minutes.

ADDITIONS & ALTERNATIVES
Serve with new potatoes and a green vegetable.

Use a block of prepared pastry and roll it yourself. Full instructions are in the 'How to' chapter.

HAMBURGERS

Serves 4   ① *Preparation 15 min, Cooking 10 min – Easy*

You know what a hamburger is, and now you are going to get a chance to make your own.

INGREDIENTS
1 onion
Small bunch parsley
750 g (1^1/$_2$ lb) minced beef
1 tablespoon soy sauce
1 tablespoon Worcestershire sauce
Salt and pepper to taste
1 mild onion
1 tomato
1 or 2 tablespoons flour to dust hands
2 tablespoons sunflower oil for shallow-frying
4 sesame seed baps

EQUIPMENT
Sharp knife
Chopping board

Set of measuring spoons
Bowl
Wooden spoon
Food processor or liquidiser (optional)
Hamburger press
Frying-pan

METHOD

Peel and chop the onion. Wash, shake dry and finely chop the parsley to give 2 tablespoons. Put the onion, parsley, mince, soy sauce, Worcestershire sauce, salt and pepper to taste in the bowl. Mix thoroughly and leave to stand for 5 minutes. You can put it in the liquidiser or food processor and blend to mix it. Peel and slice the mild onion. Slice the tomato.

Use the hamburger press to make the burgers, or divide the hamburger mixture into 4, dust your hands with flour and shape into thick burgers, pressing as hard as you can.

Put the oil in the frying-pan over a moderate heat. Fry the burgers for about 5 minutes on each side.

Serve hot, in a bap, between onion rings and tomato slices.

ADDITIONS & ALTERNATIVES

Mild mustard, relish and chips and salad are traditional with burgers, but some people like chips and baked beans.

TIPS

Mild onions are often Spanish or South American. A lot of supermarkets have ones which are rated for mildness. Numbers 1 and 2 are sweet and mild.

The better the mince, the better the burger. You can buy steak and use a food processor to grind it up if you want the very best. Chuck steak is a suitable cut of beef, with not too much fat, and reasonably cheap. Any steak type can be ground up into mince. If you grind your own you know what you are getting, or you can buy beef from your butcher and get him to mince it.

The hamburger press is a steel or plastic contraption which you fill with minced meat and press. It gives uniform size and thickness to your burgers. If using the hand-made version try to make sure the mixture is firmly pressed together and that the burger is the same thickness all the way across. The harder you press the greater the chance it will stay in one piece when cooking.

MEATBALLS IN TOMATO SAUCE

Serves 4   ① *Preparation 15 min, Cooking 50 min – Easy*

As eaten by the Godfather, at least mine. And those godfathers know a thing or two.

INGREDIENTS
1 onion
1 clove garlic
1 egg
Small bunch parsley
3 slices wholemeal bread
500 g (1 lb) pork mince
2 tablespoons water
Salt and freshly ground pepper to taste
4 tablespoons sunflower oil
Small carton (142 ml, 5 fl oz) sour cream

Tomato sauce
1 clove garlic
400 g tin plum tomatoes
2 sprigs parsley

1 tablespoon tomato purée
1 teaspoon Worcestershire sauce
1 teaspoon sugar

EQUIPMENT
Sharp knife
Chopping board
Food processor or liquidiser (optional)
Bowl
Set of measuring spoons
Frying-pan
Slotted spoon
Oven-proof dish
Tin opener

METHOD
Deal with the ingredients for the meatballs first. Peel and roughly chop the onion. Peel and crush the garlic. Break the egg into a bowl and pick out any bits of shell. Wash and shake dry the parsley. Keep a couple of sprigs for the sauce and chop enough to make 1 tablespoon for garnish. Cut the bread into cubes.

Put the bread and 6 sprigs of parsley including the stalks in the liquidiser or food processor and blend until it is crumbly. If you are using a food processor, add the onion, garlic, egg, pork, water, salt and pepper and blend until mixed. If using a liquidiser, just add the onion and garlic then mix with the other ingredients in a bowl. Wet your hands and shape the mixture into balls the size of walnuts. Put them on a plate as you do them.

Heat the oil in a frying-pan. Add the meatballs in batches, and fry until browned, shaking the pan frequently. Lift them out and put in the oven-proof dish.

Peel and crush the garlic for the tomato sauce. Put all the sauce ingredients in the liquidiser or food processor and blend until smooth. Pour the sauce over the meatballs, cover and cook at 180° C, 350° F, Gas mark 4 for 40 minutes.

Serve with a dollop of sour cream and a sprinkle of parsley.

ADDITIONS & ALTERNATIVES
Serve with spaghetti or other pasta, or potatoes.

PORK & CIDER

Serves 4   ① *Preparation 10 min, Cooking 60 min – Easy*

This is a slap-it-in-the-oven job. Then sit back and relax.

INGREDIENTS
2 Spanish onions
4 pork chops
Salt and freshly ground black pepper to taste
2 tablespoons olive oil
2 tablespoons butter
1 teaspoon mixed dried Mediterranean herbs
$^1/_2$ cup cider
$^1/_2$ cup water

EQUIPMENT
Sharp knife
Chopping board
Set of measuring spoons
Frying-pan
Casserole with lid
Set of measuring cups

METHOD

Preheat the oven to 170° C, 325° F, Gas mark 3.

Peel and finely chop the onions. Trim the excess fat from the chops and season with salt and pepper. Put the oil and butter in the frying-pan over a moderate heat. Fry the chops for about 3 minutes on each side until brown. Lift out the chops and put in the casserole. Sprinkle the herbs on top. Fry the onion for about 3 minutes until golden. Add to the pork chops. Pour in the cider and water. Put the lid on and cook in the preheated oven for 50 minutes until tender.

ADDITIONS & ALTERNATIVES

Serve with new potatoes and vegetables.

If you do not have a casserole with a lid you can use aluminium foil.

PORK & APPLE

Serves 4.   ① *Preparation 10 min, Cooking 40 min – Easy*

Here is how to get your roast pork and apple sauce together. Cook them in one dish.

INGREDIENTS

4 thick pork chops
Salt and freshly ground black pepper
4 tablespoons butter
4 eating apples
2 teaspoons dried rosemary

EQUIPMENT

Sharp knife
Chopping board

Set of measuring spoons
Frying-pan
Oven-proof dish

METHOD
Preheat the oven to 180° C, 350° F, Gas mark 4.

Trim the excess fat from the chops. Season with salt and pepper. Put 2 tablespoons butter in the frying-pan over a low heat. Fry the chops gently for about 5 minutes on each side until brown.

Peel and core the apples. Cut each into eight. Put the chops in the oven-proof dish with the rosemary, salt and freshly ground black pepper, and put the apples round them. Put blobs of the remaining butter on top. Cook in the preheated oven for about 30 minutes until tender.

ADDITIONS & ALTERNATIVES
Serve with couscous, or new potatoes and a green vegetable, or salad, or mashed potatoes.

BACON & VEG COUSCOUS

Serves 4   ① *Preparation 15 min, Cooking 20 min – Easy*

This is a really balanced flash meal. You get your meat, veg and farinaceous material all together.

INGREDIENTS
$^1/_2$ × 500 g pack (1 cup) couscous
$1^1/_4$ cups boiling water
2 to 3 tablespoons olive oil
1 tablespoon lemon juice
$^1/_2$ × 250 g pack fine green beans

1 large carrot
250 g pack smoked back bacon
1 medium onion
$1/2 \times 15$ g pack chives
1 clove garlic
Salt and freshly ground black pepper to taste

EQUIPMENT

Sharp knife
Chopping board
Set of measuring cups
Set of measuring spoons
Bowl
Saucepan
Vegetable peeler
Garlic crusher
Frying-pan
Wooden spoon

METHOD

Put the couscous in a bowl and pour over the boiling water, 1 tablespoon of olive oil and the lemon juice. Cover with a plate and leave to stand for 10 minutes. If it looks too dry add a second tablespoon of oil. Fluff up with a fork. Chop the beans in half and cook for 10 minutes in boiling water. Drain. Peel and chop the carrot, cutting off both ends and slicing thinly. Chop the bacon. Peel and chop the onion. Finely chop the chives. Put 1 tablespoon of oil in the frying-pan over a moderate heat. Peel and crush the garlic into the pan. Add the carrot, onion and bacon and fry for about 5 to 7 minutes until it is golden and cooked through, stirring to stop it sticking. Take off the heat. Mix in the couscous, beans and chives, salt and pepper.

Serve immediately.

ADDITIONS & ALTERNATIVES
Serve cold.

Serve with pitta bread and salad.

Try a bit of harissa with this. It is a chilli sauce in a tube and widely available.

PORK & BLUE CHEESE RELISH

Serves 4   ① *Preparation 10 min, Cooking 15 min – Easy*

This lumpy cheese relish melts over the pork steaks in a delicious puddle.

INGREDIENTS
2 spring onions
Small pack chives
4 tablespoons natural yoghurt
2 tablespoons Stilton cheese or 2 × 17 g individual portions
4 lean pork steaks
1 tablespoon sunflower oil

EQUIPMENT
Sharp knife
Chopping board
Set of measuring cups
Set of measuring spoons
Bowl
Wooden spoon

METHOD
Clean and prepare the spring onions. Cut the root end off, trim the leaves. Peel off and discard any dried up or slimy leaves. Chop into

thin slices. Wash, shake dry and finely chop the chives to give 1 tablespoon. Mix the onion, chives and yoghurt. Crumble the cheese into this mixture and mix well.

Spread a little oil on the steaks and grill, turning once, adding more oil when turning. Grill for about 7 minutes, on each side.

Serve with the relish.

ADDITIONS & ALTERNATIVES
Serve with new potatoes and salad or oven chips.

Use Roquefort or Gorgonzola for an even more cheesy version.

ROAST LAMB WITH BASIL SALSA

Serves 6   ① *Preparation 20 min, Cooking 90 min – Easy*

Think ahead – this is best if left to chill overnight.

Captain flash feeds your friends. This is the answer to any Sunday lunch gathering.

INGREDIENTS
6 cloves garlic
1.75 kg (3–4 lb) leg of lamb
2 × 15 g pack basil
12 olives stuffed with pimento
4 tablespoons olive oil
Salt and freshly ground black pepper to taste
4 tablespoons dry sherry

EQUIPMENT
Sharp knife
Chopping board

Set of measuring cups
Set of measuring spoons
Bowl
Aluminium foil if the roasting dish has no lid
Roasting dish or tin
Garlic crusher

METHOD

Peel 4 cloves of garlic and cut into thirds. Cut 12 deep slits at regular intervals in the lamb. Stick a large basil leaf, a stuffed olive and a piece of garlic into each slit. Rub half the olive oil over the lamb and season with salt and pepper. Put in a roasting dish, cover with clingfilm and chill overnight.

Peel the remaining 2 cloves of garlic and crush into the bowl. Wash, shake dry and finely chop the remaining basil. Mix with the crushed garlic and the remaining oil.

Remove the clingfilm, pour the sherry over the lamb and cover the dish (with foil if necessary). Cook at 190° C, 375° F, Gas mark 5 for 1 hour. Take off the cover or foil and cook for 20 minutes more. Leave to stand for 5 minutes before carving. Serve with the garlic and basil sauce.

ADDITIONS & ALTERNATIVES

Serve with new potatoes, green vegetable or salad.

Make the salsa verde with parsley or coriander instead of, or as well as, the basil.

AUBERGINE & LAMB STEW

Serves 4   ① *Preparation 10 min, Cooking 65 min – Easy*

A stew with a Mediterranean flavour.

INGREDIENTS

2 medium-sized aubergines
2 large onions
1 green pepper
500 g (1 lb) lean stewing lamb or beef
2 rounded tablespoons butter
$1/2 \times 400$ g tin chopped tomatoes
Juice of $1/2$ lemon
Salt and freshly ground black pepper to taste
4 tablespoons sunflower oil

EQUIPMENT

Sharp knife
Chopping board
Set of measuring spoons
Wooden spoon
Tin opener
Saucepan with lid
Frying-pan

METHOD

Cut the ends off the aubergines, and cut lengthways into 1 cm ($1/2$ in) slices. Peel and chop the onions. Chop the end off the green peppers and cut out the core and seeds. Cut the pepper into rings. Cut the meat into 2 cm (1 in) cubes.

Put the butter in the saucepan over a moderate heat. Fry the onion, pepper rings and meat for about 3 minutes, stirring to stop it sticking. Add the tomatoes, lemon juice, salt and pepper. Bring to the boil, then turn down the heat until it is just boiling (simmering). Put a lid on and cook very gently for 40 minutes. Check the liquid level from time to time and add a little water if needed.

Heat the oil in a frying-pan. Add the aubergine and fry for 5 minutes on each side until lightly browned and soft. Put the aubergines on top of the meat mixture. Put the lid on and cook gently for 20 minutes. If it is too wet take the lid off for the last few minutes.

ADDITIONS & ALTERNATIVES
Serve with new potatoes, a green vegetable or salad.
Use $^1/_2$ tin of peeled plum tomatoes and chop them yourself.

CIDER LAMB CASSEROLE

Serves 4   ① *Preparation 15 min, Cooking 1$^3/_4$ hr – Easy*

Don't say we don't make it easy for you. Another slow-cook dish using drink, that more or less takes care of itself.

INGREDIENTS
1 lamb stock cube
$^1/_2$ cup boiling water
1 clove garlic
Small bunch parsley
2 small onions
$^1/_2$ cup cider
1 tablespoon Worcestershire sauce
Salt and freshly ground black pepper to taste
1 kg (2 lb) lamb shoulder, off the bone
2 heaped tablespoons flour
2 rounded tablespoons butter

EQUIPMENT
Bowl
Set of measuring cups
Sharp knife
Chopping board
Garlic crusher
Food processor or liquidiser (optional)
Set of measuring spoons
Plastic bag
Frying-pan
Wooden spoon
Slotted spoon
Casserole with lid

METHOD
Dissolve the stock cube in the water. Peel and roughly chop the onions. Peel and crush the garlic. Wash, shake dry and finely chop the parsley to give 2 tablespoons. Peel the onions and either finely chop and mix with the stock, garlic, parsley, cider, Worcestershire sauce, salt and pepper, or roughly chop, then process with the other ingredients in a liquidiser or food processor.

Cut the meat into big bite-sized pieces. Put the flour in the plastic bag with a little salt and pepper. Put a few lumps of meat in the bag and holding the top tightly closed shake them up. They will get coated in flour. Pick them out. Repeat until all the meat is coated. Put the butter in the frying-pan over a moderate heat. Fry the meat for about 3 minutes to brown, stirring to stop it sticking. Lift out and put in the casserole. Put the onion mixture in the frying-pan and cook gently for 5 minutes. Add to the meat. Put a lid on and cook at 170° C, 325° F, Gas mark 3 for 1^1/$_2$ hours.

FRENCH LAMB CHOPS

Serves 4 ⏱ *Preparation 15 min, Cooking 75 min – Easy*

Elegant lamb chops that will lose none of their glamour when
teamed with oven chips.

INGREDIENTS

1 lamb stock cube
1$^1/_2$ cups boiling water
175 g (6 oz) button mushrooms
250 g (8 oz) small shallots
2 cloves garlic
1 teaspoon sunflower or olive oil
4 lamb chops (about 500 g, 1 lb together)
2 tablespoons cornflour
1 bouquet garni (looks like a herb tea bag)
$^1/_2$ teaspoon dried rosemary
1 bay leaf
Salt and freshly ground black pepper to taste
2 or 3 fresh bay leaves and a sprig of rosemary to garnish

EQUIPMENT

Set of measuring cups
Bowl
Sharp knife
Garlic crusher
Chopping board
Set of measuring spoons
Frying-pan
Wooden spoon
Slotted spoon

Casserole with lid
Cup

METHOD

Dissolve the stock cube in the water. Wipe the mushrooms clean. Discard any nasty ones. Chop the end off the stalks. Peel the shallots. Peel and crush the garlic.

Put the oil in the frying-pan over a moderate heat. Fry the chops for about 2 minutes on each side to brown. Lift out with slotted spoon and put in the casserole. Add the shallots, garlic and mushrooms to the frying-pan and fry for 3 minutes until golden. Transfer to the casserole. Add the cornflour and stir. Scrape this into the casserole.

Add the chops, bouquet garni, rosemary, bay leaf, stock, salt and pepper to the casserole. Put a lid on and cook at 180° C, 350° F, Gas mark 4 for 1 hour. Fish out the bay leaf and bouquet garni before serving.

Garnish with fresh bay leaves and a sprig of rosemary.

ADDITIONS & ALTERNATIVES

Serve with new potatoes, a green vegetable or salad.

Use half a cup of red wine instead of some of the stock.

Add 2 tablespoons of brandy with the stock.

TIPS

You can buy ready-made stock in cartons from most supermarkets. You can also buy Swiss vegetable bouillon powder (vegetable stock), if you are worried about the stuff that goes into stock cubes.

Bouquet garni has a mixture of herbs in it, so you can substitute a teaspoon of mixed dried Mediterranean herbs. It means you get little specks of herb in the dish, but no matter.

LAMB & LEEK CASSEROLE

Serves 4   ① *Preparation 20 min, Cooking 1³/₄ hr – Easy*

A meal on its own. Just thinking about it is making my mouth water . . .

INGREDIENTS

1 lamb, chicken or vegetable stock cube
1¹/₂ cups boiling water
8 spring onions
8 medium leeks
1 large tomato
4 potatoes
1 clove garlic
¹/₄ × 15 g pack fresh dill
1 kg (2 lb) cubed lamb (leg or shoulder)
4 tablespoons butter
Salt and freshly ground black pepper to taste
1 teaspoon paprika

EQUIPMENT

Set of measuring cups
Bowl
Sharp knife
Chopping board
Casserole with lid
Frying-pan (optional – see TIPS below)
Set of measuring spoons
Wooden spoon

METHOD

Dissolve the stock cube in the water. Clean and prepare the spring onions. Cut the root end off, trim the leaves. Peel off and discard any dried up or slimy leaves. Discard the green bits. Clean the leeks. First take off the outer leaves, cut the roots off and trim the green part off. Split the leeks in half lengthways. Hold the leeks under running water and wash any grit out. Shake them dry. Cut them crossways in half. Seed and chop the tomato. Peel the potatoes, cutting away any nasty bits, and cut out any eyes. Chop the potatoes into 5 mm ($^1/_4$ in) slices. Peel the garlic then chop it into tiny pieces. Wash, shake dry and finely chop the dill to give 1 tablespoon.

Heat the butter in the frying-pan on a moderate heat and fry the lamb for about 3 minutes to brown, stirring to stop it sticking. Put the meat in the casserole. Lay the spring onions and leeks on top, followed by the tomato, garlic and dill. End with a layer of potato slices. Add the salt, pepper and paprika. Pour in the stock, cover and cook at 150° C, 300° F, Gas mark 2 for 1 $^1/_2$ hours. Check after $^3/_4$ hour. If it looks too dry add another half a cup (125 ml, 4 fl oz) of water.

ADDITIONS & ALTERNATIVES

Use 2 or 3 tinned plum tomatoes, drained, seeded and chopped, instead of the fresh one. If using tinned tomatoes use the juice instead of $^1/_2$ cup of stock.

Use half a cup of white wine instead of some of the stock.

TIPS

Some casseroles, for instance cast-iron ones, are flame-proof so you can use them instead of the pan for frying and then put them in the oven. Otherwise do the frying in the frying-pan and then transfer the meat to casserole.

You can buy ready-made stock in cartons from most supermarkets. You can also buy Swiss vegetable bouillon powder (vegetable stock), if you are worried about the stuff that goes into stock cubes.

LAMB CASSEROLE WITH DUMPLINGS

Serves 4   ① *Preparation 20 min, Cooking 1³/₄ hour – Easy*

Uncomplicated dumplings are the eighth wonder of the world, particularly if you had been forced to work your way through some of my early attempts. They masqueraded as light fluffy things and then at some stage in their digestion became cannon-ball impersonators. These are not like those.

INGREDIENTS

1 lamb stock cube
2 cups water
1 leek
2 carrots
1 parsnip
1 small swede
¹/₄ × 15 g pack fresh parsley
1 onion
500 g (1 lb) lamb
1 tablespoon olive oil
1 cup red wine
1 tablespoon horseradish sauce
2 teaspoons dried thyme
Salt and freshly ground black pepper to taste
1 cup self-raising flour (125 g, 4 oz)

2 heaped tablespoons shredded suet (50 g, 2 oz)
4 tablespoons cold water

EQUIPMENT
Set of measuring cups
Bowl or jug
Sharp knife
Chopping board
Vegetable peeler
Frying-pan (optional – see TIPS below)
Casserole with lid
Set of measuring spoons
Wooden spoon

METHOD
Dissolve the stock cube in the water. Clean the leeks. First take off
the outer leaves, cut the roots off and trim the top. Split the leeks in
half lengthways. Hold the leeks under running water and wash any
grit out. Shake them dry. Cut into 1 cm ($^1/_2$ in) slices. Peel and slice
the carrots. Peel and dice the parsnip and swede. Wash, shake dry
and finely chop the parsley to give 3 tablespoons. Peel and chop the
onion.

If you have bought lamb in a piece chop it into 2.5 cm (1 in)
cubes. Put the oil in the frying-pan over a moderate heat. Fry
the lamb for about 5 minutes to brown, stirring to stop it sticking.
Transfer it to the casserole. Fry the carrot, swede and parsnip for
5 minutes then add them to the casserole. Add the stock, wine,
horseradish sauce , 2 tablespoons of the parsley, 1 teaspoon thyme,
salt and pepper. Cover and cook at 150° C, 300° F, Gas mark 2 for
$1^1/_2$ hours. Check after $^3/_4$ hour. If it looks too dry add another cup
water.

To make the dumplings, mix the flour, suet, 1 tablespoon of

parsley, 1 teaspoon of thyme and seasoning in a bowl. Add the cold water and mix with a fork to make a soft dough. Divide into 8 and roll into balls. Put them in the casserole about 20 minutes before the end of the cooking time.

ADDITIONS & ALTERNATIVES
Use fresh thyme (1 tablespoon for 1 teaspoon), rosemary or oregano as alternative herbs.

TIPS
Some casseroles, for instance cast-iron ones, are flame-proof so you can use them instead of the pan for frying and then put them in the oven. Otherwise do the frying in the frying-pan and then transfer the meat to the casserole.

You can buy ready-made stock in cartons from most super-markets. You can also buy Swiss vegetable bouillon powder (vegetable stock), if you are worried about the stuff that goes into stock cubes.

LAMB ROAST

Serves 4   ① *Preparation 20 min, Cooking 60 min – Easy*

This is very economic and goes a long way. It is best eaten hot, and if we have not managed to get across how to tie it into a sausage shape then use your imagination.

INGREDIENTS
500 g (1 lb) breast of lamb, off the bone
1 small onion
15 g pack (small bunch) parsley

1 egg
2 slices bread
2 teaspoons mixed dried Mediterranean herbs
2 tablespoons brandy (optional)
Salt and freshly ground black pepper to taste
2 teaspoons Dijon mustard

EQUIPMENT
Sharp knife
Chopping board
Set of measuring cups
Set of measuring spoons
Food processor or liquidiser (optional)
Bowl
Oven-proof dish

METHOD
Get the butcher to take the bones out of the breast of lamb. This is a fatty cut and benefits from having the stuffing mixture. Peel the onion and chop into quarters. Wash, shake dry and roughly chop the parsley to give 1 tablespoon. Break the egg into a cup and pick out any bits of shell.

Cut the bread into cubes. Put the bread in the liquidiser or food processor and blend until crumbed. Pour into the bowl. Blend the parsley, onion, egg, herbs, brandy, salt and pepper until the onion is finely chopped. Add to the breadcrumbs and combine.

Make a few shallow cuts in the breast of lamb. Spread the mustard on the skin-side of the lamb.

Cut five lengths of string longer than the breast of lamb and lay them with the breast of lamb on top, skin-side down. Spoon the stuffing onto the breast of lamb along a line 5 cm (2 in) from the shorter edge. Starting from this edge, roll the breast of lamb into a sausage. Secure it. Tie the strings round the breast of lamb, then put it in the oven-proof dish. Cook in the preheated oven at 180° C, 350° F, Gas mark 4 for 1 hour.

ADDITIONS & ALTERNATIVES

Serve with jacket potato, gravy and haricot beans.

Serve with a rich brown gravy and oven-baked jacket potatoes. Boiled butter beans or haricot beans dressed with butter and chopped parsley are also good with lamb.

You can eat this cold but it needs a lot of pickle to go with it as it can be very fatty.

LANCASHIRE HOTPOT

Serves 6   ① *Preparation 25 min, Cooking 2¹/₂ hr – Easy*

Traditionally made in a big tall earthenware pot in the oven so that there were lots of layers. Cold weather comfort food and an important part of our food heritage.

INGREDIENTS

1 kg (2 lb) middle neck of lamb chops
3 lambs' kidneys
8 medium potatoes
3 medium onions
10 button mushrooms, about 100 g (4 oz)
2 teaspoons vegetable oil
3 tablespoons butter
2 tablespoons flour
1¹/₂ cups water
Salt and freshly ground black pepper to taste

EQUIPMENT
Sharp knife
Chopping board
Vegetable peeler
Frying-pan
Set of measuring spoons
Deep casserole with lid
Set of measuring cups
Bowl
Wooden spoon

METHOD
Trim the fat from the chops and keep for later. Get the butcher to take the outer membrane from the kidneys and cut out the hard, white core, or do it yourself. Some supermarkets do ready-prepared kidneys. Cut the kidneys into slices. Peel the potatoes, cutting away any nasty bits, and cutting out any eyes. Thickly slice the potatoes. Peel and slice the onion. Wipe the mushrooms clean. Discard any nasty ones. Chop the end off the stalks and slice.

Put the oil in the frying-pan over a moderate heat. Fry the chops for about 3 minutes on each side until browned. Lift out and fry the onions for 3 minutes, stirring to stop them sticking.

Rub half the butter on the inside of the casserole. Put in half the sliced potatoes, and add salt and pepper. Add the chops. Cover with the onions and some more salt and pepper. Next put in the kidneys and mushrooms, ending up with a layer of potato.

Add some of the fat trimmings to the frying-pan and fry for 3 minutes, then remove and discard. Add the flour and stir round. Gradually add the water, stirring to get the bits off the bottom of the frying-pan. Boil for 3 minutes to thicken a little and pour over the potato. Season the top layer, dot with the remaining butter and cover. Cook at 170° C, 325° F, Gas mark 3 for 2 hours, then take the lid off and cook for another 30 minutes.

ADDITIONS & ALTERNATIVES

Pickled red cabbage is the traditional accompaniment for Lancashire hotpot.

In Victorian times oysters were a food of the poor, and they used to make this go further by adding a few shelled oysters with the kidney. You can do the same. It is great, but an expensive option.

CHILLI MUSTARD LAMB WITH COUSCOUS

Serves 4   ① *Preparation 15 min, Cooking 15 min – Easy*

Really quick to make. You only need to grill the lamb and then spread the topping on it for the last few minutes.

INGREDIENTS

15 g pack parsley
3 tablespoons sultanas
$^1/_2 \times$ 500 g pack (1 cup) couscous
$1^1/_4$ cups boiling water
1 tablespoon olive oil
1 tablespoon lemon juice
4 lamb steaks
4 teaspoons Dijon mustard
2 teaspoons soft brown sugar
$^1/_4$ teaspoon chilli powder

EQUIPMENT

Sharp knife
Chopping board
Set of measuring cups
Set of measuring spoons

Bowl
Wooden spoon

METHOD
Wash, shake dry and finely chop the parsley. Soak the sultanas in enough boiling water to cover. Put the couscous in a bowl, pour over the boiling water, olive oil and lemon juice. Cover with a plate and leave to stand for 5 minutes. If it looks too dry add a second tablespoon of oil. Fluff up with a fork. Add the parsley and the drained sultanas.

Grill the steaks on one side for about 6 minutes. Turn and cook for 2 minutes. Mix the mustard, sugar and chilli powder together and spread on the steaks. Cook for 5 minutes.

Serve hot with the couscous.

PAN FRIED LAMB

Serves 4 ⏱ *Preparation 20 min, Cooking 25 min – Easy*

We like wine, and not just for cooking. If you have some extra, use it in this great sauce.

INGREDIENTS
$^1/_2$ lamb stock cube
$^1/_2$ boiling water
4 oyster mushrooms, about 75 g (3 oz)
10 button mushrooms, about 100 g (4 oz)
4 shallots
15 g pack parsley
1 teaspoon cornflour
3 tablespoons cold water
1 tablespoon olive oil
1 level tablespoon butter

MAGIC MEAT

4 lamb steaks
$^1/_2$ cup red wine
2 tablespoons Greek yoghurt (optional)
Salt and freshly ground black pepper to taste

EQUIPMENT
Set of measuring cups
Bowl
Sharp knife
Chopping board
Set of measuring spoons
Cup
Frying-pan
Wooden spoon

METHOD
Dissolve the stock cube in the boiling water. Wipe the mushrooms clean. Discard any nasty ones. Chop the end off the stalks. Slice. Peel and finely chop the shallots. Wash, shake dry and finely chop the parsley to give 2 tablespoons. Mix the cornflour and water together in the cup until smooth. Add the water slowly or it will go lumpy.

Put the oil and butter in the frying-pan over a moderate heat. Fry the lamb steaks for about 5 minutes on each side until brown and cooked, stirring to stop them sticking. Lift out of the pan and keep warm in the oven. Add the mushrooms and shallots to the pan and fry for about 5 minutes. Add the stock and wine and bring to the boil. Turn down the heat. Add the cornflour mixture, stirring to stop it going lumpy. Cook for 3 minutes. Stir in the yoghurt if using. Pour over the steaks. Sprinkle with the parsley before serving.

ADDITIONS & ALTERNATIVES
Serve with new potatoes, a green vegetable or salad.

POSH PASTA

Probably the best-known pasta dish is spaghetti Bolognese, and we think that our recipe is the very best of all the recipes for it. You do not even have to use beef, but you can if you like. The other recipes are more exotic and unusual but, as you would expect, still easy.

SUPER BOL SPAGHETTI

Serves 3 to 4   ① *Preparation 5 min, Cooking 25 min – Easy*

INGREDIENTS
2 medium to large onions
3 or 4 cloves garlic
1 tablespoon olive oil
500 g (1 lb) pack minced turkey or beef
400 g tin of tomatoes
2 tablespoons tomato purée
1 teaspoon each dried rosemary and dried oregano or 2 teaspoons dried Mediterranean herbs
2 bay leaves
$1^1/_2$ teaspoons sugar
1 tablespoon vegetable (Marigold) bouillon or $^1/_2$ vegetable stock cube

1 cup water
Salt and freshly ground black pepper to taste
500 g pack spaghetti

EQUIPMENT
Sharp knife
Chopping board
Set of measuring spoons
Large frying-pan
Wooden spoon
Tin opener
Large saucepan
Colander or sieve
Set of measuring cups
Serving bowl
Grater

METHOD
Peel and chop the onions and the garlic. Heat the oil in a large frying-pan and add the chopped onions and garlic. Cook on a low heat for 2 to 3 minutes. Add the minced turkey and stir around with a wooden spoon so that the mince does not all stick together. Cook for 3 to 5 minutes on a low heat until the meat has changed colour slightly. Open the tin of tomatoes and pour the juice off into the pan with the meat. With the wooden spoon mash the tomatoes in the tin and then add them to the pan. Stir the mixture well together. Cook for 2 to 3 minutes then add the tomato purée and mix together. Add the dried herbs, bay leaves, sugar and the vegetable bouillon, stirring well together, then add $1/2$ cup of cold water. If you are using the vegetable stock cube then crumble it into $1/2$ cup of boiling water to dissolve before adding to the mixture and don't add the $1/2$ cup of cold water. Keep the second

$^1/_2$ cup of water in case the Bolognese sauce gets too dry. Add some black pepper, depending upon your taste, but do not add salt as vegetable bouillon and some stock cubes can taste quite salty. Cook on a low heat for 10 to 15 minutes. Add extra water if you need to.

Meantime, bring some salted water to the boil in a large saucepan. When it is boiling add the spaghetti and cook rapidly for about 10 to 12 minutes (approx. check packet for details) until done but not soft.

When cooked drain and put into a large serving bowl. Pour the Bolognese sauce over the pasta and mix together lightly so that all the pasta is covered in the sauce. If you would rather serve with the sauce on top of the pasta, then stir 1 tablespoon of olive oil into the pasta, coating evenly, and then top with the Bolognese sauce.

Serve immediately with a small bowl of grated Parmesan cheese and some salad.

PESTO

① *Preparation 10 min – Easy*

We know you can buy it in tubs and jars, chilled and long-lasting, but a lot of them put vinegar in the mixture, which does not taste too good with the basil and the Parmesan. So here is your chance to try pesto the way it is meant to taste.

INGREDIENTS
30 g pack basil
35 g pack parsley
1 clove garlic
1 tablespoon pine nuts
2 tablespoons grated Parmesan cheese

4 tablespoons olive oil
Salt and pepper to taste

EQUIPMENT
Sharp knife
Chopping board
Set of measuring cups
Set of measuring spoons
Food processor or liquidiser (optional)
Jar for storage or bowl for serving

METHOD
Wash, shake dry and remove the stalks from the basil and parsley. Peel and roughly chop the garlic. Place all the ingredients in the liquidiser or processor, with salt and pepper to taste. Blend on maximum speed for 30 to 40 seconds.

This recipe makes 175 ml (6 fl oz). If you want to store it pour it into a screw-topped jar and cover the surface with a thin layer of olive oil. Keep in the fridge, but do not keep it too long.

ADDITIONS & ALTERNATIVES
You can use 25 g (1 oz) of walnuts instead of the pine nuts.

Use this sauce on pasta, in minestrone soup, on lamb chops or baked potatoes.

PESTO PASTA SALAD

Serves 4　　① *Preparation 15 min, Cooking about 10 min – Easy*

Now you know how to make the pesto, indulge yourself with this recipe.

INGREDIENTS

1 tablespoon coarsely chopped fresh parsley
3 tablespoons prepared pesto (previous recipe or ready-made.)
4 tablespoons olive oil
1 tablespoon fresh lemon juice,
Salt and freshly ground pepper to taste
500 g pack pasta shapes of your choice
100 g packet salami or Spanish chorizo, ready sliced
1 small tin or $1/2 \times 450$ g tin pitted black olives

EQUIPMENT

Sharp knife
Chopping board
Large salad bowl
Set of measuring spoons
Large saucepan
Colander or sieve

METHOD

Wash and shake dry the parsley and then chop it quite finely. In a large salad bowl mix together the pesto, olive oil, lemon juice, pepper and chopped parsley.

In a large saucepan bring some salted water to the boil. When it is boiling add the pasta and continue boiling until it is done, probably about 10 to 12 minutes but check the packet for details. When cooked, drain the pasta and add to the ingredients in the bowl and gently stir together to make sure that the hot pasta is evenly coated. Allow the pasta to cool.

Cut the salami into strips and open and drain the pitted olives and add both to the pasta. Mix together to make sure that salami and olives are equally dispersed.

ADDITIONS & ALTERNATIVES

Stir in any of the following: halved cherry tomatoes, diced feta cheese, green olives, a 200 g drained tin of tuna, sliced smoked sausage or frankfurters.

CREAM SCALLOP TAGLIATELLE

Serves 3 to 4
① Preparation 25 min, Cooking about 20 min – Easy

You can use China Bay scallops or the larger and more expensive pink and white ones. Try the recipe with the cheaper ones first to see if it is to your taste.

INGREDIENTS
12 to 18 scallops (ready shelled)
15 g pack parsley
2 large red peppers
1 medium onion
2 cloves garlic
1 rounded tablespoon butter
2 tablespoons olive oil
1 cup (250 ml) fish stock or $^1/_2$ stock cube (fish or vegetable) dissolved in 1 cup boiling water
Medium carton (284 ml, 10 fl oz) single cream or crème fraîche
$^3/_4 \times$ 500 g pack green tagliatelle or 375 g pack
Salt and freshly ground black pepper to taste

EQUIPMENT
Sharp knife
Chopping board
Set of measuring spoons

Food processor or liquidiser
Small frying-pan
Large bowl
Set of measuring cups
Large saucepan and small saucepan
Saucepan with lid

METHOD

Rinse and slice the scallops. Wash the parsley and shake dry. Remove the stalks and chop the leaves. Wash the peppers and cut in half, remove the core and seeds and stalk. Lightly grill the peppers, skin-side up, until they start to brown and the skins start to loosen. Remove as much of the skins as possible and then dice. Peel and finely chop the onion and garlic.

Put the butter and olive oil in a pan on a moderate heat, add the onion and garlic and fry for 2 to 3 minutes. Put the diced peppers, salt and pepper in the pan with the onion and garlic and cover. Simmer for 5 minutes.

Remove from the heat and allow to cool for a few minutes. Then add to the liquidiser with $^1/_2$ cup of the stock and liquidise until the mixture is very smooth.

Pour the mixture into a small saucepan, add the cream and the sliced scallops and simmer slowly for 7 to 8 minutes while stirring. If the sauce is too thick add some of the remaining fish stock.

Meanwhile, bring some salted water to the boil in a large saucepan. When the water is boiling add the pasta, and continue to boil until cooked but not soft, about 10 to 12 minutes. Drain the pasta and mix in a bowl with the sauce. Sprinkle with the chopped parsley and serve.

MUSSEL & MUSHROOM PASTA

Serves 4   ⏲ *Preparation 20 min, Cooking about 25 min – Easy*

This is a delicious and unusual pasta dish. It is most important to throw away any mussels that are not closed when you wash them and any that do not open during cooking. (If using ready-cooked someone else has already done that.)

INGREDIENTS
1 clove garlic
1 large handful of parsley
10 to 20 button mushrooms (about 150 g, $^1/_4$ to $^1/_2$ lb)
1 kg (2 lb) mussels in the shell (or 2 × 500 g bags pre-cooked in shells)
5 tablespoons olive oil
2 teaspoons anchovy paste or anchovy sauce
$^1/_2$ cup dry white wine
Salt and pepper to taste
$^3/_4$ × 500 g pack spaghetti
2 teaspoons virgin olive oil (to toss pasta in)

EQUIPMENT
2 saucepans, 1 large with lid for mussels and pasta
Set of measuring spoons
Sieve
Bowl
Sharp knife
Chopping board
Set of measuring cups
Wooden spoon

METHOD

Peel and finely chop the garlic and wash and finely chop the parsley. Wipe the mushrooms clean. Discard any nasty ones. Chop the end off the stalks. Slice finely.

If using fresh mussels clean and prepare the mussels by washing and scraping clean. Throw away any that are open. Place in a wide saucepan with 3 tablespoons of the oil. Put the lid on and cook over a high heat for a minute or two to open the mussels. Throw away any that do not open. Take the mussels out off their shells. Save the cooking juices and oil and strain it. Put the strained cooking juices in a deep dish and add the shelled mussels. If using ready-cooked mussels, then reheat and remove them from their shells, keeping the cooking juices, and then follow the rest of the recipe.

Pour the remaining oil into a saucepan and add the anchovy paste, blending it into the oil over low heat. Add the finely sliced mushrooms and stir well. Pour in the wine, add a little salt if necessary and a generous amount of freshly ground pepper and cook gently for 10 minutes, stirring occasionally.

Meantime, cook the spaghetti in plenty of boiling salted water in a large pan until just done but not soft, about 10 to 12 minutes. Check the pack for times. A few minutes before it is done, add the mussels to the mushroom mixture together with the garlic and parsley. Heat through. Drain the spaghetti and place it in a serving bowl with 2 teaspoons of olive oil. Turn the pasta in the oil, making sure that it is evenly coated. Then mix in the mussel and mushroom mixture and serve at once.

ADDITIONS & ALTERNATIVES

If you are very hungry and have a very large saucepan then use all the 500 g of pasta.

TIPS

Always buy fresh mussels on the day you intend to eat them. You should deal with them as soon as you can after getting home, but if this is not possible put them to soak in a large bowl of cold water until you are ready. Discard the water and rinse the mussels when you are ready to prepare them.

MORTADELLA PASTA

Serves 3 to 4
① Preparation 5 min, Cooking about 20 min – Easy

There are lots of different mortadella sausages and they all have got inclusions such as olives or pistachio nuts, so pick your favourite combination of flavours.

INGREDIENTS
Salt
500 g pack tagliatelle
125 g (4 oz) mortadella (about 15 slices)
4 tablespoons butter
Freshly grated Parmesan
2 teaspoons olive oil

EQUIPMENT
Large saucepan
Colander or sieve
Sharp knife
Chopping board
Set of measuring spoons
Frying-pan
Wooden spoon

Serving bowl
Grater

METHOD

Bring some salted water to the boil in a large saucepan. When it is boiling add the pasta and continue to boil until it is cooked but not too soft. Check the packet for cooking time, probably about 8 to 10 minutes. Drain.

Meanwhile, cut the mortadella into strips. Melt the butter in a thick-bottomed frying-pan, add the mortadella and fry for 3 minutes.

Put the drained hot pasta into a serving bowl, add some of the freshly grated Parmesan and the olive oil and mix together so that the pasta is coated with olive oil. Then add the mortadella and butter sauce and stir together. Sprinkle with more Parmesan cheese and serve immediately.

PASTA & MASCARPONE WALNUT SAUCE

Serves 3 to 4　　　① *Preparation 10 min, Cooking 25 min – Easy*

Crunchy and creamy, and because it is pasta it is incredibly easy.

INGREDIENTS

75 g (3 oz) walnuts
Salt and freshly ground pepper to taste
$3/4 \times 500$ g pack conchiglie or other pasta shapes
2 teaspoons virgin olive oil
1 rounded tablespoon butter
250 g tub of mascarpone or other full fat soft cheese
2 tablespoons freshly grated Parmesan cheese

EQUIPMENT
Sharp knife
Chopping board
Large saucepan
Colander or sieve
Large bowl
Set of measuring spoons
Wooden spoon

METHOD
Chop the walnuts roughly. In a large saucepan bring some salted water to the boil. When boiling add the pasta and cook until just tender, about 10–12 minutes (check packet for cooking times). Drain well. Empty into a large bowl and add the olive oil. Mix together, making sure that the pasta is evenly coated with the olive oil.

In the same pan that you cooked the pasta in, melt the butter, add the mascarpone cheese and stir for about 2 to 3 minutes until heated through. Do not boil. Add the Parmesan and walnuts, stir, then add the pasta. Mix well until evenly coated with sauce. Season to taste and serve immediately.

GOLDEN CHEESE PASTA

Serves 4 to 6   ① *Preparation 20 min, Cooking 40 min – Easy*

It is golden on top, it is creamy underneath, it is cheesy inside and you finish it off in the oven. And it is a really filling meal.

INGREDIENTS
1 small onion
2 cloves garlic

4 fresh basil leaves or $^1/_2$ teaspoon dried basil or dried mixed herbs
$^1/_2$ × 250 g pack butter
2 tablespoons olive oil, plus extra for oiling
400 g tin tomatoes
Salt and freshly ground pepper to taste
$^1/_2$ × 500 g pack large macaroni
3 tablespoons plain flour
1 pint milk
1$^1/_2$ cups grated Gruyère cheese, about 75 g (3 oz)
4 tablespoons freshly grated Parmesan cheese
3 tablespoons dried breadcrumbs
2 teaspoons freshly grated nutmeg

EQUIPMENT
Sharp knife
Chopping board
Garlic crusher
3 saucepans, 1 heavy-based and 1 large
Tin opener
Wooden spoon
Grater
Set of measuring cups
Set of measuring spoons
Oven-proof dish

METHOD
Begin with the tomato sauce. Peel and finely chop the onion and peel and crush the garlic. If using fresh basil chop the leaves. Melt half the butter in a heavy-based saucepan with the olive oil. Add the onion and garlic and fry gently for 5 minutes until soft but not coloured.

Add the tomato juice from the tin together with the basil. With a wooden spoon break up the tomatoes in the tin and then add them to the pan with seasoning to taste. Stir everything together and bring to the boil. Lower the heat and simmer for 10 minutes, stirring occasionally.

Meanwhile in a large saucepan bring some salted water to the boil. Add the macaroni and return to the boil. Cook for about 10 minutes or until just tender.

To make the cheese sauce, first grate the Gruyère cheese if not ready-grated then melt the other half of the butter in a third saucepan, add the flour and cook over low heat, stirring with the wooden spoon for 2 minutes. Remove the pan from the heat and gradually add the milk, stirring all the time to stop the sauce from going lumpy. When all the milk is added return to the heat and slowly bring to the boil. Continue stirring all the time until the sauce thickens. Add the Gruyère cheese and stir until it is all melted.

Drain the macaroni and mix with the tomato sauce. Put half this mixture in a large oiled or buttered oven-proof dish. Pour half the cheese sauce over the macaroni, and then repeat with the remaining macaroni and cheese sauce. Finally sprinkle with the Parmesan and breadcrumbs. (You can make your own breadcrumbs by crumbling up some dry slices of bread. This is most easily done by rubbing one slice against another.) Sprinkle with nutmeg. Bake in the oven at 190° C, 375° F, Gas mark 5 for 15 minutes. If is not brown enough you can finish it off for 5 minutes under a hot grill.

Serve hot with salad.

ADDITIONS & ALTERNATIVES
Gruyère is sold ready-grated as well as in lumps. If Gruyère is not available replace with Gouda, Edam or mild Cheddar cheese.

TAGLIATELLE & GORGONZOLA

Serves 3 to 4
① *Preparation 15 min, Cooking about 20 min – Easy*

More flash pasta and really flash cheese and wine. It's like a wine and cheese party on your plate.

INGREDIENTS
15 g pack fresh sage
1 rounded tablespoon butter
$1^{1}/_{2} \times 125$ g packs Gorgonzola cheese
Small carton (142 ml, 5 fl oz) double cream
2 tablespoons dry white wine
Salt and freshly ground black pepper to taste
$^{3}/_{4} \times 500$ g pack or 375 g pack dried tagliatelle
2 teaspoons olive oil

EQUIPMENT
Sharp knife
Chopping board
Set of measuring spoons
Small heavy-based saucepan for sauce
Whisk
Wooden spoon
Large saucepan for pasta
Colander or sieve
Large bowl

METHOD
Starting with the sauce, wash, shake dry and finely chop the sage to make 1 tablespoon. Melt the butter in the heavy-based saucepan

and crumble the Gorgonzola into the pan. Stir together over a gentle heat for 2 to 3 minutes until the cheese has melted.

Add the cream and wine, mixing vigorously, preferably with a whisk. Stir in the sage, season, and continue cooking and stirring until the sauce has thickened. Remove the saucepan from the heat.

Meanwhile, put some slightly salted water into a large saucepan and bring to the boil. When it is boiling add the pasta and continue to cook for about 10 minutes until just cooked but not soft. Drain the pasta and put into a serving bowl with the olive oil. Toss the pasta in the olive oil to make sure that it is evenly coated.

If the Gorgonzola sauce has cooled, gently reheat it, stirring or whisking vigorously all the time. When reheated pour over the pasta in the bowl, stir lightly together and serve.

ADDITIONS & ALTERNATIVES
Serve with focaccia or other Italian bread and salad.

AWESOME ORIENTAL

The recipes in the first half of this chapter are all easy to cook Japanese dishes. There are a lot that are not easy to cook, but we have never managed to master them either, and so they are not here. Presentation is very important with Japanese food and it should look good as well as taste good. You may want to buy some Asian chilli oil as a condiment to go with the soy sauce, as it certainly enhances some of the flavours. But that does not mean smother everything in it. The same goes for wasabi, a very hot green horseradish powder, where even more caution is advisable.

The second half of the chapter zips round the rest of the Orient, for more dishes that are one step beyond the take-away.

SUSHI GINGER & CHICKEN STIR-FRY

Serves 4 to 5   ⏲ *Preparation 10 min, Cooking 15 min – Easy*

Plunge into the Japanese section with cooked sushi ginger. This is a real cheat. It is so simple, and no one will ever believe you cooked it yourself.

INGREDIENTS
50 g packet sushi ginger (pickled ginger)
1 kg (2 lb) skinless and boneless chicken breast pieces

1$^1/_2$ tablespoons sunflower oil
2 tablespoons Furikake Japanese seasoning (optional)

EQUIPMENT
Cup
Sharp knife
Chopping board
Set of measuring spoons
Frying-pan or wok
Serving bowl

METHOD
Open the sushi ginger packet carefully, drain the juice into a cup.
Keep it as you will need it later. Put the sushi ginger on a chopping
board and chop it roughly.

Slice the chicken breasts very thinly. Heat the oil in the frying-
pan over a moderate heat and add the sliced chicken. Cook the
chicken for 3 to 5 minutes, stirring to stop it sticking or burning.
When it has changed colour (got lighter) add half the sushi ginger
and all the juice that you have saved in the cup. Turn the heat
down very low and cook for another 2 minutes, stirring the chicken
mixture. Add the remaining sushi ginger, stir over low heat for
1 minute, sprinkle with the Furikake seasoning and serve.

Serve with plain boiled white rice (recipe below).

PLAIN BOILED RICE

Serves 4   ① *Preparation 2 min, Cooking 10 to 15 min – Easy*

Just a reminder of the simple things in life to go with the fancy
ones.

INGREDIENTS
1$^1/_2$ cups white long-grain rice
3 cups water
1 teaspoon salt

EQUIPMENT
Saucepan with lid
Measuring cups and spoons

METHOD
Read the packet to get the correct cooking time.

Put the rice, water and salt in the pan. Bring the water and rice to the boil, stirring once to stop the rice sticking.

Turn down the heat to low and put the lid on the pan. Cook for the correct time until all the water is absorbed (about 10 to 15 minutes for long-grain or Basmati rice). Do not stir! After the cooking time, take it off the heat and let it stand for a couple of minutes. Fluff it up with a fork to separate the grains and serve.

CHICKEN & HORSERADISH

Serves 2 to 3 main course, 4 to 6 as a starter or as part of a bigger meal.   ⏲ *Preparation 25 min, Cooking 5 min – Easy*

Rumour has it is that Japanese cooking is hard, and some of it is, so almost any Japanese dish will impress a lot of people. The fact that this looks and tastes great will guarantee that cooking this meal will certainly impress someone, and it may even be you.

INGREDIENTS
2$^1/_2$ teaspoons wasabi powder
2 boned skinless chicken breasts (about 250 g, 8 oz)

1 sheet of packaged nori seaweed
100 g (4 oz) bunch flat-leaf parsley
5 tablespoons sake or dry sherry
1^1/$_2$ teaspoons salt
1 cup water
2 tablespoons Japanese soy sauce

EQUIPMENT
Cup and teaspoon
Set of measuring spoons
Sharp knife
Chopping board
2 saucepans
Mixing bowl
1 large serving bowl or several small bowls

METHOD
Add just enough water to the wasabi to make a thick paste. Put
aside for at least 15 minutes to let it rest. Cut the chicken breast
horizontally into paper-thin slices, and then cut into shreds about
^{1}/$_2$ cm (^{1}/$_4$ in) wide. Cut the sheet of nori into shreds a bit thinner
than the chicken. Wash and shake dry the parsley but leave whole.

Put the shredded chicken, sake and 1 teaspoon salt in the
small saucepan. Stir well and bring to the boil over a moderate heat.
Once boiled remove from the heat. Allow to cool to room temperature.

In another small saucepan put 1 cup of water and ^{1}/$_2$ teaspoon
of salt and bring to the boil over a high heat. Add the parsley and
cook for 1 minute. Drain and rinse it in cold water. Squeeze it dry
and then chop it roughly.

Put the wasabi paste and soy sauce in a mixing bowl. Add the
chicken and its cooking liquid and the chopped parsley. Mix
together.

Serve in either one large bowl or in individual ones. Top with the shredded nori.

TIPS

Wasabi powder is Japanese horseradish. It is a lot stronger than the horseradish sauce you have with roast beef, and is bright green. You can buy it in packets from health food shops and some supermarkets.

JAPANESE BEEF

Serves 4   ⏱ *Preparation 25 min, Cooking 30 min – Easy*

A full meal in a pot. This is a sort of Japanese meat and potato pie.

INGREDIENTS

350 g (12 oz) sirloin steak
4 or 5 medium potatoes, about 500 g (1 lb)
4 cups (1 litre) water
2 medium onions
2 cm (1 in) fresh root ginger
2 tablespoons vegetable or sunflower oil
3 tablespoons sake
2 tablespoons sugar
3 tablespoons soy sauce

EQUIPMENT

Sharp knife
Chopping board
Vegetable peeler
Set of measuring cups
Large bowl

Plate
Set of measuring spoons
Large saucepan

METHOD

Cut the beef across the grain into very thin slices, 2 to 3 mm (¹/8 in). Cut each slice into 4 cm (2 in) lengths. Peel the potatoes and cut into quarters, then cut the quarters into 2 cm (1 in) pieces. Put the potatoes with 3 cups of the water in a large bowl. Soak for 5 minutes, then drain.

Peel the onions, cut in half lengthways and then cut the halves into thick slices. Peel the ginger and cut it into thin strips. Put on one side on a small plate.

Heat 1 tablespoon of oil in a large heavy saucepan over medium to high heat. Add the beef and cook for 2 minutes, stirring occasionally, until it is just brown. Put on one side on a plate.

Add the remaining oil to pan and cook over medium to high heat until hot. Add the onions and potatoes, cooking for about 2 minutes, stirring constantly. Add the remaining water, the sake and sugar to the pan and heat to boiling. Reduce the heat to medium and boil gently for 10 minutes. Add the soy sauce and the beef to the pan and cook until the potatoes are tender, 10 to 15 minutes. Serve immediately, with cooking liquid, garnished with ginger strips.

ADDITIONS & ALTERNATIVES

It is easier to slice meat thinly if it is partially frozen. Pop it into the freezer for 30 minutes before slicing.

CHICKEN LOAF SAUTÉ

Serves 4   ① *Preparation 25 min, Cooking 8 min – Easy*

This is a kind of chicken omelette with lots of chicken and very little egg.

INGREDIENTS
1 teaspoon ginger juice or 2 cm (1 in) fresh root ginger
1 small egg
1 leek
2 teaspoons white sesame seeds
500 g (1 lb) pack chicken mince
2 teaspoons sugar
2 teaspoons soy sauce
2 teaspoons sake
2 teaspoons vegetable or sunflower oil
4 sprigs watercress (optional)

EQUIPMENT
Vegetable peeler
Sharp knife
Chopping board
Small bowl or cup
Fork
Food processor (optional)
Set of measuring spoons
Small frying-pan
Medium bowl
20 cm (8 in) frying-pan
Fish slice or spatula

METHOD

If no fresh ginger juice is available use a 2 cm (1 in) piece of ginger. Peel it and chop it up very small. Break the egg into a small bowl or a cup and beat lightly with a fork. Remove the root end from the leek and top dark green leaves. Run a knife down the length of the leek and hold it under running water to make sure that you rinse out any soil that sometimes gets trapped between the leaves. Shake the leek dry and then chop it up very small. If you have a food processor chop into chunks and put it into the processor for this chopping. Heat the sesame seeds in the small frying-pan over a medium to high heat for 2 minutes, stirring or shaking the pan constantly until the seeds are light brown and they start to pop. Put on one side.

Put the minced chicken, chopped leek, ginger or ginger juice, sugar, soy sauce, sake and egg in a medium bowl and stir well. Heat the oil in the frying-pan over a medium to low heat for 1 minute. Put the chicken mixture into the pan and spread it evenly to a depth of about 1 cm ($^1/_2$ in). Cook it until it is brown, about 3 to 5 minutes. Cut the chicken into quarters and turn each quarter to cook the other side for 2 to 3 minutes more. When cooked sprinkle evenly with sesame seeds.

Cool for 5 minutes and serve with a little watercress.

WINE-SIMMERED CHICKEN

Serves 4   ① *Preparation 15 min, Cooking 25 min – Easy*

This is a very different chicken dish. The wine and the soy combined with the daikon give this an individual flavour.

INGREDIENTS

500 g (l lb) skinned and boned chicken breasts or thighs, or
ready-cubed
1 medium to large daikon (Japanese/Chinese white radish), about
250 g (8 oz)
1³/₄ cups (430 ml) water
1¹/₂ tablespoons soy sauce
1¹/₂ teaspoons sugar
1 tablespoon mirin
Pinch salt
3 tablespoons dry red wine
If the daikon is very hot, increase amount of red wine to 4
tablespoons

EQUIPMENT

Sharp knife
Chopping board
Vegetable peeler
Set of measuring cups
Large saucepan
Set of measuring spoons
Serving bowl

METHOD

Cut the chicken into 4 cm (2 in) square pieces. Peel the daikon and
cut it into 2 cm (1 in) chunks.

Bring the water to the boil in the large saucepan over a medium
heat. Add the chopped chicken and daikon and boil gently for 10
minutes. Add the soy sauce, sugar, mirin and salt and boil gently
for 10 to 15 minutes, until the chicken is tender. Add the red wine
and cook for 1 to 2 minutes more. Serve immediately with the cooking juices in a large serving bowl.

ADDITIONS & ALTERNATIVES
Serve with plain boiled rice.

JAPANESE ROAST CHICKEN

Serves 4   ⓘ *Preparation 10 min, Cooking 1 hour 30 min – Easy*

Think ahead. This needs to stand in the fridge for 4 hours before cooking.

Slow roasting for this chicken lets the flavour soak in.

INGREDIENTS
1 clove garlic
2 cm (1 in) root ginger
2 shallots
1 small lemon
3 to 4 tablespoons soy sauce
5 to 6 tablespoons sake, or 4 tablespoons dry sherry and 2 tablespoons water
1 tablespoon brown sugar
1¹/₂ kg (3 lb) chicken pieces
1 to 2 tablespoons cornflour
4 tablespoons groundnut or sunflower oil

EQUIPMENT
Sharp knife
Chopping board
Set of measuring spoons
Large bowl
Plastic bag
Oven-proof dish

METHOD

Peel the garlic and chop it coarsely. Peel the ginger and shallots and chop them into small pieces. Wash the lemon, slice it and then chop into chunks. Combine the soy sauce, sake, sugar, lemon, chopped ginger root, shallots and garlic in a large bowl.

Dust the chicken pieces with the cornflour by putting the cornflour and chicken into a plastic bag and shaking them together. When the chicken pieces are dusted in the cornflour put them into the bowl with the soy sauce mixture and leave to marinate them there for 4 hours or more. Turn the chicken pieces from time to time to ensure an even coating.

Place the chicken in the oven-proof dish, sprinkle with the oil and bake for 1¹/₂ hours in a slow oven 170° C, 325° F, Gas mark 3. Baste the chicken every half-hour or so.

ADDITIONS & ALTERNATIVES

Serve with plain rice, a slice of orange and nori flakes, or lemon sweet potato, the next recipe.

LEMON SWEET POTATO

Serves 4   ① *Preparation 15 min, Cooking 30 min – Easy*

This is a vegetable dish to accompany any of the meat dishes.

INGREDIENTS

2 or 3 small to medium sweet potatoes, about 500 g (1 lb)
Water
1 medium lemon
3 tablespoons sugar
¹/₄ teaspoon salt

EQUIPMENT

Vegetable peeler
Sharp knife
Chopping board
Bowl
Sieve or colander
Set of measuring cups
Set of measuring spoons
Large saucepan

METHOD

Peel the sweet potatoes and cut them into 2 cm (1 in) thick slices.
Place them in the bowl and cover with water. Soak them for 5
minutes. Change the water and soak for another 5 minutes, then
drain in a sieve or colander.

Rinse the lemon and slice it thinly.

Put the potatoes, $2^1/_2$ cups water, the sugar and salt in a large
saucepan. Bring to the boil over a high heat. Reduce the heat and
boil gently for 10 minutes. Add the lemon slices. Continue cooking
for another 20 minutes or until the potatoes are tender, adding
more water if necessary. Drain and serve hot or at room temperature as an accompaniment to a chicken or beef dish.

SEAWEED & TUNA

Serves 4   ① *Preparation 20 min, Cooking 5 min – Easy*

I must go down to the sea again to clamber across the rocks, or nip
in to the health store and buy it in a box. Seriously, you can get
seaweed in lots of supermarkets, and tinned tuna almost every-
where.

INGREDIENTS
10 stems dried wakame
6 cups water
3 tablespoons rice vinegar or white wine vinegar
2 tablespoons soy sauce
1 teaspoon sugar
$^1/_2$ tablespoon sesame oil
2 × 200 g tins tuna steak in brine
$^1/_2$ tablespoon lemon juice
1 small cucumber, preferably unwaxed
1 large tomato

EQUIPMENT
Set of measuring cups
Large bowl
Large saucepan
Sharp knife
Chopping board
Set of measuring spoons
Tin opener
Large serving bowl or individual bowls

METHOD
Place the wakame stems and 3 cups of water in a large bowl. Leave
to stand for 20 minutes and then drain the wakame. In a large
saucepan heat the remaining water to boiling and simmer over
medium heat. Add the wakame and simmer for 30 seconds. Rinse
under cold running water and drain well. Lay the wakame out flat
and remove any hard veins. Cut wakame into 2 cm (1 in) lengths.

Mix the vinegar, soy sauce, sugar and oil in a small bowl and stir
to dissolve the sugar. Put on one side. Open the tuna and drain off
the brine. Put the tuna in a largish bowl and break it up with a fork
into bite-sized pieces. Sprinkle with lemon juice.

Cut the cucumber into very thin slices and cut the tomato into cubes. Add the wakame, cucumber and tomato to the tuna. Add the vinegar and soy sauce mixture and toss lightly until everything is evenly coated.

Serve in a medium bowl or 4 individual bowls.

TIPS
You can buy wakame from health food shops and many supermarkets.

TERIYAKI SALMON

Serves 4   ① *Preparation 25 min, Cooking 15 to 20 min – Easy*

Salmon kebabs. You can get these sorted well before you cook them. They will not be spoilt by standing in the marinade in the fridge.

INGREDIENTS
1 kg (2 lb) salmon steaks
2 medium onions
$^1/_2$ cup light soy sauce
$^1/_2$ cup sake or dry sherry
1 teaspoon sugar
Salt

EQUIPMENT
Sharp knife
Chopping board
Bamboo or metal skewers
Large fairly deep dish

Bowl
Set of measuring cups
Set of measuring spoons
Grill or griddle pan or barbecue

METHOD

Remove the skin and centre bone from the steaks, and cut the salmon into small, even-sized cubes. Peel the onions and cut into quarters. Separate the onion chunks into layers and thread the onion layers and salmon cubes alternately onto skewers (bamboo satay sticks or steel skewers). Place the skewers in a large, fairly deep dish.

In a bowl make up the marinade by mixing the soy sauce with the sake (or sherry) and the sugar until the sugar has dissolved. Pour the marinade over the salmon skewers and leave to stand for 15 to 20 minutes. Turn them once or twice to make sure that all the pieces are evenly coated. Remove the salmon skewers from the marinade and drain well. Save the marinade – you will need it to baste the skewers. Cook the salmon skewers under the grill or on a griddle pan or barbecue for about 15 minutes until done. Baste with the marinade and turn the skewers at frequent intervals.

FRIED TOFU SALAD

Serves 4   ℗ *Preparation 20 min, Cooking 18 min – Easy*

Hot tofu, crunchy cold bean sprouts and lettuce make an interesting combination.

INGREDIENTS

$^1/_2 \times$ 200 g bag of bean sprouts
3 large iceberg lettuce leaves

$^{1}/_{2}$ cup sunflower oil

2 tablespoons raw peanuts

250 g (8 oz) slab tofu or Agé (marinaded tofu available in health shops)

Soy sauce dressing

1 small clove garlic

3 tablespoons soy sauce

2 tablespoons rice vinegar or white wine vinegar

2 tablespoons sugar

$^{1}/_{2}$ teaspoon cayenne pepper

EQUIPMENT

Sharp knife

Chopping board

Set of measuring spoons

Bowl

Wooden spoon

Garlic crusher

Slotted spoon

Small saucepan

Serving bowl or plate

Kitchen paper

METHOD

To prepare the soy sauce dressing, peel and crush the garlic and then combine all soy sauce dressing ingredients in a small bowl and let stand for 30 minutes or longer to blend the flavours.

Wash and drain the bean sprouts and the lettuce leaves. Cut the lettuce leaves into $^{1}/_{2}$ cm ($^{1}/_{4}$ in) slices. Mix the bean sprouts and lettuce in a bowl. Cover and refrigerate.

Heat the oil in a small saucepan and add the peanuts. Fry for 3 minutes until they are browned. Be careful not to burn them.

When browned remove them with a slotted spoon and drain on kitchen paper. Save the oil. When the nuts have cooled a bit put them into a plastic bag and crush them with something heavy. Shake out of the bag and put aside on a plate. Cut the slab of tofu into slices, about $^1/_2$ cm ($^1/_4$ in) thick or thinner. Reheat the oil and fry the tofu slices 2 or 3 at a time until they are lightly browned and a little puffy, about 5 minutes. Drain on kitchen paper.

To serve, put lettuce and bean sprout mixture on a serving plate. Sprinkle with the soy sauce dressing and pile fried tofu around the edges or on top. Sprinkle everything with the crushed peanuts.

ADDITIONS & ALTERNATIVES

You can fry 2 cm (1 in) cubes of tofu and have them as an accompaniment to a Chinese dish with noodles.

BEEF IN GINGER

Serves 2 or 3   ① *Preparation 25 min, Cooking 15 min – Easy*

How many dishes do you know from Kuala Lumpur? Answer: at least one after you have tried this stir-fry.

INGREDIENTS

500 g (1 lb) trimmed rump or sirloin steak, 1 to 2 cm ($^1/_2$ to $^3/_4$ in) thick
1 large onion
3 cm ($1^1/_2$ in) fresh root ginger
4 large cloves garlic
2 to 3 medium tomatoes
15 g pack fresh coriander
2 tablespoons sunflower oil
$1^1/_2$ teaspoons ground coriander

1 teaspoon sugar
1 teaspoon salt
$^{1}/_{4}$ teaspoon cayenne pepper
$^{1}/_{4}$ teaspoon black pepper

EQUIPMENT
Sharp knife
Chopping board
Vegetable peeler
Deep frying-pan or wok
Wooden spoon
Set of measuring spoons
Small bowls

METHOD
Put the beef in the freezer for half an hour (this makes it easier to cut into thin slices) and then cut into thin slices about 2 mm ($^{1}/_{8}$ in) thick. Peel and chop the onion. Peel the ginger and garlic and chop very small. Wash and chop the tomatoes. Wash the bunch of coriander, shake dry and pull the leaves off.

Heat the oil in a wok or large frying-pan over a medium heat. Add the chopped onion and cook, stirring often, until it starts to brown. Add the ginger and garlic and cook for 3 minutes, stirring to prevent it sticking. Increase the heat, add the beef and cook for 5 minutes until it is browned. Keep stirring to mix with the seasonings. Stir in the chopped tomatoes and cook for another 3 minutes until the sauce is well mixed. Stir in the ground coriander, sugar, salt, cayenne pepper and black pepper. Reduce the heat and simmer for 3 minutes. Just before serving, stir in the coriander leaves.

Serve with rice.

BRAISED PORK

Serves 4 or 5   ⏱ *Preparation 15 min, Cooking 1 hr 15 min – Easy*

Think ahead – 2 hours marinating time.

A Spanish Oriental stew, ideal for a winter dinner. You get this rich thick gravy with tender pork.

INGREDIENTS
3 cloves garlic
1 kg (2 lb) boneless lean pork or 2 × 500 g packs diced pork
1 medium onion
2 medium potatoes
1 medium green pepper
2 slices of stale dry bread or 2 tablespoons fine dry breadcrumbs
5 tablespoons soy sauce
$^1/_4$ cup white wine vinegar
1 bay leaf
$^1/_4$ teaspoon black pepper
2 tablespoons sunflower oil
400 g tin tomatoes

EQUIPMENT
Garlic crusher
Sharp knife
Chopping board
Vegetable peeler
Set of measuring cups
Set of measuring spoons
Large bowl
Large saucepan with lid
Tin opener

Small bowl or cup
Wooden spoon

METHOD

Peel and crush the garlic. If the pork is in one piece cut it into 2 cm (1 in) chunks. Peel and slice the onion. Peel the potatoes and then cut them into chunks about the same size as the pork. Wash the green pepper, cut it in half and cut out and discard the core and seeds. Chop the pepper into 2 cm (1 in) square pieces. Crumble up a couple of slices of stale and dry, but not mouldy, bread to make the breadcrumbs.

Combine the soy sauce, vinegar, garlic, bay leaf and pepper in a large bowl. Add the pork and stir to coat it in the mixture. Cover and put in the fridge for 2 hours or longer. Stir it up every half-hour or so. In a large saucepan heat the oil and add the onion. Cook on a low heat until it becomes transparent. Open the tin of tomatoes and pour the juice into a cup. With the wooden spoon mash the tomatoes in the tin. Add the mashed tomatoes to the pan. Bring to the boil and cook for 3 minutes. Add the pork and the marinade. Bring to the boil again, then cover and simmer for 35 minutes. If the mixture become too thick add the tomato juice that you have saved. Add the potatoes and green pepper and continue to simmer, covered, for another 20 minutes, until the potatoes are tender. Add the breadcrumbs, and cook uncovered for 5 minutes more.

GINGER PORK

Serves 4   ① *Preparation 25 min, Cooking 10 min – Easy*

Pork and cabbage does not seem appetising. It reminds me of school. However, this is another thing entirely. We were not brave enough to call it pork and cabbage in case it put you off.

INGREDIENTS

1 tablespoon ginger juice or 2 cm (1 in) fresh root ginger

500 g (1 lb) boneless pork loin or tenderloin

$1/4$ × Chinese cabbage, about 100 g (4 oz)

3 tablespoons soy sauce

1 tablespoon sake or dry sherry

1 teaspoon sugar

2 tablespoons vegetable or sunflower oil

EQUIPMENT

Vegetable peeler

Sharp knife

Chopping board

Set of measuring spoons

Bowl

Large frying-pan or wok

Wooden spoon

Plate

METHOD

If using fresh ginger instead of ginger juice peel the ginger and chop into very small pieces. Slice the pork thinly and then cut into 5 cm (2 in) pieces. Remove the hard central stalk sections from the cabbage leaves, if necessary. Cut the cabbage into 2 cm (1 in) squares.

Mix the soy sauce, ginger juice or chopped ginger, sake and sugar in a small bowl and stir until the sugar dissolves.

Heat 1 tablespoon of oil in the frying-pan over high heat. Add the pork and cook for about 3 minutes, stirring constantly, until the pork is half-cooked. Remove the pork from the pan and put on one side on a plate.

Add the remaining oil to the pan and add the cabbage and cook for 1 to 2 minutes, stirring constantly, until almost tender. Return the pork to the pan and add the soy sauce mixture. Cook for 2 to 3 minutes, stirring occasionally, until the pork is cooked through. Serve immediately.

ADDITIONS & ALTERNATIVES
Serve with rice or noodles.

TIP
Put the pork into the freezer for half an hour before slicing. This will make it easier to cut into thin slices.

GALLOPING HORSES

Serves 4   ℗ *Preparation 25 min, Cooking 10 min – Easy*

No horses were harmed in the making of this salad. This is traditional salad with a traditional name, but we do not know why it is named as it is. But it is great. By any other name it would taste just as good.

INGREDIENTS
$^1/_2$ pineapple (halved lengthways) or tinned pineapple slices (minimum 4 slices)
1 tablespoon roasted peanuts
1 small red chilli
1 clove garlic
2 tablespoons sunflower or groundnut oil
125 g (4 oz) pork mince
1 tablespoon fish sauce or soy sauce
1 tablespoon sugar
$^1/_2$ teaspoon white vinegar
15 g bunch coriander

EQUIPMENT
Sharp knife
Chopping board
Tin opener
Serving bowl or plate
Plastic bag
Fork
Set of measuring spoons
Garlic crusher
Frying-pan
Wooden spoon

METHOD
Cut the pineapple half in half lengthways into 2 equal pieces. Remove the core. Peel and remove the eyes. Cut the pineapple crosswise into slices $^1/_2$ cm ($^1/_4$ in) thick. Or open the tin, drain, cut the slices into quarters and arrange as for fresh pineapple. Overlap the slices on a plate and set aside.

Put the roasted peanuts into a plastic bag and crush with something heavy. Remove from the bag and keep on a plate.

Wash the chilli and chop the end off. Split in half, and scrape out the seeds. Hold the chilli down with a fork and cut the chilli into tiny bits and wash your hands afterwards. Chilli juice really stings if you get it anywhere sensitive. Peel and crush the garlic.

Heat the oil in the frying-pan over a medium heat. Add the garlic and fry for a few seconds. Increase the heat, add the pork and cook until it is no longer pink, about 5 minutes. Stir while cooking to break the meat up. Stir in the peanuts, fish sauce, sugar and vinegar. Cook for about 5 minutes until most of the liquid has boiled away but the pork is suntil moist. Do not overcook or the meat will be dry. Spoon the pork over the pineapple slices.

Meanwhile, wash and shake dry the coriander and pull the

leaves off the stalks. Throw the stalks away. Arrange the coriander leaves on top of the pork and decorate with the chilli bits. Serve at room temperature.

RED THAI DUCK

Serves 4   ① *Preparation 25 min, Cooking 60 min – Easy*

Roasty duck in thick red coconut sauce. This is one recipe where it is much easier to buy the paste than go for full authenticity.

INGREDIENTS
1 kg (2 lb) duck breast fillets
1 tablespoon water
400 ml tin coconut milk
2 tablespoons red Thai curry paste
15 g pack fresh coriander
Juice of 1 lime or 2 to 3 tablespoons lime juice
1 teaspoon light soft brown sugar

EQUIPMENT
Oven-proof dish
Set of measuring spoons
Aluminium foil
Tin opener
Saucepan
Sharp knife
Chopping board
Lemon juicer
Wooden spoon
Serving bowl

METHOD

Preheat the oven to 180° C, 350° F, Gas mark 4.

Put the duck breast fillets into the oven-proof cooking dish with the water. Cover the dish with foil and cook in the middle of the preheated oven for 45 minutes. Check that the duck is cooked but still succulent. If the duck is still a little pink after this time remove the foil, baste with some of the juices, turn the heat up to 220° C, 425° F, Gas mark 7 and cook for another 5 to 10 minutes.

Meanwhile, tip the coconut milk into the saucepan, add the red Thai curry paste and bring to the boil. Boil for about 10 minutes until the sauce has reduced by half and thickened. Halve the lime lengthways to juice it. For some reason this is easier. Put the juice to one side. Wash the coriander and shake it dry. Chop most of the stalks off and throw them away. Chop the leaves and the rest of the stalks roughly and put on one side. Cut the cooked duck into slices and add it to the sauce with the chopped coriander, the lime juice and sugar. Stir together to make sure all the ingredients are mixed. Simmer gently for 1 to 2 minutes, then tip into a serving bowl.

ADDITIONS & ALTERNATIVES

Serve with plain boiled rice or yellow rice (recipe below) to soak up the juices.

YELLOW RICE

Serves 4　　　　　① *4 Preparation 5 min, Cooking 25 min – Easy*

Adapted from traditional Asian recipes, this is an easy way to cook rice and get it right every time.

INGREDIENTS

1 cup long-grain rice, washed and drained

1 tablespoon butter
1 teaspoon salt
1 teaspoon curry powder
$^1/_2$ teaspoon ground turmeric
2 cups boiling water

EQUIPMENT
Oven-proof dish with lid
Set of measuring spoons
Set of measuring cups
Aluminium foil if no lid

METHOD
Preheat the oven to 190° C, 375° F, Gas mark 5. Put the rice in the oven-proof dish. Add the butter, salt, curry powder and turmeric. Add the boiling water and stir until the butter melts. Cover tightly with a lid or with foil and bake for 25 minutes until the water is absorbed. Let the rice stand covered for 5 minutes and fluff with a fork before serving.

SUMMER HAKE

Serves 4 ⓘ *Preparation 20 min, Cooking 25 min – Easy*

Pre-cooked chilled fish served with a light sauce.

INGREDIENTS
1 kg (2 lb) hake fillets
$^1/_4$ cup soy sauce
$^1/_4$ cup sweet sherry
2 star anise
Salt

4 spring onions
$^1/_2$ cup sunflower oil
1 teaspoon sugar
$^1/_4$ cup water

EQUIPMENT
Shallow dish or bowl
Set of measuring spoons
Set of measuring cups
Saucepan
Sharp knife
Chopping board
Frying-pan
Kitchen paper
Wooden spoon
Shalow serving dish

METHOD
Place the hake fillets in the shallow dish. Mix 3 tablespoons of the soy sauce with the sherry, star anise, and salt, and sprinkle over the fish slices. Leave the fish to stand for 10 minutes, turning 2 or 3 times. Clean and prepare the spring onions. Cut the root end off, trim the leaves. Peel off and discard any dried up or slimy leaves. Chop into thin slices.

To make the sauce, gently heat $^1/_4$ cup of the oil and $^1/_4$ cup of the water in a saucepan. Mix them together with the spring onions and cook for 2 to 3 minutes. Add the remaining soy sauce and the sugar and continue to cook over a low heat for another 5 to 10 minutes.

Pour the remaining oil into a frying-pan and heat gently. Take the fish out of the marinade and lightly pat dry with kitchen paper. Add the fish to the frying-pan and fry over a fairly high heat for 5 to 6 minutes each side after which they should be golden brown and

230

crisp on the outside. Place on a shallow serving dish. Spoon a little of the sauce over the fish and leave to cool.

Serve cold with salad.

TAMARIND FISH

Serves 4   ⏲ *Preparation 30 min, Cooking 15 min – Easy*

Think ahead. This needs to stand in the fridge for 1 hour before cooking.

Fried fish without the batter and with a warm sauce of its own, so put the ketchup down.

INGREDIENTS

1 small onion
500 g (1 lb) cod, haddock or hake fillets
1 teaspoon ground turmeric
$1/4$ teaspoon salt
3 tablespoons sunflower oil

Tamarind sauce
1 teaspoon tamarind extract or 2 cm (1 in) cube of dried tamarind
$1/2$ cup boiling water
8 spring onions
2 large cloves garlic
1 small fresh red chilli, chopped
$1/2$ teaspoon shrimp paste (optional)
1 tablespoon sunflower oil
$1^1/2$ teaspoons sugar
$1/2$ teaspoon salt

EQUIPMENT

Set of measuring cups
Sharp knife
Chopping board
Fork
Set of measuring spoons
Food processor or liquidiser (optional)
Saucepan
Large frying-pan or wok
Serving plate
Spoon

METHOD

Peel the onion and cut it into thin slices. Cut the fish into 4 portions and rub turmeric over both sides of each fillet. Sprinkle with salt, cover and put in the fridge for an hour or so.

To make the tamarind sauce, use the tamarind extract or tamarinds to make $^1/_2$ cup of tamarind liquid. If using the extract then just dissolve it in $^1/_2$ cup of hot water. If using dried tamarinds put them into a bowl and add $^1/_2$ cup of boiling water, let them stand for 20 minutes. Then squeeze the tamarinds to get as much flavouring as possible into the water. Strain and throw away the pulp but keep the liquid.

Cut the root ends off the spring onions and the very tips of the green leaves, then roughly chop. Peel the garlic. Chop the end off the chilli, split in half, and scrape out the seeds. Roughly chop the chilli, holding it down with a fork, and wash you hands afterwards. Chilli juice really stings if you get it anywhere sensitive. Put the spring onions, garlic, chilli and shrimp paste (if using) in a food processor or liquidiser and process until very fine. Heat the oil in a small saucepan. Add the mixture from the processor and cook gently for 3 minutes. Add the tamarind liquid, sugar and salt. Bring to the boil. Reduce the heat and simmer gently, uncovered, for 5 minutes or until thickened, stirring frequently. Keep warm.

Heat the oil in a frying-pan large enough to hold the fish in a single layer. Add the fish and fry for 2 to 3 minutes on each side, depending upon thickness, until the fish has changed in colour and turned from translucent to opaque. Place the fish on a heated plate and spoon the sauce over the fish. Garnish with the onion rings. Serve warm.

ADDITIONS & ALTERNATIVES
The sauce can be prepared in advance and then reheated.

IMPECCABLE INDIAN

Because curry is often cheap we think it is undervalued, although it is now the country's favourite meal. We have included these recipes for their variety of flavours. You will find some of them have quite long lists of spices but this gives you more flexibility and lets you experiment with the balance of flavours. What we have tried to do here is get away from simply adding curry powder or having things burning hot.

BALTI CHICKEN

Serves 4   ① *Preparation 20 min, Cooking 35 min – Easy*

A balti is a metal dish used for cooking, widely available nowadays. If you do not have one use a wok or a big frying-pan instead.

INGREDIENTS
2 onions
10 tomatoes or 2 × 400 g tins tomatoes
$^1/_4$ × 15 g pack fresh coriander
3 tablespoons sunflower oil
4 green cardamom pods
2 teaspoons cumin seeds
2 cloves garlic

8 small chicken pieces
1 teaspoon chilli powder
$^1/_2$ teaspoon salt
1 teaspoon garam masala
6 tablespoons water

EQUIPMENT

Sharp knife
Chopping board
Set of measuring spoons
Deep frying-pan, balti dish or wok
Garlic crusher
Wooden spoon

DEFROSTING

Make sure frozen chicken is completely thawed before use.
This means leaving it in the fridge overnight, or out of the fridge,
covered, for 6 hours.

METHOD

Peel and slice the onions. If using tinned tomatoes, drain off the
juice and keep for later and then mash the tomatoes in the tins with
a wooden spoon. Chop fresh tomatoes coarsely. Wash, shake dry
and chop the coriander to make 2 tablespoons.

Put the oil in the frying-pan over a moderate heat. Fry the cardamom and cumin for about 2 minutes until the seeds pop. Peel
and crush the garlic into the pan. Add the onions. Fry for about
5 minutes until golden brown. Add the chicken and stir-fry for 5
minutes until brown. Add the tomatoes, chilli powder, salt, garam
masala and water (if using tinned tomatoes use the juice instead of
the water). Bring to the boil, then turn down the heat until it is just
boiling (simmering). Cook for 15 minutes. Turn the chicken over.
Cook for 10 minutes. Check that the chicken is cooked. The juices

should run clear when you stick a knife in the thickest part of the chicken. Sprinkle with the coriander and serve.

ADDITIONS & ALTERNATIVES
Serve with rice or naan bread.
   Using the whole spices gives a different flavour.

CHICKEN & BLACK EYED BEANS

Serves 4   ① *Preparation 20 min, Cooking 45 min – Easy*

Think ahead – you need to soak the beans for 2 hours if using dried beans.

Another blow for freedom against chicken tikka masala, which we have already done anyway in our first book.

INGREDIENTS
$^1/_2$ × 500 g pack (1 cup) dried black eyed beans or $1^1/_2$ × 400 g tins
2 onions
2 cloves garlic
2 cm (1 in) fresh root ginger
1 green pepper
$^1/_4$ × 15 g pack fresh coriander
1 teaspoon ground turmeric
1 teaspoon ground cumin
1 teaspoon salt
$1^1/_4$ kg (3 lb) chicken, jointed into 8 pieces, or 8 small chicken portions
2 tablespoons sunflower oil
2 teaspoons coriander seeds

$^{1}/_{2}$ teaspoon fennel seeds
2 teaspoons garam masala

EQUIPMENT
Bowl
Tin opener
Sharp knife
Chopping board
Garlic crusher
Vegetable peeler
Grater
Sieve or colander
Deep frying-pan, balti dish or wok
Frying-pan
Set of measuring spoons
Wooden spoon

METHOD
If using dried beans, put them in a large bowl, pour on enough boiling water to cover and leave to soak for 2 hours. If using tinned beans, drain the liquid off. Peel and chop the onions. Peel and crush the garlic. Peel and grate the ginger. Chop the end off the green peppers and cut out the core and seeds. Chop the pepper. Wash, shake dry and finely chop the coriander to give 1 tablespoon.

Drain and rinse the beans. Put the beans, onions, garlic, turmeric, cumin and salt into the deep frying-pan. Cover the beans with water. Bring to the boil and cook for 20 minutes. If using tinned beans put the ingredients in the pan with 1 cup (250 ml, 8 fl oz) of water (do not cover with water), and cook for 5 minutes and then follow the rest of the recipe.

Add the chicken and green pepper. Bring to the boil, then turn down the heat until it is just boiling (simmering). Cook for 15 minutes. Turn the chicken over. Cook for 15 minutes. Check that the chicken is cooked. The juices should run clear when you stick a knife in the thickest part of the chicken.

Put the oil in the frying-pan over a moderate heat. Fry the ginger, coriander seeds and fennel seeds for 30 seconds, shaking the pan to stop it sticking. Add to the chicken and stir in with the garam masala. Cook for 5 minutes. Stir in the chopped coriander before serving.

ADDITIONS & ALTERNATIVES
Serve with pickle, naan or rice.

INDIAN CHICKEN BALLS

Serves 4   ① *Preparation 25 min, Cooking 20 min – Easy*

OK, our best lines go unsaid, which may even include this one.

INGREDIENTS
1 clove garlic
2 cm (1 in) fresh root ginger
$^1/_2$ green pepper
$^1/_4$ × 15 g pack fresh coriander
2 fresh green chillies
1 teaspoon garam masala
$^1/_2$ teaspoon ground turmeric
$^1/_2$ teaspoon salt
500 g (1 lb) chicken or turkey mince
6 tablespoons sunflower oil
1 lemon
1 jar hot mango pickle, to serve

EQUIPMENT

Sharp knife

Chopping board

Set of measuring spoons

Food processor or liquidiser (optional)

Deep frying-pan, balti dish or wok

Wooden spoon

Slotted spoon

Kitchen paper

METHOD

Peel and crush the garlic. Peel the ginger. Chop the end off the green peppers and cut out the core and seeds. Wash and shake dry the coriander and chop to give 2 tablespoons. Chop the end off the chillies, split in half, and scrape out the seeds. Hold the chilli down with a fork and wash your hands afterwards. Chilli juice really stings if you get it anywhere sensitive.

Put all the ingredients except the lemon, oil, chicken and mango pickle into the liquidiser or food processor and blend until the mixture is chopped finely. Otherwise, finely chop the pepper, ginger, coriander and chillies, and mix together in a bowl with the garlic, garam masala, turmeric, coriander and salt. Put the chicken in a bowl. Add the ingredients from the liquidiser and mix together with a fork. Wet your hands and fashion into balls the size of walnuts.

Put the oil in the frying-pan over a moderate heat. Fry the balls for about 10 minutes until brown, shaking the pan frequently. If you have to cook them in batches, keep the others warm in the oven. Drain them on kitchen paper. Cut the lemon into wedges. Serve with the lemon wedges and pickle.

ADDITIONS & ALTERNATIVES
Serve with naan and salad.
You could use lamb or beef mince instead of chicken or turkey.
Try other pickles like lime pickle.

CHICKEN PANEER

Serves 4   ① *Preparation 25 min, Cooking 25 min – Easy*

This chicken curry has a wonderful creamy taste. Do not worry about the paneer – lots of supermarkets sell it.

INGREDIENTS
700 g pack chicken breasts (5 or 6 breasts)
200 g pack paneer
2 fresh green chillies
1 clove garlic
3 medium tomatoes
15 g pack fresh coriander
$^1/_4$ cup flaked almonds (25 g, 1 oz) or ready-toasted
$^1/_2$ cup ground almonds (about 50 g, 2 oz)
1 teaspoon poppy seeds
Small carton (142 ml, 5 fl oz) natural yoghurt
3 rounded tablespoons butter
1 teaspoon ground cumin
$^1/_4$ teaspoon ground cinnamon
1 teaspoon paprika
1 teaspoon garam masala
$^1/_2$ teaspoon salt

EQUIPMENT
Sharp knife

Chopping board
Fork
Set of measuring spoons
Baking tray
Set of measuring cups
Food processor or liquidiser (optional)
Bowl
Deep frying-pan, balti dish or wok
Wooden spoon

DEFROSTING
Make sure frozen chicken is completely thawed before use.
This means leaving it in the fridge overnight, or out of the fridge,
covered, for 6 hours.

METHOD
Cut the chicken into 2.5 cm (1 in) cubes. Cut the paneer into 1 cm
($^{1}/_{2}$ in) cubes. Chop the end off the chillies, split in half, and
scrape out the seeds. Hold the chilli down with a fork and wash
your hands afterwards. Chilli juice really stings if you get it anywhere sensitive. Cut the chilli roughly. Peel the garlic. Chop
the tomatoes. Wash, shake dry and chop the coriander to give 2
tablespoons for garnish. Toast the flaked almonds until golden by
putting them on a baking tray in the oven for 3 to 5 minutes at
170° C, 325° F, Gas mark 3.

Put the chillies, garlic, tomatoes, ground almonds and poppy
seeds in the liquidiser or food processor and blend until smooth. If
you do not have a processor press the mixture through a sieve with
the back of a spoon into a bowl, finely chopping the chilli and garlic
first. Add the yoghurt.

Put the butter in the frying-pan over a moderate heat. Fry the
chicken for about 5 minutes, stirring to stop it sticking. Add the
paneer, cumin, cinnamon, paprika, garam masala and salt and fry

for 1 minute. Add the tomato and yoghurt mixture. Bring to the boil, then turn down the heat until it is just boiling (simmering). Cook gently for 15 minutes. Check that the chicken is cooked. The juices should run clear when you stick a knife in the thickest part of the chicken.

Sprinkle with coriander and toasted almonds before serving.

ADDITIONS & ALTERNATIVES

Serve with rice, naan bread, pickle and salad.

Use $^1/_2$ cup tinned chopped tomatoes instead of the fresh ones.

TIPS

Paneer is a kind of mild Indian cheese. If you cannot find it then use tofu instead.

You can buy ready-toasted flaked almonds.

CHILLI PRAWN

Serves 4   ① *Preparation 10 min, Cooking 11 min – Easy*

This is an Indian chilli prawn dish not to be confused with garlic prawns. It is very quick to make, and very quick to eat.

INGREDIENTS

500 g pack peeled cooked prawns
4 cloves garlic
2 cm (1 in) fresh galangal root or root ginger
2 fresh red chillies
15 g pack fresh coriander
2 tablespoons sunflower oil
1 tablespoon lemon juice
1 tablespoon tomato purée

$^1/_2 \times$ 400 ml tin coconut milk
1 teaspoon garam masala
1 teaspoon salt

EQUIPMENT
Sieve or colander
Sharp knife
Chopping board
Garlic crusher
Grater
Fork
Set of measuring spoons
Deep frying-pan, balti dish or wok
Wooden spoon
Set of measuring cups
Tin opener

METHOD
If using frozen prawns put them in a colander or sieve and stand in a sink or on a plate so that they defrost before cooking. Otherwise all the melted water will dilute the sauce. Peel and crush the garlic. Peel and grate the galangal. Chop the end off the chillies, split in half, and scrape out the seeds. Hold the chilli down with a fork and wash your hands afterwards. Chilli juice really stings if you get anywhere sensitive. Chop the chilli. Wash, shake dry and chop the coriander to give 2 tablespoons to garnish.

Put the oil in the frying-pan over a moderate heat. Fry the garlic and galangal for about 3 minutes, stirring to stop it sticking. Add the prawns and chillies and fry for 3 minutes. Add the lemon juice, tomato purée, coconut milk, garam masala and salt. Bring to the boil, then turn down the heat until it is just boiling (simmering). Cover and cook for 5 minutes.

Sprinkle with coriander before serving.

ADDITIONS & ALTERNATIVES

Serve with rice, naan bread, pickle and salad.

Use ginger instead of galangal.

TIPS

You can buy prepared galangal in jars and bottles. It will keep for 6 weeks in the fridge or longer, just check on the pack.

MONKFISH WITH CHILLI & COCONUT

Serves 4   ⏱ *Preparation 15 min, Cooking 25 min – Easy*

Monkfish has been called the poor man's lobster, which is a bit rich since it is expensive itself. It does have a very firm texture and the ability to take other flavours well.

INGREDIENTS

500 g (1 lb) monkfish tail fillets
1 medium onion
1 small cooking apple
2 cm (1 in) fresh root ginger
1 green chilli
2 tablespoons olive oil
$^1/_2$ teaspoon ground coriander
$^1/_2$ teaspoon ground cumin
$^1/_2$ teaspoon ground turmeric
4 tablespoons white vermouth
1 medium carton (284 ml, 10 fl oz) single cream
1 cup water
50 g (2 oz) creamed coconut, about $^1/_4 \times$ 200 g block
1 lemon

EQUIPMENT

Sharp knife
Chopping board
Vegetable peeler
Apple corer
Grater
Set of measuring spoons
Large frying-pan
Slotted spoon
Set of measuring cups

METHOD

Cut the monkfish into 2 cm (1 in) pieces. Peel and finely chop the onion. Peel, core and dice the apple. Peel and grate or finely chop the ginger. Chop the end off the chilli, split in half, and scrape out the seeds. Hold the chilli down with a fork and wash your hands afterwards. Chilli juice really stings if you get it anywhere sensitive. Cut the chilli into tiny bits.

Put the oil in the frying-pan over a moderate heat. Add the monkfish and fry gently for 2 minutes until it goes white on the outside. Lift out from the pan using a slotted spoon.

Put the pan back on a low heat. Add the onion, apple, ginger and chilli. Stir for about 10 minutes until soft. Add the coriander, cumin and turmeric and stir over the heat for a minute. Add the vermouth, cream and water. Return the fish pieces to the pan. Bring to the boil, then turn down the heat until it is just boiling (simmering). Cook gently for 10 minutes. Chop the creamed coconut and stir into the sauce. Continue to cook until the coconut is melted. Serve with the lemon cut into quarters.

KEEMA & SWEET POTATO

Serves 4   ⏲ *Preparation 15 min, Cooking 30 min – Easy*

Keema is mince by another name, but keema sounds so much nicer. This is the only recipe in the book combining sultanas and spinach, but it is a combination that works.

INGREDIENTS
1 lamb stock cube
1 cup boiling water
3 cloves garlic
1 cm ($^1/_2$ in) fresh root ginger
1 medium sweet potato, about 250 g (8 oz)
250 g (8 oz) pack fresh spinach
2 onions
2 tablespoons sunflower oil
500 g pack lamb mince
1 cup sultanas, about 100 g (4 oz)
1 tablespoon garam masala
$^1/_2$ teaspoon salt
1 tablespoon sugar

EQUIPMENT
Set of measuring cups
Bowl
Sharp knife
Chopping board
Garlic crusher
Vegetable peeler
Saucepan with lid
Deep frying-pan, balti dish or wok

Wooden spoon
Set of measuring spoons

METHOD

Dissolve the stock cube in the water. Peel and crush the garlic. Peel and chop the ginger into tiny cubes.

Peel the sweet potato, cutting away any nasty bits. Chop into 2 cm (1 in) chunks. Wash, shake dry and chop the spinach. Peel and slice the onions. Boil the sweet potato for 5 minutes. Drain.

Put the oil in the frying-pan over a moderate heat. Fry the onion, garlic and ginger for about 5 minutes until it is golden, stirring to stop it sticking. Add the lamb and fry for 5 minutes, breaking it up with the spoon. Add the sweet potato and spinach and stir round to coat them. Add the stock, sultanas, garam masala, salt and sugar. Bring to the boil, then turn down the heat until it is just boiling (simmering). Cook for 10 minutes.

ADDITIONS & ALTERNATIVES

Serve with rice or naan bread, pickle and salad.

Use galangal instead of ginger.

TIPS

You can buy ready-made stock in cartons from most supermarkets. You can also buy Swiss vegetable bouillon powder (vegetable stock), if you are worried about the stuff that goes into stock cubes.

LAMB & LENTIL CURRY

Serves 4 ⏱ *Preparation 20 min, Cooking 1 hr 15 min – Easy*

Think ahead – you need to soak the split peas for 1 hour.

A substantial hearty curry, thick with lentils and seasoned with cinnamon and cumin.

INGREDIENTS

$^1/_4$ × 500 g pack ($^1/_2$ cup) yellow split lentils
750 g (1$^1/_2$ lb) lean lamb, off the bone
1 clove garlic
2 fresh red chillies
1 medium onion
15 g pack fresh coriander
2 tablespoons sunflower oil
2 teaspoons cumin seeds
2 cm (1 in) piece cinnamon stick
$^1/_2$ teaspoon ground turmeric
1 bay leaf
1 teaspoon salt
4 cups (1 litre, 2 pints) water
1 teaspoon garam masala

EQUIPMENT

Bowl
Sieve
Sharp knife
Chopping board
Garlic crusher
Fork
Set of measuring spoons

Deep frying-pan, balti dish or wok
Wooden spoon
Set of measuring cups

METHOD

Pick over the lentils and rinse several times in a sieve. Place in a bowl and cover with boiling water while you prepare the rest of the ingredients. Cut the lamb into 2.5 cm (1 in) cubes. Peel and crush the garlic. Chop the end off the chillies, split in half, and scrape out the seeds. Hold the chilli down with a fork and wash your hands afterwards. Chilli juice really stings if you get it anywhere sensitive. Chop the chilli. Peel and slice the onion. Wash, shake dry and chop the coriander to make 2 tablespoons for garnish.

Put the oil in the frying-pan over a moderate heat. Fry the cumin and cinnamon for about 1 minute until the seeds pop. Add the garlic and onions. Fry for about 3 minutes until golden brown. Add the lamb and fry for 3 minutes to brown on all sides, stirring to prevent it sticking.

Drain the lentils and add to the pan with the chilli, turmeric, bay leaf, salt and water. Bring to the boil, then turn down the heat until it is just boiling (simmering). Cook gently for 1 hour. Check the water level from time to time and top it up if getting too dry. Add the garam masala and coriander, stir in and serve.

ADDITIONS & ALTERNATIVES

Serve with rice or naan bread, pickle and salad.

MUSHROOM PANEER

Serves 4   ① *Preparation 20 min, Cooking 15 min – Easy*

Paneer is a kind of mild Indian cheese. We were surprised to find our local supermarket had become so cosmopolitan as to keep it boxed in the chiller cabinet. If your supermarket is not as cosmopolitan as ours try tofu instead.

INGREDIENTS
500 g (1 lb) mixed mushrooms, such as button, oyster, shiitake, brown
About $^1/_2$ × 200 g pack paneer
1 chicken stock cube
$^3/_4$ cup boiling water
2 cloves garlic
2 cm (1 in) fresh root ginger
1 green chilli
1 medium onion
15 g pack fresh coriander
3 tablespoons sunflower oil
2 teaspoons mustard seeds
1 tablespoon garam masala

EQUIPMENT
Sharp knife
Chopping board
Bowl
Set of measuring cups
Garlic crusher
Grater
Fork
Set of measuring spoons

Bowl
Deep frying-pan, balti dish or wok
Wooden spoon

METHOD

Wipe the mushrooms clean. Discard any nasty ones. Chop the end off the stalks. Cut the paneer into 1 cm ($^1/_2$ in) cubes. Dissolve the stock cube in the water. Peel and crush the garlic. Peel and grate the ginger. Chop the end off the chilli, split in half, and scrape out the seeds. Hold the chilli down with a fork and wash your hands afterwards. Chilli juice really stings if you get it anywhere sensitive. Chop the chilli. Peel and chop the onion. Wash, shake dry and chop the coriander to make 2 tablespoons for garnish.

Put the oil in the frying-pan over a moderate heat. Fry the garlic, ginger, chilli, onion and mustard seeds for about 3 minutes until the onion is golden, stirring to stop it sticking. Add the mushrooms and paneer and stir round to coat in the mixture. Add the stock and garam masala. Bring to the boil, then turn down the heat until it is just boiling (simmering). Cook gently for 10 minutes.

Sprinkle with coriander before serving.

ADDITIONS & ALTERNATIVES

Serve with rice or naan.

POTATO CURRY

Serves 4   ⏱ *Preparation 15 min, Cooking 25 min – Easy*

You should have no problem getting the major ingredient, potato, for this dish as it is widely available. Indeed we saw some in our local supermarket only the other day.

INGREDIENTS

8 to 10 small new potatoes, about 400 g (1 lb)
1 clove garlic
1 cm ($^{1}/_{2}$ in) fresh root ginger
1 medium onion
3 tablespoons sunflower oil
1 teaspoon cumin seeds
1 cardamom pod
$^{1}/_{2}$ teaspoon chilli powder
2 tablespoons brown mustard seeds
1 teaspoon garam masala

EQUIPMENT

Saucepan with lid
Sharp knife
Chopping board
Garlic crusher
Vegetable peeler
Grater
Set of measuring spoons
Deep frying-pan, balti dish or wok
Wooden spoon

METHOD

Scrub the potatoes clean. Boil the potatoes in salted water for 15 minutes until just done. Drain and cut in half. Peel and crush the garlic. Peel and grate the ginger. Peel and slice the onion.

Put the oil in the frying-pan over a moderate heat. Fry the cumin, cardamom, chilli powder and mustard seeds for about 1 minute until the seeds start popping. Add the garlic, ginger and onion and fry for 3 minutes until the onion is golden, stirring to stop it sticking. Add the potatoes and garam masala. Fry for about 5 minutes, stirring.

ADDITIONS & ALTERNATIVES

Serve with rice or naan.

You can serve this cold as a flash salad with chicken or bar-becued meat. Try adding 3 tablespoons of natural yoghurt and 2 tablespoons of chopped coriander.

Try sweet potato instead of new potatoes.

TIPS

Potatoes are cooked when a fork will go into them without pushing hard. If you push too hard they will fall apart.

COOL CAKES & COOKIES

Well, this is a day we thought would never come, and we have to admit we do not cook these every day ourselves. Cakes are not just for the rich and famous, you can have some too. These are not sticky sweet, anaemic, cardboard rubbish cakes. These cakes are proper cakes and would be approved by CARC (Campaign for Real Cakes) if such an organisation existed.

But they are not that difficult to make, and everybody has a birthday. The real problem about making cakes is that some people make a judgement about your machismo, but we say, if you are macho enough to make a cake, you are macho enough.

Beware don't mix your measures.

FLORENTINES

Makes 25   ① *Preparation 15 min, Cooking 20 min – Easy*

A flashy chocolate nut biscuit. Perhaps they originated in Italy or were invented by a woman called Florence. Just think they might have been called zebedines.

INGREDIENTS
100 g tub crystallised mixed peel
2 × 100 g pack sliced almonds

$^1/_4$ × 100 g tub glacé cherries
Small carton (142 ml, 5 fl oz) double cream
3 level tablespoons butter (45 g, 1$^1/_2$ oz), plus extra for greasing
$^1/_2$ cup caster sugar (125 g, 4 oz)
$^1/_2$ cup plain flour (60 g, 2 oz), plus extra for flouring
250 g (8 oz) plain chocolate

EQUIPMENT
Sharp knife
Chopping board
Saucepan
Bowl
Set of measuring cups
Set of measuring spoons
Wooden spoon
Teaspoon
Baking trays (you will need several or cook a few at a time)
Knife
Pyrex bowl
Fork
Cake rack
Palette knife
Kitchen paper

METHOD
Preheat the oven to 180° C, 350° F, Gas mark 4.

Finely chop the mixed peel and about half the almonds. Quarter the cherries, wash in warm water and dry on kitchen paper.

Put the cream, butter and sugar in the saucepan and heat gently until just boiling, stirring. Take off the heat and stir in the peel, sliced and chopped almonds, cherries and flour.

Wipe the baking trays with the wrapper from a block of butter or a small blob of butter or margarine and then shake a little flour into

255

the baking tray trying to get it to stick to the thin film of butter/ margarine. Throw any excess flour away and then add the cake mixture from the bowl by dropping teaspoonfuls of the mixture onto the baking tray(s), leaving lots of room for spreading.

Cook in the preheated oven for 5 minutes. Remove from the oven and push the edges in with a knife. Cook for another 5 minutes until slightly browned at the edges. Lift onto a cake rack with a palette knife to cool.

Put the glass bowl on top of a saucepan of hot water (not boiling) over a low heat. This stops the chocolate from getting too hot, but steam-heats it through the bowl. Add the chocolate and beat as it melts. Spread the chocolate on the bottom of the biscuits and draw wavy lines with a fork when it is about to set. Leave on the rack, chocolate side up, to harden.

TIPS
Look for the chocolate in the baking section of the supermarket. Buy the chocolate with the highest percentage of cocoa solids.

BLENDER CAKE

Serves 4 to 6   ⓘ *Preparation 10 min, Cooking 25 min – Easy*

A magic one mixer cake. Use this as the base of fruit cakes and desserts. Let your imagination go, or look in the additions section for a few starting points.

INGREDIENTS
3 level tablespoons butter (40 g, 1¹/₂ oz), plus extra for greasing
1 cup plain flour (125 g, 5 oz)
1 teaspoon baking powder

$^1/_4$ teaspoon salt
1 egg
5 tablespoons milk
$^1/_4$ teaspoon lemon essence
$^1/_2$ teaspoon vanilla essence
$^1/_2$ cup caster sugar (100 g, 4 oz)

EQUIPMENT
Cup
Bowl
Sieve
Set of measuring cups
Set of measuring spoons
Liquidiser or food processor
25 × 18 cm (10 × 7 in) square baking tin
Skewer

METHOD
Preheat the oven to 180° C, 350° F, Gas mark 4.

Put the butter in a small cup and stand the cup in a bowl of boiling water until the butter has melted. Sift the flour, baking powder and salt through a sieve into the bowl. Put the egg, milk, melted butter and essences into the liquidiser or processor. Blend until smooth. Add the sugar and blend for 5 seconds. Add the sifted flour mixture to the processor. Cover and mix for 10 seconds. Using either the wrapper from a block of butter or a small blob of butter or margarine grease the square baking tin. Pour the mixture from the processor into the tin and bake in the preheated oven for 25 minutes. Test that it is cooked by pushing a skewer, or a fork or small knife into the centre of the cake. If the skewer comes out clean it is cooked.

Cut into squares while still in the tin and serve and eat warm.

ADDITIONS & ALTERNATIVES
You can treat this cake as a cake or as a pudding. If treating it as a pudding eat with cream or custard.

Try adding some of the following to the top of the cake before baking it: stoned fresh plums, prunes, a layer of thinly sliced apples, walnuts and stoned dates sprinkled with 2 tablespoons of sugar.

Try covered with chocolate or coffee butter icing (see page 264), after it has cooled.

BLUEBERRY CAKE

Serves 4 to 6   ① *Preparation 10 min, Cooking 1 $1/2$ hour – Easy*

This is a colossal muffin, technically known as a batter cake. Try it for breakfast and any other time you like.

INGREDIENTS
4 level tablespoons butter, softened (60 g, 2 oz), plus extra for greasing
$2^1/_2$ cups self-raising flour, sifted (300 g, 10 oz), plus extra for sprinkling
$1^1/_2$ teaspoons baking powder
$1^3/_4$ cups caster sugar (400 g, 14 oz)
2 eggs
1 cup milk (250 ml, $1/_2$ pint)
350 g (12 oz) blueberries

EQUIPMENT
Set of measuring spoons
Food processor or liquidiser (optional)
Mixing bowl
Set of measuring cups

Small bowls or plates
Sieve
Wooden spoon
Cup or small jug
Fork
Palette knife
25 cm (10 in) cake tin
Cake rack

METHOD

Preheat the oven to 180° C, 350° F, Gas mark 4.

If you are going to use a food processor then follow the steps below up to adding the blueberries. Do not mix them into the mixture in the processor. Instead empty the cake mixture without the blueberries into a bowl and then add the blueberries and stir with a spoon. If no processor is available this cake is pretty easy without one, just follow the steps below.

Take the butter out of the fridge and put into a medium-sized bowl at least 30 minutes before you start to make this cake. Measure out the flour and baking powder into a sieve and shake into a small bowl. Measure the sugar into a small bowl or onto a plate.

Add the sugar to the butter and with a wooden spoon force the sugar and butter together by pushing the mixture against the sides of the bowl. Continue to cream the mixture until it is light and fluffy.

Crack the first egg into a cup or jug and beat with a fork until the white and yolk are mixed. Slowly add this egg mixture to the butter and sugar mixture, stirring the butter and sugar mixture all the time. Repeat this process with the second egg. If the mixture begins to look lumpy or starts to separate add 1 or 2 tablespoons of the flour and stir it in. This should return the mixture to a creamy texture.

Add the flour and milk once you have added the eggs. Mix until well blended, then stir the blueberries into the mixture.

Wipe the inside of the cake tin with the wrapper from a block of butter or a small blob of butter or margarine and then shake a little flour into the baking tray trying to get it to stick to the thin film of butter or margarine. Throw any excess flour away and then, turn the mixture into the cake tin and level the top with a palette knife. Bake in the preheated oven for 1 $^{1}/_{2}$ hours or until the centre of the cake is firm to the touch. Be careful though – it will be hot. Place on a wire rack to cool for a few minutes, then take out of tin.

COFFEE & WALNUT CAKE

Serves 4 to 6   ① *Preparation 10 min, Cooking 60 min – Easy*

Think ahead: take the butter out of the fridge at least 30 minutes before making this recipe.

This is a self-explanatory cake and fabulous.

INGREDIENTS
$^{1}/_{2}$ cup strong coffee (125 ml, 4 fl oz)
2 × 100 g packs walnut pieces
$^{1}/_{2}$ × 250 g block butter (125 g, 4 oz), softened, plus extra for greasing
1$^{1}/_{4}$ cups caster sugar (300 g, 10 oz)
2 eggs
1 $^{1}/_{2}$ cups (generous) plain flour (200 g, 7 oz), plus extra for sprinkling
1 tablespoon baking powder

EQUIPMENT
2 cups

Sharp knife
Chopping board
Food processor or liquidiser (optional)
Large bowl
Set of measuring cups
Set of measuring spoons
Small bowl
Sieve
Bowl
Fork
Wooden spoon
20 cm (8 in) cake tin
Palette knife
Skewer or small knife
Cake rack

METHOD

Preheat the oven to 180° C, 350° F, Gas mark 4.

Take the butter out of the fridge at least 30 minutes before you start to make this cake.

To make this recipe in a food processor just follow the steps below, using the processor bowl as the large bowl. To make this recipe without a processor just follow the steps below.

Make a strong cup of coffee and drink half of it or make half a cup specially for this recipe. Chop the walnut pieces very finely with a sharp knife.

Put the butter into a large mixing bowl. Measure the sugar into a small bowl. Measure the flour and the baking powder into the sieve and shake them through the sieve into another bowl. Break the eggs into a cup and lightly beat them with a fork. Put the sugar into the bowl with the butter and with a wooden spoon force the sugar and butter together by pushing the mixture against the sides of the bowl. Continue to cream the mixture until light and fluffy, then beat in the eggs. Add the flour alternately with the coffee until the mixture is soft and smooth. Add the nuts.

With the wrapper from a block of butter or a small blob of butter or margarine wipe the inside of the cake tin.

Pour the mixture into the tin and level the top with a knife. Bake for 1 hour in the preheated oven until the cake is cooked. To make sure that the cake is cooked push a skewer or a small knife into the centre of cake and if it comes out clean, it is cooked. If not cooked, give it another 5 minutes and test again. Place on a wire rack to cool for a few minutes, then take out of tin.

CHOCOLATE CAKE

Serves 4   ① *Preparation 10 min, Cooking 50 min – Easy*

Five recipes into this chapter and you have hit a rich chocolate vein.

INGREDIENTS
3/4 cup self-raising flour (75 g, 3 oz), plus extra for sprinkling
1 level teaspoon baking powder
2 level tablespoons cocoa
2 level tablespoons dried milk
6 level tablespoons soft brown sugar (75 g, 3 oz)
1/2 cup soft margarine (125 g, 4 oz), plus extra for greasing
2 eggs

EQUIPMENT
Set of measuring cups
Set of measuring spoons
Sieve
Food processor or liquidiser (optional)
2 large bowls

Wooden spoon
Cup
Fork
Spoon
15 cm (6 in) cake tin or 500 g (1 lb) loaf tin
Palette knife
Cake rack

METHOD

Preheat the oven to 170° C, 325° F, Gas mark 3.

To make this recipe in a food processor just follow the steps below, using the processor bowl as the large bowl. To make this recipe without a processor just follow the steps below.

Put the flour, baking powder and cocoa into a sieve and shake into a large bowl.

Put the dried milk, sugar and the margarine into another large bowl and with a wooden spoon force the sugar, powdered milk and margarine together by pushing the mixture against the sides of the bowl with the spoon. Continue to cream the mixture until it is well blended.

Break the eggs into a cup, and beat lightly with a fork. Add the flour mixture to the margarine mixture and stir well together. Make a well in the middle of the mixture. Pour the lightly beaten eggs into the well and then stir them in slowly.

Wipe the inside of the cake tin with the wrapper from a block of butter or a small blob of butter or margarine Pour the mixture into the cake tin and smooth the top with a palette knife, making a little dip in the centre.

Bake the cake in the preheated oven for 50 minutes. Cool on a wire rack for a few minutes, then take out of the tin.

ADDITIONS & ALTERNATIVES

To remove a cake from a loose-bottomed tin stand the tin on a jar and push the sides down.

Try this cake with a cherry and walnut topping. When the cake has been cooked and has cooled a little spread a thin film of apricot jam or plum jam on top of it and arrange the cherries and walnuts on top. The jam should hold them in place.

Try covered with chocolate or coffee butter icing (see recipe below) once it has cooled.

CHOCOLATE BUTTER ICING

① Preparation 5 min – Easy

This is the magic joining mixture for putting between cakes or all over the top of them.

INGREDIENTS

1 tablespoon cocoa powder
1 tablespoon hot water
$^1/_2$ cup icing sugar (50 g, 2 oz)
3 level tablespoons of butter 45 g ($1^1/_2$ oz)

EQUIPMENT

Set of measuring spoons
Bowl
Sieve
Set of measuring cups
Wooden spoon

METHOD

Dissolve the cocoa in the water in a bowl. Allow to cool. Sieve the icing sugar into the bowl. Add the butter. Blend together with the wooden spoon and then beat until well mixed, 2 to 3 minutes.

ADDITIONS & ALTERNATIVES

Use soft margarine instead of butter.

For different flavours use orange juice or coffee essence instead of the cocoa and water.

CHOCOLATE CHIP COOKIES

Makes 50   ① *Preparation 15 min, Cooking 10 min – Easy*

Fancy a chip off the old block? Well that is the chocolate block actually. This will make 50 cookies and you will never know who your true friends are ever again.

INGREDIENTS

1¹/₂ cups flour (175 g, 6 oz), plus extra for sprinkling
1 teaspoon bicarbonate of soda
¹/₂ teaspoon salt
1 cup brown sugar (250 g, 8 oz)
¹/₂ × 250 g pack softened butter or margarine, plus extra for greasing
2 eggs
100 g pack of chocolate chips or bar of chocolate
100 g pack chopped hazelnuts or almonds
1 teaspoon vanilla extract

EQUIPMENT
Set of measuring cups
Set of measuring spoons
Sieve
2 bowls
Wooden spoon
Cup or jug
Fork
Metal spoon
Sharp knife and chopping board, if using a bar of chocolate
Teaspoon
Baking trays (you will need several or cook a few at a time)
Cake rack
Palette knife

METHOD
Preheat the oven to 190° C, 375° F, Gas mark 5.

Put the flour, bicarbonate of soda and salt into a sieve and shake through into a large bowl.

Put the sugar and butter into another large bowl and with a wooden spoon force them together by pushing the mixture against the sides of the bowl with the spoon. Continue to beat to cream the mixture until it is well blended, light and fluffy.

Crack the first egg into a cup or jug and beat with a fork until the white and yolk are mixed. Slowly add this egg mixture to the butter and sugar mixture, stirring all the time. Repeat this process with the second egg. If the mixture begins to look lumpy or starts to separate add 1 or 2 tablespoons of the flour and stir it in. This should return the mixture to a creamy texture.

Add the flour and fold into the mixture with a metal spoon. Add the chocolate chips, nuts and vanilla and stir in. If using a bar of chocolate first break it into pieces and then chop to the size of small orange pips before adding to the mixture.

Wipe the baking trays with the wrapper from a block of butter or a small blob of butter or margarine and then shake a little flour into the baking tray trying to get it to stick to the thin film of butter/margarine. Throw any excess flour away and then add the cake mixture from the bowl by droping teaspoonfuls of the mixture onto the baking sheets, leaving lots of room for spreading. Bake in the preheated oven for 10 minutes. Lift onto a cake rack with a palette knife to cool.

CHOCOLATE ECLAIRS

Makes 12   ① *Preparation 30 min, Cooking 20 min – Easy*

This is three recipes in one. There is the choux pastry, and then the cream filling and lastly the icing. Have a read through it all before you start. Once you have made these you will be able to make profiteroles (see page 6).

CHOUX PASTRY

INGREDIENTS
$^1/_2$ cup plain flour (75 g, 3 oz)
$^1/_4$ teaspoon salt
$^1/_2$ cup water (125 ml)
4 level tablespoons unsalted butter (60 g, 2 oz)
2 eggs

EQUIPMENT
Sieve
Greaseproof paper
Set of measuring cups

Set of measuring spoons
Saucepan
Wooden spoon
Cup
Piping bag with a plain tube
Baking tray
Cake rack

METHOD

Preheat the oven to 190° C, 375° F, Gas mark 5. Grease 2 or 3 baking sheets with butter. Sift the flour and salt onto the grease-proof paper. Put the water and butter in the saucepan on a low heat until the butter has melted. Bring the water to the boil. Take off the heat, and shoot all the flour off the paper into the pan. Stir the mixture vigorously over a medium heat until it forms a ball that comes away cleanly from the sides of the pan. Take off the heat and leave to cool for a few minutes. Break an egg into a cup and pick out any bits of shell. Add to the pan, beating with a spoon to incorporate the egg thoroughly. Repeat with the other egg.

Fill the piping bag with the pastry, and pipe 10 cm (4 in) thin sausages onto the baking tray. Bake in the preheated oven for 20 minutes. Lift off with a palette knife and cool on a rack.

CHOCOLATE CREAM

for 12 eclairs   ① *Preparation 25 min, Cooking 4 min – Easy*

INGREDIENTS

6 eggs
$^1/_2$ cup sugar (125 g, 4 oz)
5 level tablespoons flour (40 g, $1^1/_2$ oz)
$^1/_4$ teaspoon salt

2 cups milk (500 ml, 16 fl oz)
100 g plain chocolate

EQUIPMENT
Egg separator
2 cups
2 bowls
Tablespoon
Fork
Set of measuring cups
Set of measuring spoons
Saucepan
Wooden spoon
Whisk

METHOD
Separate the eggs. Break the eggs one at a time into a cup and pick out any bits of shell. Hold the egg separator over a cup. Put the eggs one at a time into the egg separator and let the white fall away into the cup beneath. Put the yolks into a bowl. Keep about 2 egg whites in another bowl. Or break the eggs one at a time into a cup and then lift out the yolk with a large spoon and put it in a small bowl. Empty the egg white out and repeat until all the eggs are done.

Add the sugar to the egg yolks and mix with a fork, then beat until the mixture is thick and cream-coloured. Gradually work in the flour, and season with a pinch of salt.

Heat the milk in the saucepan with the chocolate until the chocolate has melted. Heat to boiling point, stirring constantly. Slowly pour the milk into the egg mixture, stirring. Put the mixture back into the saucepan. Stir vigorously and bring to the boil, then turn down the heat until it is just boiling (simmering). Cook for 2 minutes. Cool the mixture, stirring from time to time. Whisk the 2 egg whites until stiff and fold into the cream before it cools.

ADDITIONS & ALTERNATIVES

Use 4 drops of vanilla essence instead of the chocolate.

Use a medium carton (284 ml, 10 fl oz) of double cream instead of this recipe.

Add 2 tablespoons of caster sugar and then whip until stiff.

TIPS

You can use this in the profiteroles.

You can separate the yolks by cracking the egg in half and then juggling the egg from one eggshell half to the other but this takes practice. The downside is that the yolk can get popped on the shell, and of course your fingers tend to get covered with egg white.

CHOCOLATE ICING

for 12 eclairs   ⏱ *Preparation 5 min – Easy*

This icing can be used on other cakes as well as the eclairs.

INGREDIENTS

1 cup icing sugar (125 g, 4 oz)
1 tablespoon cocoa
1 tablespoon warm water

EQUIPMENT

Saucepan
Glass bowl
Sieve
Set of measuring cups
Set of measuring spoons
Spoon

METHOD

Heat some water in the saucepan. Put the bowl on top and sieve in the icing sugar and the cocoa. Gradually add the warm water and stir. Cool slightly and spread on the eclairs. If it is too runny add a bit more sugar, and if too stiff a little more water.

ADDITIONS & ALTERNATIVES

Try coffee icing. Use $^1/_2$ teaspoon instant coffee instead of the cocoa in the icing.

GINGER CAKE

Serves 4 to 6   ① *Preparation 12 min, Cooking 45 min – Easy*

This is a moist and sticky ginger cake which is as good as any we have tasted.

INGREDIENTS

$^1/_2$ × 100 g tub candied mixed peel
2 eggs
500 g (1 lb) bag plain flour, plus extra for sprinkling
3 tablespoons ground ginger
1 teaspoon bicarbonate of soda
$^1/_2$ × 250 g block butter (125 g, 4 oz), plus extra for greasing
458 g (1 lb) tin treacle
4 level tablespoons brown sugar
$^3/_4$ to 1 cup milk (about 200 ml, 7 fl oz)

EQUIPMENT

Sharp knife
Chopping board
Small bowl

Fork
Sieve
Set of measuring spoons
Large bowl
Saucepan
Set of measuring cups
Wooden spoon
25 cm (10 in) shallow cake tin
Palette knife
Skewer
Cake rack

METHOD

Preheat the oven to 180° C, 350° F, Gas mark 4.

Chop the mixed peel into small pieces. Break the eggs into a bowl and pick out any bits of shell. Add the peel and beat with a fork or whisk until slightly frothy. Sieve the flour, ground ginger, and bicarbonate of soda into larger bowl.

Put the butter, treacle and sugar in the pan over a low heat. Warm until melted.

Gradually stir the eggs into the flour mixture, then the hot treacle followed by the milk.

Wipe the inside of the cake tin with the wrapper from a block of butter or a small blob of butter or margarine. Pour the mixture into the cake tin and smooth the top with a palette knife. Cook in the preheated oven for 45 minutes or until a skewer cruelly poked into it comes out clean. Cool on a cake rack then take out of the tin.

GINGER NUTS

Makes 50   ① *Preparation 15 min, Cooking 15 min – Easy*

We do not believe in doing things by halves. If you are going to make ginger biscuits worth eating, then make a lot of them and use real ginger. Of course you could do things by halves for more manageable amounts.

INGREDIENTS
2 cm (1 in) fresh root ginger or 2 teaspoons ground ginger
500 g (1 lb) bag plain flour
$^1/_2$ teaspoon salt
1 cup brown sugar (250 g, 8 oz)
1 cup treacle (250 g, 8 oz)
$^3/_4 \times$ 250 g pack butter (175 g, 6 oz)

EQUIPMENT
Vegetable peeler
Grater
Set of measuring spoons
Sieve
Bowl
Set of measuring cups
Saucepan
Wooden spoon
Tablespoon
Baking trays (you will need several or cook a few at a time)
Cake rack

METHOD

Preheat the oven to 170° C, 325° F, Gas mark 3.

Peel and grate the ginger. Put the flour and salt into a sieve and shake through into a large bowl.

Put the sugar, treacle and butter in the saucepan over a low heat. Melt together and then allow to cool. Add the ginger and flour and mix together well. Take about a tablespoon of the mixture and roll into a ball. Put onto the ungreased baking tray allowing spreading room. Repeat until all the mixture is used.

Bake in the preheated oven for 15 minutes. Lift onto a cake rack with a palette knife to cool.

ORANGE SPONGE CAKE WITH COCONUT ICING

Serves 4 to 6 ① *Preparation 15 min, Cooking 25 min – Easy*

This cake has a strong American influence, including the icing made with boiling water.

INGREDIENTS

1 unwaxed orange, preferably organic
$^1/_2$ × 200 g block coconut cream
1 cup wholemeal flour (150 g, 5 oz), plus extra for sprinkling
1 teaspoon baking powder
$^1/_2$ cup brown sugar (100 g, 4 oz)
$^1/_2$ × 250 g pack butter or margarine (100 g, 4 oz), softened, plus extra for greasing
$^1/_2$ cup milk (125 ml, 4 fl oz)
2 tablespoons boiling water
1 tablespoon icing sugar

EQUIPMENT
Zester or grater
Sharp knife
Chopping board
Juicer
Set of measuring spoons
2 bowls
Whisk or hand mixer
25 cm (10 in) shallow cake tin
Palette knife
Cake rack

METHOD
Preheat the oven to 180° C, 350° F, Gas mark 4.

Zest or grate the orange, or peel and cut into little strips. Juice the orange. Grate the block of creamed coconut.

To make this recipe in a food processor just follow the steps below, using the processor bowl as the large bowl. To make this recipe without a processor just follow the steps below.

Put the flour and baking powder into a sieve and shake into a large bowl. Put the sugar and softened butter into a large bowl and with a wooden spoon force the sugar and margarine together by pushing the mixture against the sides of the bowl with the spoon. Continue to cream the mixture until it is well blended, light and fluffy. Add the flour mixture and orange peel to the butter mixture alternately with the milk and orange juice. Beat together.

Wipe the inside of the cake tin with the wrapper from a block of butter or a small blob of butter or margarine. Pour the mixture into the cake tin and smooth the top with a palette knife.

Cook in the preheated oven for 25 minutes until firm and springy to the touch. Cool on a wire rack then take out of the tin.

When the cake is cold mix the coconut, water and sugar to a smooth paste and spread on top.

ADDITIONS & ALTERNATIVES
For a chocolate sponge, leave out the orange and add 1 table-spoonful of cocoa to the mixture, sifting it with the flour and baking powder. Cover the sponge with chocolate icing.

TIPS
Creamed coconut is a white solid which is available in tubs and packets from health food shops and supermarkets. Not to be confused with coconut cream which is a thick liquid available in cartons.

ORANGE BISCUITS

Makes about 50   ① *Preparation 12 min, Cooking 10 min – Easy*

Not easy to buy in the shops. In fact it would take you longer with your yellow pages and telephone trying to locate a shop which sold orange biscuits than it would to make them yourself. These are in the book because we like them. A lot.

INGREDIENTS
$2^1/4$ cups plain flour (300 g, 10 oz), plus extra for sprinkling
$^1/2$ teaspoon bicarbonate of soda
$^1/4$ teaspoon salt
1 cup sugar (250 g, 8 oz)
$3/4$ cup butter or margarine (175 g, 6 oz), plus extra for greasing
2 eggs
$3/4$ cup orange juice, (175 ml, 6 fl oz)
$3/4$ cup desiccated coconut (75 g, 3 oz)

EQUIPMENT

Set of measuring cups
Set of measuring spoons
Sieve
2 bowls
Wooden spoon
Cup
Fork
Metal spoon
Teaspoon
Baking trays (you will need several or cook a few at a time)
Cake rack

METHOD

Preheat the oven to 200° C, 400° F, Gas mark 6.

Put the flour, bicarbonate of soda and salt into a sieve and shake into a large bowl.

Put the sugar and butter into another large bowl and with a wooden spoon force them together by pushing the mixture against the sides of the bowl with the spoon. Continue to cream the mixture until it is well blended, light and fluffy.

Crack the first egg into a cup or jug and beat with a fork until the white and yolk are mixed. Slowly add this egg mixture to the butter and sugar mixture, stirring all the time. Repeat this process with the second egg. If the mixture begins to look lumpy or starts to separate add 1 or 2 tablespoons of the flour and stir it in. This should return the mixture to a creamy texture.

Add the flour alternately with the orange juice and desiccated coconut and fold into the mixture with a metal spoon.

Wipe the baking trays with the wrapper from a block of butter or a small blob of butter or margarine and then shake a little flour into the baking tray trying to get it to stick to the thin film of butter/margarine. Throw any excess flour away and then add the cake mixture from the bowl by dropping heaped teaspoonfuls of the mixture onto the baking trays, leaving lots of room for spreading. Bake in the preheated oven for 10 minutes. Lift onto a cake rack with a palette knife to cool.

VICTORIA SPONGE CAKE

Serves 4 to 6
① *Preparation 15 min, Cooking 25 to 35 min – Easy*

This is the secret cake that only comes out at coffee mornings. Now most blokes miss out on coffee mornings, and so do not get to taste the real thing.

INGREDIENTS

1 cup self-raising flour (125 g, 4 oz)
1 teaspoon baking powder
$^1/_2$ cup caster sugar (125 g, 4 oz)
$^1/_2$ cup soft margarine (125 g, 4 oz), plus extra for greasing
2 medium eggs

EQUIPMENT

20 cm (8 in) sponge tin
Greaseproof paper
Sieve
2 bowls
Set of measuring cups
Set of measuring spoons
Wooden spoon
Cup or jug
Fork
Palette knife or spoon

METHOD

Preheat the oven to 190° C, 375° F, Gas mark 5.

Wipe the inside of the sponge tin with the wrapper from a block of butter or a small blob of butter or margarine. Cut a circle of greaseproof paper to fit the bottom and put in the tin.

Put the flour and baking powder into a sieve and shake into a large bowl.

Put the sugar and margarine into another large bowl and with a wooden spoon force them together by pushing the mixture against the sides of the bowl with the spoon. Continue to cream the mixture until it is well blended, light and fluffy.

Crack the first egg into a cup or jug and beat with a fork until the white and yolk are mixed. Slowly add this egg mixture to the butter and sugar mixture, stirring all the time. Repeat this process with the second egg. If the mixture begins to look lumpy or starts to separate add 1 or 2 tablespoons of the flour and stir it in. This should return the mixture to a creamy texture.

Add half the flour and fold into the mixture with a wooden spoon. Repeat with the other half of the flour.

Pour the mixture into the sponge tin and smooth the top with a palette knife or a spoon, making a little dip in the centre.

Cook in the middle of the preheated oven for 20 to 25 minutes. It is done when it looks golden and springs back to the touch. Cool on a wire rack, then take out of the tin.

ADDITIONS & ALTERNATIVES

If you want a double layer cake just double the quantities. Cook for the same time. When cool spread the bottom cake with raspberry jam.

You can make a fruit version by adding the grated rind of a lemon, orange or lime with the butter.

For a coffee cake add 2 teaspoons instant coffee with the flour.

Try covered with chocolate or coffee butter icing (see page 264) or chocolate icing (see page 270).

SMART SNACKS, DIPS & DRESSINGS

This is easy quick stuff to fill a gap or perk up other dishes. We have also got a recipe for real mayonnaise, an added flash luxury, and variations for prawn cocktail and fresh tartare sauce.

TARAMASALATA

Serves 4   ① *Preparation 10 min – Easy*

Fresh taramasalata is not like the prepared versions you will have tasted. It tastes of smoked fish and is not shocking pink, which can only be an advantage.

INGREDIENTS
75 g (3 oz) smoked cod's roe
3 slices bread
1 clove garlic
2 tablespoons water
Juice of 1 lemon
4 tablespoons olive oil

EQUIPMENT
Sharp knife
Chopping board

Lemon juicer
Set of measuring spoons
Set of measuring cups
Food processor or liquidiser (optional) or bowl and wooden spoon
and fork

METHOD
Skin the outer membrane from the roe, if it has been left on. Cut
the crusts off the bread then cut the slices into cubes. Peel and
roughly chop the garlic. Place the cod's roe, bread, water, lemon
juice and garlic in the food processor or liquidiser and blend on
minimum speed for 30 seconds, scraping the mixture back off the
sides if necessary. Or put in a bowl and mash it up with a fork
then mix with a wooden spoon. Turn it up to medium speed and
gradually add the oil over a minute or so.

ADDITIONS & ALTERNATIVES
Serve with pitta bread, olives and slices of lemon.

TIPS
You can buy prepared garlic but fresh is always better.

BAKED AUBERGINE & YOGHURT DIP

Serves 2   ⏲ *Preparation 10 min, Cooking 15 min – Easy*

Here is an easy one to do. Really no more difficult than a dip for
pitta bread or raw vegetables, you can use it to go with that bought
kebab. It could also be used with or instead of hummus and taramasalata for a snack. Flash for parties – just make loads.

INGREDIENTS
1 clove garlic
1 lemon or 4 tablespoons of lemon juice
15 g pack fresh parsley
2 medium aubergines
4 tablespoons olive oil
Small carton (142 ml, 5 fl oz) natural yoghurt
Salt and freshly ground black pepper to taste
$1/4$ teaspoon paprika

EQUIPMENT
Sharp knife
Chopping board
Garlic crusher
Bowl
Lemon juicer
Set of measuring spoons
Wooden spoon
Fork for mashing
Food processor or liquidiser (optional)

METHOD
Peel and crush the garlic into the bowl. Halve and juice the lemon. Wash, shake dry and finely chop the parsley to make 1 tablespoon.

Grill the aubergines whole until soft, turning occasionally. Strip off the skin while hot to avoid discoloration of the flesh. Mash the flesh with a fork in a bowl or purée in a processor. Mix in the oil, yoghurt, garlic, salt, pepper and lemon juice to make a smooth thin paste. Serve with a sprinkling of paprika and chopped parsley.

ADDITIONS & ALTERNATIVES
Add 1 tablespoon tahini.

Instead of grilling, bake the aubergine in a moderate oven,

180° C/350° F/Gas mark 4 until soft, turning once while cooking.
Use a liquidiser or food processor to mix it all up.

TAHINI DIP

① *Preparation 10 min – Easy*

This dip for pitta bread can also be used with falafel (see page 93)
or as a salad dressing. It gives the humble baked potato an exotic taste.

INGREDIENTS
$^1/_2$ cup tahini
3 or 4 tablespoons water
2 cloves garlic
15 g pack fresh parsley
2 lemons
Salt and freshly ground black pepper to taste

EQUIPMENT
Sharp knife
Chopping board
Lemon juicer
Set of measuring spoons
Set of measuring cups
Bowl
Spoon
Garlic crusher
Herb mincer (optional)
Food processor or liquidiser (optional)

METHOD
Mix the tahini to a smooth paste with the water in the bowl. Peel

and crush the garlic into the bowl. Wash, shake dry and finely mince up or chop the parsley. Juice the lemons. Add the lemon juice, parsley, salt and pepper and mix together.

ADDITIONS & ALTERNATIVES
You can use a food processor or liquidiser to do the mixing if you have one.

MAYONNAISE

① *Preparation 10 min – Easy*

The mayonnaise you can buy is pretty good, but your own can be amazing. You might think it is difficult to do but if you have gone for the power tool food processor or liquidiser option it takes moments. It is also possible without the power tool, it just takes a bit more effort.

INGREDIENTS
1 egg
1 tablespoon vinegar or lemon juice
$^1/_4$ teaspoon dried mustard
1 teaspoon sugar
$^1/_2$ teaspoon salt
$^1/_4$ teaspoon pepper
1 cup sunflower or olive oil

EQUIPMENT
Set of measuring spoons
Set of measuring cups
Food processor or liquidiser or bowl and whisk

METHOD

Put the egg, vinegar or lemon juice, mustard, sugar, salt and pepper into the food processor or liquidiser. Put the lid on and blend on medium speed for 5 seconds, or whisk until the ingredients are well mixed. Start to pour the oil gently through the hole in the cover while the processor is running. Continue blending for about 1 minute until the oil has been mixed in. You may have to stop the processor and scrape the mixture off the sides with a spatula.

ADDITIONS & ALTERNATIVES

You can make this thicker by using two egg yolks instead of the whole egg.

You can do a version of this by hand by using a bowl and whisk instead of the food processor. Just add the oil a bit at a time, preferably while still beating.

Tartare Sauce. You can make this sauce for fish by adding 50 g pack fresh parsley, 6 gherkins, 6 stuffed green olives and 3 teaspoons capers after the oil.

Pink Mayonnaise for prawns or other fish. Add 2 tablespoons of tomato purée, 1 tablespoon of lemon juice and 1 teaspoon of cayenne pepper to the mayonnaise after you have finished.

Fresh mayonnaise will keep covered in the fridge for 3 days.

BAKED EGG POTATOES

Serves 2   ① *Preparation 10 min, Cooking 1 1/4 hr – Easy*

Don't say we never have any healthy options. This is a flash version of egg and chips.

INGREDIENTS
2 large potatoes
2 eggs
2 teaspoons butter
Salt and freshly ground black pepper to taste
2 tablespoons single cream
2 tablespoons freshly grated Parmesan cheese

EQUIPMENT
Fork
2 skewers
Aluminium foil
Oven gloves
Spoon
Set of measuring spoons

METHOD
Preheat the oven to 230° C, 450° F, Gas mark 8.

Wash the potatoes. Prick the surface with a fork. Stick the skewer through the potatoes – it helps them to cook in the middle. Wrap the potatoes in aluminium foil. Cook in the preheated oven on the top shelf for an hour. They are ready when they give if pressed. Remember to use oven gloves when testing! Take out the skewers. Wait a few minutes for them to cool a bit.

Make a hole in the top of each potato and scoop out enough of the insides to make room for an egg. Put in a teaspoon of butter, salt and pepper. Break an egg into each, add a little cream and Parmesan and bake in the oven for another 15 minutes or until the eggs are set.

TIPS
Parmesan comes ready-grated in bags or tubs. You can grate your own but be warned, it is a very hard cheese. Consider using the rotary grater power tool.

EGG & BACON BAKES

Serves 4   ⏱ *Preparation 10 min, Cooking 15 min – Easy*

This is bacon and eggs without the frying. What makes it flash is the cream and the cheese and the fact you do not get splashed with hot fat when you try to cook the eggs.

INGREDIENTS
4 slices bacon
8 eggs
4 tablespoons grated Cheddar cheese
Salt and freshly ground black pepper
Small carton (142 ml, 5 fl oz) double cream

EQUIPMENT
Sharp knife
Chopping board
4 ramekins (small pots)
Set of measuring cups

METHOD
Preheat the oven to 170° C, 325° F, Gas mark 3.

Grill the bacon and chop into pieces. Butter 4 individual ramekins. Put a quarter of the grated cheese and diced grilled bacon in the bottom of each dish. Break 2 eggs into each dish. Season to taste with salt and freshly ground black pepper and finish off with 2 tablespoons double cream on each one. Bake in the preheated oven for 15 minutes, or until the egg whites are firm.

TIPS
You can buy grated cheese in packets or grate your own.

A ramekin is a small circular pot roughly 5 cm (2 in) tall, and

8 cm (3 in) across. They are good for making individual desserts, like chocolate mousse or cream caramel.

FRITATA

Serves 4   ① *Preparation 5 min, Cooking 12 min – Easy*

Now we have got into a bit of an eggs and bacon theme let's add a bit of sausage, well flash Italian sausage, actually. Eat in the heat of the summer with salad and chilled wine or beer. Enough of a different taste to be flash and exotic.

INGREDIENTS
6 eggs
2 tablespoons grated Parmesan cheese
Salt and freshly ground black pepper to taste
2 level tablespoons butter
1 tablespoon olive oil
100 g pack sliced mortadella sausage
100 g pack Mozzarella cheese

EQUIPMENT
Bowl
Fork
Frying pan, preferably with a heavy base
Set of measuring spoons
Sharp knife
Chopping board

METHOD
Break the eggs into a bowl and pick out any bits of shell. Add the Parmesan, salt and pepper to taste and mix it all up with a fork.

288

Melt the butter with the oil in a large frying pan over a moderate heat. Add the eggs. Cook on low for about 5 minutes until the mixture is half set underneath but the top of the omelette is still runny.

Cut the sliced mortadella sausage into thin strips, and slice the Mozzarella cheese. Scatter the mortadella and Mozzarella over the omelette, then cook for 5 minutes or so until eggs are set. Put the pan under the grill for 2 minutes until the top of the omelette is light brown. Serve hot, cut into wedges.

ADDITIONS & ALTERNATIVES

Serve with crusty bread and salad.

Vegetarian version. Omit the mortadella. Chop the end off a red pepper and cut out the core and seeds. Cut the pepper into thin slices. Thinly slice 2 courgettes. Skin and roughly chop 2 tomatoes. Fry the red pepper in olive oil and butter for 2 minutes until lightly coloured. Add the courgettes and tomatoes and cook for 10 minutes until slightly reduced and thickened. Add this when you would add the mortadella.

TIPS

Parmesan comes ready-grated in bags or tubs. You can grate your own but be warned, it is a very hard cheese. Consider using the rotary grater power tool.

TOMATO OMELETTE

Serves 2   ① *Preparation 5 min, Cooking 20 min – Easy*

Another recipe for those sunny days, or alternatively turn the central heating up and dream.

FLASH COOKING FOR BLOKES

INGREDIENTS
4 tomatoes
2 onions
15 g pack fresh parsley
3 tablespoons sunflower oil
Salt and freshly ground black pepper to taste
4 eggs

EQUIPMENT
Sharp knife
Chopping board
Set of measuring spoons
Frying pan
Wooden spoon
Set of measuring cups
Bowl
Spoon
Garlic crusher
Food processor or liquidiser (optional)
Fork for mashing
Grater
Small bowls or plates

METHOD
Slice the tomatoes. Peel the onion and cut into rings. Wash, shake dry and finely chop the parsley to make 2 tablespoons. Break the eggs into a bowl and pick out any bits of shell. Beat the eggs lightly with a fork.

Put the oil in the frying pan and heat over a moderate heat. Fry the onion for about 5 minutes until it is really golden brown, stirring to stop it sticking. Add the tomatoes, parsley, salt and pepper, and cook for 5 minutes more. Add the eggs and cook for 5 to 10 minutes until the eggs are set.

ADDITIONS & ALTERNATIVES
If you like your omelettes golden, brown under the grill for a few
minutes. Serve with bread and salad.

HERB OMELETTE

Serves 4   ① *Preparation 10 min, Cooking 35 min – Easy*

This omelette is green. It has a subtle herby taste and is another
dish for a warm day.

INGREDIENTS
4 leeks
250 g pack fresh spinach
15 g pack fresh parsley
15 g pack fresh dill or 1 tablespoon dried dill
2 tablespoons sunflower oil
2 cloves garlic
5 large eggs, lightly beaten
$^1/_2$ teaspoon bicarbonate of soda
Salt and freshly ground black pepper to taste

EQUIPMENT
Sharp knife
Chopping board
20 cm (8 in) frying pan
Set of measuring spoons
Garlic crusher
Wooden spoon
Bowl
Fork
Herb mincer (optional)

METHOD

Clean the leeks. First take off the outer leaves, cut the roots off and trim the top. Split the leeks in half lengthways. Hold the leeks under running water and wash any grit out. Shake them dry. Chop into small bits. Wash the spinach, and shred finely. Wash, shake dry and finely chop the parsley and dill to make 2 tablespoons of each.

Heat the oil in the frying pan. Peel and crush the garlic into the pan. Add the leeks, spinach, parsley and dill, and fry gently for about 3 to 5 minutes, stirring with a wooden spoon, until the leeks soften. Take off the heat.

Break the eggs into a bowl and pick out any bits of shell. Beat the eggs with a fork. Add the bicarbonate of soda, leek mixture, salt and pepper to the beaten eggs, then return the mixture to the frying pan, and cook gently for about 20 minutes until the underside is well browned and crisp and the mixture firm. Turn the omelette over and cook this side for about 5 minutes until just beginning to brown. Serve hot or cold, cut into wedges.

ADDITIONS & ALTERNATIVES

Serve with salad.

TIPS

If you find it hard to turn the omelette put a plate on top and then turn the pan and plate together. Slide the omelette back into the pan. Alternatively cut the wedges before turning and turn one wedge at a time.

DYNAMITE DRINKS

First the good news, only the first recipe has any cooking in it, but it is well worth the effort. And the rest of the good news is that everything else is fabulous too.

RUDI'S RUM PUNCH

Serves MANY ⏱ *Preparation 10 min, Cooking 30 min – Easy*

This is the authentic, partially cooked version. It is very pink, and does not look very serious, but it is.

INGREDIENTS
1¹/₂ cups ginger mixture (see below)
3 cups orange juice
¹/₂ cup grenadine
1 cup rum

Ginger Mix
10 cm (4 in) fresh root ginger
1 stick cinnamon
3 cloves
3 tablespoons sugar
2 mace blades
2 cups water

EQUIPMENT
Vegetable peeler
Sharp knife
Chopping board
Set of measuring cups
Set of measuring spoons
Saucepan
Wooden spoon
Sieve
Bowl
Very large bowl or clean 2 litre bottle
Spoon
Funnel

METHOD
First make the ginger mix. Peel the ginger and slice it roughly, then add it and all the other ginger mix ingredients to a saucepan and boil for 30 minutes. Allow the liquid to cool and then strain through a sieve into a bowl. If there is not $1^{1}/_{2}$ cups of the mixture make it up with cold water.

Put the cooled and strained ginger mixture, orange juice, grenadine and rum in a very large bowl or in a large (2 litre) clean and dry bottle. If using a bowl mix together with a spoon. If using a bottle pour in with the aid of a funnel and mix by putting the top on the bottle and shaking gently. Do not shake it up vigorously. If possible chill until you are ready to serve.

RUM PUNCH

Serves 2 or 3   ① *Preparation 5 min – Easy*

This rum punch does not need any cooking.

DYNAMITE DRINKS

INGREDIENTS
1 orange
1 lime
2 slices pineapple
1 tablespoon brown sugar (preferably Muscovada)
2 tablespoons rum
2 ice cubes
$^1/_2$ cup soda water
Mint sprigs to decorate

EQUIPMENT
Sharp knife
Chopping board
Orange juicer
Set of measuring spoons
Liquidiser
Glasses
Strainer
Set of measuring cups

METHOD
Cut the orange and lime in half and juice them. Save the juice.
Chop the pineapple slices roughly. Place all the ingredients, except
the soda water and the mint, in the liquidiser and blend on maximum speed for 30 seconds. Strain into the glasses and top up with
soda water. Decorate with the mint to serve.

CHOCOLATE FROTH

Serves 2 　　　　　① *Preparation 5 min, Cooking 5 min – Easy*

Alcoholic hot chocolate for those really cold days.

INGREDIENTS
$1/4$ × 100 g bar plain chocolate
1 cup milk
2 tablespoons rum or whisky (optional)
Ground cinnamon

EQUIPMENT
Sharp knife
Chopping board
Liquidiser
Set of measuring cups
Saucepan
Set of measuring spoons
Cups

METHOD
Chop the chocolate roughly and then place it in the liquidiser. Heat the milk in a saucepan and add it to the chocolate in the liquidiser. If you are going to add alcohol add it now. Blend on maximum speed for 15 seconds. Pour into mugs and sprinkle with cinnamon to taste.

ICED COFFEE

Serves 4   ① *Preparation 10 min – Easy*

Alcoholic iced coffee for those really hot days.

INGREDIENTS

Small carton (142 ml, 5 fl oz) whipping or double cream, or aerosol cream
1 pint chilled milk (500 ml, 2 cups)
3 tablespoons coffee essence (Camp coffee or Cafinesse)
4 ice cubes
1 tablespoon Kahlua (coffee liqueur) or 1 Cadbury's flake (optional)

EQUIPMENT

Small bowl
Whisk or fork
Set of measuring cups
Set of measuring spoons
Food processor or liquidiser (optional)

METHOD

If using double or whipping cream place in a bowl and beat with a whisk or a fork until it stands in peaks. Place the milk, coffee essence and ice cubes in the liquidiser. Blend on maximum speed for 30 seconds.

Pour the coffee into tall glasses, top with the cream. If using squirty cream squirt some on the top of each glass. Trickle 1 tablespoon of Kahlua over the cream in each glass or some crumbs from a Cadburys flake. Serve.

SANGRIA

Serves Many   ⏱ *Preparation 20 min – Easy*

This needs to chill for 2 hours.

Party time.

INGREDIENTS
3 large ripe peaches
$^1/_4$ cup sugar
$^1/_4$ cup brandy
1 lemon
2 bottles light, dry Spanish red wine
1 vanilla pod
$^1/_4$ teaspoon grated nutmeg
500 ml–1 litre sparkling mineral water (depending on taste)

EQUIPMENT
Sharp knife
Chopping board
Very large bowl
Set of measuring cups
Large bowl or very large jug
Set of measuring spoons
Sieve

METHOD
Cut the peaches in half and take the stone out, then peel them. Slice thinly, and place in a very large punch bowl or decorative (non-metallic) bowl. Sprinkle in the sugar and brandy and leave to stand for 2 hours.

Meanwhile, peel the lemon carefully, taking the skin off in one spiral piece. Remove any white pith that may have come off with the skin. Pour the wine into another bowl or very large jug and add the vanilla pod, a small pinch of freshly grated nutmeg, and the lemon peel spiral. Leave this to stand for 2 hours too. After the two hours strain through a sieve into the bowl with the peaches and chill for 1 hour. Add the chilled sparkling mineral water to taste just before serving.

MANGO MARGARITA

Serves 1 or 2   ⏲ *Preparation 10 min – Easy*

A nice thick fruity drink.

INGREDIENTS
1 mango
$1^1/_2$ tablespoons sugar
$1^1/_2$ tablespoons water
6 tablespoons tequila
2 tablespoons Triple Sec or Cointreau
3 tablespoons lime juice
6 ice cubes

EQUIPMENT
Sharp knife
Chopping board
Liquidiser
Set of measuring spoons
Small bowl or cup

METHOD
Cut the mango in half and remove the stone (this is tricky, just do

your best) and the peel, and keep the other half until later. (For the next time you mix this drink). Roughly chop the mango and put it in the liquidiser. Mix the sugar and the water together in a cup or bowl until the sugar has dissolved. Put all the other ingredients in the liquidiser too and blend them together until they are slushy. Then serve and drink.

Adjust the sugar and water mixture to taste. For a very sweet tooth add more, not so sweet add less.

MANGO SHAKE

Serves 1 or 2   ① *Preparation 10 min – Easy*

Very slushy and refreshing.

INGREDIENTS
1 medium, green (unripe) mango
1 cup cracked ice
3 tablespoons water
3 tablespoons sugar
4 tablespoons white or pale rum or vodka (optional)

EQUIPMENT
Sharp knife
Chopping board
Set of measuring cups
Set of measuring spoons
Small bowl or cup
Food processor or liquidiser (optional)

METHOD

Cut the mango flesh away from the stone and then remove the peel. To crack the ice put a few ice cubes (4 to 6) into the liquidiser and whiz it until the ice is cracked up but before it becomes slush. Mix the water and the sugar together in a cup and stir until the sugar is dissolved. Place the mango and all the other ingredients in the liquidiser and blend at high speed until puréed and thoroughly mixed. Pour into glasses.

Adjust the sugar and water mixture to taste. For a very sweet tooth add more, not so sweet add less.

ADDITIONS & ALTERNATIVES

Ripe mangoes can also be used.

SINGAPORE GIN SLING

Serves 1–2 ⏱ *Preparation 10 min – Easy*

This famous drink originated at the Raffles Hotel and has made its way around the world. Here is your chance to try it without having to travel, or find your way home afterwards.

INGREDIENTS

4 tablespoons gin
2 tablespoons cherry brandy
2 teaspoons orange juice
2 teaspoons lime juice
2 teaspoons pineapple juice
1 teaspoon Benedictine liqueur
1 teaspoon Triple Sec or Cointreau
$^1/_2$ teaspoon grenadine

4 drops angostura bitters
Ice cubes
3 tablespoons club soda
Pineapple wedge and maraschino or cocktail cherry for decoration

EQUIPMENT
Set of measuring spoons
Cocktail shaker or a large improvised jar

METHOD
Combine the gin, cherry brandy, orange, lime and pineapple juices, Benedictine, Triple Sec, grenadine and bitters in a cocktail shaker. Add 3 or 4 ice cubes (if there is room), shake well and strain into a large glass. Add soda and additional ice. Decorate with the pineapple wedge and cherry on a cocktail stick.

CHINESE NEW YEAR COCKTAIL

Serves 1   ① *Preparation 10 min – Easy*

A cocktail fit to toast any new year.

INGREDIENTS
2 tablespoons gin
1¹/₂ tablespoons Cointreau or Triple Sec
2 tablespoons orange juice
1¹/₂ tablespoons lime juice
1 tablespoon sugar
1 tablespoon water
1 tablespoon grenadine
3 or 4 ice cubes

EQUIPMENT
Set of measuring spoons
Cocktail shaker or a large improvised jar or wide mouthed bottle

METHOD
Put all the ingredients except the ice cubes in a cocktail shaker. Shake thoroughly and put the ice cubes into the glass and pour the mixture over the ice cubes. Now it's ready to enjoy.

POWER TOOLS

For kitchen use

Our definition of 'power tools' for the kitchen is rather loose. It includes any tools that are powered, have a spring or any moving part. Some of them are powered by electricity and some are manually powered but are similar in nature to the ratchet screwdriver. For us, power tools means small effort in, big effect out.

Manually operated tools

In the manually operated section, a kind of power tools for a power cut, there are several devices that you may remember from childhood. Less than perfect design and manufacturing made using some of these a sad affair. We have fearlessly returned to this plastic and metal world and to our surprise things have improved. We have found all of these machines really useful at some time. We both think the onion and vegetable chopper is particularly great. It is onions without tears.

ONION AND VEGETABLE CHOPPER
This is a plastic cylinder that has a zigzag blade inside with a plunger-like device on the top. You push down on the plunger knob on the top and the blades inside the cylinder come down on whatever is beneath them. With ours there is a small plastic dish that doubles as a cap to the plastic cylinder, the item you want to

chop is placed in this dish and then you bring the blades down. And nowadays this chopper really works. It is fantastic for onions and garlic, but particularly for the onions, because you can put some thickish slices of onions in and then chop away. It is easy, and means you can chop onions without getting sore, red, runny eyes. Fantastic for curries when there are loads of onions to chop. It is also fantastic for chopping up those little garlic cloves that like to act like small bars of soap when you try to chop them. They cannot get away and shoot off at odd angles with this device. Even if you have a food processor this is worth having, because it's not worth getting the processor out just to chop onions. We've used ours for chopping onions, garlic, carrots and chillies. It only works well with the chillies if they are really crisp, otherwise it seems rather to fold or squash, but it has been so good with the onions and garlic as to make that unimportant. The name of the maker has rubbed off ours but we have seen a similar one made by Culinaire. We would not be without this tool.

HERB CHOPPER
Made by several manufacturers, the one we have is French, made by Moulin-Legumes, and is called a *Mouli Parsimint*, but we have seen other versions of the same device. You wash and shake dry your herbs and put them into a small trough at the top of either a table top or hand-held device that has a little handle attached to very very small blades that look like wires. Turn the handle and your herbs are chopped. Perhaps not the cleanest type of chopping, more shredding, and sometimes a little squashed too, but much finer than you could accomplish in the time by hand. Good for dealing with large amounts of parsley, mint or coriander.

HAND-HELD ROTARY CHOPPER AND GRATER
This a double hinged tool. The first hinge forms almost an elbow. At one end is a sort of clamp or hand and at the other are two semi-circular pieces. This becomes a cylindrical shape when the hinged piece at this end is folded up. Inside this cylinder shape fit a series of metal drums (we have 3 but may have lost 1) with variously sized

and shaped (fine, coarse and slots) grating holes. It works by popping the thing to be sliced or grated in a small cup which is held in place by the hand/clamp part. The metal drums have small handles, and you turn these handles moving the drum against the thing to be sliced or grated. We have used this for grating and slicing cheese and carrots, slicing cucumbers and garlic, and even for turning lumps of bread into breadcrumbs. It has the edge over stand up square graters because your knuckles never come into contact with the grating bits. Also because it can hold fiddly little pieces of hard cheese like Parmesan in place and can do the same with garlic cloves, which are almost impossible to hold and slice on the stand up grater. Ours is called a *Mouli grater* there are other makes. We like ours and although we don't use it every day we use it enough to make it worth having.

MOULI

This is the fancy equivalent of working a soup or sauce through a sieve with a wooden spoon. The name Mouli has already been used in this section and it is actually a brand name of a company called Brevette, so it probably seems strange to call a tool a Mouli, but we don't know any other name for it. It is probably the best-known kitchen tool made by the company, but it is probably more widely used in France than here. A Mouli is a bit like a sieve, but the base of it is removable, this is so the size of the holes can be changed. The interchangeable bottoms have a larger hole in the centre of the base. A semicircular, sloping piece of metal with a spindle attached and a handle has a little notch that fits into this hole, and with the aid of a spring-loaded bar is held in place so that it almost touches the pierced base. The handle at the top of the semicircular piece of metal is turned and that moves the semicircular piece of metal. There are several sizes available and some come with two handles like a colander (very big ones) and others with one handle like a saucepan or sieve. You put cooked soup or vegetables like tomatoes, carrots, or perhaps leeks and cauliflower into the sieve-like tool and then you turn the handle. The vegetables are forced down by the metal semicircle and pushed through the holes in the base, turning the vegetables into a purée as the mixture comes out through the holes in the bottom. A good tool to use to make soups, but it seems only to work on cooked, softened vegetables so it will not be any help with gazpacho or raw vegetables. The one thing that a Mouli will do that a liquidiser or food processor will not do is separate the skins and pips from the pulp of the vegetables, because those skins and pips do not go through the holes.

SALAD SPINNER

A salad spinner consists of two plastic bowls, one solid and one very far from solid inside the other. It also has two lids, one very solid and the other far from solid, and yet again the less solid is inside the more solid. The bowls are not fixed together but the lids are. There is a handle on the top of the lids and there is a small spindle inside the bottom of the solid bowl that the other bowl rests on. When you have washed your lettuce, spinach, cabbage, cauliflower or broccoli or all of them, you put them in the bowl with the very large perforations, put the lid on and turn the handle at the top, turning the handle actually turns the lid, and this revolves the perforated bowl within the solid one and as the speed builds up the excess water on the salad leaves is flung off and collects in the bottom of the bowl. Thus you have a bowl of washed and spin-dried lettuce leaves to eat, and now you have got rid of the water the salad dressing will not become diluted and will stick to the salad. Also the salad seems to go soggy less easily. You can certainly shake the water off of your lettuce leaves without this tool, but you may not be able to shake it off quite so completely, and it certainly will not all be shaken off into the bottom of a bowl that you can then conveniently empty down the sink. You could certainly live without this, and only you know whether you want to.

ROTARY HAND WHISK

This is for whipping cream or egg whites. A rotary whisk has two handles, one at the top that is big enough to get your hand inside and another smaller handle which is below and at right angles to the first. The smaller handle is attached by a small number of cogs and wheels to a balloon type whisk. The tool is held by the large handle and the small handle is turned in a circular motion and the rotary whisk rotates. Great for beating eggs, for making sponge type cakes, for whisking cream, mixing together thin and thick liquidish ingredients. But not good for anything lumpy. Less strenuous than a balloon whisk and not expensive, but how many cakes, omelettes, pancakes or crêpes will you make? If your answer is enough, but not enough to justify buying an electric hand-held double balloon type whisk or anything more expensive, then go for it. But if the answer is either tons or none then it is probably not for you.

Electrically operated tools

HAND-HELD MIXER OR WHISKS
More useful for making cakes or whisking up eggs or mixing soft or liquid items together. This has a larger holding piece than the small mixer above, and it has one or two rotary type whisks suspended from the piece that you hold.

HAND BLENDER OR STICK BLENDER
Slender long wand-shaped device with a small double blade in the bottom. Very useful for mixing things in small containers. Will even purée tomatoes in the tin or a cup, or in the pan.

LIQUIDISER
A lot of liquidisers come with a coffee grinder, so in a way you get two for the price of one. But that's only useful if you are going to grind your own coffee or if you are going to use it for chopping nuts. If not, then concentrate on finding the best liquidiser you can. If you are going to make a lot of soups then go for a liquidiser with a larger capacity. Some only do a pint or so, and others do a litre.

FOOD PROCESSOR

A food processor in some ways doubles as a food mixer and a liquidiser. It has a several attachments that allow you to attach whisks, slicing discs, or a double metal blade. We have not heard of anyone mixing their cocktails in a processor but in principle it is probably possible. Fruit cake may be quite hard to make in a processor because those metal blades which would do the mixing of a stiff mixture would probably chop up your glacé cherries and mixed fruit. But the processor comes into its own for making pâtés, liver pâté, smoked salmon pâté, or smoked mackerel pâté. They also excel at turning large quantities of lumpy soup smooth and creamy. You can use it instead of a mincer to make your own prime hamburger mince. It will chop large quantities of onions and if you add other vegetables like chillies and peppers will chop the lot up and mix them together.

FOOD MIXER

A food mixer is probably not a very blokish piece of kitchen furniture. Although they are really useful, they seem to suggest the middle of the 20th century and not the end of it or the beginning of the 21st. It is hard to say why that should be. They do seem to suggest people who are very serious about cooking. The large number of attachments is probably responsible for this and this seriousness implies spending a lot of time making cakes, pastry, pies, making your own mince and sausages and liquidising vast quantities of things. The food mixer is a large and specialised piece of equipment, probably not for the beginner in the kitchen. Go for the hand-held mixer first.

DISHWASHER

Once bought you're hooked for life. It is hard to understand why it took so long to buy one and it is hard to remember the inside of those tea and coffee mugs, clean but stained. This is a true power tool and it is also liberating in a way that seems unimaginable to those who suntil get crinkly fingers, or who pile washing-up in the sink and have trouble finding something to drink from.

It is part of a truth we wish to acknowledge that a bloke in the kitchen can make a huge, some would say a disproportionately huge, amount of washing-up and simple mess. I have found that having the dishwasher means that I can put a load of stuff in it as I go along, and it helps with the organising as well. I am now happy to use a bowl for the chopped tomatoes and another one for a different ingredient and a plate to put the spices on, because I do not have to wash them up. If there was a launderette for washing-up it would not be so much of a problem.

MICROWAVE

Some things cook much faster in the microwave. Christmas pudding for instance takes about 3 minutes. Every one knows about baked potatoes being done in about 10 minutes, and of course there are a lot other vegetables that it cooks just as quickly. They are also good for rapid defrosting of chicken pieces or warming toruntilas. There are also some things that take just as long or even longer in the microwave. There are a lot of microwave cookbooks, and there are a lot of microwave packaged convenience foods in the supermarkets. And there is more than one kind of microwave – some combine browning, or grilling or even some conventional heating elements. There's no doubt that they are brilliant for defrosting, warming through and reheating, for making treacle puddings, and are also good for bread sauce. Not so good for making custard as they are for heating up cartons and tins of ready-made custard, or tins of ready-made almost anything.

DEEP FAT FRYER

Although we do not include any instructions for deep fat frying in this book because in general it is quite a hazardous activity, this is the machine if you must have fish and chips, if tempura is the only Japanese food you love, and if doughnuts are the only cakes you will to make or eat.

Unfortunately, none of the recipes in this book will show you how to cook any of these things but we will say buy a deep fat fryer with a maker's recipe book. There are severally different models of the deep fat fryer. For safety's sake you want one with an external cool wall, and one with special safety features for lowering the basket into the hot fat after the lid is closed. The deep fat fryer takes quite a lot of work to keep the cooking oil up to scratch, what with draining and filtering, but it's probably easier than walking to the chippy once or twice a day. The exercise level is not so good, and with such a lot of fried food you will have to exercise more. Perhaps buy a deep fat fryer and a cycle or join a gym.

TOASTER
You probably know all that you need to know about the electric toaster, but even these basic pieces of kitchen equipment have a vast range. There are those that toast a standard piece of sliced bread and that is all. Then there are those that will take varying thicknesses of bread, or even buns or crumpets, and ones that have a device that you put the would-be toasted item into and then lift out. That of course means no lost pieces of toast that have refused to pop up adequately to clear the machine.

ELECTRIC KETTLE
What can we tell you about the electric kettle? It's a quick way to boil water. Some come with cords and some are cordless. They come in standard designs and brightly coloured retro-futuristic designs. Most of them turn themselves off once they have boiled. The only problem seems to be scaling up.

PERCOLATOR
A percolator mixes water and coffee in the same vessel and brings them to the boil together. Some people think that this makes the coffee taste bitter or stewed. Some prefer freshly 'perked' above all other kinds.

COFFEE FILTER MACHINE

The water and the coffee are kept separate until the water boils, then it travels up the tube and drips onto the coffee, runs through the coffee and drips out the bottom into the jug waiting to catch it. The coffee never boils and the water has probably stopped boiling by the time it reaches the coffee. The water is not forced through the coffee nor is the coffee compressed in any way.

ESPRESSO MACHINE

The electric espresso machine keeps water and coffee separate until the water boils. Once the water boils it is forced through the coffee which is in a confined space, and forced out into the cup below. It is much stronger than filter coffee. Some espresso machines have small steam nozzles that you put into a jug of milk, the steam from the nozzle boils and froths the milk. Some of these machines are a bit dangerous if you are not careful because the coffee is really boiling, as is the frothy milk.

TOOLS

THE BASICS

In this book all the tools you need for a particular recipe are listed after the ingredients. The information in this chapter should help you decide which are the most suitable for you.

Sharp knives

Knives are the most important tools. They must be sharp. They do not need sharpening every day, or even every week, but they will eventually get blunt. Just as some tools are better than others, and generally more expensive, so it is with knives. Within reason, more expensive knives last longer and keep a sharp edge longer.

If you only buy one knife choose a 'kitchen knife' or 'chef's knife'. The blade should be about 16 to 20 cm ($6^1/_2$ to 8 in) long with a comfortable handle. It should have a gently curved edge. It should have a smooth chopping blade rather than be serrated. This size and kind of knife can be used for chopping vegetables and meat as well as carving. The next most important kind is a small knife for cutting up smaller things. This can double as a vegetable peeler. The blade should be about 10 cm (4 in) long.

Knife sharpeners

Buy a cheap one and follow the instructions.

One kind looks like crossed fingers. You pull the knife through a few times and it puts an edge on both sides of the knife at the same time. 'Butcher's steels' (the long pointed sharpeners with a handle) need a lot of practice to use properly and can lead to injury in the overconfident starter.

Electric sharpeners, like a lot of labour-saving ideas can be an expensive waste of space.

Chopping boards & hygiene

These should be made of plastic.

A plain round wooden board is all right for cutting bread on, but unhygienic for meat, fish or vegetables. Basic hygiene and the state of some food (remember salmonella in eggs and chickens) gives two rules for using chopping boards. First, keep them clean. Wash them every time you use them. Second, chop the vegetables, salad or cheese before chopping any meat or fish. This is because the salad may get infected with bugs from the meat. The bugs are killed by cooking. Two other obvious bits of hygiene advice. Wash your hands before doing any cooking. Don't let the juice from raw meat fall on cooked meat, salad or cheese in the fridge. This means storing raw meat at the bottom of the fridge, and not letting it dribble.

Measuring spoons & cups

Recipes in this book use spoonfuls or cupfuls rather than weights for most things. If you look in any kitchen you will see that tea-spoons and cups come in several sizes. This means the amounts and so the taste may be very different if you just use any cup or spoon. To get round this problem buy a set of measuring spoons and cups in standard sizes. Look in the cooking section of your local supermarket. They come in plastic or stainless steel.

One teaspoonful is 5 ml
One tablespoonful is 15 ml

The cup set looks like a very large spoon set, and has four sizes:

1 cup	250 ml	approx. 9 fluid ounces
Half a cup	125 ml	4 fl oz
Third of a cup	80 ml	3 fl oz
Quarter cup	60 ml	2 fl oz

This makes for some easy conversions. A pint is 20 fl oz, and is approximately two and a quarter cups.

Some cups are based on 240 ml to the cup. Either sort will do. The difference between them is only about 5% and well within the tolerance of the recipes.

All of the recipes in this book are flexible and forgiving. You do not need to be obsessional about getting the exact amount of an ingredient to the nearest gram. Lots of the ingredients come in standard size packs, tins or tubs. The recipes take advantage of this. Some use half a standard pack, for instance for dried pasta. With meat and fish just ask for the amount you want, or look for a pack of about the same size.

Wooden spoons, spatulas and other spoons

Minimum requirements are a wooden spoon and a spatula (it gets into the corners better).

Next most important are a cooking spoon for getting stuff out of pans and onto plates, and a slotted spoon, which is the same but lets any fluid drain off.

Next is a fish slice which lets you lift out the flatter items.

If you buy a set, make sure it is not going to melt if it gets warm or scratch your nice non-stick pans.

Bowls

You need bowls to mix things in. If the bowl looks OK you can use it to serve food in as well. Heatproof glass like Pyrex and some ceramic bowls will be OK in the oven so they could lead a triple life, first as a mixer, second as a cooker and third as a server. Plastics are generally harder to break than glass or ceramic so you may choose them for the most vigorous mixing activity.

Colander or sieve

This is useful for draining vegetables after they have been washed, and again after they have been cooked, or for draining cooked pasta.

Colanders come in metal and plastic, with and without bases. The ones with bases will stand up on their own so you can put them in the sink and keep your hands away from the boiling substances you pour in. Plastic ones are cheaper.

Sieves can do most of what a colander does. They don't come with stands, but do have long handles. You can drain rice in them. You can also use a sieve as a fine strainer, to get the lumps out of gravy or sauce. You can push some cooked soups (particularly vegetable ones) through them to make them smooth.

Vegetable peeler

A small sharp knife will do, but there are some specially made vegetable peelers which are slightly safer and easier to use.

One is a bit like a knife and sometimes has an apple corer at the end furthest from the handle.

Another looks a bit like a letter D with the straight edge of the D being a slotted blade.

Apple corer

A sharp-ended tube on a handle. You push the corer through the apple from the top of the apple where the stalk would be. When you pull it out it takes the core and seeds out. Much easier and safer than trying to use a knife.

Garlic crusher

There's not a lot to say about these. In general you put the peeled garlic in and squeeze the handles together. The garlic gets pulped up. You poke the residue out and throw it away. The latest garlic crushers peel the garlic too.

If you don't have a garlic crusher just squash it with something suitable or chop it up small. Prepared garlic is sold in tubes, jars and bottles. This makes the crusher an optional item. Some people say you should only slice or chop garlic because crushing makes it bitter. We're not sure.

Grater

These are made from metal or plastic and have a range of cutting surfaces for getting different sizes of gratings. Use these for grating breadcrumbs, cheese, carrots or whatever. Be careful when using them. The main problem is that you can end up with grated fingernail or finger if you lose your concentration.

You can buy pretty well everything we say needs to be grated already prepared, including cheese and even carrots.

Lemon zester

This is for getting the rind off lemons and oranges. It has four or five holes in a little scraper. There is no other tool which does it as quickly, or that makes such long strips of rind. If you use a knife and then slice it, the shreds come out a bit big. You can try using a grater, but it's not as easy.

Lemon juicer

There are various sorts of these. Some look like an upturned half lemon with ridges in the middle of a bowl to catch the juice, generally made of plastic. You can use them for oranges and limes as well. Another electrical gadget purchase failure was the motorised version which sits in the back of a cupboard smirking at our gullibility. You do not have to squeeze lemons to get lemon juice. Lemon juice comes in bottles. 1 lemon gives about 2 to 4 tablespoons of juice. Fresh juice does have the edge.

Pans – overall advice

Buy a cheap set and then go looking in street markets or car boot sales for second-hand cast-iron pans with enamelled insides. This is where being a bloke will be an advantage. People buy these and then decide they don't like them because they are too heavy. You, on the other hand, will have no trouble with them. This has become a bit more difficult since we gave the same advice in *Cooking for Blokes*. The supply seems to have dried up a bit. The cheapest sets are aluminium non-stick.

Saucepans

Buy pans with lids.

How many?
At least one and preferably two.

What size?
22 cm (8^1/$_2$ in) across. 2 litres (3^1/$_2$ pints). This is big enough to cook pasta or rice or stew.
16 cm (6^1/$_2$ in) across. 1 litre (13/$_4$ pints). This is big enough for tomato sauce for pasta, custard or frozen peas.

Stick or non-stick?
Go for non-stick. Most aluminium pans have a non-stick coating. But remember, this is easy to remove with forks, metal implements and scouring pads. It can also make an interesting chemical burning smell if you heat it up too much with nothing in the pan, which may put you off eating for some time.

What metal?
Aluminium The cheap ones will wear out in a couple of years. By this time you will have decided if you want to continue to cook and whether to keep buying cheap ones or go for something better.

Stainless steel Very shiny. Quite expensive. Longer lasting. Thicker bases distribute the heat more evenly. This means that if you forget to stir the food sticks evenly to the bottom of the pan rather than in the shape of the heating element. Thinner bases mean more stirring. Stainless steel saucepans can be soaked in hot soapy water and burnt on food will come away fairly easily.

Cast-iron with enamel interior (e.g. Le Creuset) These are expensive, very durable and heavy. They cook very evenly. The enamel lining makes them practically non-stick. They do not like being heated up with nothing in them and the enamel may crack if you move them too quickly from heat to cold water. They can be soaked in water but the wooden handles don't like it. The handles can char if you cook on too high gas. Handles and casserole lids can be bought separately and replaced.

Frying-pans

Size should be about 25 to 28 cm (10 to 11 in across).

If you want to cook a lot of omelettes buy a smaller one as well, say 20 cm (8 in).

Sauté pan

This is a large deep frying-pan or a large shallow saucepan depending on how you look at things. Some come with lids and some don't. The ones with lids are very useful but do seem a little rare. You could always use the lid of a similar-sized saucepan if you should have one of an equal circumference.

Wok

A wok is like a combination of a frying-pan and saucepan. There are a number of wok kits which include the wok itself (a sort of metal bowl with a handle), lid, chopsticks, spoon and whatever else is thought to be useful. They are the best thing to cook Chinese stir-fry in. Authentic woks do not have a non-stick coating, but others do. Get one with a non-stick coating, but remember not to use metal tools on it. Buy one with a flat bottom (round ones can be unstable). Make sure it has a lid.

Larger woks are particularly useful. You can use them to cook larger quantities of food like chilli con carne or curries.

Casserole with lid

There are three sorts: ceramic, oven-proof glass or cast-iron. These are used for cooking in the oven. Cooking this way is an easy option because you can just put it in the oven and leave it to cook while you do something else.

If you go and look in a shop you will see some oven-proof glass (Pyrex type) casseroles. These and the ceramic ones are both OK, just don't move them from one temperature extreme to another, like from oven straight into the sink.

There are a bewildering number of sizes, but get one that holds at least 2 litres or 4 pints.

Our personal recommendation must be for a cast-iron casserole. This is the 'flame-proof' kind. You can use it like a saucepan on the hob and then transfer it to the oven. This is very useful as it saves you having to use a frying-pan and then an ordinary casserole. The ideal size is a 25 cm (10 in) oval casserole with straight sides. It holds 4 litres (7 pints) and can take a chicken, a small leg of lamb or most beef roasts, as well as being OK for all the casserole dishes in the book. It is fairly foolproof. It also means there is lots of juice for making gravy.

Large oven-proof dish

These come in all sizes. They can be made from ceramics, glass or metal. If you get a big enough one it can be used as a roasting dish as well. The most useful one we use is 30 × 18 cm (12 × 7 in) and 5 cm (2 in) deep and is made of glass. It is big enough to roast a chicken in, or make lasagne or shepherd's pie.

Metal baking tray about 25 cm (10 in) across

This can be used for warming things quickly in the oven or cooking things that don't create a lot of liquid. It will also do as a tin to cook or heat pizzas and pizza bases.

Pie dish

A metal dish, coated with non-stick material. It should be about 22 cm (8$^1/_2$ in) across, with sloping sides at least 2.5 cm (1 in) deep.

The best have lots of holes in the bottom which help make the pastry base crisp. Pastry needs to get hot enough to evaporate the water from it and then cook. This cannot happen if it is full of something wet like pie filling and squashed against the bottom of a ceramic dish, and so you have to cook the pastry shell empty first, which is a bit of a pain. The dish with the Aertex look lets the heat into the bottom and the steam out and so there is no need to pre-cook the case.

You can buy ceramic pie dishes. Pies should have a pastry lid but tarts are topless.

Round oven-proof glass dish 25 cm (10 in) diameter

This is used for cooking tarts or quiches, and doubles as something you can roast chicken pieces on.

EMERGENCY RATIONS

Having some emergency rations in store will give you the basics to cook an unplanned meal, forgotten invitation or some other non-specific emergency. These rations will also be there for you when those unpredicted feelings of starving hunger overwhelm you and you are too weak to leave home without food. There is no need to go and get them all at once unless that's the only way that you'll remember to do it. Our recommended emergency meal is one of the simple pasta dishes like Super Bol spaghetti (see page 188) which you can make without the meat at a pinch.

There are some things which you don't finish every time you cook a recipe, and if you treat them well they will be there in the short-term future for further cooking adventures. With dried ingredients like pasta, flour and rice you must reseal the bags by twisting or clipping or sticking. This keeps out the dust and the other creatures that would be happy to compete with you for the pleasure of eating them. Never keep the contents of an opened tin like tomatoes or bamboo shoots in the tin, even if you do put it in the fridge. You must always take things out of the tin and store them in mugs or bowls or something similar.

Cans, jars, bottles and bags

Salt and pepper, preferably a pepper grinder
400 g tin of plum tomatoes
200 g tin of tuna

400 g tin of baked beans
400 g tin of red kidney beans
50 g tin of anchovies
Bottle of sunflower oil
Small bottle of olive oil
Bottle of soy sauce
Bottle of white wine vinegar
Tikka powder or your favourite curry powder
Packet of mixed Mediterranean herbs
Pack of bouquet garni
500 g pack of pasta
500 g pack of long-grain rice like Basmati
Vegetable stock
Carton of custard

Fridge

Tube of garlic paste
Mayonnaise
Small bottle of lemon juice
Butter or low fat spread
100 g tube tomato purée
Eggs
Cheese such as Cheddar
Small carton of grated Parmesan or Pecorino cheese

Frozen food

1 pack of chicken pieces, (thighs, breasts or quarters)
1 pack of white fish (cod, hake or hoki)
1 pack of minced turkey or beef

Vegetables

Onions
Potatoes

These basics will provide the ingredients for more than one of the recipes in this book. It is important to remember to replace the emergency rations quickly because you don't know when the next emergency will be.

HOW TO . . .

This may be 'Flash Cooking for Blokes' but we still think a reminder of the basics may be helpful so here is the basic information on cooking vegetables, rice, pasta, noodles, pastry and dried beans. We have also included how to make breadcrumbs and the defrosting times for meat and chicken.

HOW TO COOK VEGETABLES

Frozen

For frozen peas, sweetcorn and other vegetables, follow the instructions on the bag. In general these will include adding the vegetables to boiling water with half a teaspoon of salt, and cooking for a few minutes. Cooking times are approximately 3 minutes for sweetcorn (off the cob) and 5 minutes for peas.

Fresh

Fresh vegetables take a bit more preparation than frozen and sometimes take longer than frozen vegetables to cook. There are times in the year when fresh vegetables will be much cheaper than frozen, and other times when they will be more expensive or simply unavailable.

Wash all fresh vegetables thoroughly. Throw away any leaves which are slimy and cut out any bits that look bad.

Potatoes

Potatoes are probably amongst the most widely used and versatile vegetables. They can be boiled, baked, roasted, mashed, deep-fried as chips or pan-fried in butter. They can be grated to make pancakes or rosti.

New potatoes have thin flaky skins which almost come off when the potatoes are scrubbed. They are smaller, often called 'Jersey' or 'Cyprus'. They are good for boiling or salads. Large new potatoes are delicious roasted with garlic and rosemary in a little oil.

Old potatoes are larger, and go under such names as Whites, King Edwards or Desirree Reds or Romanos. Good for mashing, roasting or baking.

Boiled potatoes

Potatoes can be cooked with their skins on or off. They are better for you with the skins on, but if you are worried about chemical fertilisers or pesticides and they are not organic then you should peel them. If you are leaving their skins on be sure to give them a thorough wash or scrub and dig out any eyes or unpleasant looking bits.

Cook small to medium potatoes whole. Large ones should be cut in half or quarters, so that all the pieces of potatoes in the saucepan are about the same size. Generally speaking the smaller the potato piece the quicker it will cook. Put the potatoes in a saucepan of water with 1 teaspoon of salt, bring to the boil, turn the heat down and simmer for 20–25 minutes. Test them with a fork to see if they are done. When they are done the fork will easily pierce the potato. If they start to fall apart they are overdone. When they are done drain off the water and serve.

Mashed potatoes

Peel and cook as for boiled potatoes (above), and then drain off the water. Put them in a bowl or return them to the saucepan, then mash the potatoes up with a fork or a potato masher.

Add small blobs of butter, margarine or cream if you have some left over, and fresh ground pepper to taste. If you like them creamier add a little milk and mix well into the mashed potatoes. Grated cheese added to mashed potatoes is also really nice.

Baked potatoes

Pick large old potatoes for this. Get about 3 potatoes to the kilo. Do not peel, but give them a good scrub. Stick a metal skewer through each potato, which helps them to cook in the middle. If you like the skin very crispy then prick the skin with a fork and place on the top shelf of the oven on 230° C, 450° F, Gas mark 8 for about an hour.

To check if they are done, cover your hand, preferably with an oven glove, to protect it from the heat and squeeze the sides gently. If it gives easily it is done. If you like it less crispy cover in foil and remove 10 minutes before taking from the oven. If not crispy at all leave the foil on.

Roast potatoes

Peel the potatoes, cutting away any nasty bits, and cutting out any eyes. Chop the potatoes in half if medium-sized or into quarters if large. Put the potatoes in an oven-proof dish with the some sunflower oil. Turn over the potatoes to coat them in oil.

Cook in the top of a preheated oven at 180° C, 350° F, Gas mark 4 for 60 minutes or so if you like them really well done. Turn over halfway through cooking.

You can heat the oil first by putting the dish with the oil in the oven for about 10 minutes before adding the vegetables. It helps to reduce sticking.

Pan-fried potato in butter

This is a good way of using up cooked, leftover potato. Just put a couple of spoons of butter in a frying-pan. Slice the potato and fry for about 10 minutes.

Chips

Our advice is go for the oven chips or your local chippy every time. It's not worth the hassle and risk of cooking them. Chip pans are the most common cause of household fire in the country.

Carrots

This is a vegetable that is good eaten raw. Add grated carrot to salad, or cut them into large matchstick shapes to dip into things like guacamole.

They are good roasted, and can be peeled and cooked together in the same dish as a joint of meat.

To cook separately just peel and chop into quarters lengthways, and put in an oven-proof dish with half a cup of water, a tablespoon of butter and a teaspoon of sugar. Cover with foil and cook in a preheated oven at 180° C, 350° F, Gas mark 4 for 30 minutes.

Cauliflower or broccoli

Break into 'florets', cover in water, add a teaspoon of salt and cook for about 10–15 minutes. Test the florets with a fork to check if they are ready. Cauliflower and broccoli can be eaten raw, and the longer you cook them, the softer they get. Sprouting broccoli should be broken into single stems and then cooked in 5 cm (2 in) of water with a teaspoon of salt for 5–10 minutes. It's also very good in stir-fries.

Cabbage

This comes in several colours: red, white and green. Treat them all the same. Throw away any nasty looking outer leaves. Cut out the central hard core and discard. Chop the cabbage roughly and cook in 2 cm (1 in) of water with a teaspoon of salt for about 10 to 15 minutes.

Red and white cabbage are good shredded raw in salads, particularly in the winter when lettuces are very expensive or hard to find. All of them are good shredded and stir-fried.

Spinach

This is good raw as a salad leaf or lightly cooked. It shrinks when cooked so you will need at least 500 g (1 lb) of spinach for two people. First wash the spinach and shake off the excess water. Put the spinach into a saucepan with salt to taste and a blob (the size of small walnut) of butter. There is no need to add any more water. Cook the spinach in a medium-sized saucepan over a medium heat. As soon as the water on the leaves starts to hiss and bubble, and the butter to melt, stir the spinach gently. When it is floppy and transparent, 2 to 3 minutes later, it is cooked. Strain off the liquid and serve.

Broad beans, runner beans, fine beans, sugar snaps and mangetout

All these small beans and peas are eaten in the pod. Cut off both ends, and pull any stringy bits from down the side. Cut them into pieces, except the sugar snaps and mangetout which should be cooked whole. Just cover with water, add salt to taste and boil rapidly for 5 to 10 minutes until tender, testing them with a fork.

Corn on the cob

This is a cheap vegetable in the summer and is almost a meal in itself. There are several ways to cook corn: it can be boiled, baked or barbecued. If boiling, pull all the leaves off and boil in salted water for 20 to 30 minutes. Check with a fork to see if the corn is soft enough to eat. The fork should pierce the corn easily. Serve with a blob of butter and freshly ground black pepper.

If barbecuing, keep the leaves on, and barbecue for 10 to 20 minutes, turning a couple of times. If the leaves have been removed by the shop don't worry, just turn the corn more often.

If baking the corn, pull the leaves off as for boiling, place on a baking tray, put a little oil or butter on the corn, sprinkle with salt and pepper and bake for about 45 minutes.

Courgettes

Courgettes are quick and easy to cook. Wash them and slice either across or lengthways. Put them in a pan with some oil or butter and some seasoning. Cook on a medium heat for about 5 minutes and serve. If you cook with 1 teaspoon cumin seed, it goes well with curries.

HOW TO MAKE SALAD

Salads are quick and easy, and are some of the simplest things to experiment with.

Preparing salads

Make sure you have a clean chopping board or knife if you need them. You must not prepare salad on a board you have just used to cut raw meat or fish, because you can transfer bugs which cause food poisoning if they are not cooked.

Lettuces

The simplest salad is lettuce. There are a lot of different lettuces. Each has its own characteristics but they all make a good base for a green salad. Green salads are a lot less hassle than vegetables.

Go to your local street market or supermarket. Look at different lettuces, smell them and try them.

Iceberg lettuce is crisp and has a neutral taste. It can be sliced or cut into chunks. It keeps well in the fridge.

Webb's Wonder is a crispish round lettuce.

Cos lettuce has long, crisp leaves good for dipping in things.

Round lettuce has more floppy leaves.

Oak leaf has crisp, bitterish, brown and green leaves.

Radicchio is small and slightly bitterish, the colour of red cabbage with white veins.

Frisée and Lollo Rosso have wobbly edges to the leaves. The Lollo Rosso has purple or red edges to the leaves. Both are very decorative.

Mixing together lettuces of different colour and textures works well. If lettuce is not available, try shredding white or red cabbage. Put the washed and dried cabbage in a bowl and put vinaigrette on top.

Herbs

Fresh herbs can be used in salads, either as decoration or to give a more interesting flavour.

Basil is an aromatic herb, often used in Italian food.

Rocket has small leaves with a distinct taste like watercress.
Other herbs like parsley and coriander work well.

Tomatoes

Ordinary tomatoes can be a bit tasteless but are available all year.

Cherry tomatoes are small, sweet and expensive.

Beef tomatoes are large and good with steak.

Italian plum tomatoes are good for pasta sauces. They are the ones sold in tins, but are also available fresh in many shops. If you want a really tasty tomato it should ripen on the vine in the sun. If a tomato smells like a tomato then it may well have more flavour than a lot of those available today. A lot of those grown in greenhouses taste and smell of very little at all.

Other ingredients

You can combine many raw vegetables to make a salad. Salad ingredients include: cucumber, green, red or yellow peppers, spring onions, olives and shredded carrot.

Other possible ingredients

If you want a more substantial salad try adding some of the following:

Hard-boiled eggs, tinned tuna, cheese or ham.

Fruit such as chopped apples, pears, oranges or bananas.

Walnuts, peanuts or even a few pecan nuts, cashew nuts or almonds.

Dried fruit like a couple of tablespoons of sultanas, raisins, apricot and dates.

Cooked vegetables like potato, green beans or French beans.

HOW TO COOK RICE

The most important thing to know about cooking rice is that you should use twice as much water as you do rice. Below is a recipe for plain boiled rice for two people.

Serves 2
① *Preparation 1 min, Cooking depends on sort of rice – Easy*

INGREDIENTS
1 cup rice
2 cups of water
1 teaspoon salt

EQUIPMENT
Saucepan with lid
Measuring cups and spoons

METHOD
Read the packet to get the correct cooking time. Put the rice, water and salt in the pan. Bring the water and rice to the boil, stirring once, to stop the rice sticking. Turn down the heat to low. Give it one more quick stir to stop the rice sticking to the pan. Put the lid on the pan. Cook for the correct time until the fluid is absorbed (10 –15 minutes for long-grain or Basmati rice). Do not stir!

After the cooking time, take it off the heat and let it stand for a couple of minutes. Fluff it up with a fork to separate the grains and serve.

TIPS
The cup referred to is a standard measuring cup of 250 ml. It is approximately the same as a mug. For larger quantities use 1 cup of water and half a cup of rice per person.

Basmati is more fragrant than long-grain, and also more forgiving, because it holds together better during cooking.

Approximate cooking times (read the packet for more accurate timings)

Basmati   10 to 12 minutes
American long-grain   10 to 15 minutes
Organic long-grain brown rice   30 to 35 minutes
Brown quick cook   20 to 25 minutes

HOW TO COOK NOODLES

Serves 2   ① *Preparation 1 min, Cooking 4 min – Easy*

INGREDIENTS
2 sheets dried noodles
1 tablespoon sesame oil

EQUIPMENT
Saucepan
Sieve or colander to drain the noodles

METHOD
Check the cooking time on the packet because these times seem to
change all the time. Boil at least 2 $^1/_2$ cups (600 ml, 1 pint) water in
a saucepan. Put the noodles in the water. Boil for about 4 minutes.
Drain the noodles. Return to the pan. Add 1–2 tablespoon of sesame
oil, and stir round to coat evenly and serve.

Tip
You get three sheets of noodles in a 250 g pack of Sharwoods medium
noodles

HOW TO COOK PASTA

Serves 2   ① *Preparation 1 min, Cooking 2–10 min – Easy*

INGREDIENTS
250 g dried pasta (generally half a pack or 2 $^1/_2$ cups)
1 teaspoon salt

EQUIPMENT
Saucepan
Wooden spoon
Sieve or colander

METHOD
Read the packet for the correct cooking time. Put at least 2 $^1/_2$ cups (600 ml, 1 pint) of water and a teaspoon of salt into the saucepan and bring to the boil. Put the pasta in the boiling water. Stir the pasta once to stop it sticking to the bottom of the pan. Bring back to the boil and simmer for as long as the packet says, anything from 6–15 minutes depending on variety. The best way to judge if the pasta is cooked is to bite it. This is tricky, because if you fish out a bit and stick it in your mouth you may burn your mouth with the boiling water. Wait a bit and blow on it, then bite it. You can trust the cooking time if you want to or put a bit on a plate and cut it with the edge of a fork. If it is hard it needs longer. If it is like mush it is overcooked.

HOW TO ROLL PASTRY

INGREDIENTS
Half a 500 g pack of pastry, chilled or frozen
2 tablespoons flour

EQUIPMENT
Rolling pin

METHOD
Make sure the pastry is well thawed, 4 hours in the fridge being typical. Keep the pastry in the fridge before rolling. Make sure that the surface that you are going to roll on is clean, dry and flat. Pastry can stick to the surface or rolling pin unless it is kept dry, so sprinkle the surface and the pastry and the rolling pin with flour.

Roll and then turn the pastry through a quarter of a circle. Roll and turn, scattering more flour if needed.

It is remarkably easy.

HOW TO MAKE DRIED BEANS TURN OUT SOFT AND NOT LIKE BULLETS

① Preparation 5 min, Cooking time depends – Easy

INGREDIENTS
$1^1/_2$ cups dried beans or chickpeas is equivalent to 2×440 g tins.

EQUIPMENT
Saucepan with lid
Set measuring cups
Bowl

METHOD
Check over the dried beans. Throw away any stones or odd looking ones. Put the beans in a plastic bowl or one made from heatproof glass. Pour boiling water ontop of them, and cover to a depth of about 5 cm (2 in). This takes about 1 litre or 2 pints. (Don't add any salt until the beans are cooked or they won't soften). Leave the beans for 2 to 12 hours to swell up, preferably in a fridge. Drain and rinse the beans.

Put them in the saucepan with at least $2^1/_2$ cups (600ml, 1 pint) of fresh water. Bring to the boil and boil vigorously for 10 minutes. Turn down the heat until the water is just simmering gently. Cook the beans until they are soft. This may take anything between 30 minutes and $2^1/_2$ hours, for a rough idea see the chart below. Add more water if it gets low.

When the beans are done, take off the heat. Add salt to taste. Drain the beans and leave to cool down.

ADDITIONS & ALTERNATIVES

Approximate cooking times (read the packet for more accurate timings)

Red kidney beans	60 to 90 minutes
Chickpeas	150 minutes
Rose coco (borlotti) beans	150 minutes
Red split lentils	30 minutes
Green lentils with skin on	90 minutes

TIPS

Parsley is reputed to reduce the wind generating capacity of beans. So if possible add some freshly chopped parsley just before serving the beans.

HOW TO MAKE BREADCRUMBS

You may have noticed how bread starts off really soft and moist and ends up rock hard as it dries out. Breadcrumbs are best made with bread that is not totally fresh but rock hard is not good either. Go for something in between.

1 slice of bread makes a cup of breadcrumbs.

Method 1: Rub two bits of bread together and you will get some breadcrumbs.
Method 2: Use a grater. Rub the bread against the grater. The main

problem with this is that you can end up with grated fingernail or finger in the breadcrumbs if you lose your concentration. Scraped knuckles hurt.

Method 3: Cut the crust off the bread. Cut the bread into cubes and put in a food processor or liquidiser and process for about 15 seconds.

Method 4: Give up and buy some from your local baker or super-market.

HOW TO DEFROST THINGS

CHICKEN PIECES
Overnight in the fridge or 6 hours at room temperature.

CHICKEN LIVERS (225 G OR 8 OZ TUB)
Four hours at room temperature or overnight in the fridge.

LAMB CHOPS
Defrost in a single layer for 4 hours at room temperature or over-night in the fridge.

HALF LEG OF LAMB
Overnight in the fridge or 4 hours at room temperature.

WHOLE CHICKEN (1.5 KG)
24 hours in fridge, 12 hours in a cool room.

PACKET OF EXTRA LARGE PRAWNS
3 hours at room temperature.

PLAICE, COD AND HADDOCK
Cook from frozen.

KNOW YOUR ONIONS

In this chapter you will find information about some of the ingredients used in the recipes in this book.

Anchovy

These salty brown fish fillets come in 50 g tins and are seen on the top of some pizza varieties. They are used in quite a few Italian dishes.

Basil

This herb is the basis of pesto, and typical of Italian food, though also used in Thai cooking. It can be used raw in a salad of sliced Mozzarella and tomatoes, or cut or torn up and added to pasta sauces. You can add a bit of it to salads. It comes in packets or bunches. Floppy leaves can be revived by putting them in cold water for 30 minutes.

Bouquet garni

These mixed herbs come in a pouch like a tea bag. It has a mixture of herbs in it, so you can substitute a teaspoon of mixed Mediterranean herbs. It means you get little specks of herb in the dish, but so what. You should lift out the tea bag before serving the dish.

Calvados

This is a kind of apple brandy from France. You can buy Calvados for cooking in small bottles in supermarkets. You can use it in any dish where you have cooked apples to zip up the flavour.

Capers

They look like small green bullets and taste a bit like pickled gherkins but spicier. They are the edible flower buds of a spiny shrub, and are the flavouring in the fish and meat accompaniment, Sauce Tartare. They turn up in some French and Italian dishes. You can buy them preserved in brine in jars.

Cardamom

This beautiful spice can be bought ready ground or as pods, which contain the seeds. It is used in curries but also in the sweet yoghurt dessert shrikand.

Cheese

There are lots of different kinds of cheese. There are even lots of varieties of different strength of Cheddar from round the world. Many of the cheeses on sale have already been prepared by being sliced or grated.

Mozzarella is the one to put on top of pizza and in some Mexican recipes. It comes whole in a bag with some fluid (which helps to keep it fresh) which you drain off before using. Mozzarella also comes ready-grated from some supermarkets.

The usual cheese sprinkled on pasta is Parmesan. It is a hard Italian cheese which needs to be grated before use. Fortunately it comes in tubs ready-grated. If you buy it in a slab, grate with a normal grater or take long paper-thin curls off it with a vegetable peeler which some may say looks more flash. A slightly cheaper alternative is Pecorino, which also comes ready-grated.

In recipes which need Cheddar you can use Red Leicester.

Lancashire, Cheshire and Caerphilly are almost interchangeable, all being crumbly mild cheese. The people of Lancashire, Cheshire and Caerphilly probably won't agree with this.

Edam, Gouda, Emmental and Gruyère are another group of similar cheeses, and they are often available ready-sliced and grated.

Paneer is a full-fat soft Indian cheese included in some of the recipes in this book. Substitute tofu if you can't find any paneer.

Chilli

Some like it hot, but some don't. The cartoon image of someone sitting with steam coming out of their ears after the first mouthful of chilli or drinking the contents of the fire bucket is not too inaccurate, but it is only half of the story. Persistent hot chilli use will lead you to experience the ring of fire. The answer is be moderate.

Cooling it. You can add coconut milk or a carton of yoghurt to the dish. The heat of chillies develops with cooking, and the main source of heat is in the seeds, so you can scrape out the seeds before adding it to the dish.

If you like it simple you can buy tubes or jars of prepared chilli. They should be kept in the fridge after being opened and used within 6 weeks. There are more than a dozen types of chilli, but you will only see a limited number in the shops. Check the pack to see how hot they are. The information should be on the label. Bird's eye chillies are small, about 3 cm (1 in) long, thin and red and are very hot. These are favourites for Chinese, Thai and for our Universal Salsa recipe. Cayenne chillies are slightly bigger and marginally less hot. Jalapeño chillies are less hot again and you can buy them in jars for Mexican cooking. They make a good addition to pizza and even salads. Green or red chillies about 1 cm (^{1}/$_2$ in) across and 5 cm (2 in) long are good for Indian food.

FRESH CHILLI — A WARNING! When you chop up the chillies be careful and avoid getting juice on your hands. It will sting. If you touch your eyes, mouth or other sensitive areas even an hour after chopping them they will smart and burn. So wash your hands or wear rubber gloves.

If you want the flavour but don't want to chop or run the risk of chilli burn use whole chillies (a little more than the recipe says) and prick them several times with a fork. When the dish is cooked throw the chillies away.

Cinnamon

This burnt-orange coloured spice comes from the bark of a tree. You can either buy it as a stick which looks like a dark orange cigarette, or ground up. If you use the stick version you should take it out of the dish you are cooking before serving. Although it gives up its flavour it never goes soft. You can put a stick of it in a cup of hot chocolate, and in the USA they dust a bit on buttered toast to make cinnamon toast.

Cloves

This is another spice which comes in whole and ground form. The same thing applies. If you use the whole stuff take it out before serving. It is about 1 cm (^{1}/$_2$ in) long and has a stalk with a small bobble on the end. It looks a bit like a miniature of the mace that medieval knights used. We use them in risotto and some curries. You can also stick them in ham before roasting.

Coconut

Coconut has a subtle flavour, and can also take some of the heat out of a curry if you have added too much chilli.

You can buy coconut milk in 400 ml tins, or you can buy it powdered. If you use the powdered sort, you can keep the rest in the cupboard for next time you want it. Read the instructions on the packet, but in general they say mix it up beforehand with warm water, to make sure it dissolves. 2 tablespoons of powder in 1 cup of warm water gives a reasonable thickness. Coconut powder is easy to make and measure in small quantities.

Desiccated coconut is dried grated coconut flesh. It comes in packs and may be in the cake ingredient section of the supermarket.

Creamed coconut comes in a solid block and dissolves in warm water to make a thick creamy paste which is used in a lot of Thai and Indian food.

Coriander

Fresh coriander has a subtle but distinctive flavour which goes well in lots of oriental food and sauces. You will find it in Chinese, Oriental, Indian and Mexican recipes. You can buy coriander leaves in packets or in bunches. If you buy a packet it will have been washed and partially prepared. If you buy a bunch you will need to check and wash it. For price the bunches win, with about three times as much usable coriander as a packet. You can use both the leaves and the stems. Some Chinese recipes even use the root, but not ours. Floppy leaves can be revived by putting them in cold water for 30 minutes.

Coriander powder is used in curries, and is ground from the seeds.

Couscous

Couscous is made from fine granules of semolina covered with wheat flour. It comes in packets, and is widely available. It is very easy to prepare. As well as making a fine accompaniment to any meat or fish dish, particularly if it has a little sauce, it makes a good salad. Dishes you might serve rice with you could experiment with couscous instead, with the exception of Thai or Chinese dishes.

Cream

Buy this in cartons. Single cream is fairly thin, the kind you pour on a piece of pie. Double cream is the one you can whip up so it becomes stiff, and is served in a dollop by the side of a slice of pie. By the way, when you are whipping up double cream don't overdo it – butter is the end stage of whipping cream. Sour cream is a bit sharper and goes well with sweet things, as well as being a good accompaniment to baked potato, particularly if you chop up a 15 g pack of chives and mix it in.

There are some cream alternatives that you might like to try. Fromage frais is like sour cream and crème fraîche is like thick cream. There is also wholemilk Greek yoghurt which is the creamiest, and there are low-fat alternatives. There is even a non-dairy soya alternative to cream.

Cumin

This spice is used in curries and Mexican food. You can add it to tomato sauces to perk them up. It is not overpowering. It is called 'Jeera' in Punjabi, and you may find some better value packets of it if you go to the right shop.

Curry leaves

A whole leaf used in Indian cooking. Try to fish it out before eating. Sold dried.

Curry powder

Lots of different sorts are sold here. They range from the mild through medium to hot. There are even named specific ones like Madras, Rogan Josh or even Tikka or Tandoori. This variety lets you tailor any curry to the heat and degree of spiciness you want.

Dry sherry v rice wine or sake

Chinese and oriental food uses quite a lot of dry sherry. You can try to be more authentic by using rice wine, but it doesn't really make a lot of difference. There is one thing though, don't buy the cheapest sweet sherry. You must use a dry sherry (it may well have a number on the back to indicate sweetness). With sherry as with the rest of the products from the wine department, you generally get what you pay for. So buy a proper Spanish sherry.

Fish sauce

This is used in Thai cooking. It is made, though you probably don't want to know this, from some anchovy concoction. It comes in bottles and is the colour of whisky. It is used as a salt substitute, and you can get away with using soy sauce instead. There are often recipes on the bottle. The one on the bottle we have requires four different products to be bought from their range to make it. We think this is a record.

Five-spice powder

A Chinese ground spice which you can experiment with adding to a lot of dishes. Use very sparingly. It is a pungent mixture of star anise, Szechuan pepper, fennel, cloves and cinnamon.

Garam masala

This is a mixture of a number of spices and saves the trouble of having some of each. Typically it may include turmeric, ground coriander, ground cumin, cinnamon and ground cloves. It can make every meal taste the same if you use it as the only flavouring, as can using curry powder. It does not go off but it does lose some of its flavour if you keep it too long.

The flavours are enhanced if you warm them gently in a pan or on a baking tray for 5 minutes before cooking with them.

Ginger

Fresh ginger is a light brown irregular branched bulbous root. It is generally sold by weight, but most recipes say use a piece say 2 cm (1 in) long. Buy firm, smooth ginger roots. Do not buy shrivelled up or mouldy stuff. It keeps for at least a month. You do not have to keep it in the fridge. Fresh ginger is one of the tastes together with chilli and garlic which make freshly made curries and Chinese meals taste better than anything you can buy. It is very different from ground ginger, which is the flavour of ginger biscuits.

Golden syrup and maple syrup

This is the stuff of steamed puddings. Maple syrup is the stuff the Americans pour on their breakfast pancakes. When you buy it read the label carefully. There is proper maple syrup and then a maple-flavoured syrup which is just a flavoured sugar solution. The real stuff is much better.

Honey

There are two kinds, set and runny. Set is cloudy and hard and the best for sandwiches. Runny is a light brown liquid and better for cooking with.

Lemon grass

OK. It looks like a kind of tough spring onion and it tastes of lemon. It is one of the central ingredients in Thai cookery. You can buy it freeze-dried but fresh is best. Choose ones that look green and not brown. To prepare it, cut the ends off and then crush the stalk. A Thai cook would put it on a flat surface and then lay his chopper flat on the lemon grass and then hit the knife with his hand. The idea is to flatten it to let the flavour out. Anyway, hit it lightly with a hammer or a rolling pin.

Lentils

There are lots of different kinds of lentils. Puy or Puy type which are small and dark green with the skins on hold together better than other sorts and are less likely to go to mush. Red lentils are good for dahl, as are other split peas because they do get mushy quickly and that's what you want for a dahl.

Maple syrup

See golden syrup

Mortadella

Italian pork slicing sausage with fantastic inclusions like olives and pistachio nuts and little lumps of white stuff that might be fat. mortadella comes in several sizes from just larger that the standard salami to as big as your head!

Mushrooms

The most commonly available are button mushrooms. You can also buy bigger ones (flat field mushrooms) which you chop up or stuff. Oyster mushrooms are used in Chinese dishes and come with yellow or white tops. They are more solid and shrivel less. Shiitake mushrooms are available dried or fresh. They have longish stalks and dark brown tops. They can be a bit tough if dried and if not soaked or cooked or shredded properly. Chanterelle and porcini mushrooms are European mushrooms and are worth looking out for. You can put them in with pasta sauces (the simpler the better, for instance, oil and garlic) for an unusual and authentic taste. And then there are morels, fantastic just lightly sautéed in butter, bought dry and very expensive but a few make a real treat and a great starter.

Mustard

English mustard is the bright yellow stuff, and hot. Dijon French mustard is a reasonable equivalent and Meaux wholegrain is excellent with meat. French and German mustards are darker, sweeter and less hot. American mustard comes in squeezy bottles and seems to be a bit too much like wallpaper paste for us, but is handy for squeezing on hot dogs.

Nutmeg

This spice which looks like a nut is available whole or ground. If you grate it yourself it tastes better. It is a good addition to cooked fruit and on top of rice pudding.

Oils

The best cooking oils are sunflower, corn oil and groundnut (which is made from peanuts). The cheapest are vegetable and rape seed oils. Olive oil is good for cooking Italian dishes. Make sure that you use an ordinary olive oil for this. 'Virgin' and 'Extra Virgin' are the best and most expensive but should be kept for making vinaigrette, adding to salads or tossing things in after they have been cooked. If you heat them up, the subtle flavourings which separate them from the ordinary will just boil off. There are other oils which can add flavour to salad dressings, or to Chinese noodles, such as walnut or sesame oils.

Olive oil

There are books (many, big and long) about olive oils. For in depth knowledge consult one of them or see our oils paragraph above.

Olives

There are many kinds available. They come loose, in jars or tins, whole and pitted (with the stones out), or stuffed. They have varied flavours and textures. Generally the green ones are sharper in flavour and more solid in texture than the black ones. We suggest using pitted olives, because olive stones are strong enough to break teeth. We can show you the teeth. If you ignore our advice and go for the ones with stones you can always cut the olive flesh from round the stone or use one of the tools sold to push the stone out.

Onions

How could we have a chapter called 'Know your onions' without a section on onions? So here are some things you may not know about onions. Did you know they were part of the lily family? There are several kinds of onion. There are strong, mild, and sweet, sweet Spanish, and flat Italian. There are small pearl and pickling onions, shallots and banana shallots. There are spring onions and green onions and they all make you cry when you slice them. You can eat them cooked or raw and they are supposed to be good for your chest.

Oregano

This herb is widely used in Italian dishes. You can substitute mixed Mediterranean herbs for it. You can add it to tomato sauces. It's great with lamb, pork, chicken, eggs or soups. It comes fresh, in which case pull off the leaves and discard the stalks, or put the whole lot in and lift it out at the end, and dried, in which case just add.

Oyster sauce

This is a thick brown sauce used in Chinese cooking. You can add it to a stir-fry and it comes in bottles.

Paneer

Is an Indian full-fat soft cheese sold in blocks (a bit like blocks of butter). The blocks are 200 g (7 oz) and easily sliced. If you can't find paneer substitute tofu in its place.

Parsley

This comes in two types. There is curly-leafed parsley which is the standard kind, and flat-leaf which looks similar to coriander. Both come prepared in packets or are available in bunches. The packets are supposedly ready to use and you should be able to use most of them. The bunches may need to picked over. Floppy leaves can be revived by putting them in cold water for 30 minutes.

The easy way to tell the difference between coriander and flat-leaf parsley at a market stall is that the coriander generally has the roots on and the parsley has the roots cut off. You can smell the difference by rubbing a leaf between your fingers, but this may not endear you to the stallholder.

Pasta

This is available dried or fresh from the chilled cabinet. Cooking times are on the packet. There are full instructions on cooking pasta in the 'How to' chapter (see page 336).

There are the long thin ones such as spaghetti, linguine and fidelini (like spaghetti with a hole up the middle) and long flat ones like tagliatelle and tagliolini. There are dozens of shaped pastas, from tiny ones for putting in soup like stelline, through to tubes, twists and weird extruded shapes.

Useful ones are the tubular penne, the twisted fusilli and the shell-shaped conchiglie. All of these pick up more of the sauce. Then, of course there are the flat (lasagne) and rolled tubes (cannelloni) ready for stuffing and then there are all the ready-stuffed ones like ravioli and tortellini.

Pepper

Buy a grinder for black pepper. It is ten times better than ready ground.

Paprika pepper is red and less hot, cayenne pepper is hotter, and chilli pepper the hottest. They all look similar. Make sure you use the right one.

Szechuan pepper is a black pepper used in Chinese cooking. If you cannot find any just substitute the same amount of black pepper.

You can also buy peppercorns in brine in jars. Whole mixed coloured peppercorns, pink, green and black, are available and they are quite good because they give a subtle mix of pepper tastes. You have to grind these in a pepper mill.

Pine nuts

Sometimes called pine kernels these little nuts come from pine cones, and are fried and added to couscous and some other dishes. They are also used in Italian recipes in pesto sauce and in other dishes. You can substitute walnuts in the pesto and fried cashews or almonds with the couscous.

Pomegranate

Pomegranate is a pinkish coloured fruit on the outside and a deep pink mass of seeds on the inside. It is a strange looking fruit. You can use the seeds in cooking Indian and Middle Eastern dishes and you can use the juice too. Juice by cutting in half and pressing in the same way as a citrus fruit. One or two recipes call for dried pomegranate seeds. If you can't find them, fresh will do.

Poppy seeds

Tiny black seeds, bought in packets and sometimes seen on the top of bread. Used in curry.

Prawns

These are available frozen or sometimes fresh. The cooked ones are pink. The raw ones are greyish-blue and come with the shells off or on. The bigger the prawn the more expensive. Raw prawns should be kept in the fridge and cooked the same day you buy them.

Rice

There are several kinds of rice, long-grain rice, round grain, pudding rice, sushi rice, risotto rice, Basmati rice, white rice, brown rice, wild rice, flaked rice and ground rice. In general in this book we use a white long-grain rice like Indian Basmati rice. It is a little more expensive than ordinary long-grain rice but it is worth it.

There is information on some different kinds of rice and how to cook them in the 'How to' chapter (see page 334).

Rosemary

This herb comes dry or fresh. It comes from a low shrub which you can grow on a windowsill and so have it free all the time. It is particularly good with meat, and you can throw in a couple of bits with any lamb you are cooking in the oven.

Sesame oil

This is sold in little bottles and comes from sesame seeds. You can add it to Chinese noodles after cooking.

Sesame seeds

These come in small packets in supermarkets but big bags in Asian/Middle Eastern stores. They have a subtle nutty flavour which is improved by putting them in the oven for 3 minutes to toast them. Throw them ontop of Chinese food.

Shiitake mushrooms

See mushrooms

Soy sauce

Soy is a thin sauce, made from fermented soya beans. The best is naturally fermented and has a distinctive salty flavour. Take care when you are buying it. There is more than one kind. There is 'dark' soy sauce and 'light' soy sauce and sweet soy sauce, Chinese and Japanese soy sauces and there are others as well but generally only available from specialist Chinese or Japanese shops. One brand which is reliably good is Kikkoman's which is Japanese, but is good wherever you need soy sauce.

Squid

These are used in a lot of Mediterranean and Asian dishes. They may be an acquired taste but they are worth getting to know. You may know the battered calamari already.

Cleaned and almost ready to use squid tubes are stocked in many supermarkets and some fishmongers. Don't buy unprepared squid unless you like slimy things and know how to take the quill out. But check the prepared ones as you chop them for a strip of clear plastic-like stuff. If you find it, throw it away. It is the quill.

Just make sure they are fresh. Once thawed, keep in the fridge and cook the same day. Wrap up any uncooked bits in paper and don't leave them in the bin in the kitchen. They start to smell really badly almost immediately.

Star anise

Spice with a distinctive aniseed taste used in Chinese cooking. Comes whole as a star-shaped seed pod or ground. Take the pods out before serving. The powdered version is part of Chinese five-spice.

Stock cubes

Stock cubes are concentrated extracts of beef, chicken, lamb, fish or vegetables. They are a handy way of adding a bit of extra flavour but you can't be sure which part of the animal has been used to make them.

You can buy ready-made stock in cartons from most supermarkets. You can also buy Swiss vegetable bouillon powder (vegetable stock), if you are worried about the stuff that goes into meat or fish stock cubes.

Sunflower oil

See oils.

Tahini

This is ground-up sesame seeds which form a thick paste. Used in various dishes, you should stir it up to get the oil back into the paste before use. You can add a teaspoon to bought hummus to make it more exciting. Spread the hummus on a plate, make a dimple in the middle and put the tahini in, and then dribble a tablespoon of olive oil round the edge. This is a fantastic snack or starter with warmed pitta bread and pitted black olives. In recipes you can substitute peanut butter (unsweetened) instead of tahini.

Tamarind

This is the brown pulp surrounding the seed from the tamarind tree. It has a slightly acid taste like a cross between a date and apricot. It is used in Thai, Indian and other similar dishes. You either buy it in blocks in which case you soak it and squeeze the pulp to mush the flavour out, or you can buy an instant version in a plastic pot, where you add by the teaspoonful. Tamarind is one of the main components in HP sauce.

Tarragon

This herb has a subtle aniseed flavour. It is good with chicken and meat. You can buy it dried, but fresh is better.

Tofu

This is a solid cake made from soya bean curds. There are several degrees of solidity in the world of the tofu. It is a bit like a jelly in its ordinary state and tends to fall apart if stirred about too much. Sometimes it comes in cartons like small milk cartons. You can use it in Chinese food instead of meat. You can fry cubes of it and then warm them in the oven, and serve it as a side dish. Agé (pronounced agai) is a firmer textured form which you can buy in health food shops where you can also buy smoked tofu and some also sell deep-fried tofu. Generally speaking the tofu from health shops seems more solid than that from supermarkets and it comes in clear vacuum packs. We prefer the health shop kind.

Tomato purée

This thick concentrated tomato sauce can be added to a tomato sauce for pasta, or meat to improve the flavour. It comes in tubes. It keeps for 4 weeks in the fridge. You can also buy little tins of it, but you have to throw away what you don't use.

Turmeric

This yellow powder spice is used to colour a lot of curries. It is called 'Haldi' in Punjabi, and you may find some better value packets and tins of it if you go to an Indian shop.

Vinegar

Vinegar is used in vinaigrette dressing and some recipes to give a sour taste. A good all purpose one is white wine vinegar. Alternatives are red wine vinegar – cider or champagne or sherry vinegar or even those that have had herbs added. Don't use malt vinegar – it is excellent with fish and chips or for making pickles but it is limited in its uses.

Worcestershire sauce

A mixture of flavours, it is a thin brown sauce and is sold in bottles. You can put it on steak when cooking as well as a number of other things. Incidentally it contains both anchovies and tamarind. We just looked at the label.

INDEX